The Renaissance and Reformation Movements

Lewis W. Spitz

Stanford University

The Renaissance and Reformation Movements

Volume

2

THE REFORMATION

Publishing House
St. Louis

Concordia Publishing House, St. Louis, Missouri
Copyright © 1971 Concordia Publishing House
Manufactured in the United States of America

4 5 6 7 8 9 10   TP   90 89 88 87 86 85 84 83

Library of Congress Cataloging in Publication Data

Spitz, Lewis William, 1922—
    The Reformation.

    (His The Renaissance and Reformation movements; v. 2)
    1. Reformation. I. Title.
CB359.S653 1980, vol. 2   [D228]   940.2s [940.2′2]
ISBN 0-570-03819-7   80-14461

TO
David M. Potter

Preface

CONTEMPORARY MAN is suffering from amnesia. He is drifting along in a state of mind that Sören Kierkegaard once referred to as "a kind of world historical forgetfulness." The French savant André Malraux intones somberly: "Western civilization has begun to doubt its own credentials." This condition is part of the price paid for modern man's pathetic attempt to live entirely in the "specious present," seeking relevance only in those fleeting moments that glide so quickly into the past. The loss of history means the loss of identity. The knowledge of history gives man "divine perspective." "Who I am," says the existential philosopher Karl Jaspers, "and where I belong, I first learned to know from the mirror of history."

The Renaissance and the Reformation were clearly high points of Western history. The Renaissance was an age of supreme cultural achievement and the Reformation was a time of most profound spiritual revolution. We have fallen heir to a golden age, but as St. Bernard once observed in his *De diligendo Deo,* "To possess what one knows nothing about, what glory can there be in that?" Certain implicit assumptions of this history merit explicit expression. This study emphasizes the thought, literature, art, morals, faith, and spirit of man, the culture and religion of the age, without neglecting its socioeconomic developments or political events. Highly personal ideas are as effective springboards for action as impersonal historical forces. It is not popular to cite Thomas Carlyle these days, but occasionally his observations still apply with epigrammatic force, as when he wrote in his *Essays:* "What is all knowledge, too, but recorded experience, and a product of history; of which, therefore, reasoning and belief, no less than action and passion, are essential materials?"

The age of the Renaissance and Reformation was not a static unified period within which time and history stood still. It was above all an age of movement, a time of accelerated transition. From Dante and Petrarch to Erasmus and Rabelais, from Giotto and Fra Angelico to Michelangelo and Pontormo, from Savonarola to Loyola, from Philip the Fair to Henry IV, from the Hundred Years' War to the Thirty Years' War, Europe was in motion. This critical period of history as a movement was felt in all aspects of life. In *The Future of Man*, Teilhard de Chardin accurately assigns to history its role in human knowledge:

> It is clear in the first place that the world in its present state is the outcome of movement. Whether we consider the rocky layers enveloping the earth, the arrangement of the forms of life that inhabit it, the variety of civilizations to which it has given birth, or the structure of languages spoken upon it, we are forced to the same conclusion: that everything is the sum of the past and that nothing is comprehensible except through its history.[1]

One problem with many textbooks is that no one lives longer than a few lines. It is much like dividing up the beautiful Pacific coast and assigning two inches of it to each citizen of California. A better understanding of the past can be gained by focusing most of our attention on the major protagonists, allowing the leading actors in the drama of history to speak their pieces. Nor should the men of that day, any more than those of our own, escape all moral judgment. The great Catholic historian Lord Acton criticized Bishop Creighton, author of *A History of the Papacy During the Period of the Reformation,* for going "through scenes of raging controversy and passion with a serene curiosity, a suspended judgment, a divided jury, and a pair of white gloves." The real tragedy would be for the author to get in the way of the story itself or to trivialize the universality of the human experience in those exciting centuries. "There is only one way to make love," quipped Dorothy Sayers, "but there are a thousand ways to commit a murder." If this book kills the subject or deadens its impact, it would have been better left unwritten.

For a single historian to give an account of three centuries (1300–1600) of European history requires greater temerity than anyone should possess. Perhaps only a fool would make such a bold attempt. And yet in his *Praise of Folly* Erasmus observed: "There are two main obstacles to the knowledge of things, modesty that casts a mist before the understanding, and fear that, having fancied a danger, dissuades us from the attempt." A general work such as this, after all, rests upon the research of hundreds and even thousands of specialists in the field. This book might well say with Tennyson's *Ulysses,* "I am a part of all that I have met." I am indebted to the work of many more scholars of various nations than could possibly be acknowledged in the notes. But I owe a special debt to certain colleagues, students, and friends.

For my general approach to Renaissance and Reformation history I am indebted to my loyal friend and genial graduate school mentor, Dr. Myron P. Gil-

---

[1] Pierre Teilhard de Chardin, *The Future of Man* (New York, 1964), p. 12.

more, who now serves as director of the Villa I Tatti in Florence. Dr. Gene Brucker, chairman of the history department of the University of California at Berkeley, a noted authority on Florentine social history, read the portion on the Renaissance and gave me the benefit of a detailed critique, for which I am most grateful. My able colleague Dr. Paul Seaver read and improved upon the chapters concerned with English history. My energetic assistant Mr. Mark Edwards chose the illustrations and selected the maps for this volume. My heartfelt thanks to them and to my editor, Mrs. Barbara H. Salazar, who has refined the manuscript and prepared the index with skill, grace, and literary talent. I wish to express my appreciation also to Mrs. Wilbert Rosin and to Mrs. Linda Edwards, who did the typescript. My wife, Dr. Edna Spitz, aided in many ways and at all times during the years this book was under way.

I owe an equally genuine if less immediately obvious debt to my students. The undergraduates, with their ingenuous, intelligent, critical candor, have ways uniquely their own of keeping a professor reasonably honest and humble. The graduate students have contributed not only historical knowledge but human insights and new methodology of the greatest value. Among these young scholars, many already holding important teaching and research positions across the land, I wish to mention especially the following: of the ladies, Ruth Arnon, Cissie Bonini, Patricia Covey, Virginia DeMarce, Sue Diamondstone, Lynn Hunt, Sharon Kettering, Margaret King, Arlene Miller, Anne J. Schutte, Kay Solon, Linda Taber, and Sister Marian Leona Tobriner; of the gentlemen, Darrel Ashcraft, Michael Baylor, John Biddle, Jules Bouret, Noel Brann, John Bray, James Bullard, David Bycina, Michael Carter, Theodore Casteel, Abraham Friesen, James Hinz, Larkin Kirkman, James Kittelson, William Klaustermeyer, Robert Lear, David McNeil, Steven Ozment, William Painter, Louis Reith, Charles Stinger, and Hugh West. "The young, too," said Luther, "must soon stand up and speak out after us."

I dedicate this book to my distinguished colleague David M. Potter, who has this year been honored by the entire profession, becoming at the same time the president of the Organization of American Historians and of the American Historical Association. His tremendous learning is equaled by his great strength of character and his capacity for true friendship.

LEWIS W. SPITZ

October 1970
Stanford University

Preface to *THE REFORMATION*

THE AGE OF THE REFORMATION witnessed a powerful resurgence of evangelical faith and a profound spiritual revolution that affected all the peoples of Europe and of the New World. "When God sends forth his Word," Luther declared, "it moves with power." The men of the Reformation were intensely preoccupied with the life of the inner man. "The Gospel is not preached so that we may only hear it," Calvin explained, "but so that it may as a seed of immortal life altogether reform our hearts." But their religious Reformation had a tremendous impact also upon the life of man in society.

The Reformation era was a time of social unrest, of crises, civil wars, assassinations and massacres. Europe experienced a long dynastic struggle between the Hapsburgs and Valois, the spread of Protestantism and the revivification of a great Church, the emergence of England as a major power, and a deadly duel between Catholic Spain and Protestant England for vantage at sea and the prizes of Empire. But amidst all the turmoil, wars, and rumors of wars, western man achieved some of the greatest literary, philosophical, theological, musical, geographical, and scientific triumphs and discoveries which history has to record.

So much of that history is still alive within us and has so directly helped to make us what we are that a knowledge of the Reformation movement is essential to our own self-understanding. Historical knowledge must be generative rather than self-terminating. "Life can only be understood backward," observed Sören Kierkegaard, "but it must be lived forward." If we can learn from the men of that day how to face troubled times and an uncertain future with some measure of faith, creativity, and courage, the study of Reformation history will have been very rewarding indeed.

L.W.S.

June 1972

Contents

ILLUSTRATIONS

MAPS

The maps are from Bryce Lyon, Herbert H. Rowen, and Theodore S. Hamerow,
A History of the Western World, cartography by Willis R. Heath (Chicago: Rand
McNally, 1969).

The Renaissance and Reformation Movements

CHAPTER 12

The Age
of the
Reformation

"We are at the dawn of a new era!" exclaimed Luther more prophetically than he himself imagined. For the final consequences of the Reformation movement for all of Europe went far beyond what Luther expected, and in many ways were very different from what he hoped for. "Rarely is a work undertaken out of wisdom and precaution," he declared, "but everything is undertaken out of ignorance." The man who initiates creative action can seldom know where his steps will lead him and what effect his actions will have on himself and others. Luther knew this, and was willing to leave the result to God. "God has led me as a horse having blinders so that I cannot see those who come up against me," he confessed. As an outsized historical figure, Luther cast a large shadow across the events of early modern times. But if Luther was a prime mover, the forces that soon set all Europe in motion were stronger than any single man.

Europe entered the sixteenth century at least nominally unified by the Catholic Church; it emerged from the Reformation with a variety of evangelical communities and Protestant groups competing with the old church and with each other for the faith and devotion of men. At the outset Europe still conceived of itself as Christendom, a body of believers with common goals to match their common faith; by the end of the period it openly acknowledged the particularist interests of the new monarchies and territorial principalities, and witnessed the bursting of its long-

DUTCH ENGRAVING OF THE SEVENTEENTH CENTURY. *The Candelstick: The Light of the Gospel Was Rekindled by All the Reformers.* Rijksmuseum, Amsterdam.

established bounds by colonial expansion into nearly all parts of the world. At the beginning of the century Europe had a lively but geographically limited capitalist economy on a broad agrarian base; at the end of the era its capitalism was vastly expanded and its mercantile enterprises circled the globe. Europe came to the Reformation epoch with a certain uniformity of ecclesiastical culture and still aglow with the artistic and literary triumphs of the Italian Renaissance, and at the close was moving rapidly toward new secular cultural foundations and the world of modern science. If it is no longer fashionable to refer to the Reformation, as did the historian James Froude in the nineteenth century, as "the hinge on which all modern history turns," its tremendous importance in the shaping of modern Europe must still be acknowledged. "I perceive a certain fatal change in human affairs," wrote Erasmus at the time. But the change he apprehensively saw as fatal was characterized rather by an enormous new vitality and by drives that carried European culture into new geographical and intellectual worlds.

A major historical happening like the Reformation is difficult to describe in detail, and no analysis of it can hope to be complete and final. The great historian Jacob Burckhardt, in the sixth book of his masterful work *The Civilization of the Renaissance in Italy,* candidly conceded the near impossibility of the undertaking:

> Mighty events like the Reformation elude, as respects their details, their outbreak and their development, the deductions of the philosophers, however clearly the necessity of them as a whole may be demonstrated. The movements of the human spirit, its sudden flashes, its expansions and its pauses, must forever remain a mystery to our eyes, since we can but know this or that of the forces at work in it, never all of them together.

History as the realm of freedom and of meaning is always difficult to describe and to interpret, but a movement in which the most delicate inward spiritual concerns of men are involved requires special sensitivity, a proper balance between objectivity and sympathy.

The task of understanding the period has been made more difficult by the great simplifiers, who have fixed in the popular mind clichés and half-truths that must first be cleared away. The eighteenth-century philosophers missed the real importance of the Reformation. Voltaire, for example, praised Luther only as one who resisted the Roman Catholic Church, and saw the Reformation as a squabble of monks in a corner of Saxony which plunged thirty nations into misery. Montesquieu appreciated the Reformation for its cultural by-products. Many of the nineteenth-century historians saw it as a seedbed of ideas congenial to themselves, whether they were liberal or conservative. Thus the French statesman and historian François Guizot called the Reformation an expression of the desire of the human mind for freedom and a "great effort to emancipate human reason." The German poet Heinrich Heine declared that when Luther defied the pope, Robespierre decapitated the king, and Immanuel Kant disposed of God, it was all one insurrection against the same tyrant under different names. The Prussian historian Heinrich Treitschke proclaimed in 1883 that Luther broke the shackles of "that crowned priest the pope" and became the founder of the modern secular state. And the famous nineteenth-century thinker Bertrand Russell, who lived on far into the twentieth century, once said that the Reformation had freed men religiously, but they have yet to free themselves politically and economically.

But if one were to ask the reformers themselves what gave their work its special memorable character, they would declare their service to have been the restoration of Christian truths that had been forgotten or only half remembered in the church: the sovereignty and graciousness of God, the meaning of Jesus Christ as the redeemer of estranged man, the power of faith, the essence of the Word, the freedom of the Christian, and the pure teaching of these truths against the false accretions of tradition and an erring papacy. Though the Reformation brought about social, political, and economic change, the reformers themselves concentrated predominantly on theological and religious matters. "My affair is not a joint program," Luther asserted. The study of the Reformation in its full dimensions, then, must take the religious issues seriously. "The deepest theme in history has been posed by the conflict between faith and disbelief," wrote Goethe.

During the first years of the Reformation many humanists viewed it as the religious expression of the general cultural Renaissance. The Erasmian humanist Johann von Botzheim, a canon at Constance, praised Luther as the man who, "after all the other disciplines have been renewed, is now renewing theology itself." In Augsburg another Erasmian, Bernhard Adelmann, equated the terms *doctus* and *Lutherus,* learned man and Lutheran. Erasmus' own alter ego, the young humanist Beatus Rhenanus, responded to the Reformation with the cry: "I see the whole world reviving!" And Luther himself viewed the Renaissance revival of learning as a kind of John the Baptist serving as a forerunner for the advent of the pure gospel. "No one knew," he wrote, "why God allowed the study of the languages to come forth until it was finally realized that it was for the sake of the gospel which He wished to reveal thereafter."

Many ties bound the Reformation to the Renaissance: the drive back to the pure sources, the reaction against scholastic philosophy, the criticism of formalism in religious practice, and the concern with an educational and religious revival. The humanists had sought their model in the golden age of classical letters, the reformers in the early church and the Scriptures. This drive to the sources was recognized as a characteristic mark of the Reformation by Francis Bacon, who wrote in his *Advancement of Learning* (Book 1):

> Martin Luther, conducted (no doubt) by an higher providence, but in discourse of reason finding what a province he had undertaken against the Bishop of Rome and the degenerate traditions of the church, and finding his own solitude, being no ways aided by the opinions of his own time, was enforced to awake all antiquity,

and to call former times to his succours to make a party against the present time: so that the ancient authors, both in divinity and in humanity, which had long time slept in libraries, began generally to be read and revolved.

The humanists made basic contributions to the recovery of Christian as well as classical antiquity. The new philology and linguistic studies, the discovery and editing of patristic texts as well as new critical editions of the Scriptures in the original languages, the new historical sense of distance from the pure and more perfect age, all these belonged to the Renaissance inheritance of the reformers.

The reformers shared with the humanists a low assessment of the centuries just past. If Petrarch and the humanists evolved the concept of a dark age separating them from antiquity, the reformers viewed the three preceding centuries as the nadir of the church's history, a period of corruption in the hierarchy, of abuses, ignorance, and indifference among the lower secular clergy and monks, and of gross superstition and "work righteousness" on the part of the laity. They reserved special scorn for medieval scholastic philosophy. Like the humanists, they were critical of the "barbarous" Latin of the scholastics, and elevated rhetoric above dialectic as a method for ascertaining and expressing truth. Luther's young lieutenant Philipp Melanchthon thus described medieval learning as a barbaric mixture of two evils: ignorant yet garrulous philosophy and the cult of idols. The English reformer John Bale, popularly known as "bilious Bale" for his talent for invective, declared that the mere description of this sordid, obscure, and ignoble kind of writing was enough to move generous and wellborn minds to nausea. Luther opposed scholastic logic as unsuitable to religious study. The objection of the reformers to scholastic learning went far beyond criticism of its language and dialectic to rejection of the religious presuppositions of scholastic theology, propositions they considered to be semi-Pelagian, stressing man's contribution to his salvation rather than his total dependence upon God's grace and forgiveness. The reformers' drive against the church's religious teaching and practice proved to be a far more radical and revolutionary force than Renaissance religious philosophy had generated. From 1520 on, the Reformation began to derail humanism in the religious realm.

How revolutionary was the Reformation? Edward Gibbon observed toward the end of the second volume of his monumental *Decline and Fall of the Roman Empire:* "After a fair discussion we shall rather be surprised by the timidity than scandalized by the freedom of our first reformers." Luther recognized in himself and others the difficulty of overcoming inertia and undertaking something that challenged established custom. "How very true is the saying 'To leave behind customary things is difficult and custom is second nature,'" he reflected. Moreover, the magisterial reformers viewed their program as a restoration of the ancient and honorable faith, not as an innovation or novelty. Melanchthon, in fact, believed that their moderate reforms had prevented tumults that would have been much more serious. A movement that was not revolutionary by intent, then, nevertheless turned out to have very revolutionary consequences. Revolutions are not created, they are unleashed. Controversy drove Luther to take positions more radical than any he had anticipated. Much of Europe was ready for that historical change to which the reformers gave actual form and shape. Leopold von Ranke, the great founder of modern critical history in the past century, described the Reformation as the most profound spiritual revolution ever experienced by a people in so short a period of time. Paradoxically the Reformation was moderate in intent and radical in consequence.

The Reformation was the first major historical movement of the post-Gutenberg era, and the printing press was a major instrument in its mass appeal. The printing press had an impact on two levels, among the learned and among the commoners. The printers, many of whom, such as Johannes Froben, Johannes Amerbach, and Aldus Manutius, were intellectual humanists and patrons of learning, made available to scholars a flood of classical, patristic, and medieval texts, especially devotional materials, and above all Bibles. More than one hundred editions of the Scriptures were published between 1457 and 1500. After the first printing the Bible was reduced to one-twentieth of its former price. It has been estimated that by 1500 A.D. some forty thousand works had been published, totaling around ten million precious volumes. This meant a great diffusion of knowledge, of course, but perhaps of equal importance was the improvement of textual accuracy and general consistency for the benefit of philological study. While the printed book inaugurated that phase of Western civilization which the metahistorian Oswald Spengler characterized as our "book and reading culture," and may have unduly exalted the authority of the written word, with peculiar consequences for later Protestantism, its immediate effect was a powerful impact by the reformers upon the masses through ideas that trickled down from the learned classes and through tracts and flyers distributed directly to the people. From 1500 to the start of the Reformation, German publishers issued an average of forty books a year, but once the Reformation began this number rocketed to five hundred titles a year. Beatus Rhenanus wrote to Zwingli that Luther's books were not so much sold as snatched from the hands of the booksellers. Within a fortnight after their appearance Luther's ninety-five theses had been printed and carried into all parts of Europe. Luther viewed the printing press as the ultimate gift of God by which the gospel was to be propagated. In his *Book of Martyrs* the English Protestant John Foxe praised the invention of printing as the "admirable work of God's wisdom," through which by God's grace "good wits" were stirred up "aptly to conceive the light of knowledge and judgment, by which light darkness began to be espied and ignorance to be detected, truth from error, religion from superstition to be discerned." Protestants and their opponents were very quick to seize upon this revolutionary instrument.

Brosamer. *The Seven Heads of Martin Luther.* Title page for Cochlaeus' blast against Luther. One head is a fanatic with wasps in his hair.

Why the Reformation Happened

WHY DID the Reformation originate in Germany? Why, for that matter, did it happen at all?

A common elementary explanation of the occurrence of the Reformation is that it came as a reaction against abuses in the church. "The church" was hopelessly corrupt, arousing the wrath and indignation of right-minded men. This simple argument, which appeared in much early humanist and Protestant polemical historiography, was matched on the Catholic side by assertions that Luther acted as a wicked or misguided and rebellious son of mother church, a grand example of what the philosopher Alfred North Whitehead has described as "the fallacy of misplaced concreteness." Actually an explanation on this level is not without some truth, for there were gross and offensive abuses in the church, and Luther and the reformers did seek to bring about changes while remaining within the fold.

A second explanation, a variation of the first, is that the Reformation was a result of doctrinal deviation. On the eve of the Reformation the church was, so the argument goes, wallowing in theological uncertainty. Doctrine was imprecisely defined, allowing as legitimate many theological statements that were no longer really Catholic, since they were not compatible with the Roman missal or liturgy. This uncertainty was heightened by the battle of the *viae* in scholastic theology— that is, the philosophy of the nominalist followers of William of Occam, known as the *via moderna*, and that of the moderate realist supporters of Thomas Aquinas, known as the *via antiqua*. The Occamists are said to have pressed their nominalist epistemology to the extreme of skepticism and nearly to the point of the doctrine of double truth: that some things are true in theology that are not true in philosophy and vice versa. They put such emphasis on God's will and sovereignty that they made him seem arbitrary and unaccountable. Yet man's role in attaining salvation and a stress upon the authority of the church were paradoxically elevated to new heights. Luther studied *via moderna* theology in the works of Gabriel Biel (d. 1485), the last significant Occamist. The opposition by Johannes Eck and other poor representatives of the faith also schooled in nominalism led to the doctrinal deviations of the Reformation. Against this negative interpretation of scholasticism it may be argued that the scholastics from Robert Holcot (d. 1349) to Gabriel Biel did not press Occam's presuppositions to extremes of skepticism or basic doctrinal deviation, and that Luther criticized the tendency of both scholastic *viae* to stress man's contribution to his own salvation in contrast to reliance on God's grace alone. Thanks to the schism and the conciliar movement, the primacy of the pope and his monarchical episcopate were no longer so securely fixed in the popular mind. But beyond the debates that still remained within the bounds of ecclesiastical permissiveness lay the acknowledged heresies of the Cathari, Waldensians, Wycliffites, Hussites, and a welter of other sects and mystic cults, many of which persisted into and beyond the first decades of the Reformation and contributed to radical deviation.

Behind the medieval variations in theology and the Reformation leap into new dimensions of religious thought lay what seems to be a characteristic of the collective mind. Systems of thought such as the great *summa* of St. Thomas seem to have certain limits of extension and longevity; when these are reached, the restless intellect presses beyond them. This has been true of all dogmatic systems as well as of the great synthetic philosophies. Perhaps, too, there is something worth pondering in Carl Jung's suggestion that the great archetypal configurations in the collective unconscious lose their hold upon man after a time and are replaced by others.

Still another and more prosaic explanation of the Reformation looks to its sociological roots. Europe in 1500 had between 65 million and 80 million people and possibly sixty or more kings, princes, archbishops, and other rulers in strategic positions of power. New social forces such as capitalism and the bourgeois classes that rose with it, the new technology in printing, mining, shipping, and other enterprises and the new working classes that maintained it, and the further growth of the cities were changing the real lines of power and dependency. Some classes, such as the lower nobility, were losing their traditional status and, except for a relatively few individuals of extraordinary adaptability, were being pushed aside. The church, which had adapted all too well to feudalism—some bishops, for example, were little more than feudal overlords—found it necessary to adopt new capitalist devices in order to support her hierarchy and the bureaucracy that had developed to meet the exigencies of curial government. The papacy's desperate and frustrated attempts to increase its income from the time of the Avignonese popes through the Renaissance popes gave the church the appearance of rapacious avarice, contributed to its loss of prestige and moral influence, and enraged the moralists, humanist critics, and reformers.

Finally, by one of those peculiar developments that precipitate cataclysmic events in history, at the very time when the official church was least able to provide moral leadership and a satisfying spiritual experience for the people, a new wave of religious devotion broke over Europe. For a century and a half before the Reformation, an increase in religious fervor was in evidence throughout most of Europe, including Italy. This increasing religiosity, principally touched off by the horrors of the Black Death and fear of the Turks, was evident in the growing number of shrines and pilgrimages, new prayers and increased use of candles, a renewed popularity of the rosary promoted by the Dominican Alain de la Roche (d. 1475), and the appearance of the stations of the cross in churches.

The veneration of saints increased, and each craft and trade guild adopted its own patron saint. St. George and St. Martin were popular with soldiers, St. Dorothea with gardeners, St. Barbara (who had been imprisoned in a tower)

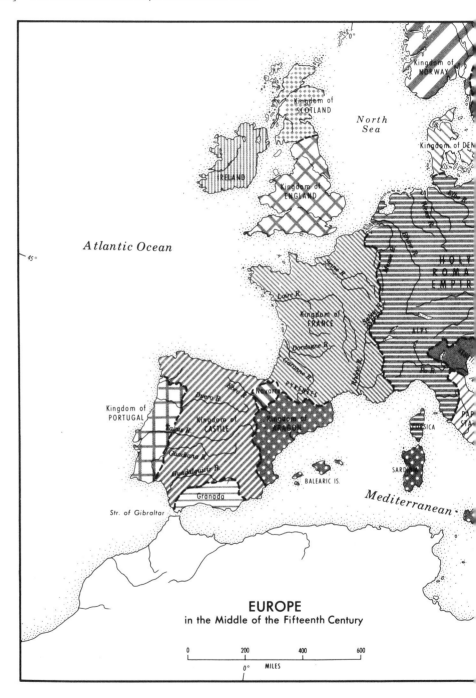

EUROPE
in the Middle of the Fifteenth Century

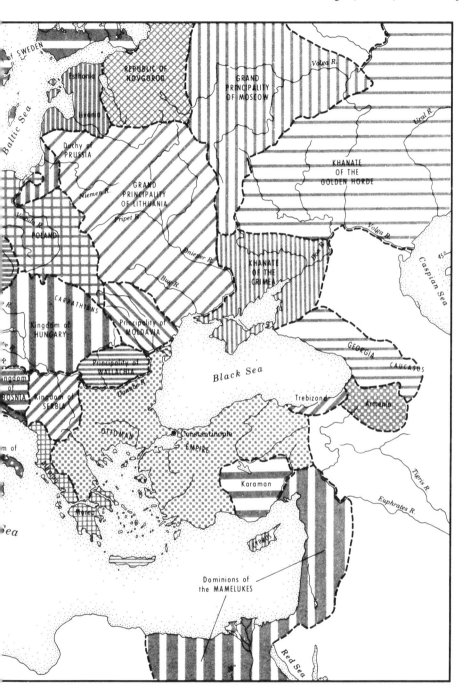

with cannonaders, and St. Bartholomew, skin in hand, with butchers. In Germany saints' names superseded all but the most popular old German names for children during the fifteenth century. The cult of St. Anne, Mary's mother, was widespread during that century and at the start of the next. Devotion to Mary increased enormously during the late fourteenth and fifteenth centuries. New masses were established commemorating every detail of her life, piety, and seven sorrows. The Franciscans, with the support of many of the humanists and against the opposition of the Dominicans, promoted the doctrine of the immaculate conception of Mary, an idea destined to become Catholic dogma many centuries later. Scores of new churches, especially in the new lands in northeast Germany, from Lübeck eastward, were named in her honor.

Endowed brotherhoods were organized for the pooling and sharing of good works. The Brethren of St. Ursula in Cologne in the sixteenth century amassed a spiritual fortune of 6,000 masses, 3,000 psalters, 20,000 *Te Deums,* and 100,000 rosaries, paternosters, and *Ave Marias.* Grotesque collections of relics in various parts of Europe attested to the gullibility and superstition of the people as well as to the commercial advantage of such attractions. Two such treasures, which played a direct part in setting the stage for the Reformation, were the collection of Frederick the Wise in Saxony, which included among its five thousand relics such gems as straw from the manger in Bethlehem, wood from the true cross, and the thumb of St. Anne, and the collection in the cathedral chapter at Noyen in Picardy (where John Calvin spent his childhood), which boasted a fragment of the crown of thorns and a lock of John the Baptist's hair. Pilgrimages to the shrines at Canterbury in England and Compostela in Spain remained popular, and newer shrines such as those in Regensburg and Alt-Ötting in Bavaria drew increasingly large numbers, including many crippled and sick people looking for cures.

The sale of indulgences multiplied, allegedly for church building or crusades against the Turks, though often for debt reduction by higher clergy or the papacy. The fact that they were sold and bought on such a grand scale is an index of the admixture of piety and superstition that proved to be such an explosive compound. Many new churches were built in the fifteenth and sixteenth centuries, first in an elaborate late Gothic style and then in the Renaissance style. The success of such popular preachers as John of Capistrano (d. 1456) and Johann Geiler von Kaisersberg (d. 1510) in swaying tens of thousands of people was an indication of the surcharged spiritual atmosphere and the response awaiting a clear call and more certain trumpet.

The great irony, indeed the great danger, of the situation was that in this time of increased religious fervor, the church was in no position to provide inspiring leadership or a constructive channel for this new force, but was itself the object of criticism and even ridicule. In religion, Dean Inge observed, nothing fails like success. At the Council of Nicea in 325 A.D. the Spanish bishops were reprimanded for being too worldly and too concerned with material things. In 1215, at the height of the Middle Ages, the great pope Innocent III charged the Fourth Lateran Council with introducing reforms. *Ecclesia semper reformanda* (the church which must always be reformed) was a phrase perennially applicable to a human institution of such wide scope. During the fifteenth century the slogan formulated by William of Durand during the conciliar movement, calling for a "reformation in head and in members," was repeatedly heard. Signs of discontent and disaffection were everywhere.

When the church appeared to be most opulent, it actually stood most in need of money to finance its burgeoning bureaucracy, elaborate juridical processes, and ambitious building programs and activities. It has been asserted that one-third of the landed wealth of Europe was held by the church, by means of a legal fiction known as the incorporation of the church, whereby the title was vested in God while the property was administered by churchmen. It was widely believed that two-fifths of the German income was siphoned off to Rome through ecclesiastical channels. Great ingenuity was employed in devising new sources of ecclesiastical income. From the thirteenth century on, by canonical provision, if the holder of an ecclesiastical post died while in Rome, his benefice was reassigned by the pope (not by the bishop in whose see the post was located). The practice of reservations, or payments for nominations to vacant benefices, and the collection of annates, the first year's revenue from a benefice, increased opportunities for simony, the buying of church offices. Nepotism in ecclesiastical appointments seemed to be on the increase. Under Pope Leo X (1513–1521) the number of church offices available for purchase rose to an all-time high, and he employed his Medici talent in founding new offices for financial gain. The acrostic *Radix Omnium Malorum Avaritia* (the love of money is the root of all evil) = ROMA was popular. Conrad Peutinger, the Augsburg city secretary sent to Rome during the pontificate of Innocent VIII, wrote in 1491 of the shocking venality in the capital of Christendom:

> I see that everything here can be bought from top to bottom. Intrigues, hypocrisy, adulation are highly honored, religion is debased; vulgarities occur without number; righteousness sleeps. Whenever I see the ruined monuments of antiquity, I deplore the fact that this famous city is ruled by a foreign race which under pious pretenses practices every deed of violence and other unheard-of outrages, and they wish thereby to be praised instead of the deserved censure. When I rebuke them they say that fate has so ordained it![1]

In marked contrast to the splendor of many of the upper clergy in key positions, a great many priests, especially in rural areas, were wretchedly provided for. The income from many prebends was so small that a cleric either held several of them, which involved him in the abuse of plurality of incomes, or lived in poverty

---

[1] Peutinger to Valentin Eber, August 5, 1491, in *Konrad Peutingers Briefwechsel*, ed. Erich König (Munich, 1923), p. 9.

as great as any monk's. Vicars of parishes attached to monasteries had extraordinarily small incomes. In Scotland over half the vicars were extremely poor. In Flanders the priests were so poorly paid that many had to work at other jobs. The bishop of Clermont reported to the Council of Trent in 1546 that of eight hundred parishes in his diocese, only sixty had regular parish priests, and the rest were cared for by vicars, whose incomes amounted to a mere ten or twelve guldens a year.

The education of a majority of priests was minimal. Most of them had learned the elements of Latin and basic catechismal theology and the rite of the mass as apprentices to local priests; only a few were privileged to attend cathedral and monastic schools prior to ordination. A very small proportion of priests studied theology at a university, although the number increased during the second half of the fifteenth century. Felix Faber was exaggerating, though not greatly, when he wrote in his *Chronicle of Ulm* at the end of the fifteenth century that in his youth, of a thousand clergymen there was hardly one who had so much as seen a university town, and the holder of a degree was stared at as a prodigy. Of course, this was an unfair thrust, for ever since the high Middle Ages it had been the custom for most local clergymen to be educated in local houses of study that served the purpose, though they never claimed to produce scholars. In some dioceses candidates for the priesthood were required by their bishops to study in the diocesan schools of the regular clergy. The social status of the common clergy was depressingly low. These conditions help to explain not only the poor morale of the clergy on the eve of the Reformation, but also the fact that recruits for the evangelical movement came by the thousands from the secular and regular clergy of the church itself.

One of the abuses most corrosive of the spiritual life of the church was the absenteeism of key clergy. The holding of multiple prebends and offices was necessitated in part by the low income produced by endowments in the depressed economy and in part by the extravagant living by higher clergy, many of whom were actual feudal overlords or functionaries of civil government. Cardinal Wolsey, the butcher's son who rose to be Henry VIII's chancellor, was also archbishop of York, bishop of Durham and Winchester, deputy for nonresident alien bishops at Worcester, Salisbury, and Llandaff, and abbot of St. Albans. As a boy his bastard son was already dean of Wells and archdeacon of York and Richmond, with two rectories, six prebends, and one appointment as chancellor. Even Henry VIII's humanist physician Thomas Linacre had been a canon of three cathedrals, rector of four parishes, and precentor of the York cathedral prior to ordination into the priesthood. Government was exploiting church income for the monarch's political or personal ends, but the church as keeper of the public conscience suffered the moral opprobrium of a situation not always of its own making. A scandalous instance in France was the case of Antoine Duprat, a diplomat who was rewarded with the archbishopric of Sens, but entered the cathedral there for the first time on the occasion of his own funeral. In Italy Cardinal Ippolito d'Este, who was archbishop of Milan, never once visited this important diocese in thirty years. In Germany the most blatant case of plural offices was that of Albert of Brandenburg, who was not content to be merely archbishop of Magdeburg and bishop of Halberstadt, but in addition purchased the archbishopric of Mainz, since this office made him both one of the imperial electors and secretary of the Holy Roman Empire. The clergy, said the preacher Johann Geiler von Kaisersberg, had become fishers of prebends rather than of souls. Because the rewards of high church offices were great, the aristocracy preempted them. Many enterprising young men took degrees in both canon and civil law, so that they would be prepared for any opportunity. The social requirements of some cathedral canons were so severe that Erasmus commented that Christ himself could not have become a member of the chapter at Strassburg.

A peculiar dichotomy existed in the general attitude toward the clergy. The late scholastic Gabriel Biel placed priests higher than the angels, for in the blessed sacrament they were dispensers of a mystery and could allow or prohibit God to come into being, which angels could not do. The father of German humanism, Rudolf Agricola, in his *Exhortation to the Clergy at Worms,* waxed eloquent over the majesty, mystery, and glory of the priesthood. But these very decades witnessed a marked increase in the immorality of the clergy and a widespread breakdown of celibacy as a viable system. Sixteenth-century visitation reports reveal that one-fourth of the clergy in the Netherlands and one-third of all Catholic clerics in the lower Rhine region were living with concubines. In rural areas a woman was considered a natural and necessary helpmate to the working priest. The reform-minded bishop of Constance decreed that priests' children were not to serve as altar boys or take walks with their fathers. Bishop Christoph von Stadion composed a long report on the clergy's loss of virtue. Archbishop Albert of Brandenburg kept a house of courtesans in Halle until it was stormed and dismantled by a mob of Protestants. As late as 1539 Luther had to admonish him for smuggling a mistress into the archepiscopal palace inside a relic box. In the popular mind corruption was seen to be spreading from Rome outward, subverting the simple, purer people across the Alps. "The nearer to Rome, the worse the Christians," they said. The author of *The Ship of Fools,* Sebastian Brant, a half-medieval humanist, summarized much popular sentiment in his foreboding couplet:

> Saint Peter's ship I fear I'm thinking
> May very shortly now be sinking!

The medieval religious principles of the virtue of self-denial and the spiritual value of the ascetic life remained the theoretical ideals of society into the sixteenth century. On this basis the regular clergy (those who lived by the *regula,* or rule, of a monastic order) were the truly "religious," bound by their threefold vows of poverty, chastity, and obedience. "To become a priest is worthy of honor," wrote Trithemius, abbot of Sponheim, "but to become a monk out of love of God means to achieve a greater perfection." But this same Trithemius who held such high regard for the monastic way decried the pride, power drive, and corruption of the orders and their houses. He attacked the abbots who ruled as feudal overlords of the vast possessions of the monasteries:

> Dare we believe, my brothers, that St. Benedict had such expensive horses and mules as we now see many an abbot possess? Certainly not! And do we not read of St. Martin that he rode in on a lowly donkey using a cord for a rein, not on such a proud steed as our heads of orders today, who dash about here and yon on their noble horses holding in their hands a bridle with silver and gold ornamentation! O vanity of vanities, what does this pride mean?[2]

Preachers such as Johann Geiler von Kaisersberg were critical of the worldliness and lack of spirituality of the monks. "The walls do not make a monastery!" he exclaimed. "It must be within the heart." Popular humor often turned on the theme of monastic corruption. "She longs for the cloister for she wants a lover" was a standard witticism.

The humanists assaulted especially the mendicants for their tyranny, which made even popes fear them, and for their obscurantism. Because of their reputation for mendacity and lechery, they were depicted in popular art as foxes and wolves wearing cowls. The controversy over Johannes Reuchlin defined the issues clearly in the humanists' minds. They saw the Dominicans of Cologne as treacherous reactionaries intent on martyring Reuchlin, who had achieved so much for Hebrew studies and the cause of scholarship. There was clearly a loss of élan, a displacement in the heart of the medieval ascetic system, due to a corrosion in the monastic and mendicant orders themselves and to a shift away from the ascetic ideal as an expression of the good life and of religion's highest worth.

Yet the reputation of the orders, thanks to the exaggerations of the humanists, Protestants, and later Whiggish historians, was certainly much worse than the actual conditions warranted. The orders, in fact, made repeated efforts at fundamental reforms. The Carthusians had a near-perfect record of adherence to their rule. The Benedictines had such centers of reform as Melk on the Danube. The Dominican reform effort began in Italy under Cajetan, the master general of the order. A Franciscan "observant" movement began in France, and in 1517 Pope Leo X allowed two independent orders to organize: the Observantines, who believed in strict observance of the rule of St. Francis, and the Conventuals, who followed a modified rule. The Augustinian hermits developed an Observantine group of houses, organized by the Saxon Andreas Proles and continued by Johannes Staupitz, Luther's confessor, after Proles's death in 1503. It was in connection with

---

[2] Cited in Willi Andreas, *Deutschland vor der Reformation: Eine Zeitenwende*, 5th ed. (Stuttgart, 1948), p. 126.

a dispute about bowing to a nonreformed provincial that Luther was sent to Rome to represent the Observantine Augustinians in 1510. The lay order of the Brethren of the Common Life, founded by Gerard Groote (d. 1384), established many houses from Utrecht and Deventer across northern Europe and up the Rhine in the course of the fifteenth century. The Brethren, closely associated with the more mystical Augustinians, showed tremendous vitality, maintained dozens of famous secondary schools where the "safe" classics were taught, kept hospices for poor students, and educated a surprisingly large number of men who later became famous, among them Desiderius Erasmus and, it seems, Martin Luther. They were so useful and enjoyed such an excellent reputation that even after the church was wrenched apart, Luther and Melanchthon defended them, and they were allowed to teach in such Protestant lands as Brandenburg. Recent research has revealed that moral conditions had not deteriorated so badly in the English monasteries as had been popularly believed since their closing by King Henry VIII. The same is true of monasteries on the continent. And yet all the evidence suggests that in much of northern Europe the monastic system was played out as a vital religious force. In city after city, as in Nuremberg and Augsburg, the same mothers who had tearfully delivered their unmarried daughters to the cloisters descended upon these establishments to free them again when the Reformation erupted. More than coincidence is involved in the fact that literally thousands of evangelical preachers and teachers were recruited from the ranks of the monks, friars, and hermits; Luther himself was only the first of many.

The church missed its last big chance at a general reform that would have met the demands for restoration and renewal when, at the opening session of the Fifth Lateran Council (1512–1517), the general of the Augustinian order, Egidio da Viterbo, a distinguished Platonist, called for an inner spiritual reform that would be reflected in an outward improvement. His approach was in the tradition of the Christian humanist program, but the council failed to respond to this or to any of the other demands for reform. It was comprised mostly of Italian prelates, and thus fell somewhat short of being ecumenical, even though a New World bishop from Santo Domingo did attend. It called for perpetual peace among Christian princes and made a loud clamor for a financial assessment on all kingdoms and states for a crusade against the Turks, even permitting the taxation of the clergy in some lands. But the response was cynical, for the Venetians, for example, declared that the money would be used by Pope Leo X to finance his war against Urbino, where he hoped to gain territory for the Medici family. In the final session, which ironically came in the year in which the Reformation began, the council reaffirmed the bull *Unam sanctam* (1302), in which Pope Boniface VIII had asserted his claim to a fullness of spiritual power and real, though indirect, authority over all rulers. The ecclesiasts had, it seems, forgotten nothing, but they were about to learn a great deal.

After the outbreak of the Reformation the earnest Dutch pope Adrian VI instructed Chieregati, his legate to the Diet of Nuremberg in 1522 and 1523, to confess:

> God has let this persecution of His church occur because of men and especially because of the sins of the priests and prelates. The Holy Scriptures loudly proclaim that the sins of the people have their origin in the sins of the religious leaders. We know all too well that also in the case of this Holy See for many years many reprehensible things have taken place: abuses in spiritual things, breaking of the commandments, yes, that everything has taken a turn for the very worst! We therefore have no cause to wonder that the disease has been transplanted from the head to the members, from the popes to the prelates.[3]

If the disappointing pronouncements of the Fifth Lateran Council and the failure to implement even these was a matter of too little, too late, the public confession of Pope Adrian was a matter of too much, much too late, for by 1523 the Protestants simply used his statement to prove the truth of their allegations against Rome. The church entered the Reformation with its spiritual power sadly diminished.

Why the Reformation Happened in Germany

LEOPOLD VON RANKE formulated the postulate that ecclesiastical and political history are indissolubly connected. In the case of the Reformation this truism is even more obvious than usual, for the political conditions in the Germanies contrasted in many essential ways with those in other lands. The special circumstances in Germany constituted preconditions favorable to the success of the Reformation movement. Certainly they do not of themselves offer a causal explanation for the Reformation or for its religious nature and theological substance.

The Holy Roman Empire was not yet so effete as it was to become in the seventeenth century, when the political philosopher Samuel Pufendorf called it a ghost, but its claim to universality was already empty and its ancient members could hardly bestir themselves to effective action. The very name Holy Roman Empire did not come into widespread use until the twelfth century, and the fact that the empire's jurisdiction was really limited to the German lands was at last acknowledged when the qualifying phrase "of the German Nation" came into semi-official use during the reign of Emperor Maximilian I (1493–1519). Various efforts at the constitutional reform of the empire, such as those of its secretary Archbishop Berthold von Henneberg, who hoped to make it a more effective political force in the late fifteenth century, failed because of the particularist interests of the territorial principalities and the dead weight of tradition. Von Henneberg pressed for

---

[3] Carl Mirbt, ed., *Quellen zur Geschichte des Papsttums und des römischen Katholizismus,* 4th ed. (Tübingen, 1924), p. 261.

an executive college of electors, an effective imperial supreme court, and a common imperial tax to promote centralization. But the princes were unwilling to sacrifice any sovereignty, and neither Maximilian nor Charles V succeeded in getting any reforms through the diet. In 1519 the elector of Mainz referred to the empire as a princely aristocracy with the diet as the actual sovereign.

The historian can argue with some plausibility that the last real chance for a unified Germany under effective imperial rule was lost at the time of the investiture controversy in the late eleventh and early twelfth centuries, when in his struggle for "the right order of things in the world" Pope Gregory VII freed the feudal vassals of their oaths of allegiance to the emperor and gave the princes their chance at virtual autonomy. The empire had failed as a political force long before the Reformation; there is no truth in the old cliché that Luther did what Pope Innocent III and Emperor Frederick II had failed to do—break up the Holy Roman Empire and the Holy Roman Church. The very most that can be said is that the Reformation accelerated a process of dissolution already far advanced. By the end of the eighteenth century Goethe's whimsical query in *Faust* could be understood by all: "The dear old Holy Roman realm, how does it hold together?" The ignominious end came at last in August 1806, when a diminutive Corsican corporal pronounced its demise, speaking as Emperor Napoleon of France.

During the fifteenth and sixteenth centuries the Holy Roman Empire of the German Nation moved in a direction precisely opposite to the trend in western Europe. While England, France, and Spain moved toward national consolidation under strong dynastic monarchies, the empire experienced a strengthening of the territorial principalities, the social upsets of a dying feudalism, and a further weakening of the emperor's position. The very universality of the Habsburg dynastic holdings kept them from concentrating their efforts upon the Holy Roman Empire as such. Charles V was Charles I of Spain, though his first language was French, part of his Burgundian heritage and upbringing. His election as emperor in 1519, secured with loans from the Fugger banking house and the manipulation of the electors, brought to him a decentralized state with virtually none of the instruments of government that could serve as centripetal forces. For revenue and military power he was almost entirely dependent upon his dynastic lands. The *Reichstag* or diet was composed of the usual three estates, but it was dominated by the nobility, with lesser influence wielded by the upper clergy and especially the prince-bishops with great landed holdings, such as the three episcopal electors, the archbishops of Mainz, Trier, and Cologne; little or no power was exercised by the cities. For such enterprises as defense against the Turks the emperor was dependent upon voluntary contributions voted ad hoc and seldom paid when they were due.

Like the territorial principalities, the cities of the empire were in the ascendancy. In 1521 the imperial registry listed some eighty-five cities, of which sixty-five were directly under the empire. Governed by city councils and mayors who were

Der Buchdrucker.

Der Teppichmacher.

Der Papyrer.

Der Organist.

Der Schrifftgiesser.

Der Uhrmacher.

Der Apoteccker.

Der Buchbinder.

really controlled by the merchant oligarchies, with some influence being exercised by lesser guilds, the cities enjoyed a large measure of freedom and independence. During the fifteenth and early sixteenth centuries they enjoyed great prosperity, especially those in southern Germany and along the Rhine. Augsburg, Nuremberg, Constance, Freiburg, Strassburg, Mainz, Cologne, and Erfurt hummed with commercial activity. They were veritable beehives, observed the humanist Conrad Celtis, where German merchants returned from Italy and the north to store their honey. But the cities were not organized to protect their mutual interests and had little collective political power, no matter how prosperous they became.

While the princes and cities rose to new eminence, the knightly class lost its military utility and went into decline as a vestigial remain of feudalism. Some of the nobility adjusted to the new society, but many turned to robbery and pillage, making raids upon merchants, towns, and monasteries until their castles were reduced to rubble by artillery fire or they were hanged or imprisoned in city dungeons. Goethe has immortalized in a play one such robber baron, Goetz von Berlichingen, the man with the iron arm, who struck fear into the hearts of prince-bishops and merchants until he was finally captured while leading a peasant revolt. There were many like him. To this superfluous class belonged also the humanist Ulrich von Hutten; perhaps his class background goes far to explain the bitterness of his attacks upon the ecclesiastical establishment.

Much of the empire, especially in the central and northern territories, was still agrarian and feudal in economic organization and mentality. While the peasants had less personal freedom than in many parts of France and England, they had greater independence than they had enjoyed in earlier centuries. They still shouldered many of the traditional burdens: annual dues, tithes, death taxes, restrictions on hunting and fishing, and limitations on personal movement. But payment in kind was increasingly commuted to payment in money, so that more and more peasants became renters rather than serfs. In a money economy their position seemed unenviable compared with that of the city dwellers, even though on an absolute scale they were much better off than ever before. Paradoxically their very prosperity and gains in personal liberties made the remaining restrictions more irksome. And in the southwest upper Rhineland, where the position of the peasants was better than elsewhere, their unrest was greater. It was in these regions that the dreaded *Bundschuh,* a secret revolutionary society of peasants, had its greatest strength. With social tensions mounting, the empire was a tinderbox ready for the revolutionary spark.

Ironically, much of the resentment of various social classes was directed against the church. The princes, who needed ever larger revenues for their modern weapons, mercenary troops, law courts, and finery, eyed the property and income of the church and coveted the wealth that was siphoned off to Italy. The cities struggled to wrest power away from neighboring overlords who were often prince-bishops, as much feudal rulers as churchmen. The city councils, like the princes, were opposed to the juridical privileges and immunities of the clergy, who were subject only to ecclesiastical courts and could carry their cases out of the empire all the way to Rome. The knights harbored hostility against the prince-bishops and exploitation by foreigners. Why should German gold be used to build churches in Rome, asked Ulrich von Hutten, when so many churches in Germany needed rebuilding? The peasants hated the ostentatious bearing of silk-clad prelates. When they labored on church lands, the abbots and bishops were themselves the hated oppressors, and it was very easy to identify the church with feudal exploitation.

The Roman church was much less restricted in Germany than in neighboring France. The Pragmatic Sanction of Bourges, agreed to by the French king Charles VII in 1438, had given the Gallican church many special privileges, among them the right to limit judicial appeals to Rome, to restrict the papal control of benefices, and to substitute voluntary contributions for official dues. In 1516 King Francis I concluded the Concordat of Bologna with Pope Leo X, securing to the French king the right to make nominations to vacant bishoprics and abbacies in his realm, while granting the pope the right to collect the annates or first years' incomes from these offices. The emperor had no such privileges. He could never act with the force and effectiveness of the French king, to say nothing of the English monarch Henry VIII on his tight little island.

On the other hand, for a century and a half prior to the Reformation the rising new powers in the empire, the princes and the cities, had been strengthening their control over the church on the local level. In their drive to establish centralized control over their territories the princes introduced where they could the newly revived Roman law, which elevated the absolute power of the *princeps,* for it had, after all, been codified under Justinian. It is true that arguments from Roman law could be used to limit the power of princes, as in the frequent citations in the treatises on the right of resistance in the sixteenth century, but officially it was usually exploited in behalf of princely power. Humanist chancellors and secretaries worked with Roman legists to strengthen the authority of the prince at the expense of the traditional rights of the territorial estates and in opposition to the loosely organized bodies of common law such as the *Sachsenspiegel,* or Saxon folk law. Long before the Reformation some jurists of the territorial courts decided that the *princeps,* after the example of the *pontifex maximus* in ancient Rome, should be concerned also with religious affairs. Thus the old Germanic *Eigenkirche,* or proprietary church tradition, reinforced by the Renaissance legal development, grew into a system of princely control over the church in the princes' territories. The domination of church life by the princes was most thorough in the larger states: Austria, the Palatinate, Bavaria, Brandenburg. In Ducal Saxony the two archbishops took their fiefs from Duke Georg and paid him feudal dues. When Lutheranism threatened to penetrate Ducal Saxony, it was one of Georg's lawyers,

Melchior von Aussa, who first enunciated that principle so important in later centuries: *Cuius regio, eius religio*—whoever rules the realm, his shall be the religion. In tiny Jülich and Cleves the dukes had the right of visitation as though they were bishops. And in Electoral Saxony Duke Frederick the Wise made ecclesiastical and academic appointments. Though he saw Luther only once, at the Diet of Worms in 1521, as a good German ruler he would not tolerate Roman persecution of his professor.

In the imperial cities a very similar pattern of secular control developed. The city councils preempted one prerogative of the hierarchy after another until they were virtually in control of the church. The councils took over the administration of charity, sick care, hospices for the aged, the ordering of church and cloisters, regulations on ethical questions, and punishment for blasphemy, swearing, religious disturbances, and superstitious excesses. Education too became the concern of secular authorities: the cities and princes founded eighteen of the twenty universities established in Germany before the Reformation, including the University of Erfurt, a city foundation, and the University of Wittenberg, established by Frederick the Wise. The political fragmentation of the empire, coupled with the proprietary church situation, made the Reformation possible in the Germanies.

Lay control opened the door further to ecclesiastical abuses, so that, ironically, animosity against the Roman Catholic Church increased sharply in these decades. Erasmus wrote of the common hatred of the name of Rome among the Germans, intensified by the cultural nationalism of the German humanists. Year in and year out the imperial diets were flooded with complaints about exploitation, false jurisdiction, immorality, and other abuses. From 1415 to 1521 the *gravamina*, or grievances of the German nation against the Roman church, were voiced at the diets. In 1452 the archbishop of Mainz, as secretary of the Holy Roman Empire, drew up the first official statement of such grievances. In 1493 the nobles submitted their own list of grievances. The din grew loud and shrill. When at the Diet of Nuremberg in 1522 the papal legate Chieregati asked why the Edict of Worms of 1521 had not been enforced against Luther, he was answered with a list of a hundred grievances against the church about which nothing had been done either. Years later Cardinal Contarini had to tell Pope Paul III that if all the Protestant divines, including Luther himself, were reconciled to the church, the situation would in no way be affected, and the rebellion would go on as bitterly as before.

The religious situation in the Germanies in the early sixteenth century, however, does not bear an easy causal relationship to the outbreak of the Reformation. Quite the contrary, it offers rather the startling paradox that when disenchantment with the Roman hierarchy was most complete and resentment against abuses burned most fiercely, religious fervor and popular piety were most intense. Philosophers and historians have noted this phenomenon and have speciously attributed it to some quality in the Germans themselves. The German philosopher Hegel

ALBRECHT DÜRER. *Knight, Death, and the Devil*. Grey Collection, Fogg Art Museum, Harvard University.

ascribed the force of the Reformation to an "ancient and constantly preserved in-wardness of the German people." The Swiss Protestant historian Merle d'Aubigné wrote of "the peculiar character of the Germans, which seemed especially favorable to a religious reformation, for they had not been enervated by a false civilization."

Certainly there is nothing peculiarly Teutonic about religious intensity. For most people life was grim. As a result of poor diet, repeated outbreaks of the plague, and feudal warfare, life expectancy was not much over forty years, and many men of that age referred to themselves as "old men." The Germans, moreover, stood directly in the line of advance of the fearful Turks as they pressed up the Danube. A somber mood predominated, perhaps best illustrated in Albrecht Dürer's wood-cut of the four grinning horsemen of the apocalypse riding roughshod over hu-manity, or in his portrait of a knight in armor accompanied by death and the devil. The most striking characteristics of the German people in the years that ushered in the Reformation were a deep piety, a concern with the afterlife, and a zealous loyalty to the church as keeper of spiritual treasures. Heresies seemed ac-tually to be in decline and church activities increased, from the building of chapels to the publication of a great volume of religious literature. Mysticism gained a new power through the spread of tracts and treatises. The heartfelt tenderness of per-sonal religious faith is reflected in the one major contribution of the Germans to late medieval art, the Pietà, the representation of Mary holding in her lap the life-less body of her crucified son. The traditional economy of salvation was firmly held to and a genuine concern for the restoration of the church to its primal purity was everywhere in evidence among the humanists as well as among popular preachers. Matthias Grünewald's Isenheim altar painting of the suffering Christ on the cross was a typical expression of German faith in the crucified Redeemer. Germany was in the medieval religious mold in a way unique among the larger lands of Europe.

The churchmen, both German and Italian, failed to respond to this renewed piety. Not only did they fall behind lay humanists in culture and lay devotees in faith and ethics, but they continued as before to use the church for material gain and for political ends. They employed the dreaded ban or power of excommunica-tion to force payment of debts and to gain political concessions, and were insensitive to the giving of offense. The hostility to the Roman church that poured forth when the floodgates were opened by Martin Luther was largely the bitterness of the dis-appointed lover.

Luther, the Man of the People

SELDOM HAS ONE MAN so shaken the world as did Martin Luther as leader of the Reformation movement. In his own person he embodied both of the major reformatory drives surging through the German people: a demand for external reform to end abuses and pressure for a genuine spiritual renewal on the deepest level.

As an orator and publicist who enjoyed extraordinary rapport with his public, he became the spokesman for all of their pent-up feelings of frustration, moral indignation, and downright anger at the Roman hierarchy, from the pope to the exploiting clergy and ignorant monks. The people were carried away with his powerful thrusts at the greedy "tyrants." His declarations ring with revolutionary force, as do these lines from his "Address to the Christian Nobility of the German Nation" in 1520:

> How is it that we Germans must put up with such robbery and extortion of our goods at the hands of the pope? If the kingdom of France has prevented it, why do we Germans let them make such fools and apes of us? . . . And we still go on wondering why princes and nobles, cities and endowments, land and people grow poor. We ought to marvel that we have anything left to eat![4]

The people could not resist a voice so tuned to their thinking. Alfonso Valdés, secretary to Emperor Charles, reported that the Germans were generally exasperated against the Roman see. The people did not seem to attach great importance to the emperor's edicts, he observed, for Lutheran books were sold with impunity on every street corner and marketplace.

But even more important than the negative attack was Luther's own evangelical religious fervor. A religious genius of profound faith and theological insight, he had made a deeper plunge into the meaning of the gospel than perhaps any other man since St. Paul. As a prophet he reached the heart of a people longing for purity and spiritual renewal. The great artist Albrecht Dürer wrote to Georg Spalatin in January or February of 1520: "If God helps me to see Dr. Martin Luther, I shall diligently make his portrait and engrave it as a lasting memory of the Christian man who has helped me out of great anxieties!"[5] And Hans Sachs, the simple cobbler and *Meistersinger* of Nuremberg, saw a new stirring and a new hope, and hailed Luther as the "nightingale of Wittenberg." The Reformation was under way, and no one could possibly know where it would lead Western man.

Bibliography

ATKINSON, JAMES, *The Great Light: Luther and the Reformation*. Grand Rapids, Mich., 1968.
BAINTON, ROLAND H. *The Reformation of the Sixteenth Century*. Boston, 1952.

---

[4] *Luther's Works*, ed. James Atkinson (Philadelphia, 1966), vol. 44, pp. 142–43.
[5] Erwin Panofsky, *The Life and Art of Albrecht Dürer* (Princeton, 1955), p. 198.

————. *The Age of the Reformation*. New York, 1956.

BRANDI, KARL. *Deutsche Geschichte im Zeitalter der Reformation und Gegenreformation,* 3rd ed. Leipzig, 1941.

BÜHLER, JOHANNES. *Deutsche Geschichte: Das Reformationszeitalter*. Berlin and Leipzig, 1938.

CHADWICK, OWEN. *The Reformation*. Baltimore, 1964.

DICKENS, A. G. *Reformation and Society in Sixteenth-Century Europe*. New York, 1966.

DILLENBERGER, JOHN, ed. *Martin Luther: Selections*. Garden City, N.Y., 1961.

ELTON, G. R. *Reformation Europe, 1517–1559*. Cleveland, 1963.

————, ed. *The Reformation, 1520–1559,* vol. 2 of *The New Cambridge Modern History*. Cambridge, 1958.

GRIMM, HAROLD J. *The Reformation Era, 1500–1650,* rev. ed. New York, 1965.

HARBISON, E. HARRIS. *The Age of the Reformation*. Ithaca, N.Y., 1955.

HARTUNG, FRITZ. *Deutsche Geschichte im Zeitalter der Reformation, der Gegenreformation und des 30 Jährigen Krieges,* 2nd ed. Berlin, 1963.

HILLERBRAND, HANS J. *The Reformation: A Narrative History Related by Contemporary Observers and Participants*. New York, 1964.

————. *The Protestant Reformation*. New York, 1968.

————. *Men and Ideas in the Sixteenth Century*. Chicago, 1969.

HOLBORN, HAJO. *The Reformation,* vol. 1 of *A History of Modern Germany*. New York, 1959.

HULME, E. M. *The Renaissance, the Protestant Revolution, and the Catholic Reformation in Continental Europe*. New York, 1921.

HURSTFIELD, JOEL, ed. *The Reformation Crisis*. New York, 1966.

JOACHIMSEN, PAUL. *Die Reformation als Epoche der deutschen Geschichte*. Munich, 1951.

KOENIGSBERGER, H. G., and MOSSE, G. L. *Europe in the Sixteenth Century*. New York, 1968.

LAU, FRANZ, and BIZER, ERNST. *A History of the Reformation in Germany to 1555*. London, 1969.

LÉONARD, ÉMILE G. *A History of Protestantism,* vol. 1, *The Reformation,* ed. H. H. Rowley, trans. Joyce M. H. Reid. London and Camden, N.J., 1965.

LINDSAY, THOMAS M. *A History of the Reformation,* 2 vols. New York, 1951.

LORTZ, JOSEPH. *How the Reformation Came*. New York, 1964.

————. *The Reformation in Germany,* 2 vols. New York, 1969.

LUTHER, MARTIN. *Luther's Works,* ed. J. Pelikan and H. Lehmann, 56 vols. St. Louis and Philadelphia, 1958–

MOUSNIER, R. *Les XVIᵉ et XVIIᵉ siècles,* vol. 4 of *Histoire générale des civilisations*. Paris, 1954.

SMITH, PRESERVED. *The Age of the Reformation*. New York, 1920.

SPITZ, LEWIS W., ed. *The Reformation: Material or Spiritual?* Boston, 1962.

————, ed. *The Protestant Reformation*. Englewood Cliffs, N.J., 1966.

THULIN, OSKAR. *Illustrated History of the Reformation*. St. Louis, 1967.

WHALE, J. S. *The Protestant Tradition*. Cambridge, 1955.

WHITNEY, J. P. *The History of the Reformation*. London, 1940.

CHAPTER 13

Luther's Evangelical Thrust

About six o'clock in the evening of April 18, 1521, the imperial herald led a pale and inwardly fearful and trembling Augustinian brother into the crowded torchlit episcopal hall next to the towering Romanesque cathedral of Worms in Germany. There Martin Luther stood before Emperor Charles V, the princes and estates of the diet, the cardinals and the powers of this world, to attest to his other-worldly faith. It was hardly a fair judicial trial, for he had been cited to recant publicly, or, as Luther put it, to "rechant," or sing a new song. A day earlier Luther had been asked whether he acknowledged the books placed before him to be his and whether he was willing to retract and recall them. Much to everyone's surprise, Luther had requested twenty-four hours in which to consider his reply. Now his time was up, and as a great throng milled about outside, everyone within strained to hear his decision. In a high, clear voice he spoke for ten minutes in German and in Latin, acknowledging his books and declaring his loyalty to the word of God. When the emperor's spokesman then demanded a simple answer declaring whether or not he would recant, Luther answered:

> Since then your serene majesty and your lordships seek a simple answer, I will give it in this manner, neither horned nor toothed: Unless I am convinced by the testimony of the Scriptures or by clear reason (for I do not trust either in the pope or in councils alone, since it is well known that they have often erred and contra-

dicted themselves), I am bound by the Scriptures I have quoted and my conscience is captive to the word of God. I cannot and I will not retract anything, since it is neither safe nor right to go against conscience.

I cannot do otherwise, here I stand, may God help me. Amen.

This simple declaration changed the state of Christendom and the course of human affairs. "Luther at Worms," wrote the Catholic historian Lord Acton, "is the most pregnant and momentous fact in our history. . . . The great fact which we have to recognize is that with all the intensity of his passion for authority he did more than any single man to make modern history the development of revolution."[1] But the twenty-one-year-old emperor Charles V was not impressed by this Saxon monk; "He will not make a heretic out of me!" he declared.

Luther left the hall with German soldiers muttering approval and the Spanish horsemen at the street gate shouting, "Into the fire!" Some witnesses reported that as Luther made his way out of the hall, he held his hand over his head like the victor in a tourney and cried out, "I am finished!" But what he thought to be the end turned out to be only a beginning.

Luther was warned to leave by friends who remembered the fate of Jan Hus at Constance. On April 26 he left Worms by a side gate and was spirited away by retainers of Elector Frederick of Saxony to a hideaway in the Wartburg Castle. Emperor Charles had the papal legate Girolamo Aleander prepare the famous Edict of Worms against Luther as an obstinate schismatic and manifest heretic. It was passed by a small group of delegates after the diet had officially adjourned and was signed by Charles on May 26, joining to the church's excommunication the great ban and overban of the secular arm and making Luther an outlaw who could be seized at will. But could the edict be enforced?

Luther's trip from Wittenberg to Worms had turned into a triumphal procession. He had left home on April 2, and on entering Erfurt he was greeted by his old friend Crotus Rubeanus, the rector of the university, with a large delegation of faculty and students, who hailed him as a righteous judge come to redress the grievances of the nation. He was repeatedly warned not to enter Worms. People held up to him pictures of Savonarola, a sobering reminder. At the last minute Elector Frederick himself, through the chancellor Spalatin, urged him not to enter Worms, for he had already been condemned. But Luther declared he would enter the city if there were as many devils in it as tiles on the roofs. As the procession moved along, Luther riding in a simple wagon with two or three companions, preceded by the imperial herald Kaspar Sturm in ceremonial costume and accompanied by a troop of a hundred armed men, thousands of people poured out to cheer the man who had become a national hero. In the dispatches that Aleander sent to Rome he estimated that three-fourths of the common people were on

---

[1] Lord Acton, *Lectures on Modern History* (London, 1906), pp. 101, 105.

Luther's side. The trip to Worms had been tense and fearful, but Luther's long road from his early years to Wittenberg had been even more arduous.

Luther's Religious Reformation

Luther's ancestral home was Moehre, a small village of some fifty families on the western slope of the Thuringian forest. His forebears had emigrated to this region of Saxony from western Germany centuries before and had become free peasants. His grandfather Heinrich owned considerable property, including a small estate. The family lived in comfortable circumstances, but according to Saxon custom the younger son inherited the land and the eldest, Hans, had to make his own way. He moved to Eisleben, and there on November 10, 1483, Hans's second son, Martin, was born. Hans worked as a miner and rose first to foreman and then to renter. In 1491, when Martin was only eight, Hans borrowed money and became a member of a firm of copper miners. Two decades later he owned shares in six pits and two smelting companies. He supported his family of eight children well and sent Martin all the way through the university.

Martin attended school in Mansfeld to the age of fourteen, when he was sent to secondary school at Magdeburg for a year, possibly in the care of the Brethren of the Common Life. In 1498 he transferred to a similar school in Eisenach, where for three years he studied with the well-known grammarian Trebonius. He entered the University of Erfurt in 1501 and received his A.B. degree in the fall of 1502, thirtieth in a class of fifty-two. On January 7, 1505, he took his master's degree, second in a class of seventeen. As a graduation present his father sent him the expensive *Corpus iuris,* for he was to enter the legal profession, a sure ladder to wealth and social preferment. On May 20, 1505, Luther entered law school. On July 16 he threw a party for a group of university friends and as his guests were leaving after an evening of beer and high-spirited song he said to them, "After today you will never see me again." He gave away all his books, except for a copy of Virgil and one of Plautus, and the next day he entered the Augustinian monastery. Why did he take this dramatic step?

Luther was a typical product of the fear-motivated medieval piety. His home discipline had been severe, although not unusually so, and the religious training in the schools had been more somber than joyous. The way to be assured of salvation was to flee the temptations of the world, overcome the appetites of the flesh and the assaults of the devil, do the best one could to obey the commandments of God and the precepts of the church, and with the initial gift of grace work toward perfect holiness. The ideal life of perfection was the ascetic life of the hermit or monk, given over to contemplation and religious duties away from the world. Toward this end Luther chose the strict Observantine Augustinian house, and while he was there he was a perfect monk, outfasting, outpraying, and outworking the other brothers in his search for assurance that God was merciful and forgiving.

To be sure, some events in the months preceding his decision had precipitated the act. As he was returning to Erfurt after spending Easter at home he accidentally cut a blood vessel in his leg and nearly bled to death. The plague swept through Erfurt and took one of Luther's classmates. Immediately before he entered the monastery Luther made another trip home and was caught in a storm. When lightning struck a tree near him he vowed to St. Anne that if she would spare his life he would enter a monastery. But the underlying reason was really a long spiritual struggle for religious certainty and assurance. "Doubt makes a monk" was an old medieval saying. In September 1506 he was admitted to the order and was assigned an unheated cell seven feet wide by nine feet long with a window looking out over the anticipated site of his future grave in the monastic cemetery.

On the vicar general's order Luther was ordained into the priesthood in 1507, and on May 2 he celebrated his first mass, trembling as he held the sacred host in his hand. His father came with two wagonloads of friends and provisions for the customary banquet, and gave the monastery a very large cash gift. But at the end of the banquet Hans concluded his speech as host with the remark: "But have you not read 'Thou shalt honor thy father and thy mother'?" Luther commented later that this note of parental disapproval raised in him his first misgivings about the course he had chosen.

Luther's theological studies tended to reinforce the basic religious presuppositions upon which the monastic life was based. The scholastic theology at Erfurt was taught according to the *via moderna* or nominalist system. Though he did not study William of Occam himself, he did study intensely one of the late Occamist theologians, Gabriel Biel, especially his exposition of the mass. Biel and the Occamists stressed on the one hand the mighty sovereign will of God and on the other man's ability to contribute toward his own salvation. They stressed the limitations of human reason when man searches the tremendous mystery of the Divinity and emphasized the authority of the church in defining matters of dogma. God would not withhold grace from anyone who did the best that was in him. Man thus obtains a conditional merit, and with the gift of prevenient grace is enabled to lead a holy life. On the basis of his sanctified life and good deeds, his fully sufficient merit, man becomes fit to receive salvation. When Luther was unable to obtain peace of mind through his most energetic monkish works or from the sacrament of penance, his confessor, Johannes Staupitz, conceded to him the futility of attempting to attain the perfect love of God through these methods and urged him to commend himself to God's grace and forgiving love.

Staupitz saw in Luther a young man of intellectual brilliance and religious earnestness, and he recommended him to Elector Frederick for the new University of Wittenberg, founded in 1502. Luther arrived there in 1508 as an instructor of philosophy, and lectured on Aristotle's ethics. In March 1509 he received his bachelor of divinity degree and proceeded to lecture on the scholastic Peter Lombard's dogmatic *Sentences*. He returned to teach at Erfurt from 1509 to 1511, but then was reassigned to Wittenberg, where he remained for the rest of his life. The journey he made to Rome in the winter of 1510–1511, as a representative of the Observantine Augustinians, had no particular effect upon him. Pope Julius II was away from Rome on one of his many campaigns. Luther visited churches and went up the stairs to the praetorium of Pilate on his knees in order to gain indulgences for his grandfather, but the story told years later by his son—that halfway up he heard a voice saying, "The just shall live by faith," rose, and walked back down—is surely a false legend. Luther left Rome as he came, an ardent papist and obedient son of the church.

In Wittenberg again Luther rose to new positions of leadership in the order and in the university. On October 18, 1512, Luther received his doctorate, and a few days later he assumed the chair for biblical studies, taking an oath to protect and expound the word of God to the best of his ability. He lectured first on the Psalms and then in 1515–1516 on Paul's Epistle to the Romans. During the course of his exegetical studies he seems to have achieved an evangelical breakthrough, an insight into the all-encompassing grace of God and all-sufficient merit of Christ. The turning point came in connection with the exposition of Romans 1:17: "For therein is the righteousness of God revealed from faith to faith: as it is written, The just shall live by faith." This passage he understood in the light of Romans 3:24: "Being justified freely by his grace through the redemption that is in Christ Jesus." Formerly Luther had understood this "righteousness of God" as an active, retributive, punishing, essential righteousness that demands that a man keep the whole law of God. Now he understood the "righteousness of God" (*justitia*) as a passive, imputed righteousness that God gives freely to man through Christ. "I pondered night and day," he related many years later, "until I understood the connection between the justice of God and the sentence 'The just shall live by faith.' Then I grasped that the justice of God is the righteousness by which, through grace and pure mercy, God justifies us through faith. Immediately I felt that I had been reborn and that I had passed through wide-open doors into paradise!" Luther had emerged from his tremendous struggle with a firmer trust in God and love for him. This doctrine of salvation by God's grace alone, received as a gift through faith and without dependence upon human merit, was the measure against which he judged the religious practices and official teachings of the church of his day and found them wanting. He had, as Lord Acton once put it, a "lever of wonderful strength with which he moved the world." In his exegetical lectures on Galatians in 1516 and 1517 and on the Epistle to the Hebrews in 1517 and 1518, he expounded his theology with a new clarity and began to attract the attention of students and colleagues.

Luther's "theology of the cross and suffering" represented not so much a new theological system as a new way of thinking theologically. In the treatise *De servo arbitrio* he laughs at himself as a *rusticus*, but he was actually as capable of the greatest theological sophistication as he was skilled in making the most elementary catechetical explanation. He was a great scholar, not in the sense of excelling in scholarship for its own sake, but in using his gifts fully, in reading his sources carefully, in employing new humanist methods, in practical philology and the mastery of languages, his own German as well as Latin, Greek, and a respectable amount of Hebrew. Compelled by a strangely concrete dynamism, he approached theological problems directly rather than as an abstract speculative systematician. He owed something to mysticism, the stress on the necessity of inward appropriation of religious belief and experience, but he was critical of the mystics' assumptions about the divine scintilla in man and his ability to mount the heavenly ladder to reunion with God. He owed much to the discipline of scholastic theology, but he objected to the scholastics' suppositions about man's ability to keep God's law and even to Thomas Aquinas' formula of "faith fashioned by love" rather than "trust inducing love." He owed much to Renaissance humanism for its stress on languages and critical method. Halfway through his commentary on Romans, for example, he switched to Erasmus' edition of the Greek New Testament text (1516). But he sensed an excessive anthropocentrism and stoic moralism in the humanists' religious thought. He was indebted to Augustine and of course to Paul for his basic theological orientation, but he allied himself with their thought creatively, and his theology had the ring of relevance and made a powerful impact.

Luther had a Hebraic rather than a Hellenistic view of God, reinforced by many years of exegetical studies of the Old Testament. He believed that metaphysical speculation about God leads merely to a formal concept of God, such as God as pure being. To define God thus abstractly is to make him unreal, a scarecrow for timid souls. God can only be addressed, not expressed. God's will is the only truly free will, itself the rule of all things without exterior cause or reason or external norms. In 1520 Luther spoke of God as an active power and continual creativity. God is noted for willing and acting and is known by what he has done. In the *Commentary on Genesis* he wrote: "God is heroic without a rule." God's omnipotence is not that power by which he can do anything he may choose to do, but the actual doing of all that he does. His power exerts itself concretely and imbues all that exists with actuality. The world is what it is according to the contingent will of God. God willed to reveal himself in the historic Christ portrayed in the Scriptures. God in nature and in history is an awesome God, both hidden and exposed, whose intentions toward us are not known. Among unbelievers in the world he remains silent. In Christ God becomes the revealed God who shows himself to be full of grace and love. God works in a hidden way and by contrasts rather than directly, revealing lofty truth in lowly form. God's true intentions toward us can be known only if, like a man approaching us in the gathering dusk, he stops and talks with us. In his word he reveals himself to be a glowing God of love, one who deplores sin and overcomes it, abhors death and triumphs over it, and by his grace transforms alienated people into trusting men of faith. He is gracious and merciful toward man, a forgiving God.

Man stands in need of God's grace, for without God's forgiveness man remains in a state of sin. Luther heightened the conception of sin beyond the notion of sins as specific transgressions against particular commandments of God. Sin is the root condition of natural man, who is in the state of unbelief until he is acted upon by the Holy Spirit, who calls him to faith through the gospel. Sin is not, then, related to things of the body as opposed to higher things of the spirit. Luther saw man whole, as a unity, not divided by the body-soul dichotomy or body-soul-spirit trichotomy. "In my temerity," he said, "I do not distinguish body, soul, and spirit, but present the whole man unto God." The "whole man" is flesh insofar as he lives his life without God and is alienated or hostile to him, and spirit insofar as he loves God and has come to trust in him. The law is the word of the God of justice to man. He gives man commandments that man does not fulfill, such as "Be ye therefore perfect" and "Thou shalt love the Lord thy God with all thy heart and with all thy soul and with all thy mind" and "Thou shalt love thy neighbor as thyself." The gospel is the word of God in man, Christ in the heart of man, promising forgiveness to all who accept the offer. Grace in this context is not a spiritual power extended to man, but a benignity, a specific act by which God forgives a particular man at a specific point in time. Faith in God is the "life of the heart," which unsettles poise and insists on transformation. Faith is active in love and produces good works. The forgiven man, justified in God's eyes, does good works. On this earth man attains perfection only in hope, not in reality.

Certain existential emphases in Luther's theology are very striking. While he remains formally an ontologist, his distrust of metaphysical abstractions and his emphasis upon the concreteness and immediacy of religious experience indicate the new thrust of his teaching. The most important words in religion, he stressed, are the personal pronouns he, I, and you (my brother). There is no salvation by affiliation or through implicit faith in what the church teaches, but only through explicit faith in Christ. "Everyone must do his own believing just as everyone must do his own dying," he wrote. An either/or quality in Luther's theology points toward modern dialectical theology and existentialism. There is, finally, a bold facing up to the harshest realities of life, wickedness, transiency, irrationality, and death itself. For the smooth Latin rational "therefore" (*ergo*) of scholastic theology he substituted the paradoxical German agonizing "nevertheless" (*dennoch*), for it is only in spite of everything that a man can with the help of the Holy Spirit say, *"Credo,"* I believe. The kingdom of God, he once said, is like a besieged city surrounded on all sides by death. Each man has his place on the wall to defend and no one can stand where another stands, but "nothing prevents us from calling encouragement to one another." Luther's evangelical message made a tremendous impact upon a generation searching for religious assurance. He was the Copernicus of theology, who with his high Christology pointed to a Son-centered universe.

The conflagration began over a relatively simple issue, Luther's attack upon abuses in the sale of indulgences and his questioning of their validity. The granting of indulgences had undergone a considerable development since the early days of the church, when the congregation granted permission (*indulgentia*) to relax or commute the penance imposed upon a repentant sinner as an outward sign of sorrow. The power to impose private penance in place of public penance was gradually taken over by priests, bishops, and popes. The church assumed the power of remitting the temporal punishment for sins after the guilt had been forgiven on the basis of sincere repentance and by application of the merits of Christ, Mary, and the saints. Indulgences were promised to crusaders, pilgrims, and donors to the church. In 1457 Pope Calixtus decreed that indulgences were valid for the relief of souls in purgatory. The papal bull *Salvator noster* in 1476 extended the remission of temporal punishment in purgatory to include both the living and the dead. In promulgating indulgences the popes were careful to distinguish between guilt and temporal punishment, insisting that those who received indulgences must be of contrite heart and must have made oral confession. These requirements, however, were glossed over in actual practice, and often the sale of indulgences became routine huckstering.

Ironically, one of the grandest monuments in Christendom, St. Peter's Cathedral in Rome, became the occasion for and the lasting reminder of the division of the church. Pope Julius II in 1507 issued a plenary indulgence to obtain funds for building St. Peter's. In 1513 Pope Leo X renewed this indulgence and made Archbishop Albert of Brandenburg the high commissioner of the sale in the archbishoprics of Magdeburg and Mainz, promising him half of the take to help him repay the Fugger bankers some 29,000 gulden. The Fuggers had advanced this sum to Albert so he could pay for papal dispensation to assume the archbishopric when he was underage (he was only twenty-three at the time) and to hold a number of offices simultaneously, and to pay the annates and the fee for the archbishopric itself. The super-salesman of indulgences was a fat Dominican named John Tetzel. When in April 1517 Tetzel approached the borders of Electoral Saxony and many members of the Wittenberg congregation swarmed over to buy letters of indulgence, Luther urged various bishops to intervene. When they failed to act, he prepared his ninety-five theses on indulgences and sent copies to Bishop Jerome of Brandenburg and, naïvely, to Archbishop Albert of Brandenburg. According to

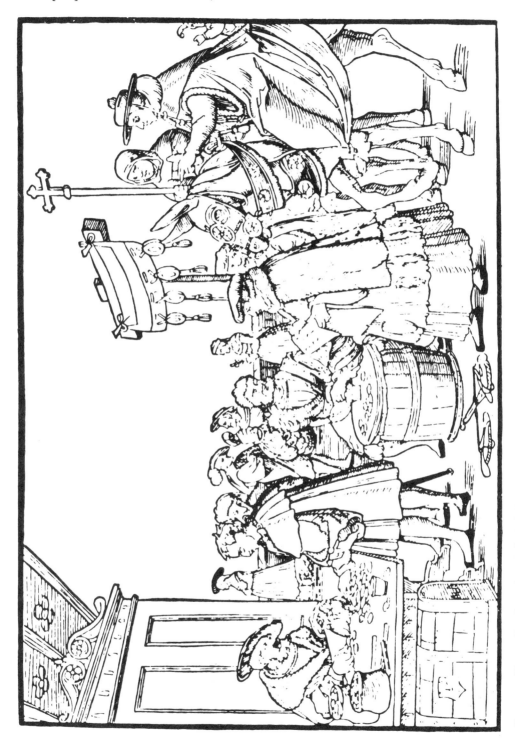

BREU THE ELDER. *Proclamation of the Indulgence.*

Melanchthon's account many years later, he posted them on the north door of the Castle Church on All Saints' Day, challenging any comer to an academic disputation. "When our Lord and Master Jesus Christ said, 'Repent' (Matthew 4:17), he willed the entire life of believers to be one of repentance," he wrote. Repentance in the New Testament meant a change of heart, not to do penance, and if God forgives the guilt of sin, why should punishment remain? The storm unleashed by this act surprised Luther most of all, for within weeks his theses were carried to the farthest corners of Europe. Luther had ruined the sale and had unknowingly launched the Reformation.

The wheels of the ecclesiastical machinery began to grind, beginning with a squeak from Tetzel, who threatened to have the heretic in the fire within three weeks. Tetzel's fellow Dominicans in Saxony preached from the pulpit that Luther would soon be burned. On February 3, 1518, the Dominicans in Germany officially denounced him to the pope. In July 1518 the Dominican master of the sacred palace, Prierias, prepared a citation summoning Luther to Rome. On August 25, 1518, the head of the Augustinian order in Germany was instructed to arrest and imprison Luther. Under pressure from Emperor Maximilian, Pope Leo, whose first reaction had been to view the theses as the irresponsible work of some drunken German who would sober up eventually, authorized Cajetan, the papal legate to the diet at Augsburg, to arrest Luther. He demanded that Frederick the Wise surrender this "son of iniquity" to Cajetan, but Luther appealed to Frederick for protection as a German citizen. Since at that time Pope Leo favored Frederick over Charles as a candidate for election as emperor after the death of the aging Maximilian, Leo agreed to a mere meeting of Cajetan and Luther at Augsburg, which took place from October 12 to 14, but left Luther unmoved. In December the papal chamberlain Miltitz arrived with the Golden Rose for Frederick and a bull against Luther. The Golden Rose was a coveted decoration blessed by the pope on the fourth Sunday in Lent and awarded only once each year to some Christian king or prince. But nothing came of the pope's maneuvering. During the course of a debate in Leipzig with Dr. Johannes Eck of Ingolstadt University, held from June 27 to July 15, 1519, Luther reminded his listeners that popes and councils had often erred and contradicted each other. The decision in points clearly went to Dr. Eck, but in preparing for the debate Luther plunged into a furious study of canon law, church history, and the church fathers, and became even more firmly convinced that the church had departed far from its early teachings.

Luther's power as a publicist now came into full play. As early as February 14, 1519, the humanist publisher Johannes Froben in Basel wrote to Luther:

> We sent six hundred copies of your collected works which I published to France and Spain. They are sold in Paris, read and appreciated at the Sorbonne. The book dealer Clavus of Pavia took a sizable number to Italy to sell them everywhere in the cities. I have sent copies also to England and Brabant and have only ten copies left

in the storeroom. I have never had such good luck with a book. The more accomplished a man is, the more he thinks of you![2]

Luther was a prolific writer, producing over four hundred treatises, an average of more than one a month, between 1516 and 1546. Charles and Aleander could not believe that Luther had singlehandedly written all the books that lay on the table before them at Worms.

In a burst of unparalleled creativity he wrote his three famous treatises of 1520. "I deliver as soon as I conceive!" he exclaimed. At one point in his career he was keeping three presses busy. He sent the first pages of his *Address to the Christian Nobility of the German Nation* to the printer while he was still writing the last pages. In it he called upon the emperor and princes as Christians in authority to reform the church, since the clergy had defaulted. The *Address,* which has been called a "cry from the heart of the people" and a "blast on the war trumpet," was Luther's first publication after he was convinced that the breach with Rome was all but irreparable. He assaulted the "three walls of the Romanists," the arguments that secular force has no jurisdiction over them, that only the pope is competent to expound Scripture, and that no one but the pope can summon a council. In *The Babylonian Captivity of the Church* he attacked the abuses in the sacramental system, through which he believed the "Roman tyranny" had exercised its control over all Christians. He discussed all seven sacraments, holding only baptism, communion, and penance to have been instituted by Christ, but paid most attention to the Lord's Supper. He held the first "captivity" to be the withholding of the cup from the laity, the second the doctrine of transubstantiation, and the third the conception of the mass as a sacrifice rather than as a spiritual communion with the Lord. The third famous treatise of 1520, *On the Liberty of the Christian Man,* was more devotional in nature and, as he put it, contained the "whole of Christian life in brief form." In it he described the liberating effect of faith in Christ upon the Christian man, for faith frees man from spiritual slavery and moves him to a life of love and service to his fellows. This treatise, conciliatory in tone, was accompanied by an open letter to Pope Leo reassuring him that Luther's intention had been to attack the corruption and false doctrine surrounding the papacy, not Leo's own person.

But Leo was not to be appeased, for by now the affair had moved far beyond the point of reconciliation. On June 15, 1520, Leo had published the bull *Exsurge domine,* citing forty-one heresies in Luther's writings, giving him sixty days in which to recant, and demanding that his books be burned. That fall the papal legate Girolamo Aleander and Johannes Eck staged a burning of Luther's books. In retaliation the Wittenberg University faculty and students gathered on Decem-

---

[2] Froben to Luther, February 14, 1519, in *D. Martin Luthers Werke: Briefwechsel* (Weimar, 1930), vol. 1, p. 332.

CRANACH THE YOUNGER. *The Last Supper of the Lutherans and the Fall to Hell of the Catholics; in the Center Luther Preaching.*

ber 10, 1520, outside the Elster gate to build a bonfire and burn copies of scholastic writings and the canon law. Luther, shaking with emotion, stepped out of the crowd and threw upon the flames the papal bull, saying softly, "Because you have destroyed God's truth, may the Lord destroy you today in this fire." Luther had spoken his final farewell to Rome. On January 3, 1521, the pope issued the bull of excommunication *Decet romanum pontificem,* declaring Luther a heretic outside the law. It remained now for Charles V, who had become emperor in 1519, to enforce the excommunication through the imperial ban, which meant death for the heretic. Luther was summoned on March 6, 1521, to appear before the emperor and the diet of the Holy Roman Empire meeting in Worms. Luther went to Worms and there took his stand.

On the way home from Worms to Wittenberg, Luther's party detoured to Moehre so that Luther could visit his grandmother and preach in the church there. In the evening of May 4 a troop of armed horsemen ambushed the wagon train near Altenstein. Luther's companions fled into the underbrush, and when they returned Luther was gone. The horsemen took him on roundabout paths for half the night, till morning found them at the Wartburg Castle, up the hill from Eisenach. Elector Frederick had instructed his men not to tell him where they took Luther, so that at the diet he could truthfully profess no knowledge of his whereabouts. Only the warden and a few trusted troopers knew the identity of the hostage. As Knight Georg, Luther wore a knight's necklace and trappings, let his beard and hair grow long, and sent letters with such mysterious addresses as "the Realm of the Birds," "the Region of the Air," and "the Isle of Patmos." Rumors ran wild that Aleander had arranged to have him assassinated, that he had been found dead in a silver mine, that he had fled to Sickingen; but there were some who suspected Elector Frederick of protecting him.

Removed from the public arena, Luther was extremely restless during his ten months at the Wartburg. He suffered from severe nervous exhaustion and attacks of indigestion after his ordeal. He wrote a number of treatises, the most important of which was *On Monastic Vows,* dedicated to his father, in which he argued that celibacy and monastic asceticism were contrary to Scriptures and contributed less to God and man than a useful life in society. But the great achievement of his enforced "idleness" was his masterful translation of the Greek New Testament into German, which he accomplished from December to the end of February 1522. Later he and his "sanhedrin" at the university translated the Old Testament from the Hebrew, completing the entire work in 1534. It was a linguistic triumph important for its direct religious impact, for its formative power in the development of New High German as the standard language of the people and of literature, and for its influence on translations of the Bible into other vernacular languages, including English.

Social Unrest and Revolts

In Wittenberg meanwhile affairs took a radical turn. Gabriel Zwilling, an Augustinian friar, and Andreas Carlstadt, a university professor, made a violent attack upon the form of the mass, favoring communion in both kinds (communicants' receiving both the bread and the wine), and upon celibacy and images. Carlstadt married the daughter of a poor nobleman, and many monks followed him in taking wives. Zwilling led an iconoclastic attack upon altars, images, and pictures in churches. On December 21 the "prophets" of Zwickau arrived in Wittenberg: Thomas Müntzer, a religious mystic with radical social ideas; Nicholas Storch, an illiterate clothmaker; and Mark Stübner, a student. These charismatic spiritualists made claims to private revelations, opposed the use of external sacraments, and preached the setting aside of all authorities. There was some talk of communism in property and in wives. Philipp Melanchthon, who assumed the role of leader in Wittenberg during Luther's absence, however timidly, was initially favorably impressed by them. Luther's reaction was that no private revelation could be valid unless it was in agreement with the Scriptures, and he quipped, "They have swallowed the Holy Ghost feathers and all."

On February 1, 1522, there was a great tumult in the town, and the city council, unable to contain it, appealed to Luther to return. He did so on March 6 and preached eight sermons on the need for moderation, the duty to proceed with love toward one's neighbor, and the need to avoid giving offense to weaker brethren not yet converted, for all eyes were on Wittenberg. The situation quieted down and changes were then made gradually: the abrogation of private mass, the change of the public mass into a reformed communion, and in the fall of 1523 the introduction of Luther's own revised liturgy.

Unrest is contagious, and since feuding was an endemic disease of the knightly class, the outbreak of the Knights' War of 1522–1523 was almost predictable. The knights had three possibilities open to them as their class lost its social utility. They could turn to farming or estate management, as they did east of the Elbe; they could adjust to the new forces of the time and serve as functionaries of the more powerful princes; or they could turn renegade and live by robbery and pillage. Franz von Sickingen, a little man with big ideas, chose the third alternative. When he was born, in the fortress of Ebernburg in 1481, his father read his horoscope and saw that the child would achieve a considerable reputation but would come to a bad end. Franz had great ability and amassed considerable wealth from the mines on his lands and by plundering merchant wagon trains; at one point he even loaned the emperor 50,000 gulden. He put himself at the service of the French king and made punitive and plundering raids with a thousand armed men all the way into Lorraine. He declared a feud with the city of Worms. His heart was with the German empire, however, and he supported Charles V, though he was disappointed when Charles failed to lead Germany to new triumphs. "Franz is a man such as Germany has not had for many a day!" wrote Ulrich von Hutten, as propagandist for the German knightly cause.[3] Sickingen fortified Ebernburg with thirty-six cannon, including a three-and-a-half-ton piece called the Nightingale.

On August 27, 1522, Franz declared a feud with the semifeudal archbishop of Trier, starting what has mistakenly gone down in history as the Knights' Revolt. He declared that he would free the people from the yoke of the priests and bring them evangelical liberty. Lutheranism had indeed penetrated far into the knightly class, but Franz's motives were as mixed as he himself was ideologically confused, for in secularizing the archbishop's territory he hoped to gain land for himself. On September 7 he attacked the city, but was defeated after an eight-day siege. Then three princes combined forces and on April 30, 1523, besieged Sickingen in a fortress called Landstuhl. Franz was mortally wounded by a missile and a broken beam finished him as the stone walls collapsed under artillery fire. The Swabian League of princes and towns in southern Germany then fielded an army under Georg Truchsesz von Waldburg which assaulted the strongholds of the Swabian and Franconian knights, destroying thirty-two castles within six weeks.

Ulrich von Hutten had at first thought Luther's cause a mere battle of the monks, and chortled, "Devour and be devoured in turn!" But without ever really appreciating Luther's theology, he soon identified himself with his cause as an anti-Roman ally. He addressed Luther as "You my dear brother!" and wrote, "They tell me that you have been excommunicated. How great, O Luther, how great you are, if this is true!" He was ready to attack the "priestly tyranny" with letters and with arms. From 1520 on he wrote a steady stream of pamphlets attacking the Roman hierarchy. His *Febris* and *Inspicientes* assaulted Luther's interrogator and judge, Cardinal Cajetan. In his glosses on *The Bull of Leo X Against The Errors of Martin Luther* he attacked the pope as the Antichrist. His tract *Bulla* was a discussion of Leo's bull, German liberty, Hutten, Franz, and other Germans. In his *Monitor I* and *Praedones* (Robbers) he identified Christian liberty with freedom from Rome. He switched from Latin to the vernacular and reached the masses with a great number of German tracts. But Luther could not condone Hutten's appeal to the sword in defense of the gospel and refused his suggestion that he take refuge with Sickingen. On January 16, 1521, Luther wrote to his friend Spalatin:

> You see what Hutten wishes. But I do not desire to do battle for the gospel with violence and murder, and I wrote him as much. Through the power of the Word

---

[3] William R. Hitchcock, *The Background of the Knights' Revolt, 1522–1523* (Berkeley and Los Angeles, 1958), p. 46.

the world is conquered, through the power of the Word the church has been created—and through the Word it will also be restored.

Hutten, too sick to fight in Sickingen's campaign, fled to Switzerland, but Erasmus refused him sanctuary in Basel. He was finally befriended by Zwingli in Zurich and died there in August 1523, still a young man.

Scarcely had the Knights' War ended than a more terrifying uprising occurred, a series of peasant revolts that racked southern and central Germany from May 1524 to July 1526. The astrologers had predicted a deluge and horrendous things for 1524 and 1525. Half of Germany was torn apart by rioting bands of peasants numbering up to twelve thousand men in some regions. In the south the revolt spread into Austria as far as Salzburg and Styria; only Bavaria was spared major uprisings. Caught up by the revolutionary spirit, interpreting Luther's Christian liberty as social freedom, urged on by erratic "prophets," and led by inept military men, the peasants rose up against their feudal overlords, ecclesiastical and secular. The uprisings were spontaneous, regional, and in no way coordinated.

In the Black Forest the peasants were stirred up and led by a soldier-agitator named Hans Müller von Bulgenbach, who was joined by an Anabaptist preacher, Balthasar Hubmaier. In Swabia Sebastian Lotzer, a tanner from the city of Memmingen, framed the famous Twelve Articles, which illustrated the concrete nature of the peasants' demands, for it was not liberty in the abstract that they demanded. They wanted the restoration of common lands to the community, the abolition of arbitrary feudal services and the death tax, elimination of the "small" or cattle tithe, the right to choose their own pastors, a return of hunting, fishing, and forest rights preempted by the nobles, an end to increases in rents and services, and the restoration of the good old law in the administration of justice in place of the Roman law codes. The demands were moderate enough, but once the revolt was under way it produced mob excesses—burning, pillaging, lynching, murder, and at Weinsberg the massacre of all the defenders of the castle after they had surrendered. The count of Helfenstein was run through with a spear before the eyes of his wife and child. The Swabian League fielded against them a veteran of the Knights' War, Georg Truchsesz von Waldburg, who killed and captured thousands at Leipheim, east of Ulm. He confronted a large army of peasants at Weingarten and induced them to sign a treaty, whereupon they disbanded and lost further bargaining power. In Franconia the peasants, led by an innkeeper, recruited the knight Goetz von Berlichingen for campaigns against Bamberg and Mainz. They even succeeded in forcing the archbishop of Mainz to accept the demands of the Twelve Articles.

In Thuringia the peasants rioted and pillaged Erfurt. In central Germany alone over forty monasteries and castles were destroyed by the rebels. Under the leadership of the fanatical spiritualist Thomas Müntzer, who made his headquarters in Mühlhausen, the peasants made the wildest assaults and suffered the most tragic slaughter imaginable. Müntzer was more a chiliastic religious extremist than a social revolutionary. He preached the imminent coming of the kingdom of God, in which all men would be equal and all property would be held in common. He encouraged the masses to kill the rulers and destroy their castles. He urged his League of the Elect to wipe out the unregenerate. "Do not listen to the cries of the godless," he exhorted in 1524. "On while the fire is hot! Do not let the blood cool on your swords!" On his banner he displayed the rainbow as a reminder of God's covenant with man. The overwrought peasants went into battle singing, "Come, Holy Ghost, God and Lord!" On May 15, 1525, Duke Georg of Saxony and Count Philipp of Eisenach attacked. One volley of artillery fire threw the peasants into a panic and the cavalry cut them down. In one of the worst massacres of the war, the princes' troops killed several thousand peasants and took hundreds of prisoners, allowing few to escape. Müntzer fled, but he was captured feigning illness in a bedroom, and was quartered. Thus ended the bloodiest and most dramatic episode of the revolts, on an eschatological note of Armageddon.

These peasant revolts fitted the pattern of such rebellions in the late Middle Ages. They swept across Flanders, France, England, and Bohemia, and there were at least a dozen such uprisings in German lands before the major one of 1525. As during the fourteenth-century revolts, the condition of the peasants was better than it had been earlier. Again improvements in their lives led to visions of greater improvements still, and to resentment against the increased wealth and growing power of princes, towns, and bishops. The crushing defeat of the knights in southwest Germany, those bullies who had despoiled and terrified the peasants for centuries, released the peasants from one group of foes, though remnants of them, including Hutten's brother and Sickingen's son, now fought in the armies against them. Population pressure was greatest in the hilly Swabian southwest, that fountain of German emigration throughout the centuries. There the only well-organized peasant movement, called the *Bundschuh,* after the sandal worn by the peasants, arose under the leadership of the skillful Joss Fritz, who was more effective as a propagandist than as a military tactician but always avoided capture. Luther's evangelical proclamations of Christian liberty led to a coalescing of economic and religious ideas which triggered revolution. During the night between his appearances before the diet at Worms the sign of the *Bundschuh* had appeared on the walls. From the beginning Luther had consistently opposed the use of force and violence in the defense either of his person or of his theology. He attacked the tyranny of the rulers, secular and ecclesiastical, but warned against mob terror. "Had I wanted to start trouble," he once boasted, "I could have brought great bloodshed upon Germany. Yes, I could have started such a little game at Worms that even the emperor would not have been safe. But what would it have been?

PETRARCA-MEISTER. *Von Adeligem Ursprung.* The peasant foundation of medieval society.

A mug's game. I did nothing. I left it to the Word!" Sensing the dangerously charged atmosphere while in refuge at Wartburg Castle, he wrote *A Faithful Exhortation to Christians to Keep Themselves from Riot and Revolution.*

That his position on armed rebellion was widely understood is evident from the famous tract of 1521 by the Swiss humanist Vadian entitled *Karsthans* (Hans the Hoeman; just as all French peasants were called Jacques by their betters, German peasants were called Hans). In this tract Mercury, Murner the Franciscan monk, and Karsthans are discussing the Leipzig debate. When it is announced that Luther is coming, Murner leaves the scene. Luther complains of persecution and Karsthans promises the protection of the peasants. But Luther denounces all "fighting and killing" and takes his leave. Luther never gave up the principle that only constituted authority had the power of the sword. A month after the appearance of the peasants' platform he wrote *An Exhortation to Peace in Reply to the Twelve Articles of the Swabian Peasants* (April 1525), in which he admonished both sides, boldly attacking the princes and bishops, against whose tyranny God's word and all history threatened a catastrophic end, and warning the peasants that God's word and all experience showed that rebellion and anarchy made conditions worse rather than better, citing Christ's warning, "All they that take the sword shall perish with the sword." Luther went personally to centers of disaffection in Thuringia at the risk of his life to mediate between the peasants and Elector Frederick, who was willing to make concessions, but his preaching was in vain. When he heard outrageous and probably exaggerated reports of mob rapine and murder and saw the peasants follow Müntzer into battle, he wrote his harsh pamphlet *Against Robbing and Murderous Peasant Bands* (May 1525), urging that the rebels be struck down, strangled, and suppressed. When the crisis passed he wrote letters and pamphlets urging clemency and moderation toward the peasants, and expressing regret for his harsh language earlier.

The peasant revolts actually had only the remotest possibility of success because of their sporadic nature, lack of organization, poor military leadership, and small staying power. The position of the peasants in reality remained little altered. The fines imposed upon them were gradually reduced or left uncollected. Not even the disarming of the peasants was everywhere insisted upon. Many lords saw that concessions to the peasants were to their own economic advantage. Only after the failure of the revolts did the peasants accept Luther's evangelical religion en masse, as evangelical preachers became willing to man the pulpits of country parishes. They seemed to understand the consistency of Luther's position and few charged him with betraying a cause he had never really embraced. The Reformation continued to spread into new areas of Germany as a spontaneous popular movement after 1525 as it had before. On the other hand, the suppression of one more major sociological group that could serve as a counterforce made the way to princely absolutism much easier. It has often been alleged that the peasant revolts alarmed the rulers and drove them closer to Catholicism out of shock at the effect of Lutheranism on the masses, but this is manifestly untrue in view of the continued spread of the evangelical church to many additional territories and countries.

The Reformation to the Diet of Augsburg, 1530

SELDOM IN HISTORY has there been such rapport and resonance between a university and the broad mass of people as existed between the new and vigorous University of Wittenberg and the Germans. The heart of the Reformation movement was a center of learning and its leader was a professor of theology who had come from among the people, which gave it a special character. "Learning, wisdom, and writers must rule the world," Luther pontificated in one of his *Table Talks*. "If God out of his wrath would take away from the world all the learned men, people would become beasts and wild animals. Then there would be no wisdom, religion, or law, but only robbery, theft, murder, adultery, and all kinds of evil!" Luther was a professor to the core, lecturing twice a week to the crowds of theological students who came for education or reeducation from all parts of Germany. One of them has given us this description of Professor Luther the exegete:

> He was a man of middle stature, with a voice which combined sharpness and soft-ness: it was soft in tone; sharp in the enunciation of syllables, words and sen-tences. [Typical Saxon!] He spoke neither too quickly nor too slowly, but at an even pace, without hesitation and very clearly, and in such fitting order that each part flowed naturally out of what went before. He did not expound each part in long labyrinths of words, but first the individual words, then the sentences, so that one could see how the content of the exposition arose and flowed out of the text itself. . . . For this is how he took it from a book of essential matter which he had himself prepared, so that he had his lecture materials always ready at hand—con-clusions, digressions, moral philosophy, and also antithesis, and so his lectures never contained anything that was not pithy or relevant. And, to say something about the spirit of the man: if even the fiercest enemies of the gospel had been among his hearers, they would have confessed from the force of what they heard that they had witnessed, not a man, but a spirit, for he could not teach such amazing things from himself, but only from the influence of some good or evil spirit.[4]

Luther felt gratified and a bit surprised that not only the students but the whole learned world listened to what he had to say. "We wished out of respect," wrote the humanist Irenicus in 1518, "to call Luther the leader of all the Germans on account of the excellent erudition possessed by such a man."

Luther led the movement for reform of the arts curriculum at the university,

---

[4] Cited in E. Gordon Rupp, *Luther's Progress to the Diet of Worms* (New York, 1964), p. 44.

supporting humanist discipline, languages, rhetoric, and history against the traditional dialectic and scholastic disputation. He accomplished reform also in the theological curricula, challenging the Thomist dictum that without Aristotle it is impossible to be a theologian. In a letter to Matthew Lang in 1517 he wrote: "Our theology and St. Augustine are beginning to prosper. . . . Aristotle is coming down little by little." The students and the young instructors at the university rallied to his ideas for educational reform and his evangelical theology, while his older colleagues for the most part opposed both. The Reformation was a young man's movement, for at thirty-four Luther had a following at Wittenberg, at other universities, and among the humanists of men thirty years old or younger. Conversely, nearly all of his major opponents except Dr. Eck were fiftyish or older. The very radical treatise that estranged some of the older humanists, *On the Babylonian Captivity of the Church*, attracted the support of the young humanists. Many students now changed their vocations from law to theology, and a stream of monks and clerics turned to the new ministry. Luther was active in organizing congregational life whenever localities turned to him for help. He recommended students for pastorates and schools, and carried on a tremendous correspondence totaling over four thousand letters.

Luther's young lieutenant Philipp Melanchthon (1497–1560), a grandnephew of Reuchlin, was already renowned as a precocious young humanist when he came to Wittenberg as professor of classics in 1518. His inaugural lecture, "On the Improvement of the Studies of Youth," called for the recovery of the wellsprings of classical literature, the ancient languages, and Christian piety. Melanchthon was a slightly built, bookish, professorial type. Urban Balduin observed in a letter to a friend, "I saw Melanchthon dance with the dean's wife and it was marvelous to behold!" Melanchthon lectured on the Greek and Latin classics as well as on the Scriptures throughout his career. At one point he was lecturing to a class of over nine hundred students. Luther, fourteen years his elder, thought him the greatest theologian who had ever lived, and declared that his *Loci* or *Commonplaces* on Christian doctrine should be esteemed next to the Bible. He was a clear systematic thinker, the primary author of the Protestant Augsburg Confession and many other systematic, rhetorical, and confessional writings. After Luther's death he became titular head of the movement, working in a conciliatory humanist fashion for concessions leading to the unity of the church.

The break between Luther and Erasmus in 1524–1525 must have been particularly painful to Melanchthon, who so keenly admired the prince of the humanists and kept up a correspondence with him even after the great debate. The older humanists had at first been favorably inclined toward Luther, believing him to be a critic and renovator of theology according to their program. Reuchlin exclaimed, "God be praised that now the monks have found someone else who will give them more to do than I!" Georg Spalatin wrote to Mutian in 1519:

I have written to you about your doctor Martin Luther, the Augustinian, toward whom I know you to be much too favorably inclined to wish him ill, that he is such a Christian that he would truly rather suffer all human danger than deny Christ and his truth and teaching. God be praised that the best learned disciplines still are so coming to life, together with that true and holy theology, that we may hope shortly to have all the fine arts and sciences clean and purified.[5]

Luther himself was perfectly clear in his own mind that although the humanities represented the flower of man's creativity and culture, they had no redemptive power. "True it is," he wrote, "that human wisdom and the liberal arts are noble gifts of God.... But we never can learn from them in detail what sin and righteousness are in the sight of God, how we can get rid of our sins, become pious and just before God, and come to life from death." Luther sensed the relative relaxation of religious intensity among the humanists as early as March 1517, when he wrote, "The human avails more with Erasmus than the divine." Erasmus recognized his own weakness when he commented that God had not given all men the strength to become martyrs—but he added that Christianity had had many martyrs but few scholars. They were, moreover, men of different temperaments. Zwingli shrewdly compared Luther with the heroic young Ajax and Erasmus with the wily Odysseus. The poet Eobanus Hessus observed that Erasmus had pointed out what needed to be done but that Luther took the knife and did the pruning.

When they came to grips it was a battle of giants, and Luther congratulated Erasmus on avoiding peripheral issues and aiming for the jugular. Erasmus, who would gladly have remained aloof from the dispute, as he had done during the Reuchlin controversy, was caught in the crossfire. When at last he was pressured into writing against Luther, he argued that man's will is conditionally free, that deeds of a conscious ethical character can be meritorious in God's eyes, and that the commandments to do good would be meaningless unless man had the ability to act as God requires. For Erasmus the way into God's presence was a compound of grace and good works by which man can climb "from the body to the spirit, from the visible to the invisible, from the letter to the mystery, from the sensible to the intelligible, from the compounded to the simple, up as on the rungs of Jacob's ladder" (*Enchiridion*). Erasmus made some damaging admissions, such as that on certain matters he would be a skeptic if the church had not defined such beliefs as necessary. To this Luther replied in his *De servo arbitrio* (*On the Bondage of the Will*), "The Holy Spirit is not a skeptic!" Luther followed Paul in stressing the divine initiative in man's salvation. God's grace is a benignity, and the giver of grace himself is always present. Grace is the divine act of full, free, and final forgiveness which justifies man, not merely an element of spiritual power to be infused and combined with man's natural free will. Man cannot of his own reason

---

[5] Spalatin to Mutian, May 17, 1519, cited in Irmgard Höss, *Georg Spalatin, 1484–1545: Ein Leben in der Zeit des Humanismus und der Reformation* (Weimar, 1956), pp. 79–80.

or strength believe in Jesus Christ. The debate, then, was not one of free will versus determinism in the content of man's life on earth. Like Erasmus, Luther believed that human reason was the greatest of God's creations and that man was quite free to decide things of an earthly nature. He did not, however, believe that man could unaided keep God's law, to love God above all things and his neighbor as himself, even though God commanded it. He did not believe that man could come to faith in Christ, which ran basically counter to reason, unless enlightened by the Holy Spirit. Only the will of the regenerate man is free in spiritual things. This great debate marked a divide between the older humanists and the reformers. From that point on Luther publicly ignored Erasmus, although he continued to read his writings. Ironically, many of Erasmus' Catholic contemporaries thought he was defending his own positions rather than the doctrine of the church. His old friend Aleander once commented that Erasmus had damaged the church more than Luther ever could.

Luther dominated his age as few other men have done, but at the same time there was an unaffected naturalism about him. Open and frank, he displayed his innermost sentiments for all to see.

In the very year in which Luther wrote *On the Bondage of the Will* (1525), he married. Luther's marriage almost caught even him by surprise. He had long resisted the idea of taking a wife, although he had energetically recommended marriage as an excellent estate—for others. He feared that if he married, his opponents would malign his intentions as a reformer. On August 6, 1521, he wrote to Spalatin, "They will never force a wife upon me." In 1524, he was of the same mind, though several of his friends in the religious life had married. He himself lived on in the Black Monastery in Wittenberg with the sole surviving monk, the prior, in real bachelor style—beds not made for as much as two years at a time, irregular hours, poor food. By springtime of 1525 his attitude was changing. Then one day his friend Wenceslas Linck received a letter from him: "Suddenly, and while I was occupied with far other thoughts, the Lord has plunged me into marriage." It may have happened suddenly, but apparently "other thoughts" had not completely crowded the idea from his mind, for he had written to another friend, "If I can manage it, I shall take my Kathie in marriage to spite the devil before I die. I trust they won't deprive me of my joy and courage!" Katherine von Bora was one of nine nuns who had fled the cloister of Marienthron under the influence of Luther's writings and had come to Wittenberg for refuge. She had a lively spirit and somewhat aristocratic bearing. The wedding took place in the evening of June 13, 1525, in the Black Monastery. The bride was twenty-six and the groom forty-two. "Thank God," Luther said years later in one of his rambling *Table Talks*, "it has turned out well, for I have a pious, faithful wife, on whom a man may safely rest his heart."

Martin and Kathie Luther had six children during their two decades of mar-

MARTHIN LVTHER.

CATHARINA.

CATHOLIC SATIRE. *Luther and His Wife Carrying and Wheeling Home the Expelled Protestant Preachers.*

ried life, and Luther spent many happy hours in the family circle. He loved music, played both the lute and the flute, and led in the singing of songs by Flemish and German masters, and occasionally of his own composition. Luther prepared a book of family devotions (*Hauspostille*), the *Small Catechism* and the *Large Catechism* (1529) for the instruction of children and the use of the clergy, and wrote hymns to be sung in congregational worship. The best known became the "marching song" of the Reformation, "A Mighty Fortress Is Our God." The house was always full of indigent students, friends, and visitors from all parts of Europe, so that only Kathie's careful household management kept them from bankruptcy. Luther learned, too, a father's sorrow at the death of a child. His daughter Elizabeth died in infancy, and when thirteen-year-old Magdalena passed away in her father's arms, he turned aside to conceal his tears and said, "Whether we live or die, we are the Lord's." His faith was tested experientially.

The ancient Spartans said of Philip of Macedon after the fall of Thebes, "To destroy a city he is able, but to build another lies beyond his power." Rebuilding the reformed church along the lines of an evangelical church order consumed much of Luther's energies during the last decades of his life. He prepared a new German order of worship (1526) for the church in Wittenberg which retained the traditional responses. The sermon, in the language of the people, was given the central place in the service, with communion in both kinds celebrated after it. Baptism was retained as the second dominical sacrament, through which infants were regenerated and engrafted into the church. He applied his idea of the priesthood of all believers, as far as it proved to be practicable, to the re-creation of a congregational form of church life on the New Testament pattern. The congregation was to exercise judgment in matters of doctrine, call pastors and teachers, manage finances, care for the needy, and exercise the office of the keys, or admonition and excommunication. The authority of the pastor to preach and to administer the sacraments was derived from the congregation that called him to his office.

In actual practice this ideal was only partially realized, for the pattern of control of the physical properties and external affairs of the church by the princes and city councils was so deeply rooted that in many areas Luther was forced to depend on them for the organization and supervision of the church. He would not, however, concede the principle, and referred to them as "Christians in authority" and as "emergency bishops" until such time as educated men were available to assume control and leadership as evangelical bishops free from the control of secular authority. In Saxony Elector John (1525–1532) appointed a visitation commission consisting of two electoral councilors and two theologians, Luther and Justus Jonas, to look into the spiritual condition of the congregations. The monastic properties and endowments for masses were now to be used for educational and charitable purposes. The next year Melanchthon prepared for the elector an *Instruction for the Visitors to the Pastors,* which outlined evangelical doctrine, provided for supervision of the clergy in four separate districts by a superintendent, and demanded an improved level of education for pastors and laymen. In the preface to this *Instruction* Luther stressed again that "his Electoral Grace" was to act "out of Christian love, for he is not responsible as secular overlord, and for God's sake for the good of the gospel and for the benefit and welfare of distressed Christians." The visitation, he wrote, was called for because of the great need of the church; it was to be undertaken as by a Christian brother, out of love, and was to be temporary, until an improved situation or better plan evolved. Luther strove manfully to preserve the distinction between the spiritual and the secular authorities. He was caught in the dilemma of choosing between the congregation as a small group of confessing believers and the idea of the people's church, embracing all members of the community, even those who were only formally Christians. In 1539 Elector John Frederick established a consistory or civil court to handle cases of ecclesiastical discipline. While Luther lived, matters of spiritual concern were still regularly referred to him for disposition, but after his death the consistory and its four commissioners became increasingly the instruments of the territorial government.

The Lutheran movement gained in strength with the addition of new cities and territories during the decade following the Diet of Worms. In 1526 Emperor Charles decided to enforce the Edict of Worms, but he was unable to attend the diet at Speyer that summer. There the evangelical estates, supported by some Catholic princes, managed to postpone action until a national council or an ecumenical council, to meet within a year and a half, could take up the question. Meanwhile each estate should act in response to its own sense of duty toward God and the emperor. The emperor was prevented by his constant preoccupation with his wars against the French, the pope, and the Turks from acting freely against Luther. But when at Speyer in 1529 he demanded that the resolution of 1526 allowing the estates discretion in the Lutheran question be rescinded, the evangelical estates, Electoral Saxony, Brandenburg, Hesse, and Anhalt, and fourteen free imperial cities under the leadership of Strassburg became "protesting estates," the origin of the name Protestant.

The emperor resolved to attend the next diet at Augsburg in 1530. Luther could not be present because of the ban, and even the city of Nuremberg did not dare give him sanctuary. He therefore stayed in the fortress of Coburg, the Electoral Saxon castle nearest to Augsburg, impatiently awaiting news from the diet; would the edict now be enforced against him? On the wall of his room high over the castle ramparts he inscribed for his own comfort the words of the psalmist: "I shall not die, but live, and declare the works of the Lord!" He kept up a steady barrage of letters to Melanchthon and the evangelical party, telling them to stand fast and be courageous. Melanchthon wished to do nothing to perpetuate the schism and would gladly have restricted the Protestant statement to criticism of abuse, but he was forced by Luther's opponents to make a doctrinal statement of the evangelical position. His Augsburg Confession, read to the diet and emperor on June 25, 1530, became the classical statement of the Lutheran faith. There was no thought of founding a new church, but an effort toward the reform of the whole Christian church on earth. "I cannot walk so soft and gently," Luther said admiringly when he read Melanchthon's words. Still hoping for unity, Melanchthon omitted from the Confession such controversial subjects as the veneration of saints, purgatory, transubstantiation, and the priesthood of all believers. Luther shared Melanchthon's concern, but he no longer believed that unity was possible while the pope remained at the head of the hierarchy. The emperor and Catholic majority rejected the Confession and would not even consider Melanchthon's *Apology* for the Augsburg Confession. On October 2, 1530, two days before he left Coburg, Luther preached a final sermon in the chapel on the events at Augsburg:

> If they are willing to be merciful toward us, then they are so in God's name. If not, then let them do as they will—what do we care? Heaven is greater than the earth, and things will hardly be so turned around that the earth rules heaven. If they have plans, they must first ask our Lord God whether it is pleasing to him. If it does not suit him, let them deliberate and resolve what they will; it is written: "He that sitteth in the heavens shall laugh, the Lord shall hold them in derision."

At Worms Luther stood alone; at Augsburg he was represented by a chorus of evangelicals, and the Confession was signed by some of the most powerful and energetic rulers in the empire.

Luther's last years were marked by restless activity and prodigious labor. He continued lecturing, began his last great commentary on Genesis in 1535, served as dean of the theological faculty, made church visitations, and prepared the Schmalkald Articles as his theological testament for a meeting of the Schmalkald League of Protestant princes in 1537. At that meeting he fell ill with kidney stones and gallstones and was brought back to Wittenberg a very sick man. But he still had nearly nine years of life in him, and devoted much of them to writing nearly 165 treatises and as many as ten letters a day. He examined doctoral candidates and staged "doctor feasts" with beer and venison for the lucky candidates. Sick and constantly apprehensive about the danger of war, he became short-tempered and even harsh, though in behalf of the cause and not from personal peevishness. In response to Kathie's chiding, "Dear husband, you are too rude," he retorted, "They teach me to be rude!"

His life came to an end where it had begun, in the town of Eisleben. An activist to the last, concerned with social issues, he traveled there in midwinter to settle a legal dispute between the counts of Mansfeld. He suffered a heart attack on arrival, but recovered and directed the negotiations for three weeks. On February 17 the affair was settled, but Luther was exhausted and suffered a series of further heart attacks. When one of his friends at the bedside asked him, "Dearest father, do you confess Christ, the Son of God, our Savior and Redeemer?" he answered with a clear "Yes!" Thus about two-thirty in the morning of February 18, 1546, there passed into history the man about whom more has been written than about any other person with the exception of Jesus. Was he an event-maker or merely a man whose life was eventful? His own last written words, jotted on a slip of paper two days before his death, reflect his appreciation of both the greatness and the limitation of every human being:

> No one who was not a shepherd or a peasant for five years can understand Virgil in his *Bucolica* and *Georgica*.
>
> I maintain that no one can understand Cicero in his letters unless he was active in important affairs of state for twenty years.
>
> Let no one who has not guided the congregations with the prophets for one hundred years believe that he has tasted Holy Writ thoroughly. For this reason the miracle is stupendous (1) in John the Baptist, (2) in Christ, (3) in the Apostles.
>
> Do not try to fathom this divine *Aeneid*, but humbly worship its footprints. We are beggars. That is true. [*Wir sein Pettler. Hoc est verum.*][6]

Luther may have had his own fascinating theories about wondermen and healthy heroes in history, but he saw himself as a humble instrument in the hands of God, not as a mere piece of driftwood thrown up by indifferent waves of history upon the sands of time.

Bibliography

Luther:

BAINTON, ROLAND H. *Here I Stand! A Life of Martin Luther*. Nashville and New York, 1950.

BOEHMER, HEINRICH. *Road to Reformation*. Philadelphia, 1946.

DICKENS, A. G. *Luther and the Reformation*. London, 1967.

ERIKSON, ERIK H. *Young Man Luther*. New York, 1958.

FIFE, ROBERT H. *The Revolt of Martin Luther*. New York, 1957.

GERRISH, BRIAN, ed. *Reformers in Profile*. Philadelphia, 1967.

GRISAR, HARTMANN. *Martin Luther: His Life and Work*. Westminster, Md., 1950.

KOOIMAN, W. F. *By Faith Alone: The Life of Martin Luther*. New York, 1955.

McGIFFERT, A. C. *Martin Luther*. New York, 1917.

MACKINNON, JAMES. *Luther and the Reformation*, 4 vols. London, 1925–1930.

OLIN, JOHN C., ed. *Luther, Erasmus, and the Reformation: A Catholic-Protestant Reappraisal*. New York, 1969.

RITTER, GERHARD. *Martin Luther: His Life and Work*. New York, 1963.

---

[6] Heinrich Bornkamm, *Luther's World of Thought*, trans. Martin H. Bertram (St. Louis, 1958), p. 291. The reference to the *Aeneid* is a quotation from the Roman poet Statius (d. *c.* 96 A.D.), *Thebaid*, XII, 816f., cited in *ibid.*, n. 4.

Schwiebert, Ernest G. *Luther and His Times.* St. Louis, 1950.
Simon, Edith. *Luther Alive: Martin Luther and the Making of the Reformation.* Garden City, N.Y., 1968.
Thiel, Rudolf. *Luther.* Philadelphia, 1955.
Todd, John M. *Martin Luther: A Biographical Study.* Westminster, Md., 1964.

Luther's religious reformation:
Althaus, Paul. *The Theology of Martin Luther.* Philadelphia, 1966.
Bluhm, Heinz. *Martin Luther: Creative Translator.* St. Louis, 1966.
Bornkamm, Heinrich. *Luther's World of Thought.* St. Louis, 1958.
———. *Luther and the Old Testament.* Philadelphia, 1969.
Elert, Werner. *The Structure of Lutheranism,* vol. 1. St. Louis, 1962.
Forell, George W. *Faith Active in Love.* New York, 1954.
Gerrish, Brian. *Grace and Reason: A Study in the Theology of Martin Luther.* New York, 1962.
Headley, John. *Luther's View of Church History.* New Haven, 1963.
Kadai, Heino. *Accents in Luther's Theology.* St. Louis, 1967.
McSorley, Harry J. *Luther: Right or Wrong?* New York and Minneapolis, 1969.
Meyer, Carl S. *Luther for an Ecumenical Age.* St. Louis, 1967.
Pelikan, Jaroslav. *Luther the Expositor.* St. Louis, 1959.
Pinomaa, Lennart. *Faith Victorious: An Introduction to Luther's Theology.* Philadelphia, 1963.
Prenter, Regin. *Spiritus Creator.* Philadelphia, 1953.
Preus, James S. *From Shadow to Promise: Old Testament Interpretation from Augustine to Luther.* Cambridge, Mass., 1969.
Rupp, Gordon. *Luther's Progress to the Diet of Worms.* London, 1951.
———. *The Righteousness of God: Luther Studies.* London, 1953.
Siggins, Ian D. Kingston. *Martin Luther's Doctrine of Christ,* Yale Publications in Religion no. 14. New Haven, 1970.
Vajta, Vilmos. *Luther on Worship.* Philadelphia, 1958.
Watson, Philip. *Let God Be God!* Philadelphia, 1948.
Wingren, Gustaf. *Luther on Vocation.* Philadelphia, 1957.
Ziemke, Donald. *Love of Neighbor in Luther's Theology.* Minneapolis, 1963.

Social unrest and the progress of the Reformation:
Althaus, Paul. *Luthers Haltung im Bauernkrieg.* Basel, 1953.
Bax, E. B. *The Peasants' War in Germany.* London, 1903.
Cranz, F. Edward. *An Essay on the Development of Luther's Thought on Justice, Law, and Society.* Cambridge, Mass., 1959.
Engels, Friedrich. *The German Revolutions: The Peasant War in Germany; and, Germany: Revolution and Counter-Revolution,* ed. Leonard Krieger. Chicago, 1967.
Franz, Günther. *Der deutsche Bauernkrieg,* 7th ed. Darmstadt, 1965.
Gritsch, Eric W. *Reformer Without a Church.* Philadelphia, 1967.
Kautsky, Karl. *Communism in Central Europe in the Time of the Reformation.* London, 1897.
Smirin, M. M. *Deutschland vor der Reformation.* Berlin, 1955.

CHAPTER 14

The Empire
in Crisis

The young emperor Charles V who sat upon the throne in the presence of the diet at Worms in 1521 was in every respect a remarkable person. The product of ancient historical forces, he had inherited from his Habsburg fore-bears the Netherlands, Luxemburg, Burgundy, Alsace, Castile, Aragon, Naples, Sicily, Austria, and the Spanish dominions in the New World, and three years earlier he had been elected Holy Roman emperor as well. He had the largest hold-ings of any ruler of his time, more than twice the realm of France, which his posses-sions now encircled. Through his veins flowed the royal blood of Christendom's oldest dynasties, mostly Hispanic, but also Burgundian, French, and German.

The young man whom Luther addressed as his "most gracious lord and em-peror" had light brown hair, a long, rather thin and melancholy face, alert eyes, and a jutting Habsburg jaw. On the walls in Worms these words appeared mys-teriously during the night of April 17: "Woe to the land whose king is a boy!" Before Charles stood Luther, the lowly Augustinian, who by sheer spiritual power had broken out of a monastery onto the stage of history. By a strange irony the forces he unloosed helped to wear down the emperor until in his last years he him-self retreated to a monastery. He was a lay brother there when he died. The reign of Charles V was for him frustrating but it was in no sense futile, for he molded

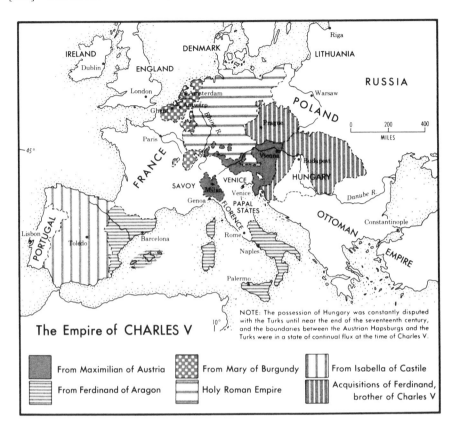

The Empire of CHARLES V

NOTE: The possession of Hungary was constantly disputed with the Turks until near the end of the seventeenth century, and the boundaries between the Austrian Hapsburgs and the Turks were in a state of continual flux at the time of Charles V.

From Maximilian of Austria

From Ferdinand of Aragon

From Mary of Burgundy

Holy Roman Empire

From Isabella of Castile

Acquisitions of Ferdinand, brother of Charles V

inherited ideas of power, behavior, and belief into new universal forms that have shaped both reality and the vision of mankind down to the present.

Born at Ghent on February 24, 1500, to Philip the Fair, son of Emperor Maximilian and Mary of Burgundy, and Joanna, later called "the mad," daughter of Ferdinand of Aragon and Isabella of Castile, Charles grew up in the Netherlands imbued with Flemish piety and Burgundian chivalric notions, which remained his two most outstanding personal characteristics throughout his life. While Charles was still an infant his parents went to Spain, leaving him in the care of Margaret of York, the widow of Duke Charles the Bold of Burgundy, who had been killed at Nancy in 1477. In 1507 Margaret of Austria moved to Malines and assumed the roles of regent and mother to Charles. From early childhood he had a high sense of his calling and the dignity and supremacy of kingship as a divine regency; it never left him. One of his tutors was Adrian of Utrecht, a pious man who later became pope. During his boyhood his policy was aimed at the recovery of Burgundy from the French. With a change of advisers and his election as Holy Roman emperor in 1519, his interest shifted to Italy.

Operating mainly from Spain after 1521, he reasserted the old imperial claims to the territories of Milan, Tuscany, and Naples and assumed the imperial responsibilities of shielding Italy from the French and dominating the papacy. With a new Madrid-Rome axis established, he reawakened a vision of European unity.

Charles was completely dedicated to dynastic policy as a means of achieving a European hegemony and world empire. To establish Habsburg rule by marriage or conquest was a solemn religious duty owed in piety to his ancestors and in conscience to his descendants. He held to the medieval ideal of one pope as the supreme spiritual head and one emperor as the highest secular power in Christendom. He was deeply hurt by the pope's betrayal and by the alliance of the Christian king of France with the Turks. His interest in the New World was centered on the extension of Christianity to the heathen and the resources that the new treasures of Mexico and Peru provided for his continental enterprises. His dream of a universal dynastic empire raised the sights of feudal and urban authorities to higher political conceptions and goals. The great lords were beckoned away from their petty personal rivalries to larger policies of empire and a statecraft based upon more lofty principles.

For over forty years Charles waged war after war and negotiated treaty after treaty in order to achieve his goals or redress losses. His campaigns were often quixotic, planned and executed like some feudal chess game or tournament. Though slightly built, he was athletic, and he directed many battlefield encounters well armored and mounted on a white horse. He sent tens of thousands of state letters, often in his own hand; many still survive, evidence of his passion for affairs of state and his devotion to duty. He left the image of a most dedicated monarch to kings for centuries to come, but his own master plan as a design from Charlemagne floundered and failed. His very strength was his weakness, for the vast extent of his holdings meant they were correspondingly exposed and vulnerable. The encircled French had the advantage of centrality and interior lines of communication. The extreme eastern lands, farthest away from his main base of strength in Spain, lay directly in the path of the advancing Turks. Above all, Charles's widespread commitments and the shift in the seat of his power to the west proved to be disastrous for the Holy Roman Empire itself, which now entered a period of severe crisis.

The imperial election of 1519 was of crucial importance to the princes and people of the empire and to all Europe. Even before the death of Maximilian on January 12, 1519, political maneuvering for the election was under way. On January 1, 1515, twenty-one-year-old Francis I had ascended the throne of France. He was a handsome, proud, somewhat vain, free-spending Renaissance king who generously supported humanists, artists, and pleasing women at his magnificent court. "A court without beautiful women," said the king, "is like a spring without roses." His fairy-tale Château Chambord still stands as one of the architectural pearls strung along the Loire valley, and the deer still roam through his hunting grounds in the woods of Boulogne. Personally courageous, he loved a campaign. He had more than a touch of bravado about him, as when he said to the Venetians, "I will come, and I will triumph or die." After his victory at Marignano in 1515 over Swiss soldiery he enjoyed a military reputation that was totally undeserved, for he was a poor strategist and an impulsive field commander. According to the Treaty of Brussels (1516), France was to receive Milan and Spain was to control southern Italy. Francis I now feared that if Charles I of Spain were to be elected emperor, his own interests in northern Italy would be jeopardized. He believed that his own election as emperor would countermand the growing Habsburg ascendancy, and from 1517 on he worked to secure the votes of a majority of the seven electors. The months prior to the election of the new emperor were filled with conniving. Archbishop Richard of Trier committed himself to Francis and Frederick the Wise of Saxony followed an independent course; but the other five electors took fantastic bribes from both sides. The Habsburgs were reduced to borrowing bribe money from the German bankers. Pope Leo X favored the French king, in line with Medici policy and out of fear of the Spaniards, and he used his influence, promising a cardinal's hat and appointment as permanent papal legate to the archbishop of Mainz for the right vote. Francis promised to make Joachim I of Brandenburg his regent for all Germany. Both Leo and Francis would have preferred any German prince to Charles, but the only likely candidate was Luther's patron, Elector Frederick the Wise, and Frederick realized that his family and Electoral Saxony lacked the resources in men and money to keep peace in the empire. Pope Leo's agents reported back their suspicion that the electors were taking French gold but would not choose a French king. Then just before the election Frederick came out forcefully for Charles I of Spain, and on June 28, 1519, the electors choose Charles with a unanimous vote. The grandson of the popular Maximilian had been chosen. To the great rejoicing of all the Germans, the Habsburg eagle had soared above the Gallic cock. On October 22, 1520, Charles rode into Aachen on a beautiful stallion for his coronation.

The Germans could not yet foresee how Charles's international policies would work to the disadvantage of their empire. But it gradually became apparent to them that Charles was shifting the main base of his power away from Germany and Burgundy to the west. He always put Spain first and gave to the Spanish branch of his dynasty a preponderance that was to last for a century and a half. He achieved an ephemeral unity of Iberia through his fifteen-year marriage with Isabella of Portugal. The control of the Habsburg Danubian lands he transferred to the younger branch of his family. He skillfully glued together the Habsburg-Jagellon lines by arranging for the marriage of his younger brother Ferdinand with Anne, sister of King Louis II of Hungary and Bohemia, and of his sister Mary to Louis himself. He made Ferdinand regent of Austria and of the adjoining lands, Tyrol,

Vorarlberg, and Württemberg, and also turned over to him Alsace, Pfirt, and Hagenau with the proviso that on Ferdinand's death they should revert to the Burgundian inheritance.

In moving his own base of power to Spain, Charles made the western Mediterranean his own sphere of interest, which involved him in dramatic sea battles with the Tunisian pirates. He tied the Netherlands in with his Spanish nexus, thus cutting them off from a more natural union with the empire. He suppressed the north German Hanse cities and accelerated their decline. He opposed Christian II of Denmark, husband of his unhappy sister Isabella, and frustrated his attempt to build a strong state in the north. By shutting France out of Italy, he diverted its expansive drives into Lorraine and toward the empire, to the discomfiture and at times the terror of the German Rhineland. By his relative neglect of the empire, he allowed the Protestant princes in the north and the Catholic princes in the south to further the development of their territorial autonomy and particularist interests. After the Diet of Worms in 1521 Charles left for the Netherlands, hurried then to Spain, and did not return to the empire again for eight long years. Three enormous challenges confronted him: the wars with France, the invasion by the Ottoman Turks, and the test of strength with the Lutherans.

The Habsburg-Valois Wars

CHARLES V found the enemy of his life in King Francis I of France. The emperor had a dual role to play in his statecraft, for he strove toward that universal dominion which would ensure the unity and the security of Christendom against all foes, and he forged a dynastic chain of Habsburg states designed to throttle France. Much was at stake, for the control of the Mediterranean, the Atlantic, and the New World would be the prize of the victor in this struggle. The Italian cities and smaller states became mere pawns in this chess game of kings. The new superstates now swallowed up many small principalities.

In Francis of Angoulême, of a second line of the house of Orléans, the emperor found a worthy opponent, brash, colorful, determined, a gambler who thoroughly enjoyed ruling his nation. When Francis learned that Louis XII would be childless, he called together his friends and celebrated with a tournament, and when the king died Francis succeeded to his throne. His mother, Louise of Savoy, had imbued him with an exalted sense of his royal worth. "I went," she once related, "on foot to Our Lady of Fontaines in order to commend to her him whom I love more than myself, my son, the glorious and triumphant caesar, conqueror of the Helvetians." The growing French feeling of cohesion and national pride worked to his advantage. He exercised all the control he possessed and found a powerful response in the people. Emperor Maximilian once commented that he was a king of kings, for no one felt obliged to obey him. The king of Spain was a king of men, for people voiced objections but did not withhold obedience. But the king of France was like a king over animals, for no one dared think of refusing obedience. When the Venetian ambassador related Maximilian's *bon mot* to Francis I, he laughed out loud, for he recognized the truth in it. He ruled with a certain flair for grandeur and worked with vigor at governing, meeting his *conseil des affaires* in his bedroom each morning shortly after he awoke. He wished desperately to establish his family firmly on the throne, and when his oldest son suddenly died at a time when the imperial armies had occupied Provence, he was in despair. But he had other heirs, including his second son, Henry, who was married to Catherine de' Medici and perpetuated the Valois line.

Once the imperial election of 1519 was decided in favor of the Habsburg, Charles and Francis jockeyed diplomatically for a favorable position and then squared off for a duel that went through four wars and lasted four decades. In August 1521 the representatives of the emperor, Francis I, the pope, and Henry VIII met in Calais, ostensibly to assure peace but in reality to win England over to one side or the other. The Spanish diplomats succeeded in isolating Francis and winning over Henry VIII to a mutual-assistance pact with promises of the return of the old Angevin holdings, while Charles would take everything in the east and south of France that once belonged to the empire, as well as Navarre north of the Pyrenees. Pope Leo X made an alliance with Charles V in order to strengthen him against the Lutherans. Leo even prepared a bull that would have empowered Henry VIII to absolve French subjects of their oaths of loyalty to Francis. Francis gave sufficient provocation to Charles, aiding rebels in Castile, trying to detach the kingdom of Navarre from Spain, and encouraging Robert von der Mark to attack the empire on the western front. When Charles heard of Robert's aggression he exclaimed, "God be praised! It is not I who starts the war! God is giving me an opportunity to defend myself!"

Georg von Frundsberg, Franz von Sickingen, and an imperial army under the count of Nassau pressed into France, but were held off with the loss of only a few forts. Italy was destined to be the main theater of action. The imperial forces, opposed by French, Swiss, and Venetian troops, took Milan on November 19, 1521. Then Georg von Frundsberg brought in twelve fresh contingents of soldiers in support of the imperial general Pescara and together they took Genoa on May 20, 1522. The following year a great French magnate, Constable Charles of Bourbon, turned against Francis I, whom he considered a threat to his land and prospects, and in July 1524 he invaded southern France and besieged Marseilles with the help of imperial troops. Francis I now made an all-out effort to retake Milan. The French were well entrenched in the park of Mirabello near Pavia, but their impetuous king, spoiling for the encounter, moved out of his protected position. "Today," he exclaimed, "I shall name myself duke of Milan!" He gambled everything in one desperate battle at Pavia and lost. Before the battle the German troops knelt until the enemy was very close, then sprang to their feet shouting, "Forward! Now is the time! In God's name!" The Spanish arquebus proved to be a formidable weapon, and hand-to-hand combat raged for an hour and a half. French losses ran to over ten thousand men. Francis I himself was surrounded and captured.

The battle took place on February 24, 1525, and at the close of the day the imperial commissioner, the abbot of Najera, sent a dispatch to Charles in Spain: "Today is the feast of the Apostle St. Matthew, on which your majesty is said to have been born twenty-five years ago. Twenty-five thousand times thanks and praise be to God for his grace! From this day on your majesty will be able to prescribe laws as you will to Christians and to Turks!"

The effect upon France of the capture of Francis I and his imprisonment in Madrid was traumatic. The leaderless troops wandered about aimlessly, shouting for Bourbon or Burgundy. The nobility had suffered heavy losses and the cities now began to assert greater independence. Francis himself indulged in posturing, declaring that honor and duty had led him into captivity, but his heart remained free. But he fell ill and became for a time demoralized. Popular opinion in France fixed the blame for the debacle more on Queen Mother Louise and Chancellor Duprat than on the king himself. A note widely distributed in the churches of France in March 1525 read: "Do you wish to know who is to blame for all this evil? It is Dame Pride and her chancellor. Through stubbornness and desire for revenge they have brought the king and his realm into this misfortune, and it will become worse if the chancellor is not punished!"

Charles V was astounded at the capture of his archrival; he was completely unprepared for such a turn of events. Henry VIII urged him to render Francis permanently harmless, but this advice did not take into account the strength of French national feeling for the young king and the terrible reaction such a step would have produced. A churchman urged him to release Francis immediately and unconditionally as a gesture of magnanimity that would elicit gratitude and friendship forever after, but this kindly approach did not take into account Francis' own Machiavellian propensities. Charles chose the middle course of releasing Francis on certain conditions. People should not say of him, he declared, that he was like Hannibal, who knew how to conquer but not how to use the victory. The Treaty of Madrid (January 14, 1526) was a severe but not an unreasonable resolution. Francis was to renounce his claims to Burgundy, the Netherlands, and Italian territories. Charles of Bourbon was to be restored to his own lands. Francis was to marry Charles's sister Eleanor. Francis' two oldest sons were to be sent to Madrid as hostages to ensure the honoring of the treaty. The treaty was signed with due ceremony, but quickly came unglued. The marriage did nothing to ensure peace between the brothers-in-law, for Francis did not allow Eleanor to influence his policy. She was ill at ease at the brilliant French court and failed to produce a child. Francis very predictably took the first opportunity to renounce the treaty on the grounds that he had signed it under duress.

The European powers now turned against Charles, fearing his power. They joined forces in the League of Cognac on May 22, 1526, with the Medici pope Clement VII, Florence, Venice, Duke Sforza of Milan, and Francis I lined up against Charles. They were bolstered further by Henry VIII, who anticipated England's later policy of maintaining a balance of power on the continent by opposing the leading force. Moreover, he was already disenchanted with his inherited wife, Catherine, who happened to be Charles's aunt. Charles was enraged at the duplicity of Pope Clement VII. He addressed a letter to him asking how the vicar of Christ on earth could justify shedding one drop of blood for the sake of worldly possessions. The pope was damaging the Christian religion, for as emperor he could not now protect Christendom from the Turks or suppress the heretics. If the pope continued to act as a factional leader rather than a father, as a robber rather than a shepherd, the emperor would appeal to a council. In less than a year the emperor had his revenge.

In November 1526 an army of fifteen thousand German troops crossed the Alps under the command of Georg von Frundsberg, the old campaigner. In February 1527 Charles of Bourbon joined him with five thousand French dissidents and Spanish soldiery. The commanders ran out of money and Frundsberg died of a stroke after a confrontation with his rebellious troops. The army stormed on toward Rome, living on loot and plunder. On May 6 they began an assault on the walls of the eternal city. Bourbon was killed by a bullet as he mounted a scaling ladder. By midnight the troops were in the city and began the sack of Rome, which still lives in Italian memory as one of the most terrifying experiences in the city's long history. Clement VII took refuge in the fortress Sant' Angelo, while on the streets below drunken soldiers paraded a comrade crowned with a triple tiara and dispensing blessings with his wineglass. Now, they shouted, they would make Luther pope! But Emperor Charles allowed the pope to keep his secular power in exchange for a promise to work for peace and to call a council.

Francis recovered his stamina and was ready for a second try at realizing his ambitions. He developed a defensive system of fortresses in two lines, employing the latest techniques in earthworks and stone construction developed in Italy against artillery fire. He organized a rudimentary system of provincial militias. In August 1527 he made peace with Henry VIII, now in love with Anne Boleyn and hostile to Charles V. With the home front secured, he plunged into another Italian adventure and the second Habsburg war. The imperial army suffered the fate of countless forces that had invaded Italy through the long millennia, debauchery and demoralization. The French retook Genoa and went on to besiege Naples on land and, with a Genoese fleet under Andrea Doria, by sea. But then the French were hit by a plague, Andrea Doria defected to the emperor over the French treatment of Genoa, and an imperial army occupied Lombardy and relieved Naples.

In the Peace of Barcelona (June 29, 1529) Pope Clement confirmed the imperial claim to Naples and guaranteed free passage of imperial troops across the Papal States in exchange for the emperor's promise to oppose the Lutherans. With the Treaty of Cambrai, or "Ladies' Peace," as it was called, because Queen Mother Louise and Charles's aunt Margaret of Austria initiated negotiations, the second war was officially ended on August 5, 1529. The terms of Cambrai were basically the same as those of the Treaty of Madrid, with Charles renouncing attempts to recover Burgundy and Francis renouncing his overlordship of Flanders and Artois and promising never again to invade Italy or the empire. Pope Clement VII saw the "great value" of the treaty in the return of Francis' sons for a huge ransom in a single gold payment, for the emperor would now be free to go to Germany and personally oppose the Turks and Lutherans. On February 25, 1530, he crowned Charles emperor in a festive ceremony in Bologna, the last time in history that a pope would crown an emperor.

Though he had obviously signed the treaty freely, Francis again claimed that he had signed it under duress and maneuvered for a resumption of hostilities. The marriage in 1533 of his second son, the future Henry II, to Catherine de' Medici, the pope's niece, cemented relations between king and pope. The gift of Francis to Pope Clement on this grand occasion aroused considerable comment: a unicorn's horn that, when placed upon a banquet table, would reveal the presence of any poison in the food or drink by breaking into a cold sweat. Charles tried repeatedly during these years to find a basis of agreement with Francis. But a sinister development was in the making, an alliance of the most Christian king of France with the infidel Turks against the most Catholic emperor.

While a prisoner in Madrid, Francis had contrived to communicate with Sultan Suleiman I, presumably urging him to invade Hungary, which he did the next year. An official French embassy was sent to the Turks in 1535. In that year Francis explained this act to the Venetian ambassador: "Orator, I cannot deny that I hope the Turks appear mighty on this sea; not that I find pleasure in their advantages, for they are infidels and we are Christians, but they keep the emperor preoccupied and thereby effect greater security for other rulers." In February 1536 he made a formal alliance with the Turks, to the general horror of Christendom. The following month Francis suddenly invaded Savoy and moved on into Italy while the Turks attacked the Habsburg lands along the Danube and the Venetians at sea. The French pressed into the Netherlands, while imperial troops invaded Piedmont and Provence. Pope Paul III, fearing the Turks, was relieved to be able to mediate a peace between the two Christian monarchs on June 18, 1538.

The fourth and last attempt of Francis to break the Habsburg power nearly ended in disaster for his own kingdom. He renewed his alliance with Sultan Suleiman, who responded by a new invasion of Hungary. A combined French and Turkish fleet ruled the Mediterranean and attacked the cities along the coast, avoiding those in France. In the summer of 1542 Francis' armies attacked Spain and Luxemburg simultaneously. Charles again made an alliance with Henry VIII against France and then launched a massive counterattack. He sent a force down the Rhine to crush an ally of the French, William of Cleves, a rebellious Protestant prince. Then in June 1544 an imperial army of some 35,000 men penetrated deep into France, coming within fifty miles of Paris by September 8. At that point cautious Charles, near exhaustion and not willing to risk a reversal, offered peace terms. Charles once again invoked his dynastic principle and agreed that if the king's third son would marry the emperor's daughter, he would give her the Netherlands or Milan as a dowry. Thus ended the fourth and final Habsburg-Valois war.

Both sides, having devoted blood and money to a massive exercise in futility, were near bankruptcy and collapse. On March 31, 1547, Francis I died and was succeeded by Henry II. Charles V retired in 1556 and the task of arranging a more lasting peace with France fell to his successors. The Treaty of Cateau-Cambrésis (April 1–3, 1559), which came just forty years after the election of Charles as emperor and less than a year after his death, formalized the relationship between Spain, the empire, and France for decades to come. According to its terms France once again renounced her claims to Italy (except for five fortresses), yielded Savoy and Piedmont, but retained the income from those fateful bishoprics in the east, Metz, Toul, and Verdun. Italy suffered a new division, with western Lombardy going to Savoy, the south and east to the Farneses and Gonzagas, and Siena to the Medicis. The fact that this peace endured was due less to the good faith of the contracting parties than to the Spanish preponderance of power in the second half of the sixteenth century. Beset by civil war and domestic troubles, the French were in no position to challenge the Habsburgs for a long time to come.

The Ottoman Turks Attack

WHAT THE GERMAN EMPIRE really needed for its own well-being was a new location. In the center of a troubled continent and with no substantial natural barriers for defense, it was constantly caught between pressures from alert, advanced forces in the west and massive, brutal powers in the east. Charles V was caught in the middle of a two-front war with an opponent in the east as colorful and as worthy as his enemy to the west. Suleiman the Magnificent (1520–1566), the only son of Sultan Selim I, succeeded to the golden throne in the same year in which Charles V was crowned emperor, and remained his lifelong opponent. Suleiman, it was widely believed, was of a quiet and calm disposition, not well versed in affairs of state. But once in power he became a ruler without peer, a lawgiver, administrator, builder, patron of letters, and military leader of enormous energy and daring. He is remembered in history and legend for his style of governing, for th "marvelous grandeur" of his face, as the Venetian Navagero observed, and for a unique combination of wisdom and ruthlessness.

When King Francis I declared war in April 1521, Suleiman I saw his chance to realize the ambition of Mohammed II and of Bayazid II, Selim's predecessor, who had made assaults on Belgrade, the key to the Hungarian plain, but had failed to take it. A tremendous force of janissaries, regular troops, siege guns, and the sultan with his personal regiments moved out of Istanbul up the Danube. Light cavalry raided the countryside and cut off Belgrade to the west and north. A heavy bombardment and assault drove the garrison of defenders into the citadel, while Ottoman boats controlled the river. The Serbian and Hungarian defenders quarreled over tactics, and on August 29 the fortress surrendered. Suleiman followed up this victory the next year with a triumphant assault on the island of Rhodes. The Knights of St. John on Rhodes received no help from the west, for the Dutch pope Adrian VI seemed not to realize the strategic importance of Rhodes, in the eastern Mediterranean. They fought until exhausted and then surrendered on condition that they be allowed to withdraw to the west. The Mediterranean was now open to Turkish galleys.

The Persians provided a temporary distraction, but in April 1526 Suleiman's armies moved out again, this time to crush Hungary. King Louis II of Hungary led his brave but badly outnumbered Magyars against the Ottoman forces on the plain at Mohács on August 29, 1526. The Danube flowed to the east, and wooded hills to the west and south screened Ottoman forces from view. The Hungarian heavy cavalry charged the center of the Turkish line and threw it back. But at a critical moment Ottoman troops came down from the woods to the west and hit the Hungarian right flank. Murderous fire from the Ottoman artillery cut down thousands and the Hungarians were routed. Those not massacred by the Turks drowned in the marshes of the Danube, among them King Louis II. While noble Magyars died at Mohács on that fateful day, the governor of Transylvania, John Zapolya, stood aside with a large army. He was rewarded by being made king of Hungary under Suleiman's protection. The claim was disputed, of course, by Ferdinand, the younger brother of Charles V, on whom the emperor had bestowed the Habsburg Danubian lands.

Rebellious Turks distracted Suleiman, but in 1529 he was ready to take another slice of Europe. Having taken Buda and gained control of most of Hungary, Suleiman set his sights on Vienna. Time and distance were now his great foes, for the campaign season lasted only from April to the end of October, and the long lines of supply and communication compounded his logistics problems. His forces moved out of Istanbul on May 10, and on September 21 the first Turks appeared before Vienna. Within a week the 20,000 defending troops within the city were surrounded by a force estimated at more than 200,000. The Turks tunneled under the walls and mined them. On October 9 they blew up a large section of wall between the Carinthian gate and the fortress and began to storm the gap. The defenders filled the breech with cannons, guns, and lances, and held off the attackers. Two days later the Turks blew up another section of wall, and Spanish and German troops fought them off in fierce hand-to-hand combat. The Turks launched three new attacks, but the scimitar could not cut through the imperial shields and heavy double-edged swords. On October 12 a third section of wall fell and two days later the Turks made their final assault, suffering heavy losses from artillery fire at close range. Suleiman decided to withdraw, for Count Frederick of the Palatinate, field marshal of the empire, had gathered a relief force in Linz, the Austrians were collecting troops in Moravia, the Swabian League was stirring, and the nights were getting longer and colder. Suleiman retreated through the snow to Belgrade and Vienna was saved. The cross and not the crescent was to glisten on the tall tower of St. Stephen's Cathedral.

In the summer of 1532 Suleiman was back in Hungary with a huge army ready for another try at Vienna. But this time the emperor and his brother Ferdinand were better prepared. The pope sent a hundred thousand gold guldens to support Hungarian and Italian troops. By the end of September the emperor had an army of eighty thousand men. The Turks failed to take the small fortress of Güns, sixty miles south of Vienna, lost some fifteen thousand men in the woods outside Vienna, and turned south toward Graz. Only a final effort was needed to drive the Turks out of Hungary, but Charles now left Vienna for Italy to negotiate with the pope, and the German Protestant princes had no interest in freeing Hungary so that Ferdinand could re-Catholicize it, so the opportunity was lost.

The struggle at sea was equally dramatic. In 1532 an imperial fleet under the great admiral Andrea Doria scored a triumph over the Ottoman fleet in the eastern Mediterranean. In 1535 Charles assaulted the Moorish city of Tunis and took it. The next summer, 1536, Charles planned to attack the Turks' stronghold of Algiers and free all of Tunis. He even planned a great naval operation from Naples against Istanbul itself, but more prudent counsel prevailed. In October 1541 Charles's fleet attacked Algiers, but only part of his landing forces had hit the beach when a storm destroyed many ships and forced a retreat. To the disgust of Christendom, the Ottoman fleet wintered securely in the French harbor of Toulon. The dramatic blow at sea was to be struck not by Charles, but by his illegitimate son, Don Juan of Austria, in the battle of Lepanto in 1571. In 1574, however, the Ottomans conquered Tunis and fixed their hold on the southern coast of what Charles had hoped would be a Spanish sea.

The Expansion of Lutheranism

THE "INFIDEL TURK," by keeping Charles and Ferdinand constantly off balance and periodically on the defensive, quite unintentionally provided the evangelical movement in the empire with the respite from repression needed for continued growth. The year in which the Turks won their great victory at Mohács, 1526, was the year in which Charles made his concession at the Diet of Speyer, when he guaranteed the security of Lutheranism for the time being by endorsing the principle of a conciliar solution to the problem of Protestantism. The pope's suspicions of Charles and opposition to a council, together with Habsburg involvement with the French in Italy and fear of the Turks in Hungary, gave to Lutheranism precious time for consolidation and expansion. The emperor's alarm at the rise of Lutheranism and his determination to deal with it, made evident at the Diet of Speyer in 1529, came late in the year of Suleiman's siege of Vienna, before the danger was entirely past. The doom pronounced against the heretics by Ferdinand and the Catholic princes at the Diet of Augsburg in 1530 was never executed, for rumors of the major Turkish offensive of 1532 were already in circulation. The religious Peace of Nuremberg, agreed to at the diet in that same year, postponed a religious settlement until the meeting of a general church council and ordered that the processes against the Lutherans in the imperial supreme court be thrown out. The Protestants responded by supporting the war effort against the Turks. The Lutherans gained such strength in those years that even their defeat in the Schmalkald War in 1546 was not fatal, and in 1555, in the religious Peace of Augsburg, they achieved legal recognition of their existence as ecclesiastical bodies. The evangelicals viewed their deliverance as the working of Providence, with Suleiman cast in the role of King Cyrus of Persia, whom God used to free Israel although he knew Him not.

The evangelical movement spread through the empire by many channels and in unseen ways. From workmen to princes, Lutherans testified to their renewed faith. By word of mouth, through tracts and books the ideas spread. Merely charting the advance of Lutheranism on a political map state by state or listing the cities and territories by the dates of their conversion does not reveal the true human story of the struggles of conscience, the strife and uproar, the sacrifices and suppression, the martyrdoms.

The establishment of the Reformation in the cities and territorial states followed a pattern. Usually there was a general spirit of criticism or hostility to the Roman church and the local bishop and hierarchy. Sometimes there was in addition an active reform group already in existence, which then metamorphosed into a Lutheran group. This was true in Nuremberg, for example, where the followers of Johannes Staupitz, Luther's confessor, turned to Luther's program, and in Augsburg and other cities. The city council or the prince would appoint or tolerate evangelical preachers, who prepared the people for the radical changes subsequently introduced. Thus in Nuremberg the council and the city secretary, Lazarus Spengler, worked with the preacher Wenceslas Linck for evangelical reform. The preacher Johannes von Zwick played a key role in the conversion of Constance, though the Habsburg armies soon took the city and reestablished Catholicism by force. The roster of cities that turned Lutheran included Esslingen, Reutlingen, Memmingen, Lindau, Augsburg, Nuremberg, and Regensburg in the south, and Magdeburg, Erfurt, Halberstadt, Danzig, and Bremen in the north.

A key city in Reformation history was Strassburg, because of its central location at the commercial crossroads on the Rhine and its moderate theological tradition, midway between the Lutheran and Swiss reformed positions. At the Strassburg cathedral the great preacher Geiler von Kaisersberg had denounced the evils of the day and called for reform. Strassburg had its sodality of humanist reformers, led by the earnest moralist Jacob Wimpfeling. Its city secretary, Jacob Sturm, a political leader of great ability, became a Lutheran. The printers published many editions of the works of Luther and Melanchthon. The earliest leaders of the Reformation in Strassburg were Matthew Zell, a priest and penitentiary who preached in a side chapel of the cathedral in 1521, and his wife, Catherine, whom he married in 1523. An eloquent folk preacher, he attacked abuses and delivered evangelical sermons to large congregations. He and Catherine were consistently protective and hospitable to sectarians such as the Anabaptists and were open to the mystical inner-light ideas of religious thinkers such as Caspar Schwenkfeld.

In 1523 Martin Bucer (1491–1551) arrived in the city, a virtual unknown who quickly assumed the leadership of the movement. He had become a Dominican while still a boy, studied in the Schlettstadt Latin school in Alsace, and associated with Erasmus' alter ego, the young humanist Beatus Rhenanus. In 1518 he heard Luther defend his theological theses before the Augustinians in Heidelberg and was completely won over. As chaplain to von Sickingen he was a participant in the Knights' War. In 1523 the Strassburg city council authorized evangelical preaching in the pulpits of the city's churches, and the next year the parishes were reorganized with new orders of church discipline under the guidance of evangelical preachers. With the public conscience thus prepared for reformed prescripts of public law and the religious precepts of the biblical reformers, Bucer worked to establish a model Christian community, ably assisted by Wolfgang Capito (1478–1541), an Erasmian humanist turned reformer. In the tradition of the Zells, the city was unusually tolerant and hospitable toward Protestant refugees of all kinds. An edict of June 27, 1527, was designed to protect the city against disturbances by fanatics.

At Augsburg in 1530 four south German cities, Strassburg, Constance, Lindau, and Memmingen, presented a doctrinal statement, the *Confessio tetra-politana,* which Bucer and Capito had written. Swiss reformed tendencies were evident in it, including a reluctance to follow the Lutheran insistence on the real presence of Christ in the Sacrament and a consequent discretionary attitude toward the question; severe criticism of ceremonies; and stress upon the authority of Scriptures over that of the church. And yet in 1536 the Strassburg reformers traveled to Saxony and worked out the Wittenberg Concord on doctrinal matters, including the Lord's Supper, to which both Luther and Melanchthon were able to subscribe. With John Calvin and Melanchthon, Bucer attended the colloquies with Catholic theologians at Worms and Regensburg in 1540 and 1541, always seeking unity. His second wife, the merry widow Wibrandis, who had outlived two husbands, the reformers Oecolampadius and Capito, kept up his morale. When the city was forced to accept the emperor's doctrinal interim after the triumph of the imperial armies in 1546, and Jacob Sturm on bended knee begged for Charles's clemency, Bucer left his city for the England of Edward VI and lived out his days as regius professor of divinity in Cambridge. His earnest book *De regno christi* described that ideal community of Christ's kingdom on earth for which he had worked with such fervor in Strassburg.

The new pattern of Protestant education emerged clearly in Strassburg. Whereas pupils formerly went directly from the cathedral, monastic, or city schools to the universities when they were only twelve to fifteen years old, under the leadership of Luther and Melanchthon a secondary school, or *gymnasium,* was established, combining studies in arts and letters with evangelical religious instruction as preparation for university work. Melanchthon was personally active in founding such a school in Nuremberg; a life-sized statue of him still stands before its front door. Nicholas von Amsdorf, who assisted Luther in translating the Old Testament, helped found a school of this type in Magdeburg, where he was pastor and reformer. In Strassburg the founder and director of the humanist-evangelical school was Johannes Sturm, Jacob's brother, who published an influential treatise on *The Correct Exposition of Letters in the Schools* in 1537. New Lutheran universities were founded as well at Marburg, Tübingen, Königsberg, and later Jena, complete with evangelical theological faculties to train a new generation of Protestant leaders.

One of the first major territorial gains of Lutheranism came when Albert von Hohenzollern, the grand master of the Teutonic Knights, on Luther's advice secularized his holdings in East Prussia into a duchy under the overlordship of the king of Poland. His marriage to the daughter of King Frederick I of Denmark was important for the spread of the Reformation to that country. The decade of the 1530s saw the addition of powerful new territories to the Lutheran side. In Württemberg Duke Ulrich, who had been driven out in 1519 and replaced by the Habsburgs, reestablished himself in power in 1534 with the help of Philipp of Hesse and the French. He turned the territory Protestant under the leadership of Johannes Brenz, who worked out a program of school and church reform, including a new liturgy. That same year Pomerania turned Lutheran and in 1535 was given an evangelical church order prepared by Johannes Bugenhagen. Elector Joachim II (1535–1571) reformed Brandenburg in 1539, although he was so conservative that he kept the episcopal constitution intact until 1543. But perhaps the greatest joy to the Wittenberg reformers was the conversion of Ducal Saxony to Lutheranism in 1539. In that year Luther's implacable foe Duke Georg died, and his successor, Duke Henry (1539–1541), quickly introduced the Reformation. One can imagine Luther's satisfaction at preaching the festive Reformation sermon in the same hall in Leipzig in which he had debated Dr. Eck just twenty years before.

Other noteworthy Protestant gains within the empire came with the conversion of Brunswick-Wolfenbüttel and part of the Palatinate. The entire northwestern part of the empire came very close to turning Protestant when the archbishop of Cologne, Hermann von Wied, called on Bucer and Melanchthon to reform the archdiocese, but he was deposed and the Protestant duke William of Cleves was forced by the armies of Charles to re-Catholicize his territories. In that part of Germany the process was reversed and the area remained firmly Catholic.

EXPANSION IN NORTHERN AND EASTERN EUROPE

The Reformation movement reached beyond the borders of the empire to the Scandinavian countries as early as the 1520s and 1530s. The Reformation in the north was imposed from the top, with very limited spontaneous response from the people. The Danish king Christian II (1513–1523), who had executed more than eighty Swedish foes in one bloodbath, attempted to introduce the Reformation into Denmark in the hope of joining with Sweden to form a strong consolidated state, but the opposition of the Danish clergy and nobility and of the Swedish aristocracy was too strong, and in 1523 the king was forced to flee. In exile he visited Wittenberg and gave Kathie Luther a beautiful ring that she always cherished—a kind act by an unscrupulous and reckless man. Frederick I (1523–1533), who succeeded him, was well disposed toward the Reformation and had the example of his successful son-in-law Duke Albert of Prussia always in mind, but he had to promise the conservative nobility not to move against the old church. In his own duchies of Schleswig and Holstein he allowed evangelical preaching, and appointed as court chaplain the evangelical preacher Hans Tausen, who had studied at Wittenberg. In 1527 he persuaded the diet at Odense to allow toleration for Lutherans pending the convening of a council. In 1529 Christian Peterson published a Danish translation of the New Testament which was very influential in the formation of the modern Danish language. A full-scale reformation was not possible until 1536, when the next king, Christian III (1533–1559), introduced the new evangelical church order prepared by the itinerant statesman of Protestantism, Luther's "Dr. Pommer," the preacher Johannes Bugenhagen of Pomerania and Wittenberg. The seven bishops became superintendents, although the title of bishop was later reintroduced in the new context. The king became the head of the church as supreme bishop, and in due course the Augsburg Confession was accepted as the official credal statement.

Christian III's success in introducing the Reformation in Denmark coincided with his political and military victory over Norway. Since the Norwegians had supported Danish dissidents in a civil war against Christian, he forced them now to surrender their independence and compelled them to accept Lutheranism as their official religion. Iceland, formerly a Norwegian province, fell under the same legislation.

By a strange turn of events, Lutheranism was allied with nationalism in the Swedish drive for independence from the Danes between 1521 and 1523. The new king, Gustavus Vasa (1523–1560), led the resistance movement against the Danes and was crowned by the Swedish diet at Strengnäs on June 7, 1523. He was personally inclined toward Lutheranism, and in addition believed that its introduction would strengthen the independence movement. In 1527 at Westerås he forced the diet to sanction the transfer of church property to the king and to allow evangelical preaching. He was greatly aided in the dissemination of Lutheran ideas by two brothers, Olaf and Lars Petri, who had been educated in Wittenberg, and by Lars Andersson. They produced a Swedish translation of the Bible based on Luther's German Bible and led in the educational reform of the country. The Swedish Reformation was very conservative, retaining the episcopacy and a claim to an apostolic succession together with many traditional Catholic rites and ceremonies, such as the elevation of the host, prayers for the dead, and exorcism. It took another generation for Lutheranism to saturate the country. That Sweden became and remained Lutheran was to be of great political significance during the following century.

As a territory of Sweden, Finland followed along into the Lutheran Church. The most able of the Finnish reformers, Michael Agricola (1508–1557), had studied and taught at Wittenberg. He translated the New Testament, the Psalms, and some of the prophets into Finnish, and thus helped to develop Finnish as a literary language.

The chief center of Lutheranism in the Baltic states was the city of Riga. German Lutheran merchants in the Baltic were among the most active missionaries of the new movement. There had been evangelical influence in Riga as early as 1523, and in 1539 an evangelical archbishop was elected. Livonia and Esthonia followed Riga's lead. In 1561 the master of the Livonian Brethren of the Sword in Courland turned Lutheran, secularized his land into a duchy, and held it as a fief under the king of Poland.

The Poland of the Jagellon dynasty extended from west of the Vistula River to east of the Dnieper, reaching nearly to the Black Sea. Ethnically and religiously heterogeneous, the land included, besides the Poles, Roman Catholic Lithuanians, Greek Orthodox Ruthenians, and in the cities of western Poland many German merchant colonies and Jews, who were very important to the economic life of the country. The king had little effective power, for the landed nobility was virtually autonomous, and the Polish diet of 1505 had passed a law providing that only with the consent of all three estates could any new business be considered by that body, and another forbidding the king to maintain a standing army. Since the state was so thoroughly decentralized, a conversion of the whole state by the king in the familiar pattern was an impossibility. With such a poor power base, King Sigismund II Augustus (1548–1572) could not help losing ground on all fronts, falling back before Ivan IV of Muscovy, tolerating the union of Brandenburg and East Prussia under the Hohenzollerns, and making ever new concessions to the gentry, especially in "Little Poland," or the southwestern lands of the Vistula valley.

It was in this province that Protestantism took strongest root, and there were reportedly some 265 reformed congregations there, compared with 120 in "Large Poland" of the northwest. Whereas in western Prussia and "Large Poland" congregations of Lutherans and Bohemian Brethren were in the majority, in "Little Poland" a church in the Calvinist style developed, with anti-Trinitarian groups breaking off from them. The anti-Trinitarians—or Socinians, as they were also called, after their leaders, Lelio Sozzini and his nephew Fausto (1539–1604)—were centered in Racow, where they had their own church school and published their own catechism and confession of faith (the second Racow catechism of 1605). In 1638 their school was destroyed and in 1658 they were driven out of Poland as an "Arian sect." The multicolored Protestant movement prospered in Poland for only some sixty years. Eventually Roman Catholicism as a national faith seemed a necessary bond of unity to differentiate the Poles from the Russian Orthodoxy of the threatening power in the east and the Lutheranism of the Prussian complex to the north and west.

At the very outset of Luther's career his ideas were often associated with those of Jan Hus, the Bohemian heretic burned at Constance. At the Leipzig debate Luther had declared that not all of Hus's propositions condemned by the Council were false. Luther even dedicated a book to the Prague city council in 1523 and encouraged it to break with Rome. It seemed natural to expect that Lutheranism would find a foothold in Bohemia. In actual fact, however, it prospered mainly among the Germans in the north and in Moravia. While the Bohemian Brethren of the Unity, the more radical Hussites, looked with favor on Lutheranism, the more conservative Utraquists, who had made their peace with the Catholic Church, effectively frustrated movements toward a union with the new Protestantism. Conrad Cordatus, a student of Luther's who recorded his *Table Talk*, brought the evangelical religion to the miners in Slovakia, where a Lutheran church was to persist during the centuries that followed.

In view of Ferdinand's determined opposition and persecution, the spread of Protestantism in the Habsburg Danubian lands is most surprising. It was not only the cities of upper Hungary, with large German populations, that turned Lutheran; so did most of the Magyar landed magnates, including eventually the family of John Zapolya, the erstwhile king under the Turkish hegemony. The most influential reformer was Matthias Biró (Dévay), a Wittenberg student and friend of Melanchthon. After his exile to Switzerland he returned in 1543 to lead the Protestant movement in the direction of the Swiss reformed Helvetic Confession. In Austria, too, many leading members of the landed nobility turned Lutheran, but the chief centers of the movement were in cities such as Graz and Klagenfurt. For a time it seemed that all Austria might move into the Protestant camp, slipping right through the fingers of the Habsburgs, until they slowly tightened their grip once again.

THE STRUGGLE FOR SURVIVAL

Luther was a fighter who recognized the inevitability of conflict between the new and the old. He prophesied the worst:

> To wish to silence these tumults is nothing else than to wish to hinder the word of God and to take it out of the way. For the word of God, wherever it comes, comes to change and renew the world. . . . You do not see that these tumults and dangers increase through the world according to the counsel and the operations of God. And therefore you fear that the heavens may fall about our ears. But I by the grace of God see these things clearly, because I see the other tumults greater than these which will arise in ages to come, in comparison with which these appear but as the whispering of a breath of air, and the murmuring of a gentle brook.[1]

Nevertheless, Luther adamantly opposed the use of force or shedding of blood in defense of his theology or his life. It was years, in fact, before the jurists could convince him that the Protestant princes had the right to fight in their own defense when the emperor sent troops against them in an aggressive war that went beyond the prerogatives of his office. In any case, the actual decision to organize defensively against the Habsburgs and the Catholic princes was not for Luther to make.

The ominous maneuvering began as early as July 1525, when several Catholic princes, notably Duke Georg of Saxony, Albert of Mainz, Joachim I of Brandenburg, and Erich and Henry of Brunswick, organized the League of Dessau to root out evangelical doctrine. The young evangelical ruler Philipp of Hesse responded by forming with Elector John of Saxony and several lesser princes the League of Gotha, also called the League of Torgau, after the town where the

---

[1] Cited in E. Gordon Rupp, *The Righteousness of God* (London, 1953), p. 273.

alliance was ratified in February 1526. That same year both Hesse and Saxony organized territorial churches with Protestant constitutions. Tension mounted when in 1528 an official of Duke Georg of Saxony, Otto von Pack, was reported to have discovered a treaty signed by Catholic princes, pledging to exterminate the Lutherans. Even though the letter allegedly substantiating the existence of the treaty was proved to be a forgery, suspicion and rancor lingered on. In February 1531 a larger group of Protestant princes organized the Schmalkald League to prevent the enforcement of the decree of the Diet of Augsburg, condemning Luther and the evangelical movement to extinction. They developed the legal fiction that the territorial princes received their power directly by divine ordination, whereas the emperor's power was merely derivative, since he was appointed by the princes through the electors. A decade of relative security and continued Lutheran advances followed.

Protestant solidarity received a body blow in the scandal of Philipp of Hesse's bigamy and his separate treaty with the emperor. Philipp's wife, Christina of Ducal Saxony, it seems, could not satisfy the volcanic prince. The *femme fatale* of the drama was Margaret von der Saal, a court beauty, whose mother held out for a proper marriage. In earlier days Philipp had been an accomplished fornicator, but now his Protestant conscience would not allow him to step so freely outside the law—or at least this particular law. His wife agreed to the second marriage, and Luther, Melanchthon, and Bucer gave the confessional counsel that bigamy was preferable to divorce, since it enjoyed Old Testament precedents. Strange as this counsel seems, it was the same that Pope Clement VII gave to Henry VIII as an escape from his dilemma. Luther naïvely believed that Philipp's pangs of conscience were real and severe, and that the second marriage would be the lesser of two evils. When the second marriage was consummated in March 1540, a great uproar arose. Philipp had violated solemn imperial law and thereby made his title and lands subject to seizure by the emperor. On June 13, 1541, recognizing his vulnerability, Philipp made a separate nonaggression treaty with the emperor. His son-in-law, Maurice of Ducal Saxony, subscribed to this pact and eventually left the Schmalkald League to side with the emperor, a mortal blow to Protestant defenses and to the balance of power in the empire. Charles prepared to strike at his foes.

A general council was summoned to assemble at Trent in 1545. On February 18, 1546, Luther died. All signs seemed propitious for the final solution of the problem of heresy in the empire. With Pope Paul III, Duke Ferdinand, Duke William of Bavaria, Maurice of Saxony, and some lesser evangelical princes as allies, Charles fielded his armies in 1546. He overran southern Germany within the year and forced the south German Protestant cities and states to capitulate. Then he moved into north Germany, and at Mühlberg on April 24, 1547, thoroughly defeated the Lutheran forces, taking captive Elector John Frederick of Saxony and Landgrave Philipp of Hesse. In the Wittenberg capitulation of May 19, 1547,

Maurice took over the electoral right from John Frederick and much territory, including Wittenberg.

In June 1548 Charles had a basically Catholic doctrinal statement prepared, known as the Augsburg Interim, which he attempted to impose upon the Germans. Melanchthon and the Catholic bishop Pflug of Naumburg worked out a substitute doctrinal formulation known as the Leipzig Interim, which they hoped would be more satisfactory to the Lutherans, but resistance was strong and many Protestant cities and estates openly defied it. At this juncture the Machiavellian Maurice, who was besieging the Lutheran stronghold of Magdeburg, saw his opportunity. He deftly insinuated himself into a position of leadership in the Schmalkald League. The league now sacrificed Metz, Toul, and Verdun to King Henry II of France in return for aid against the emperor. Emperor Charles suffered a military setback and loss of prestige when he failed to take Metz. In a surprise attack on Charles, Elector Maurice surrounded the imperial troops near Reutte and forced them to surrender. He almost captured the emperor himself near Innsbruck. Charles fled through the Brenner Pass to the south, falling back to Lienz and Villach. The disaster was a shock from which he never recovered. In the Peace of Passau, in August 1552, the emperor agreed to free Philipp, as he had John Frederick, and allowed the Lutherans to practice their religion until the next diet.

At the Diet of Augsburg in 1555 the emperor's final failure to suppress Protestantism in the empire was legally acknowledged. The Protestant princes at the diet represented a whole spectrum of particularist interests, from conservative Saxony,

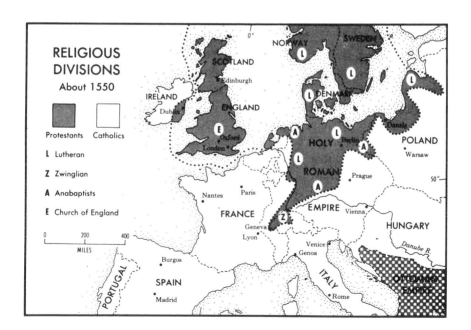

most concerned with securing a permanent peace, to Duke Christoph of Württemberg, who wanted concessions that would assure further Protestant gains. After tedious negotiations that lasted from February into September, the provisions of the celebrated Peace of Augsburg were agreed upon. The Lutheran cities and states were to be guaranteed security and all pledged themselves to an eternal and unconditional peace. The principle *cuius regio, eius religio* was to be applied to Lutherans as well as to Catholics, each estate to have the privilege of choosing its official religion. Ecclesiastical property taken by the Protestants prior to the Peace of Passau was to remain theirs, but any ecclesiastical prince who turned Protestant thereafter was to lose his title, lands, and privileges—the so-called ecclesiastical reservation. The peace also made real a privilege that Luther had urged in his day: Christians were to be permitted to move freely from one principality to another more congenial to their religious convictions. When the peace was announced the bells rang out throughout the Lutheran lands, for the right of peaceful coexistence had been won at last. And for all its compromises and weaknesses, the Peace of Augsburg did bring relative tranquillity to the land until the outbreak of the horrendous Thirty Years' War more than half a century later, a near record for Europe.

Emperor Charles was thoroughly weary and demoralized. In a dramatic and emotional scene in 1556 he renounced his worldly titles and, having made careful provision for the succession of his son Philip to the thrones of Spain, the Netherlands, and Spanish Italy and of his brother Ferdinand as emperor, he retired to a villa adjoining the monastery of San Jerónimo de Yuste in Spain to prepare for the world to come. There he died in September 1558. He had brought Habsburg power to the greatest heights it was ever to know. And yet a deep sense of tragedy and melancholy lay like a shadow upon the emperor. In victory as in defeat, the thought of the transiency of this earthly life and the hope of a better life to come had kept him from overweening pride or bottomless despair. He was a man of tremendous character, sincere and well intentioned. He has been compared, ironically enough, with Luther, who intended to reform the old church but founded a new one, and with Columbus, who searched for the ancient East but discovered the New World. For Charles was dedicated to the renewal of the medieval ideal of universal monarchy, but in reality he let the empire sink into impotence and became instead the founder of the Spanish imperium and the Spanish hegemony in Europe.

Bibliography

Habsburg-Valois wars:
BABELON, JEAN. *Charles Quint.* Paris, 1947.

BRANDI, KARL. *The Emperor Charles V*, trans. C. V. Wedgwood. New York, 1939.

CARSTEN, F. L. *Princes and Parliaments in Germany, from the Fifteenth to the Eighteenth Century*. Oxford, 1959.

CLASEN, CLAUS PETER. *The Palatinate in European History, 1559–1660*. Oxford, 1966.

FRANÇOIS, M., et al. *Charles Quint et son temps*. Paris, 1959.

FUETER, EDUARD. *Geschichte des Europäischen Staatensystems von 1492 bis 1559*. Munich, 1919.

MOUSNIER, ROLAND. *Les XVIe et XVIIe siècles*. Paris, 1956.

RITTER, GERHARD. *Die Neugestaltung Europas im 16. Jahrhundert*. Berlin, 1950.

ROSSOW, PETER. *Karl V: Der Kaiser und seine Zeit*. Cologne, 1960.

Ottoman Turks:

FISCHER-GALATI, STEPHEN A. *Ottoman Imperialism and German Protestantism, 1521–1555*. Cambridge, Mass., 1959.

LEWIS, B. *Istanbul and the Civilization of the Ottoman Empire*. Norman, Okla., 1963.

LYBYER, A. H. *The Government of the Ottoman Empire in the Time of Suleiman the Magnificent*. Cambridge, Mass., 1913.

MERRIMAN, R. B. *Suleiman the Magnificent, 1520–1566*. Cambridge, Mass., 1944.

ROUILLARD, C. D. *The Turk in French History, Thought, and Literature, 1500–1660*. Paris, 1939.

WITTEK, P. *The Rise of the Ottoman Empire*. London, 1938.

Expansion of Lutheranism:

CHRISMAN, MIRIAM. *Strasbourg and the Reform*. New Haven, 1967.

EELLS, HASTINGS. *Martin Bucer*. New Haven, 1931.

FRAENKEL, PETER. *Testimonium Patrum: The Function of the Patristic Argument in the Theology of Philipp Melanchthon*. Geneva, 1961.

HARTFELDER, KARL. *Melanchthon als Praeceptor Germaniae*. Berlin, 1899.

HOPF, C. *Martin Bucer and the English Reformation*. New York, 1946.

KITTELSON, JAMES. "Wolfgang Capito: Humanist and Reformer." Ph.D. dissertation, Stanford, 1969.

MANSCHREK, CLYDE. *Melanchthon, the Quiet Reformer*. New York, 1958.

POLL, GERRIT JAN VAN DER. *Martin Bucer's Liturgical Ideas*. Assen, 1954.

SPERL, ADOLF. *Melanchthon zwischen Humanismus und Reformation*. Munich, 1959.

STEPHENS, W. P. *The Holy Spirit in the Theology of Martin Bucer*. Cambridge, Mass., 1970.

STUPPERICH, ROBERT. *Melanchthon*. Berlin, 1960.

Northern and eastern Europe:

BENZ, ERNST. *Wittenberg und Byzanz*. Marburg, 1949.

BERGENDOFF, CONRAD. *Olavus Petri and the Ecclesiastical Transformation of Sweden, 1520–1552*. New York, 1929.

DUNCKLEY, E. H. *The Reformation in Denmark*. London, 1948.

FOX, PAUL. *The Reformation in Poland*. Baltimore, 1924.

HALECKI, OSKAR. *A History of Poland*. Baltimore, 1924.

LARSEN, K. *A History of Norway*. Princeton, 1948.

MECENSEFFY, GRETE. *Geschichte des Protestantismus in Oesterreich*. Graz, 1956.

MURRAY, ROBERT. *Olavus Petri*. Stockholm, 1952.

WADDAMS, H. M. *The Swedish Church*. London, 1946.
YELVERTON, E. E. *The Manual of Olavus Petri*. London, 1951.

Protestantism's struggle for survival:
BERGENDOFF, CONRAD. *The Church of the Lutheran Reformation*. St. Louis, 1967.
BRANDI, KARL. *Der Augsburger Religionsfriede, 1555,* 2nd ed. Göttingen, 1927.
FABIAN, EKKEHART. *Die Entstehung des Schmalkaldischen Bundes und seiner Verfassung*. Tübingen, 1962.
HARTUNG, FRITZ. *Karl V und die deutschen Protestanten, 1540–1555*. Halle, 1910.
MENTZ, G. *Johann Friedrich,* 3 vols. Jena, 1903–1908.
SCHLINK, EDMUND. *Theology of the Lutheran Confessions*. Philadelphia, 1961.
WINTERS, R. L. *Francis Lambert of Avignon*. Philadelphia, 1938.

CHAPTER 15

Zwingli
and the
Radicals

An enemy soldier looked down at the mutilated body of the reformer Ulrich Zwingli as it lay on the battlefield at Cappel on October 11, 1531, and exclaimed, "You were a rotten heretic, but a damned good Swiss!" Zwingli was indeed Swiss to the marrow of his bones, and in turn he impressed his own personality upon the national character as few Swiss have done. His reform program determined the direction of Swiss history, and the Alpine state became a microcosm presaging the way divided Europe was to go.

Although in Zwingli's day Switzerland was nominally still a part of the Holy Roman Empire, it had long since achieved very real political independence. The original union in 1291 of three forest cantons, Uri, Schwyz, and Unterwalden, had grown into a confederation of thirteen cantons in all. The confederacy was held together by mutual defense treaties and by a diet that met to discuss common problems, although it had little authority over the virtually autonomous cantons. In the Swiss War—or the Swabian War, as the Swiss preferred to call it—in 1499, the Habsburg emperor Maximilian I made a final feeble attempt to force the Swiss back under the imperial yoke. The fiction of imperial rule was maintained until Swiss independence was legally acknowledged in the Peace of Westphalia in 1648. A pattern of urban resistance to the rule of feudal episcopal authorities outside the cities developed even before the Reformation, as the bourgeois city councils assumed an ever greater authority over ecclesiastical administration within the cantons. In this unique urban republican setting the German Swiss Reformation developed under the leadership of Ulrich Zwingli.

Zwingli the Reformer

THE KEY to Zwingli's preeminence lay not in his social position but in his native ability and superior education. Ulrich Zwingli (1484–1531), the "third man" of the Reformation (after Luther and Calvin), developed from a learned humanist into an ecclesiastical reformer of great historical stature. His father, a free peasant and an official of the village of Wildhaus in the Toggenburg valley of St. Gall canton, was very ambitious for his son and kept him in the best schools available. At eight Ulrich went to school in Wesen, where an uncle of his was dean, and at ten transferred to Basel, where he studied Latin, dialectics, and music for three years under Gregor Bünzli in the School of St. Theodore. At thirteen he moved on to a school in Bern for two years (1496–1498) under the formative influence of a noted teacher, Heinrich Wölflin, a man thoroughly dedicated to Renaissance humanist educational ideals, who inspired him with a love of the classics and an appreciation for music. The Dominicans in Bern recognized in Zwingli a youth of extraordinary gifts and urged him to enter their monastery, but he had barely begun his probationary year with them when his family forced him to withdraw, and soon afterward sent him to Vienna for university study.

The Vienna of Maximilian's brilliant reign made a tremendous impression upon the young Swiss student during his two-year stay (1500–1502). The matriculation book indicates that he was expelled at one point (his name is struck out and an *exclusus* written in the margin), possibly for expressing anti-Habsburg sentiments. The liveliest spirit at the university in those years was Conrad Celtis, the German arch-humanist, active as a teacher of the classics, head of the college of poets and mathematicians, and director of humanist plays. Zwingli cultivated further his classical learning and musical prowess and was able to play a variety of instruments: lute, harp, flute, viol, reed pipe, and cornet. He became a close friend of Heinrich Glareanus, later renowned as a leading musical humanist in Switzerland. But as a good Swiss Zwingli returned to Basel, where he took his A.B. degree in 1504 and his M.A. degree in 1506. At Basel he came under the direct influence of Dr. Thomas Wyttenbach, an Erasmian reform-minded scholar who favored the study of the New Testament and the church fathers and was hostile to scholasticism, monastic vows, indulgences, and the mechanical use of the sacraments. Zwingli taught the classics at the School of St. Martin and purchased an edition of Pico della Mirandola. At the age of twenty-two he was ordained into the priesthood by the bishop of Constance. He said his first mass among his own people in Wildhaus.

Zwingli's decade as the people's priest at Glarus provided a solid foundation for his later reform activities. At the very outset he encountered a problem typical of the chicanery that characterized all too many church positions. When Zwingli was elected priest at Glarus over Heinrich Göldi, who had been appointed by the pope, he found it necessary to buy Göldi off with a hundred guldens. Zwingli was pulled in two directions during his Glarus ministry, toward scholarship and toward a real pastoral concern for his people. His library of over 350 volumes covered subjects ranging from geometry and geography to philosophy, theology, philology, and the classics. He studied Greek assiduously and began Hebrew, and read widely in patristic literature. His friends soon began referring to him as "the Cicero of our age." He was naturally attracted to Erasmus, who repaid his admiration with chillingly superior and patronizing letters. Zwingli even made a trip to Basel to meet the prince of the humanists in person. When Erasmus' edition of the New Testament appeared in 1516, Zwingli memorized Paul's epistles in Greek from his own copy. At the same time, he was devoted to his pastoral duties. He established a school for children and taught in it himself.

Zwingli accompanied Swiss mercenary troops as chaplain in such lost battles as Novara in 1513 and Marignano outside of Milan in 1515. He conducted himself on the battlefield with honor and courage, his biographer Heinrich Bullinger related, but saw clearly the evils of the mercenary system, which enriched but corrupted young Swiss, when it did not cripple and maim them. He wrote political rhymed allegories or fables and preached sermons against the degrading practice of selling blood for money. His opposition to the lucrative mercenary business, and to a treaty with France which obligated the Swiss to the French in return for financial aid, turned powerful pro-French interests against him and forced him out of Glarus.

In 1516 Zwingli was called to the monastic church in Einsiedeln, where the shrine of the Black Image of the Virgin attracted many pilgrims. But Zwingli soon began to criticize the plenary indulgence granted for the pilgrimage to Einsiedeln, and in August 1518 he managed to block the activities of the Franciscan monk Bernardin Samson, who had come to sell indulgences like Tetzel in Saxony. Late in October 1518 the possibility of a pulpit far more influential opened up in Zurich, but two things worked against Zwingli's chances of obtaining it: the rumor that as a musician he was frivolous and unreliable and the report that he had been guilty of immoral conduct. Zwingli met the charges head-on by writing a letter defending his music making but confessing his guilt of misconduct. A wanton young woman had tempted him and he had unwisely embraced the opportunity and the girl, as others had before him; the child she awaited in Zurich might indeed be his. He denied that he had violated a virgin or a woman of high standing, although, as he said ironically, her father was one of those powerful men who could even touch the emperor's beard without risk, since he was a barber. On December 11, 1518, the canons elected Zwingli to the pulpit in Zurich over a Swabian competitor who had a concubine, six children, and many benefices. It was at the Great Minster in Zurich that Zwingli was to undertake the reformation of German Switzerland.

Zwingli had an attractive personality and a warmhearted way with him, along with a quick mind, a beautiful voice, and tremendous rhetorical power. He already enjoyed a reputation as a powerful preacher. He was also keenly perceptive and had an acute sense of the right moment for action. He carefully prepared the council and the congregation before undertaking any major change. On New Year's Day of 1519, his birthday, he preached his first sermon in the great church at Zurich and announced that the following Sunday he would begin to interpret the gospel according to Matthew according to divine truth, not human vanity. Zwingli had the Greek text before him in the pulpit and presented a straightforward explication of the text. The impact was sensational. A young humanist in the congregation, Thomas Platter, recorded that when he heard the word of God proclaimed from the very source, as he put it, he felt as though he were being drawn up by the hair of his head. After this treatment of the life of Jesus, Zwingli went on to portray the early church on the basis of the Acts of the Apostles and Paul's epistles. It took him six years to go through the entire New Testament.

During his first year in Zurich Zwingli underwent an agonizing experience that almost took his life. The dreaded bubonic plague swept through the Swiss confederacy and struck Zurich in August. It has been estimated that as much as a third of the population died. Often when the plague struck in those centuries, the doctors who recognized the symptoms were the first to leave. Zwingli was away at the time, taking the waters at Bad Pfäfers, but he returned immediately to minister to the sick and dying. Death claimed his own brother Andreas, and in late August or September Zwingli himself fell sick. In November rumors of his death circulated in Basel and Constance. But after a long struggle he recovered, although it was the following summer before he fully regained his strength. In gratitude he wrote his "Song of Pestilence" or "A Christian Song, Written by Huldrych Zwingli as He Was Attacked by the Plague," and set it to music. This brush with death left him in a more serious mood and led him to search even more earnestly into the deeper dimensions of the Christian faith.

The actual break with the old church was precipitated by a purely external breach of church law, the canonically enforced abstention from the eating of meat during Lent. Zwingli had taught from the pulpit that the word of God clearly allows the eating of all food at all times, and that papal prohibition ran counter to the liberty proclaimed by the gospel. On Ash Wednesday in 1522 a number of prominent citizens, including Zwingli and Leo Jud, the people's priest at Einsiedeln, met at the house of Christopher Froschauer, a printer. They cut up two fried sausages and everyone ate some, except for Zwingli, who refrained for fear of giving offense to parishioners not yet ready for such a drastic step. The city council reacted quickly by punishing several with imprisonment and fines. Zwingli responded from the pulpit less than three weeks later in defense of those who had broken the fast, and in April he published the sermon under the title *Concerning Choice and Freedom of Food.* The same year he published a key reformatory writing, *Archeteles* (The Beginning and the End), in which he argued for spiritual freedom from the control of the bishops. Only the Holy Spirit is needed to make God's word intelligible, he now argued; no definitions by church, council, or pope were necessary or proper. With Luther's Leipzig debate in mind, Zwingli pressed for a public disputation in which the issues could be publicly discussed, and the city government agreed. The debate was to be held on January 29, 1523.

Over six hundred men, friends and foes, assembled at the town hall for the disputation. The bishop of Constance was represented by Zwingli's erstwhile friend John Faber, now diocesan chancellor and vicar general. Zwingli sat front and center with his Hebrew, Greek, and Latin Bibles open before him. As a basis for discussion he had prepared and published *Sixty-seven Articles,* which summarized most succinctly his theological platform for reform. The first sixteen articles presented his positive doctrines, proclaiming the meaning of the gospel, the all-sufficiency of the teaching and work of Christ, who made known to man the will of his heavenly father and with his innocence released men from death and reconciled them with God, and the true nature of the church as the communion of saints or company of all believers in Christ. The rest of the articles spelled out his objections to the assumption of high priestly powers by the pope, the celebration of the mass as a sacrifice rather than as a remembrance, prayer for the intercession of saints, compulsory fasting, pilgrimages, monastic vows, clerical celibacy, the misuse of the ban, gabbled prayers, the sale of indulgences, the doctrines of penance and purgatory, the priesthood, the role of the state in religion, and other teachings and practices.

> Let no one undertake here to argue with sophistry of human foolishness, but come to the Scriptures to accept them as the judge (*foras cares!* the Scriptures breathe the spirit of God), so that the truth either may be found, or if found, as I hope, retained. Amen.
> Thus may God rule.

The main thrust of Zwingli's argument in the debate that followed was that the reformers were engaged in restoring the church to its ancient purity; it was the medieval church that was the innovator, not the reformers.

The disputation resulted in a resounding victory for Zwingli's teachings and an order from the city council that all priests of the canton should promote them.

Six months later Froschauer published Zwingli's *Interpretation and Substantiation of the Conclusions,* in which he contrasted church practices with the law of Christ and expressed his dissatisfaction with traditional forms of worship and liturgical music. In September the council passed an ordinance providing for changes in the statutes of the Great Minster, reducing the number of clergy, lowering the fees for spiritual services such as baptism and the Sacrament, and providing for daily instruction in the Scriptures.

In view of the favorable result of the first disputation and the growing tensions within the city, Zwingli pressed for a second debate to deal with the question of the mass and the veneration of images. The second disputation, attended by about eight or nine hundred priests and laymen, began on October 26, 1523, and lasted for three days. This time Zwingli and Leo Jud were opposed more ably by Martin Steinli of Schaffhausen. The council voted to retain the mass, to restrain those who wished to carry images into the church or to remove them, and to appoint a commission, which included Zwingli and Jud, to instruct the people in evangelical teachings. The council was clearly moving toward reform, but it preferred to move gradually.

For the enlightenment of the clergy in the canton, Zwingli wrote *A Brief Christian Introduction,* a sharp attack on the use of images. Zwingli's ideas reflected the influence of an eighteen-page pamphlet written by Ludwig Hätzer, a priest educated at Basel in classical humanism, *The Judgment of God Our Spouse as to How One Should Hold Oneself Toward All Idols and Images, According to the Holy Scriptures.* On Monday, December 28, a third and more limited debate was held with the canons and clergy of Zurich together with the members of the small and great councils to discuss once again the problem of images and the mass, but further action was deferred until another debate could be held early the next year.

The years 1524 and 1525 witnessed the culmination of the drive toward reform with the resolution of the three vexing questions of the veneration of images, the celibacy of the clergy, and the celebration of the mass. The fourth disputation, held on January 19 and 20, 1524, marked a critical turning point, for the intellectual poverty of the defenders of the "old belief," as opposed to proponents of the new "right belief," left the field to the reformers and cleared the way for the subsequent official decrees of the council sanctioning change. The debate was conducted by fourteen men: six members of the council, five cathedral canons, and the reformers Engelhard, Jud, and Zwingli. Only Rudolf Hofmann spoke at length for the iconophile position, formulating twenty-three theses drawn almost entirely from nonscriptural sources: tradition, the church fathers, medieval scholastics, conciliar decrees, and canon law. The council was easily moved to follow Zwingli's iconoclastic recommendations. After temporizing interim decrees, on June 15 the council announced its final decision, authorizing the removal of all remaining images from the churches. The council now acted swiftly and appointed a committee of twelve, each man from a different guild, to remove the "idols" from the temples and whiten the walls, an operation that took 'from June 20 to July 2. The myopic Zwingli had never had the appreciation for the visual arts that he had for music, and so had few regrets about the loss of medieval art. Yet his personal tastes seem to have had little influence on his reform program, for it also required the elimination of choir singing, congregational singing except for psalms, organ music, and any other features not expressly authorized by the Scriptures. On December 9, 1527, after years of silence the organs of the Great Minster were removed and chopped up. Zwingli regarded this removal of images and organs as a triumph of the spirit over things corporeal and sensual, a very Puritan point of view. "In Zurich," he exclaimed in triumph, "we have churches which are absolutely luminous; the walls are beautifully white!"[1]

In 1522 Zwingli and other clerics had petitioned the bishop of Constance for permission to marry, and when they were summarily rebuffed, he was married secretly to a pious widow, Anna Reinhard Meyer. Two years later, on April 2, 1524, when the tide in Zurich was clearly moving in his favor, he made the most of it by celebrating his marriage in the Great Minster, thus publicly practicing what he had preached about the honorable estate of marriage for clergymen and the invalidity as well as the futility of the Catholic decrees on celibacy. When Zwingli once made the dramatic charge that out of a hundred or even a thousand monks, priests, and nuns, hardly a chaste one could be found, a local canon expressed regret at such public accusations but acknowledged that they were all too true.

A third major controverted dogmatic issue was the Catholic doctrine of the mass. In 1215 the Fourth Lateran Council had given official sanction to the doctrine of transubstantiation, which held that the "elements," the bread and wine used in the Sacrament, were changed in substance into the real body and blood of Christ, although the "accidents," or external appearance, remained the same. The Sacrament itself had taken on the character of a bloodless sacrifice by which the priest repeated the original sacrifice of Christ on Calvary. Participation in the mass by the faithful believer was no longer indispensable, since endowed private masses could be said by a priest, even for the benefit of souls already presumably in purgatory. Finally, communion "in one kind," with only the bread distributed to the communing laity while the priest drank the wine, was the universal practice. Zwingli objected on biblical grounds to all of these aspects of the mass, viewing them as departures from the Lord's institution as recorded in the New Testament. To the mass he opposed the reformed conception of the Lord's Supper as a memorial or spiritual communion with Christ, with the bread and wine as symbols of the body and blood of Christ. Like Luther, he objected to the doctrine of transub-

---

[1] See Charles Garside, Jr., *Zwingli and the Arts* (New Haven, 1966), pp. 146–60.

stantiation on the grounds that the distinction between essence or substance and accidents was metaphysical and not scriptural. He viewed the elevation of the host and adoration during Corpus Christi processions as the idolizing of a material object. He opposed the idea of the mass as sacrifice on the ground that Christ's original sacrifice was valid once and for all time, and because of sacerdotal misuse of the magical power of transformation and sacrifice. He believed that private masses without the congregation of believers and without the presence of communicants were invalid and misled the laity into a work-righteous or mechanical view of the Sacrament.

Zwingli carefully educated the congregation and council to his views. During Holy Week in 1525, on April 16, to be precise, communion was celebrated in Zurich for the first time according to the new form, the Lord's Supper in both kinds as a remembrance of the Last Supper and a spiritual communion of the believer with his Lord. Once again Zwingli's drive to elevate the spiritual over the material triumphed, this time in a matter of very essential doctrine. Only a month earlier he had published his *Commentary on the True and False Religion,* dedicated to King Francis I of France, in which he clearly stated his interpretation that by faith alone the Lord's presence could be received in a feast that was designed to be commemorative and symbolic.

The influence of Erasmian humanism upon Zwingli's religious thought was very evident during Zwingli's earlier years as a reformer and remained a permanent part of his theological orientation. He was deeply impressed with the humanist emphasis upon deriving truth from the original sources, so that the formal principle of his theology required the derivation of the knowledge of Christ from "the very fountains," the Scriptures themselves. The Erasmian slogan of "gospel simplicity" and the nonscholastic nature of revelation are recurrent themes in Zwingli's writing. Until around the year 1522 phrases familiar from Erasmus' "philosophy of Christ" as he had taught it in his *Enchiridion* and *Paraclesis* recur frequently in Zwingli's program for a renaissance of Christendom. The humanist's easy association of "good letters" with Christianity and with Christ the teacher is also a major emphasis in Zwingli's writing. Humanist pedagogical ideals are reflected in his treatise *On the Education of Youth* (1523).

The basic content of the theology of the young Zwingli is the "doctrine of Christ." He refers to sin more as a blindness or infirmity of the flesh than as a basic evil and the root condition of man. His Christocentrism is normative, not existential, the result of a gratifying intellectual enlightenment rather than the result of a spiritual struggle that led him to cast himself entirely upon the mercy of Christ. Zwingli preached the most extreme doctrine of divine double predestination of any of the major reformers—the doctrine that God not only had predetermined at the time of creation the souls he would save, but had also made a deliberate selection of the souls he would cast into hell. But Zwingli's writings on the point leave the impression that he embraced the doctrine simply because he believed Paul had taught it, not because he had himself trembled before the terrible decree of God. Even his assurance that God would save Heraclitus, Plato, Aristotle, Cicero, and other good pagans comes rather easily, compared with Luther's mere hope that God might find a way to save Cicero. But the most characteristically Erasmian aspect of his thought is the constant contrast of the law of the spirit and the law of the letter or flesh. The distrust of the material constitutes the basic reason for his puritanical reaction against images and ecclesiastical art, sensuous music, and the real presence of Christ in the Sacrament. The conception of the religious life as the triumph of the spirit over the flesh explains the moralistic emphasis of his "evangelical teaching" during the early years. Nevertheless, Zwingli's teaching underwent a marked change as he became ever more deeply involved in the theological issues of the Reformation and more thoroughly steeped in Pauline theology.

The Sacramentarian Controversy

WHEN IN OCTOBER 1529 Zwingli and Luther met at last face to face in the magnificent castle of Landgrave Philipp of Hesse in Marburg, towering high above the river Lahn, Luther summarized the fundamental difference between them with words addressed directly to Bucer but intended for Zwingli and the rest as well: "You have a different spirit!" The meeting, intended by the landgrave to unify the evangelicals for the anticipated Catholic assault, served only to clarify the differences among them and to render permanent the division between the German and Swiss reform movements.

In later years Zwingli liked to think of his Einsiedeln period as the time when he broke through to a true evangelical understanding of the Scriptures. How limited his advance was can be seen from the fact that as late as 1517 he personally participated in a pilgrimage as a meritorious act. Nevertheless, Zwingli was not entirely mistaken in claiming that he was preaching a reformed interpretation of the gospel before anyone in Switzerland knew anything at all about Luther. His conception of the gospel in those early years, however, was a kind of Erasmian Christocentric ethic of love, the "philosophy of Christ." It was only during his Zurich period, while he was studying Paul's epistles under the influence of Luther's writings, that he shifted his emphasis to the "law of Christ" or a higher Christology, eventually preaching with fervor of God's full, free, and final gift of salvation in Jesus Christ, bestowed upon man by God's grace alone. For this conception of the gospel, or "good news," he was clearly heavily in debt to Luther. There is no evidence that Zwingli was aware of the initial flurry of excitement over Luther's ninety-five theses in 1517, strange as it may seem in view of the fact that the humanist circles in Basel and other south German cities were so excited about the event. But it is clear that by late 1518 Zwingli knew of and corresponded about Luther's writings and thereafter assiduously read them. By 1523, however, Zwingli was protesting his own originality, declaring that he had preached the new interpretation of the gospel before he had heard of Luther, claiming to have read little of Luther, and expressing resentment at being called a Lutheran. From Luther, Zwingli averred, he had learned only the courage to do what he had already come to believe was right. Zwingli was clearly not inclined to defer to the Wittenberg reformer. The parting of the ways came over their different interpretations of the nature and significance of the Sacrament of the Altar.

Zwingli believed that the Sacrament of the Altar, or the Lord's Supper, was merely a sign or seal of divine grace already bestowed upon the communicant. The bread and wine were mere symbols of the body and blood of Christ, who was locally present in his own physical person in heaven and not on earth. The man of faith who communes in remembrance of the last supper of the Lord with his disciples gains the benefit of a spiritual communion with his Lord. Zwingli derived his conception of the Sacrament as a memorial from a Dutch humanist physician, Cornelius Hoen, who wrote to Zwingli in 1523 from The Hague that the words of institution, "This is my body," were really a figure of speech, a trope, and that the word "is" must be understood to mean "signifies." "We need to differentiate," wrote Hoen, "between the bread which is received by the mouth and Christ who is received by faith." Zwingli was impressed by Hoen's interpretation, and called it "the precious pearl" by which he found clarity in this difficult matter. It was indeed a rational solution, but was it consonant with other facets of biblical theology? Luther received a similar letter from Hoen and replied that while he was naturally inclined toward a symbolic interpretation, he could not escape the clear words of Scripture, which plainly stated, "This is my body," with no hint that a figure of speech was being employed.

Luther's catechetical definition of a sacrament, taken from St. Augustine, reads: "The Word comes to the element and makes of it a sacrament." The Sacrament, like the message of the gospel, offers to man the benefits of Christ, Luther taught, and is essentially a means of grace by which men's faith is strengthened. Christ is truly present in the Sacrament, and his real presence is assured not only by his ubiquity, since the glorified Christ is not limited by spatial dimensions, but also by virtue of his express promise in the institution of the Sacrament. It is evident that Luther felt bound by the words of Scripture, but not simply as a literalist, for the conception of the communication of attributes between the human and divine natures in Christ and the thrust against demeaning the material, as in Zwingli's doctrine, were also involved in his definition.

The sacramentarian controversy soon became a public issue. Andreas Carlstadt, the expelled Wittenberg professor with marked Puritan tendencies, brought his sacramental theories to Strassburg. Although he was not permitted to stay in the city, some of the reformed theologians there were inclined to accept a spiritual interpretation and held Christ's real presence in the Sacrament impossible because of his presence in heaven. Oecolampadius in Basel, Bucer in Strassburg, the humanist Pirckheimer in Nuremberg, and others joined in the fray until at last Zwingli and Luther themselves were drawn into the great debate. In 1526 Luther published his *Sermon on the Sacrament of the Body and Blood of Christ, Against the Fanatics.* In February 1527 Zwingli attacked his position in his *Friendly Exegesis.* In April Luther responded with a heated but substantial reply, *That These Words "This Is My Body" Still Stand, Against the Fanatics.* In June Zwingli reacted sharply in his treatise *That the Words "This Is My Body" Still Have Their Original Meaning.* In March 1528 Luther published his *Great Confession Concerning the Lord's Supper,* striking a condescending tone. Zwingli was furious and announced that he did not like being "treated like an ass." In a rage he wrote on August 30, 1528, to Conrad Sam at Ulm:

> That rash man Luther keeps killing human and divine wisdom in his books, though it would have been easy to restore this wisdom among the pious. But since the heretics, that is, his followers, together with the wicked, have become so deaf to all truth that they refuse to listen, I was for a long time doubtful about expending this enormous labor which I knew would be vain. . . . May I die if he does not surpass Eck in impurity, Cochlaeus in audacity, and, in brief, all the vices of men!

Some years before, Luther had written to a certain Gregory Casel: "In a word, either they or we must be ministers of Satan! There is not room here for negotiation or mediation." And yet on the first three days of October 1529 Luther sat with Zwingli at a massive oak table in the landgrave's castle at Marburg for a colloquy aimed at a resolution of outstanding differences in the interest of evangelical unity. The year 1529 was a hazardous one for the Protestants, who had to speak out at the diet at Speyer against the emperor's determination to nullify the temporary concessions made at the diet in 1526. Landgrave Philipp of Hesse, an energetic evangelical, who had dined on steak on a Friday at Speyer in 1526 to demonstrate his Christian liberty, was a political activist determined to unite the Protestant forces for a common defense. Luther disapproved of this political and potentially military motive for the unification efforts, since he would not condone the use of force in religious matters. But to oblige Philipp, he and Melanchthon traveled to Marburg together with Justus Jonas, Johannes Brenz, Caspar Cruciger, Andreas Osiander, and several other theologians to meet with Zwingli, Johannes Oecolampadius, Martin Bucer, Caspar Hedio, and Jacob Sturm, the Swiss and Strassburg theologians. They quickly came to a general agreement on fourteen articles, dealing with doctrines such as the person of Christ, justification by faith, baptism, and the like.

There was also a surprising amount of agreement on a fifteenth article, dealing with the Sacrament of the Altar. They rejected transubstantiation and the conception of the mass as sacrifice and favored communion in both kinds. Luther conceded that the Sacrament had symbolic character and presupposed spiritual eating and drinking, but when he insisted upon the real presence of Christ in the Sacrament, Zwingli could not concede. Melanchthon at this point seems to have opposed concessions to the spiritualists, since he was still hopeful of reunion with the Catholics. After the session ended Luther worked out a statement on the presence of Christ's body in the Sacrament "essentially and substantively," though not "qualitatively, quantitatively, or locally." But Zwingli rejected the formula and insisted upon his views of the purely spiritual and symbolic nature of the Sacrament. Perhaps Erasmus' most effective blow at Protestantism was not his frontal assault on Luther in the *De libero arbitrio,* but his subtle infusion of spiritualism into Zwingli, making him susceptible to his fellow humanist Hoen's highly rational solution to a mystery of faith. Brenz and Bucer found Luther's formula satisfying and it became the basis of the Württemberg Concord of 1534 and the Wittenberg Concord of 1536, signed by the Strassburg theologians who traveled to Wittenberg to consult with Luther. The debate between Zwingli and Luther at Marburg was not exactly a model of irenic theological discussion. At one point Zwingli buttressed his argument by referring to Christ's statement on the bread of life in John 6. "There," Zwingli exclaimed, "is an argument that will break your neck!" Luther replied, "Ah, but don't forget you are in Hesse, not in Switzerland. Necks are not so easily broken in Germany."

Sincerity and earnestness are in evidence in their colloquy. Neither would make concessions against conscience, not even for political gain or in the interest of sheer survival. Zwingli was about to pay with his life for the failure to secure a united Protestant front, or at least good allies. Luther's land of Saxony was to be despoiled and Philipp of Hesse imprisoned by the Habsburg allies of Zwingli's Catholic opponents.

Zwingli's Leadership and Civil War

ZWINGLI'S REFORMATORY ACTIVITY in Zurich served as a catalyst for the Swiss Protestant movement, even in those cantons where the beginnings were already under way. The city of Bern is a case in point, for there Berchthold Haller, strongly influenced by Luther's theology, served as a teacher and from 1519 on as preacher in the cathedral. But it was not until the marathon nineteen-day public disputation during January 1528, in which Zwingli, Oecolampadius, Capito, and Bucer presented Reformation doctrines, that the city moved into the Protestant fold.

The city of Basel was of pivotal importance both for its location on the upper Rhine and for its preeminence as a center of humanism and publishing. The printers Froben and Amerbach were leaders in the book trade. The conciliar movement had left its mark upon the city, for the second of the major church councils had met at nearby Constance (1414–1418) and the long session of the schismatic third council had met in Basel itself (1431–1449), leaving behind a residue of conciliar and antipapal feeling and a general sense of the urgent necessity for reform. Zwingli's Erasmian humanist professor Wyttenbach had urged reform, and the presence of Erasmus himself from 1521 on attracted many reform-minded men of the Christian humanist type to the city. Wolfgang Capito was active there for a while before he moved to Strassburg. But the real reformer of Basel was the Swabian whose statue still stands in front of the cathedral, Johannes Oecolampadius (1482–1531), a man influenced by both Wittenberg and Zurich. As a young humanist he was a promising student of the classics, but he turned to biblical studies and became an Erasmian reformer, then fell under the influence of Melanchthon and Zwingli and evolved into an evangelical reformer. As pastor of St. Martin's Church and professor at the university he laid the groundwork for a more radical reformation of the church. He participated in the Bern disputation in 1528 and led the popular movement that pressured the city council in February 1529 to cut off relations with the hierarchy and inaugurate a Zwinglian reformation in Basel. As superintendent, Oecolampadius saw to the reform of the churches throughout the canton. He would have been only too happy to keep the great Erasmus in the city, but Erasmus now saw that the reform had taken a radical and schismatic turn, and he left in 1528, escorted to the river boat in grand style, for Freiburg-im-Breisgau, safe Habsburg Catholic territory.

In St. Gall, Zwingli's home canton, Vadian (1485–1551) led the reform. Vadian or Vadianus, a Latinized version of his Germanic name, Joachim von Watt, was one of the most attractive personalities among the Swiss reformers. As a young man he was both a student and a professor of classical studies at the University of Vienna. Through a study of the Scriptures he was brought quite independently to an evangelical conviction. He became the wise and revered reformer of St. Gall, where a giant statue in his honor still dominates the marketplace. He was under Zwingli's spell, though he was more moderate and less belligerent than Zwingli. Zwingli's successor at Glarus, Valentin Tschudi, also worked for a reform more generous and tolerant of Catholic convictions, though Zwinglian in essence. Zwinglianism spread also to Schaffhausen, Constance, Memmingen, and other south German cities, down the Rhine to the Netherlands, and into East Frisia. It made a considerable impact also upon the English Reformation, contributing especially to its Puritan component.

Unlike the cosmopolitan Erasmus, Zwingli was a fierce patriot who wished to see all Switzerland freed from the yoke of the papacy. The forest cantons, however, remained loyal to the Catholic Church. Uri, Schwyz, and Unterwalden were jealous of Zurich's rise to prominence and were eager to preserve their traditional pre-eminence in the confederacy. They, together with Lucerne and Zug, cast about for support, and in April 1529 made an alliance with the archenemy of the Swiss, the Austrian Habsburg duke Ferdinand. On the theory that the best defense is a good offense, and without the support of his cantonal allies, Zwingli led the Zurich troops to Cappel in June 1529 for an attack on their enemies. But Swiss fraternal feelings asserted themselves, and the troops on both sides exchanged bread, milk, and banter. Bern refused to join in an offensive war at all. Zwingli had to be satisfied with the First Peace of Cappel (June 26, 1529), which called for the severance of the Catholic cantons' alliance with Ferdinand and toleration of evangelical con-gregations in common administrative circuits.

Zwingli now was drawn into a diplomatic design, devised by Philipp of Hesse, for a grand anti-Austrian alliance, to include Denmark, Venice, Saxony, and France. But no one could be induced to become involved, not even the German Protestant principalities, as the breakdown of the unity efforts at Marburg in 1529 should have made evident. That year was a critical one for the empire, and the new imperial pressure on the evangelicals at the Diet of Speyer put them on the defensive. Zwingli was reduced to a basic alliance with Bern and Basel in league with Strassburg, and an assistance pact between Philipp of Hesse, Zurich, and Basel. Arrangements were completed by January 1530. The Catholic cantons had not carried out their agreement to dissolve their Austrian alliance, and Zwingli, convinced they were planning some treachery, favored striking first. The session of the confederacy diet held in January 1531 was stormy with charges and counter-charges. Zwingli was extremely nervous, expecting an attack. He maneuvered economic sanctions against the Catholic cantons, blocking the sale of wheat, salt, wine, and iron to them. The forest cantons struck back, and with a force of eight thousand men invaded the canton of Zurich at Cappel on October 11, 1531. When word reached the city, about fifteen hundred men, Zwingli among them, marched out to meet the attackers. Seeing the badly outnumbered Zurich troops giving way, Zwingli moved into the middle of the battle and took a fatal thrust in the throat. Enemy soldiers found his body on the field, quartered and burned it, and scattered the ashes. Zurich lost over four hundred dead in that battle, including twenty-six councilmen and twenty-five pastors. The Catholic cantons knew that the city of Zurich had considerable manpower in reserve and did not press their military ad-vantage. The Second Peace of Cappel (November 20, 1531) provided that the Protestant lands were to remain as they were, the Catholic but not the Protestant minorities were to be tolerated, all entangling foreign alliances were to be abro-gated, and St. Gall was to restore the ancient Benedictine monastery to its former status. The Swiss civil war was a tragedy according to Hegel's definition: "a con-flict of right against right." It was an Alpine preliminary to the avalanche of misery and destruction that was to engulf all Europe during the decades that followed.

In Swiss Reformed Protestantism Zwingli left an important legacy to his own land and to the world. He gave to his followers an example of political activism coupled with religious legalism and extreme spirituality. The cultural ties with Protestant Germany remained strong even after the growth of Calvinism overshadowed the Zurich-centered reform. Under his successor, Heinrich Bullinger (1504-1575), his own son-in-law and biographer, the German-Swiss reform movement was turned more exclusively to ecclesiastical concerns and lost its political drive, although Zwingli's hostility to the Habsburg emperor left its mark in the continued estrangement of the Swiss from the empire. The Swiss remained aloof from the later wars of religion for the very good reason that they had experienced one of their own and had been the first among the people of Europe to do so. Luther had disapproved of Zwingli's belligerence, and he considered Zwingli's death a divine judgment upon him.

The Radical Reformation

THE TREMENDOUS CONVULSION of the Reformation movement had the effect of freeing millions of people from traditional norms and relationships at a time when time-honored and sacrosanct institutions were in the process of disintegration. Great numbers of people sought reassurance in the most improbable proclamations of bizarre prophets, or in cultlike associations that provided the company that misery seeks. These borderline individuals and marginal groups frequently had insights into dimensions of the Christian faith not at all appreciated or emphasized by the magisterial reformers.

For centuries the role of the radicals in the Reformation was largely neglected, and they were treated as Christendom's stepchildren. But in recent years they have come into their own. Unlike the major reformers, most of the radicals founded no lasting church bodies whose members were interested in promoting the study of their teachings. But now some religious groups generically or sentimentally related to Reformation sects have come of age, turned against their former anti-intellectual bias, and abandoned a largely self-imposed isolation. Scholars of smaller denominations are beginning to contribute significant knowledge about the movement. Moreover, since the Marxist historians have fastened upon Thomas Müntzer and radical religious types as the theological epiphenomena of social revolution, countless volumes have appeared interpreting the radical Reformation in the light of those remarkable scholars Engels, Marx, and Lenin. New knowledge is streaming in from all sides.

Protestantism very quickly took on the appearance of a banyan tree, sprouting a maze of roots and branches. The problem of authority as a basis of institutional or credal unity proved to be the Achilles' heel of the movement. One might have expected an infinite proliferation of splinter groups, but in reality a few major evangelical churches embraced the vast majority of Protestants. The minority was badly fragmented into small sects and even isolated individuals. A few of these were offshoots of the parent stock, but most developed as independent responses to the same basic problems as those with which the leading reformers were concerned.

The German historian and sociologist of religion Ernst Troeltsch (d. 1922) suggested that there were three main religious types in the sixteenth century. The first was the sect, a new collectivity or association in which those who could not conform to the larger society gathered to formulate their own norms. The sectarian groups aimed at holiness, though they were seldom perfectionists, and usually believed in a time-line progress toward an *eschaton,* or apocalyptic consummation of history, which would usher in the millennium, the thousand-year rule of Christ and the saints. Plotted on a right triangle, the sect would form the base line, moving out from the point indefinitely to the right. The Anabaptists belonged to this type of sect.

Then there were the religious individualists. The mystic caught up in his private system or method strove for vertical ascent through contemplation and meditation, experiencing the dark night of the soul before breaking through to momentary union with God. The whole spectrum of mystics, spiritualists, and ethical theists devoted to the inner life of the soul were of this kind. The evangelical rationalists too were often individualistic, although some of the anti-Trinitarians, such as the Socinians or Polish Brethren and the Lithuanian and Transylvanian Unitarians, formed associations or churches. Plotted on our right triangle, this second type forms the vertical line, moving upward toward individual perfection and union with the Infinite.

Between these two extremes were the church members, both those who remained in the Catholic Church and those who followed the major reformers. The ecclesiastical reformers sought to embrace the emphases of both the sects and the mystics, accommodating collective social and ethical progress along with personal religious expression. Plotted on our right triangle, the main reformed churches constitute sector lines, some inclining more toward the base line of the sectaries and others more toward the vertical line of the mystics.

Although formerly some sociologists of religion argued for the radically Protestant nature of the Reformation sectaries, scholars have come increasingly to recognize many ties between the radical reformers and medieval heretical currents of thought. In a history of pietism published in 1880, the historian Albrecht Ritschl pointed to the similarity of ecstatic sectarian ideas of the sixteenth century to the heretical notions of the Spiritual Franciscans. The localization of the sectaries in the Rhine valley and the Netherlands, the precise areas that had witnessed a proliferation of late medieval heretical groups—the Brethren and Sisters of the Free Spirit, the Beguines, the Beghards—cannot be explained as mere coincidence.

THE ANABAPTISTS

There was an important tie between some of the leaders among the Anabaptists and Renaissance humanism, for some of the most important of them came to their radical evangelism from Erasmian religiosity. The influence of the more volatile reformers, such as Luther's erstwhile colleague Carlstadt, upon radicals in Strassburg and elsewhere is also evident. Moreover, the impact of such a wild man as Thomas Müntzer, with his call for a war of extermination against the godless by his League of the Elect, had a detectable, if embarrassing, influence even upon peace-minded Anabaptists. The fact that a pejorative association of all Anabaptists with this militant leader was used to defame them should not obscure the definite relationship between them. From the very outset the Anabaptists had a bad press. They were considered by both Catholics and evangelicals to be heretical and by the magistrates to be subversive.

In Zwingli's Zurich Conrad Grebel (1448–1526), the leader of the Swiss Brethren, performed the first adult baptism, or rebaptism. On January 21, 1525, he administered the sacrament to Georg Blaurock in the home of Felix Manz. In a way, this act was a tribute to Zwingli's rhetorical impact and to his powers of persuasion, for these Swiss Brethren, as members of Zwingli's reform movement, took very seriously his injunction to search the Scriptures independently of tradition and authority. They found no warrant there for infant baptism, and concluded that baptism was a sign or symbol of the regeneration or coming to faith of adults who had reached the age of accountability and discretion. They were carrying Zwingli's own sacramental theory to its logical extreme. Grebel was a member of a fine patrician family and was a well-educated classical humanist who, like Zwingli, had studied at the University of Vienna. He was therefore able to counter the arguments that church fathers of the third to the fifth centuries, such as Cyprian, Tertullian, Gregory Nazianzen, Origen, and Augustine, had testified to the apostolic origins of infant baptism. Why are the Scriptures silent, he asked, if this is an essential aspect of the dominical sacrament, and why is there no evidence for it from the first two centuries? In opposition to the state church and the people's church, Grebel and the Brethren favored a free confessional church, a visible communion of saints living holy lives, excluding the faithless or immoral, following the injunctions of Matthew 18 literally. They tried to revive the simple forms of the apostolic church, using a low-liturgical order of worship and celebrating the Lord's Supper in private homes in the evening as a meal of solemn remembrance. In separating from the godless world they sought to live out the commands of Christ's Sermon on the Mount very literally, offering no resistance to evil treatment, refusing to take oaths, and rejecting military service. They even cultivated the concept of a suffering church in emulation of the "suffering servant" prophesied by Isaiah and embodied in Jesus.

Zwingli was amazed and distressed at this turn of events. He preached vehemently against the Anabaptists, for he opposed their rejection of infant baptism and their attitude toward civil government, and he believed the scurrilous reports of their social disorder and dissolute behavior. He directed a special blast *Against the Tricks of the Katabaptists*. The Zurich city council decided that the Anabaptists were subverting law and order in the state, and should be forced to conform or emigrate. Grebel, Manz, and Blaurock left the city, but undertook the propagation of their views elsewhere. Arrested near Zurich, they were tried and given life sentences, but escaped. Grebel died of the plague in 1526 and Manz was executed by drowning in 1527 (an imaginative sentence reminiscent of baptism by immersion). Blaurock managed to carry his message to Austria, but he was arrested in the Tyrol and burned at the stake in 1529. Their fates were a portent of the persecution that awaited their suffering churches.

Popular Anabaptist preachers were recruited from the ranks of the evangelical clergy as well as from the Catholic regular and secular clergy. The Swabian Balthasar Hubmaier (1485–1528), a Protestant minister in Waldshut, Austria, shocked his congregation in January 1525 by proclaiming that he had received a divine command to reject infant baptism. On Easter Day he had himself rebaptized together with most members of the congregation. His book on *The Christian Baptism of Believers* became an influential presentation of the Anabaptist view that baptism was to follow a profession of faith. The Zurich authorities arrested him and forced a recantation. Thereupon he set out upon a wandering mission eastward, preaching in Constance, Augsburg, Regensburg, and Nikolsburg in Moravia, where he converted the Lutheran congregation to Anabaptism and established a shelter for religious refugees from all over the empire. The Habsburg government could not tolerate such a disturbance in a well-ordered realm. So the lords of Liechtenstein turned Hubmaier over to Duke Ferdinand's officials, who burned him at the stake on March 10 outside Vienna and drowned his wife in the Danube. One hundred and five Anabaptists were executed in Vienna alone.

An even more pathetic, if heroic, case was the trial and martyrdom of Michael Sattler, a saintly man who was converted by evangelical preaching, gave up his position as prior of St. Peter's in Breisgau, went to Zurich, and there joined the Swiss Brethren. Driven out of Zurich, he became a refugee in Strassburg, and then moved to Horb in the Black Forest to do mission work for his cause. In 1527 he presided at the Schleitheim Conference of Anabaptists and was the main author of the Schleitheim Confession of Faith, which was adopted on St. Matthew's Day (February 24). The Confession was widely circulated and was perhaps the most representative statement of distinctive Anabaptist teachings. It elicited refutations from Zwingli and many years later from Calvin. The Confession established seven main points: (1) Baptism was to be given to all those who had learned repentance and amendment of life and who truly believed that their sins were taken away by Christ. (2) All those who, having professed the Anabaptist faith and been baptized, fell into error and sin, even though inadvertently, were to be excommunicated. (3) All those who wished to take part in the Lord's Supper had first to be baptized. (4) The baptized were to separate themselves from the evil and wickedness that the devil planted in the world. (5) A pastor in the church must, as Paul prescribed, be one who had a good reputation among those outside the faith. (6) No member of the church was to bear arms in any cause. (7) No member of the church was to take an oath.[2]

For this confession Michael Sattler was to die a horrible death. Arrested for sedition by the Austrian authorities, he was tried in Ensisheim. Tilman J. van Braght's *Martyr's Mirror* (1660) records the sentence passed upon this gentle person and the manner of his death:

> "In the case of the attorney of His Imperial Majesty vs. Michael Sattler, judgment is passed that Michael Sattler shall be delivered to the executioner, who shall lead him to the place of execution and cut out his tongue, then forge him fast to a wagon and thereon with red-hot tongs twice tear pieces from his body; and after he has been brought outside the gate, he shall be plied five times more in the same manner. . . ."
>
> After this had been done in the manner prescribed, he was burned to ashes as a heretic. His fellow brethren were executed with the sword, and the sisters drowned. His wife, also after being subjected to many entreaties, admonitions and threats, under which she remained steadfast, was drowned a few days afterward.[3]

Society has usually understood how to protect itself from its little people. Hans Denck called a conference of Anabaptist leaders in Augsburg in 1526, which was subsequently known as the Martyrs' Synod, since virtually everyone who attended was hunted down and judicially murdered. It was not only their beliefs that outraged the more conventional citizens; some mentally unbalanced extremists brought further discredit to the movement. One Anabaptist emulated the Old Testament prophet Isaiah by placing a red-hot coal to his lips, intending to confess with him, "Woe is me, I am undone, for I am a man of unclean lips!" but the burn left him speechless. Some eccentrics in the Netherlands ran around naked, also in emulation of Isaiah, who had done so as a sign. There were even cases of radicals indulging in sexual intercourse while lying on an altar, no doubt to demonstrate the triumph of pure spirit over the flesh. Storming the pulpit and ejecting an

---

[2] The full text of the Confession may be found in John C. Wenger, "The Schleitheim Confession of Faith," *Mennonite Quarterly Review*, 19, no. 4 (October 1945):247–52.

[3] See George H. Williams, ed., *The Library of Christian Classics* (London, 1957), vol. 25, *Spiritual and Anabaptist Writers*, pp. 138–44.

unregenerated minister was a common occurrence. One somber fellow marched through Zurich crying, "Woe! Woe! The day of judgment is at hand!" Another traveled from city to city wearing a wooden sword at his side by way of rebuke to the secular government. The persecution of the Anabaptists had the effect of producing a diaspora of religious refugees with tremendous mobility and a remarkable network of international contacts and intelligence.

The Anabaptist ideology of brotherhood and egalitarianism appealed to the poor and lowly, the dispossessed. Since they were attempting literally to reestablish the pattern of the New Testament church, a number of the leaders were almost inevitably attracted by the voluntary communism practiced by some of the early Christians. Jakob Hutter (or Huter) organized a communal society, nonviolent and collectivist, in Nikolsburg, that city of social ferment in Moravia. About fifteen thousand brethren, mostly artisans and peasants, were organized into communes of two hundred people in about eighty localities. Although the Austrian officials burned Hutter at the stake in 1536, several communities of the Hutterite Brethren survived. Hutterite settlements are still to be found in Russia and North and South America, models of cooperative and pacific living.

A strong strain of millennialism ran through the Anabaptist movement, as erratic and even hysterical eschatological types prophesied the imminent second coming of Christ and his thousand-year rule upon earth before the final destruction of this universe by fire. Luther too believed that he was living in the last age of the world, but he managed to keep a certain sense of balance about it. Once when a friend asked him what he would do if he knew for certain that the world would come to an end the next day, he replied, "I would plant an apple tree today." Unfortunately, all too many of the half-educated or highly emotional sectarians precipitated panic situations by their wild interpretations of the prophecies of Daniel and the Book of Revelation, those two main sources of apocalyptic visions. Three such millennialists were Hans Hut, David Joris, and Melchior Hofmann, who succeeded in gaining mass followings and stirring up social unrest.

Hans Hut, a Franconian bookbinder and dealer, was an important member of the Augsburg circle of Anabaptists. Rebaptized in Augsburg on Pentecost Day, 1526, he was one of those who preached the imminence of the kingdom of God. In Nikolsburg he debated with Balthasar Hubmaier, arguing for complete nonresistance to violence on the part of Christians, while Hubmaier defended a man's right to defend himself and his family. Hut was arrested in Nikolsburg in 1527, but escaped to Vienna, where he baptized fifty people. He then wandered westward to Linz, Melk, and Steyr, baptizing and proclaiming the coming of Christ to judgment. Christ would deliver into the hands of the saints the double-eged sword of justice to be wielded against priests and false prophets, the nobles and kings. Then Christ and the saints would rule in peace for a thousand years. Charged with preaching free love and communism, Hut was arrested in 1527, jailed in Augsburg, and killed during an attempted escape.

David Joris (1501–1556), a radical visionary in the Netherlands, wrote pro-
lifically in Dutch, escaped execution, and went underground to direct his movement. The son of a shopkeeper and an artisan himself, he was influenced by Luther,
but Lutheranism became only a halfway house on his road to Anabaptism. He
attacked the pope as Antichrist, and on Ascension Day of 1528 he violated the
sacramental host being carried in a procession. The authorities seized him, pilloried
him, had his tongue bored, and exiled him from Delft for three years. He was rebaptized in 1533 and wandered about Europe as an Anabaptist missionary. The
execution of his own mother as an Anabaptist in 1537 shocked him profoundly and
may have been the occasion for the release of a stream of pent-up visions and
prophecies. Like Joachim of Flora, he saw the history of the world divided into the
three great dispensations of Father, Son, and Holy Spirit. As "Christus David"
he proclaimed the last revelation, which was to supersede that of "Christus Jesus."
a historical role that the Pontius Pilates of the Habsburg regime could not accept
with equanimity. Joris left for Basel, which was to be the New Jerusalem, and lived
there for the remainder of his life under the alias of Jan van Brugge. He continued
his contacts with the Anabaptists of Frisia and the Netherlands, but kept his
identity secret until his death in April 1556. Three years after his burial in St.
Leonard's Church, his own son-in-law denounced him to the city officials, who
had his body disinterred and burned.

A religious enthusiast of the same stripe as Joris was Melchior Hofmann, a
Swabian furrier who wandered through northeastern Europe and the Rhineland
proclaiming the approaching end of the world. Attracted to Luther's teaching, he
combined missionary work with business trips to Sweden, Livonia, and Riga. He
visited Wittenberg and impressed Luther favorably on his first visit, but on his
second visit Luther began to fear the worst. There Hofmann wrote an apocalyptic
exposition of the twelfth chapter of Daniel (1527). At Kiel, where King Frederick
I of Denmark had appointed him preacher, he indulged in wild proclamations. At
a colloquy of preachers in Flensburg in 1529 he defended the Zwinglian doctrine of
the Sacrament and was subsequently banished, taking refuge in Strassburg. He
moved now progressively toward a more radical theology, under the influence of
Carlstadt and Caspar Schwenkfeld. In East Frisia he founded a community of regenerate artisans. In 1533 he returned to Strassburg to make that lucky city his
New Jerusalem, for his study of the Apocalypse revealed that he was to reestablish
apostolic Christianity. But Strassburg did not appreciate the honor, and though
efforts were made to rehabilitate Hofmann to calmer ways, he languished imprisoned in a cage in a tower for a decade until finally he died late in 1543. Through
his preaching and books of prophecy he influenced many people, especially in the
Netherlands, who came to be known as Melchiorites.

The wildest adventure of the militant Anabaptists was the proclamation of
the Kingdom of Münster. The anatomy of the revolution followed the classical
pattern: repression by the prince-bishop, a revolt against the bishop and a moderate

change in favor of Lutheranism, a more radical Anabaptist takeover, a Jacobin reign of terror, and a dictatorship, followed by the suppression of the revolution and a Thermidorian reaction. In Münster, as in other ecclesiastical estates in Westphalia, there was constant friction between the city and the prince-bishop over feudal and canonical dues. General economic distress caused by crop failures, the loss of manpower to the plague, and high prices created much unrest and a populace receptive to the Lutheran preaching of Bernard Rothmann, a persuasive pulpiteer. In the year 1532 the city council, under popular pressure, appointed Lutheran preachers to all churches in the city, and the next year the bishop recognized Münster as an "evangelical city."

Münster had already taken in the Anabaptist refugees from nearby Jülich-Cleves, and when news of its Protestantization spread, the rootless and disaffected came pouring into the city from all around. The volatile Rothmann himself turned radical and was rebaptized by two Melchiorites sent to Münster as apostles by Jan Matthys, a baker in Haarlem. Like Müntzer, Matthys was a militant radical who preached that the elect had to wield a bloody sword against the ungodly in preparation for the rule of the saints in the millennium. Persuaded by the rhetoric of Rothmann and influenced by a prominent cloth merchant and guild leader named Bernt Knipperdollinck, who had traveled in Sweden with Melchior Hofmann himself, over fourteen hundred people were rebaptized in a short time.

The arrival of a Dutch apostle, Jan Bockelson, better known as John of Leiden, marked a turning point for the movement. This handsome and eloquent young man of twenty-five had just been rebaptized by Jan Matthys and had the fervor of a convert. On February 8, 1534, John and Knipperdollinck ran up and down the streets of Münster crying out for all to repent of their sins, unleashing a flood of religious hysteria. Masses of women and men too screamed and writhed madly on the ground. At this point the Anabaptists staged a spontaneous revolt and took over the marketplace and city hall. Horrified by these excesses, many of the middle-class Lutherans moved away and were replaced by thousands of sectarian proletarians who streamed into the city from everywhere. Münster was declared the New Jerusalem, which would be spared when all the rest of the world was destroyed, before Easter of that year.

The election on February 23 of an Anabaptist city council coincided closely with the arrival of Jan Matthys in person from Holland. He immediately urged the execution of all Catholics and Lutherans remaining in the city, but they were instead driven out during a fierce blizzard. Those who refused or were unable to go were forcibly rebaptized in the marketplace. When the bishop undertook a partial siege of the city, Jan Matthys assumed dictatorial powers and began a reign of terror. He declared a communist state, and when a blacksmith protested the confiscation of private property, Matthys stabbed and shot him as an example to the crowd in the marketplace. All money and valuables were taken by the state, all houses were to be open at all times and were to be owned in common, all books except the Bible were burned, each laborer was to be paid according to his need and only in kind, and the armed men were fed at public kitchens. At this point Matthys received a vision that like Gideon of old he was to choose a handful of men and go out to destroy the army of the godless bishop. The gaunt, fierce-eyed fanatic sallied forth and was promptly cut down by the enemy.

John of Leiden's hour had come. This bastard son of a Dutch mayor and a peasant woman was a proletarian rabble-rouser, a megalomaniac with the wild imagination of an unbalanced fanatic and the peculiar lucidity of the mad. Early in May he ran naked through the streets of the city and fell into an ecstatic trance that lasted three days. When at last he roused himself he seized power, pronounced an automatic death penalty for insubordination, and established a bodyguard, a chain of command, and a system that held the whole city of ten thousand inhabitants cowed in terror. He declared that in a vision he had been commanded to establish polygamy, and, having married the beautiful young widow of Matthys, he collected a harem of fifteen wives. In August 1534, after beating off an attack of the bishop's mercenary army, John had himself proclaimed king of the New Jerusalem and the Messiah or anointed one of the last days foretold by the prophets of the Old Testament. He ruled from a tall throne covered with gold cloth in the marketplace. Rothmann, who published pamphlets significantly entitled *Restitution* and *Announcement of Vengeance,* became court orator, and Knipperdollinck became his prime minister. The royal court dined in splendor and dressed in gorgeous robes while the subjects of the king lived in want. One of John's wives, the beautiful Divora, was named queen.

The tragicomedy turned into a horror story when the bishop's army, supported by money and troops from Hesse and other states of the empire, began to besiege the city in earnest in January 1535. They surrounded it with earthworks, infantry troops, and cavalry, cut it off completely from the outside world, and settled down to wait for time to take its toll. Fierce famine raged in the city as the months dragged on; people were reduced to eating vermin and even the dead. After a siege lasting nearly half a year a few skeletal escapees from the city revealed to the besiegers vulnerable points in the defenses. On June 24 they stormed the city and captured King John and his court. He was led about on exhibition like a dancing bear on a chain as an object lesson to revolutionaries. Then in January 1536 he, Knipperdollinck, and a third man were put to death with red-hot irons. In shock or in a catatonic state, King John made no motion or sound during his torture. Their bodies were hung in cages from the Lambert Church tower in Münster, which still serves as a reminder to the city and the world of the human potential for both folly and vengeance. The city walls were torn down and the surviving inhabitants returned to the Catholic fold.[4]

---

[4] Norman Cohn, *The Pursuit of the Millennium: Revolutionary Messianism in Medieval and Reformation Europe and Its Bearing on Modern Totalitarian Movements* (New York, 1961), pp. 272–306.

The disaster at Münster thoroughly discredited militant communal and eschatological Anabaptism. The cause was rehabilitated largely by a peace-minded Anabaptist in the Netherlands, Menno Simons (1496–1561), who had lost a brother to the executioners after the fall of Münster. He had moved from the priesthood to Lutheranism and from there to Anabaptism. He believed that the biblical or apostolic church pattern called for the organization of individual congregations of the regenerated, men moved by the Holy Spirit to lead lives of peace and service. Manifest and impenitent sinners should be excluded from the congregation. The sacraments were symbolic memorials of Christ's death and of the believer's rebirth. He believed that oaths, military service, and participation in worldly government were contrary to the Lord's will. His basic beliefs were summarized in his highly influential book published in 1539, the *Book of Fundamentals*. Mennonite congregations spread from his native East Frisia through the Netherlands into northern Germany and from there into Russia and the New World.

Through their vigorous effort to return to the practices of the primitive church in the ancient Roman world, the Anabaptists actually contributed enormously to the development of principles characteristic of liberal societies in the modern world. Their insistence upon a voluntary or confessional church as opposed to an official church embracing all members of the civic community was an important step in the development of religious pluralism within the state. The separation of believers from an officially sanctioned church made a marked contribution to the modern constitutional principle of the separation of church and state. Finally, the perseverance of the Anabaptists under fierce persecution impressed even their oppressors. The Anabaptists made the gift of their own blood to the cause of religious toleration and liberty. These principles anticipated the later developments made explicit in American constitutional democracy and propagated by the French revolution.

SPIRITUALISTS AND THE EVANGELICAL RATIONALISTS

If the forty or more varieties of Anabaptists were inclined toward sectarian group organization, the Reformation also liberated many individuals who sought an independent religious life. Some of these nonconforming individuals were spiritualistic, cultivating an inwardness of religious life, while others of a more questioning or rationalistic bent became radical critics of received theological traditions and orthodoxies.

An intertwining of the various trends and tendencies can be seen in the case of Hans Denck, a spiritualist who was involved for several years with the Anabaptists. A student of the classics, he was rector of the famous school of St. Sebaldus in Nuremberg. He was attracted by the stress placed by the German mystics and Christian Neoplatonists upon the spirit and the inwardness of true religion. He believed in the coincidence of the interior word inspired by the indwelling of the

Holy Spirit and the external word recorded in the life of the spirit, and showed universalistic tendencies. The Nuremberg reformer Osiander had him expelled from the city on January 21, 1525, the same day that the first rebaptism was taking place in Zurich. In Augsburg he met Hubmaier, who won him over to Anabaptism, and in 1526 he summoned the famous Martyrs' Synod to plan the missionary efforts of the regenerate. He was soon disillusioned with the Anabaptists' undisciplined activism, however, and left them before his death in 1527, turning "the eye of his mind inward" once again. His movement merged with that of the Swiss Brethren.

A man of a very similar stripe was the Lutheran Sebastian Franck (1499–1543), best known for his historical *Chronicles*. His own form of spiritualistic mysticism showed definite pantheistic and universalistic tendencies. Though he did not approve of Anabaptism, he urged toleration in a striking statement:

> I have listed them [the Anabaptists] among the heretics that they may perceive that their church is not the true church, that they may turn to genuine unity in spirit and in truth, but I warn their persecutors not to play the part of Caiaphas and Pilate. The Anabaptists are not entirely right nor is anyone else and from each we should take the best.[5]

One of the most prolific authors of spiritualistic and mystical treatises was a Silesian nobleman, Caspar Schwenckfeld (1489–1561). Captivated by Luther's teachings, he understood faith in a highly interiorized spiritual manner. From German mysticism he learned that faith must be a moving inner experience and that regeneration must be felt within the heart. His emphasis upon the spirit over the flesh led him to stress the inward baptism of the spirit and to accept a Zwinglian interpretation of the Lord's Supper, but in a highly spiritualistic mode. Eventually he left his own estate and became a traveling evangelist, preaching to small groups of followers who huddled together under the protection of benign landed nobles of his own class.

The evangelical rationalists varied even more widely from the norm and from one another. More intellectual and critical than the spiritualists, these men tended toward radical deviations such as anti-Trinitarian tendencies and low ecclesiology. An older scholarly view once held that Anabaptism fostered anti-Trinitarianism, but this position is no longer widely held. It is true that Menno Simons avoided Trinitarian terminology, since he did not find it used in the Scriptures themselves, and in Adam Pastor or Ludwig Hätzer one can possibly find traces of the tendency, but the Anabaptists were almost all orthodox in their doctrine of God and in their Christology. The evangelical rationalists were Latin scholars and learned men, and they arrived at their ideas by the study of the sources and the patristic writers rather than through the influence of the sectaries. The greatest luminary in

---

[5] Sebastian Franck, *Chronica, Zeytbuch und Geschychtbibel* (Strassburg, 1531), cited in *The Recovery of the Anabaptist Vision*, ed. Guy F. Hershberger (Scottdale, Pa., 1957), p. 318.

this constellation was clearly Michael Servetus, who, as the American church historian Roland Bainton once put it, had the singular distinction of being "burned by the Catholics in effigy and by the Protestants in actuality."

Michael Servetus, born in Spain in 1511, the son of a royal notary, was gifted with a brilliant intellect and cursed with an argumentative and obstreperous personality. He studied law and later medicine, but became caught up in the theological turmoil of the time. His intellectual interests carried him to many parts of Europe—Toulouse, Bologna, Basel, Strassburg, Paris, Lyon, and finally to Geneva. During his law studies at Toulouse he had a moving religious experience in discovering in the Scriptures the historical person of Jesus of Nazareth, who became the object and center of his faith. He turned against the traditional credal formulations of the Trinity and of the divine and human natures of Christ. He came to hold that such theological terms as persons, substance, and essence represented a historical development, and had been imposed upon biblical conceptions from Hellenistic metaphysics. As Greek philosophical terms they were abstract, artificial, speculative, and unrelated to the living God.

When at the age of twenty he failed to convince the reformers in Basel and Strassburg of the propriety of his views, this precocious but obstinate and conceited young man proceeded to publish his treatise *On the Errors of the Trinity,* and gained an immediate and lasting reputation for religious deviationism. He argued that traditional scholastic theology introduced Greek philosophical terms and nonbiblical categories into the definitions of the Trinity. His own formulations, however, created the impression that he was reviving the ancient Arian heresy that Jesus Christ was not the preexistent *logos* or word, a person of the Trinity who was with God the Father from eternity. His book was greeted with a storm of disapproval and was nearly everywhere condemned and suppressed. In order to make his position clear, he published in 1553 a large rambling book entitled *The Restoration of Christianity,* which failed, however, to improve upon the clarity of the first work or to restore the author's reputation for orthodoxy. A fascinating part of this omnibus work was a section dealing with his theory of the pulmonary circulation of the blood. If the work had not been so thoroughly suppressed by the book burners, this section might have established Servetus as a pioneer in early modern biological science.

Servetus found it discrete to take the alias M. de Villeneufve and to travel in disguise, but his was an ill-kept secret. He was tricked into giving medical attention to prisoners in Vienne, and there in jail was himself made prisoner. Happily he escaped over the wall, discarding a nightcap and bathrobe that he had donned for a walk in the prison yard. He was condemned in absentia by a civil tribunal in Lyon on evidence in part supplied by John Calvin. Unhappily he resolved to stop in Geneva on his way to practice medicine in Naples. In Geneva the French reformer John Calvin was enjoying new prestige as the spiritual leader of the reformed city. He was a long-standing opponent of Servetus; he had tried to convince him of the errors of his ways, had written against him, and sixteen years before in Paris had invited him to a debate for which Servetus failed to appear. Now Servetus went to hear Calvin preach and was recognized, denounced, and brought to trial before a state court for blasphemy, a capital offense. Calvin argued and pleaded with him in vain to change his erroneous opinions. Finally, when he was sentenced to be burned, Calvin sought for him the less painful execution by beheading, but the law was upheld. The hunted heretic was burned at the stake on October 27, 1553. He was a victim of a misguided zeal for truth on the part of his foes, who seem to have believed that they were acting in the best interest even of Servetus himself.

One man, perhaps the greatest liberal in an intolerant age, defended Servetus and decried his oppression: Sebastian Castellio of Savoy. Castellio went as a religious refugee to Strassburg, where he met Calvin in his home. In 1541 he accompanied Calvin to Geneva and taught in the academy there, but was rejected for ordination because of his nonconformist views. He moved on to Basel, where he expected to live out his days in peace as a professor of Greek. He was an intellectual, professorial type who, unlike Servetus, did not really relish controversy. In his work *On the Art of Doubting and Being Sure, of Knowing and Being Ignorant* he argued that of the three sources of knowledge—experience, revelation, and reason—the first two must be subjected to the third. Since many traditional dogmas are not subject to reason, they must be considered matters of faith. The written word of God is the treasure-house of divine thought, to which man's inward spirituality provides the key. He shifted the emphasis away from inerrancy to sincerity as the precondition for divine favor. Defining sincerity as a man's interior loyalty to that which he believes to be true, he argued that integrity is the indispensable factor in the quest for truth. Truth must be sought with passion and utter transparency. No one, not even Calvin, has the right to sit in judgment on another; Servetus had been a martyr for the truth as he saw it.

Castellio had differed with Calvin over the credal statement on Christ's descent into hell and on the allegorical interpretation of the *Song of Solomon*, which he took to be a love song; now the Servetus affair brought them to the breaking point. In 1554 Calvin wrote his *Defense of the Orthodox Trinity Against the Errors of Michael Servetus*. That same year Castellio, using the pseudonym of Martin Bellius, wrote his most famous work, *Concerning Heretics, Whether They Are to Be Persecuted and How They Are to Be Treated*, a book that has appeared in 133 editions through the years. In the preface, addressed to Christoph of Württemberg, he asked the prince how he would feel if he were to leave his subjects and instruct them to await his return clad in white garments, and then found them, when he came back, quarreling and even stabbing each other. So will Christ be displeased to find his followers fighting and even putting one another to death, he wrote. In the text Castellio presented many quotations in favor of liberty of conscience and toleration taken from the works of Erasmus, Luther, Sebastian Franck, and many others. He decried the persecution of the Anabaptists in a moving passage: "They were miserably slain, even those who were not in arms, and what is still more cruel, the suppression was carried on not only by the sword but also in books, which reach farther and last longer, or rather forever perpetuate this savagery."[6] His thesis that tolerance and mutual love constitute a Christian imperative, however, ran counter to contemporary notions of the absoluteness of orthodox formulations. Calvin considered him a Pelagian monster and he was finally brought to trial for heresy. But he died in 1563 during the proceedings, a death that Calvin's understudy, Theodore Beza, viewed as a punishment from God.

Montaigne believed that all posterity owed Castellio a great debt. The Anabaptists, spiritualists, and evangelical rationalists, though relatively few in number, contributed enormously to some of the finest modern liberal traditions. Many heroic deeds of passive resistance to oppressive authority and much intellectual cultivation were necessary for the development of true toleration and genuine religious freedom. The Anglo-American philosopher Alfred North Whitehead once observed that the impractical ethics of Christianity constituted one of the most remarkable instruments of human progress ever devised. In trying to live out literally some of the most impractical injunctions of the Sermon on the Mount, the Anabaptists confronted society with an embarrassing image reflected in the mirror of the evangelical law. The authorities understood well how to fight this threat to their complacency and security, but failed to suppress all nonconformists or to root out their ideas. The concept of the necessity of religious uniformity within a state was to enjoy a period of dominance in the second half of the sixteenth century and a good part of the seventeenth century. But eventually the ideas of toleration and religious liberty broke through and became a basic part of the Western liberal inheritance. There are direct lines of influence from the spiritualists and evangelical rationalists to the *philosophes* of the eighteenth century. When a modern man reads the *Martyr's Mirror* or Foxe's *Book of Martyrs* and reflects on the price in human misery and blood paid by many religious folk for the limited progress made by mankind toward genuine brotherly love, he is moved to ask with George Bernard Shaw's St. Joan, "O God that madest this beautiful earth, when will it be ready to receive thy saints? How long, O Lord, how long?"

Bibliography

Zwingli and Bullinger:
Bouvier, André. *Henri Bullinger: Réformateur et conseilleur oecumenique.* Paris, 1940.
Bromiley, G. W. *Zwingli and Bullinger,* vol. 24 of *Library of Christian Classics.* London and Philadelphia, 1953.

---

[6] Cited in *ibid.*, pp. 318–19.

Courvoisier, Jacques. *Zwingli: A Reformed Theologian.* Richmond, Va., 1963.
Farner, Oskar. *Huldrych Zwingli,* 4 vols. Zurich, 1943–1954.
————. *Zwingli the Reformer.* New York, 1952.
Fast, Heinold. *Heinrich Bullinger und die Täufer.* Weierhof, 1959.
Garside, Charles. *Zwingli and the Fine Arts.* New Haven, 1966.
Jackson, Samuel M. *Huldreich Zwingli.* New York, 1901.
Köhler, Walther. *Das Marburger Religionsgespräch.* Leipzig, 1929.
————. *Huldrych Zwingli,* 2nd ed. Stuttgart, 1952.
Locher, Gottfried. *Die Theologie Huldrych Zwingli im Lichte seiner Christologie.* Zurich, 1952.
Rich, Arthur. *Die Anfänge der Theologie Huldrych Zwinglis.* Zurich, 1949.
Richardson, C. C. *Zwingli and Cranmer on the Eucharist.* Evanston, Ill., 1949.
Rilliet, Jean. *Zwingli: Third Man of the Reformation.* Philadelphia, 1964.
Rupp, E. Gordon. *Patterns of Reformation: Oecolampadius, Karlstadt, Müntzer.* Philadelphia, 1969.
Staedtke, Joachim. *Die Theologie des jungen Bullinger.* Zurich, 1962.
Stähelin, Rudolf. *Huldreich Zwingli: Sein Leben und Wirken,* 2 vols. Basel, 1895–1897.
Walton, Robert C. *Zwingli's Theocracy.* Toronto, 1968.

Anabaptists and Mennonites:
Armour, Rollin S. *Anabaptist Baptism: A Representative Study.* Scottdale, Pa., 1966.
Bax, Belfort. *The Rise and Fall of the Anabaptists.* London and New York, 1903.
Bender, Harold S. *Menno Simon's Life and Writings.* Scottdale, Pa., 1936.
————. *The Life and Letters of Conrad Grebel,* vol. 1. Goshen, Ind., 1950.
Bergsten, Torsten. *Balthasar Hubmaier: Seine Stellung zu Reformation und Täufertum.* Kassel, 1961.
Blanke, Fritz. *Brothers in Christ: The History of the Oldest Anabaptist Congregation, Zollikon near Zurich.* Scottdale, Pa., 1961.
Dyck, Cornelius J. *The Legacy of Faith: The Heritage of Menno Simon.* Newton, Kans., 1962.
Friedmann, Robert. *Mennonite Piety Through the Centuries.* Goshen, Ind., 1949.
————. *Hutterite Studies.* Goshen, Ind., 1961.
Gratz, Delbert. *Bernese Anabaptists.* Scottdale, Pa., 1953.
Hershberger, Guy F., ed. *The Recovery of the Anabaptist Vision.* Scottdale, Pa., 1957.
Hillerbrand, Hans. *A Bibliography of Anabaptism, 1520–1630.* Elkhart, Ind., 1962.
Horst, Irvin. *A Bibliography of Menno Simon (c. 1496–1561).* Nieuwkoop, 1962.
Keeney, William. *The Development of Dutch Anabaptist Thought and Practice, 1539–1564.* Nieuwkoop, 1968.
Krahn, Cornelius. *Dutch Anabaptism: Origin, Spread, Life, and Thought, 1450–1600.* The Hague, 1968.
Littell, Franklin H. *The Anabaptist View of the Church.* Chicago, 1952.
Oyer, John S. *Lutheran Reformers Against Anabaptists.* The Hague, 1964.
Peachey, Paul. *Die soziale Herkunft der Schweizer Täufer in der Reformationszeit.* Karlsruhe, 1954.
Smith, C. H. *The Story of the Mennonites,* 3rd ed. Newton, Kans., 1950.
Smithson, R. J. *The Anabaptists.* London, 1953.
Vedder, H. C. *Balthasar Hubmaier: The Leader of Anabaptists.* New York, 1905.

Verduin, Leonard. *The Reformers and Their Stepchildren.* Grand Rapids, 1964.

Williams, George H. *The Radical Reformation.* Philadelphia, 1962.

―――― and Mergal, Angel M., eds. *Spiritual and Anabaptist Writers,* vol. 25 of *Library of Christian Classics.* London and Philadelphia, 1957.

Spiritualists and evangelical rationalists:

Bainton, Roland H. *The Travail of Religious Liberty.* Philadelphia, 1951.

――――. *Hunted Heretic: The Life and Death of Servetus.* Boston, 1953.

Cohn, Norman. *The Pursuit of the Millennium.* New York, 1957.

Coutts, A. *Hans Denck, Humanist and Heretic.* Edinburgh, 1927.

Fast, Heinold, ed. *Der linke Flügel der Reformation: Glaubenszeugnisse der Täufer, Spiritualisten, Schwärmer, und Antitrinitarier.* Bremen, 1962.

Fulton, John F. *Michael Servetus, Humanist and Martyr.* New York, 1953.

Hillerbrand, Hans J. *A Fellowship of Discontent.* New York, 1967.

Kot, Stanislas. *Socinianism in Poland: The Social and Political Ideas of the Polish Antitrinitarians.* Boston, 1957.

Maier, Paul L. *Caspar Schwenkfeld on the Person and Work of Christ.* Assen, 1959.

Wilbur, Earl Morse. *A History of Unitarianism.* Cambridge, Mass., 1945.

CHAPTER 16

Calvin
and
Calvinism

The great gift of France to the Reformation was her brilliant son
John Calvin. In France he was born, educated, attracted to the evangelical faith,
arrested, driven into exile, and finally supported by a militant minority of followers
ready to fight and die for their beliefs. The campaigns of the third Habsburg-Valois
war forced Calvin to take an indirect route in his flight from Paris to Strassburg.
In a hotel room in Geneva, where Calvin intended to stay no longer than a single
night, the fiery red-haired and red-bearded French reformer Guillaume Farel, who
with Pierre Viret had driven "popery" from that city, prevailed on him to stay and
help in the reform of Geneva. Farel threatened the curse of God upon Calvin's
retirement and the tranquillity of his studies if he should refuse to assist in the
cause. "Guillaume Farel detained me at Geneva," Calvin wrote years later in the
preface to his *Commentary on the Psalms*, dated July 22, 1557, "not so much by
counsel and exhortation as by a dreadful imprecation, which I felt to be as if God
had from heaven laid His mighty hand upon me to arrest me." Calvin in his innermost being felt himself to be God's man, a conviction that, combined with his extraordinary abilities, raised him above the ranks of ordinary men. He became one
of the truly formative influences upon Western history and the character of Western man. "To omit Calvin from the forces of Western evolution," wrote the British
author and statesman Lord John Morley, "is to read history with one eye shut."

Calvin—The Man and the Message

CALVIN WAS ONE of those strong and consistent men of history whom people either liked or disliked, adored or abhorred. Shortly before his death he observed that the people of nearby Bern "have always feared me more than they have loved me." The two things that even the most untutored man of our day will presume to know about him are that he had a bad temper and that he taught the predestination of many men to hell. In actual fact, both the man and his doctrine were far more subtle and complex than the popular image would suggest.

When Calvin was born on July 10, 1509, in Noyon in Picardy, northeast of Paris, Luther had already spent four years in the monastery. While Calvin was learning to read, Luther was delivering his lectures on the Psalms, Romans, and Galatians. He was a boy of eight when Luther published his ninety-five theses. The generation that separated them explains the novel emphases in Calvin. Luther's volcanic theological affirmations needed now to be systematized and set in order. Amorphous and ineffective Protestant church organizations needed to be given a form and structure that would enable the movement to maintain itself against a militant Catholic majority and crushing blows by hostile states. Calvin and Luther were temperamentally quite different. The younger man was shy to the point of diffidence, precise and restrained, except for sudden flashes of anger. He was severe, but scrupulously just and truthful, self-contained and somewhat aloof. He had many acquaintances but few intimate friends. The older man was sociable to the point of volubility, free and open, warm and cordial with people of all stations of life. But in spite of their differences in personality, Calvin and Luther retained a mutual respect for each other that was rooted in their confessional agreement.

In 1539 Luther was tremendously pleased with Calvin's *Open Letter to Cardinal Sadoleto on Why the Reformation Was Necessary.* In a letter of October 14 in that same year Luther expressed his joy that Calvin was serving in Strassburg at the side of his other friends. Melanchthon reported that Calvin stood high in Luther's favor. In April 1545 Luther took a copy of Calvin's *Instruction and Confession of Faith* from the shelf of a Wittenberg bookstore, perused it, and observed: "The author is certainly a scholarly and pious man. If only Oecolampadius and Zwingli had been as clear from the beginning, such a terrible quarrel would never have happened." He thought Calvin to be as thorough as Zwingli was superficial. Calvin, for his part, warmly defended Luther against detractors and once wrote to counter Heinrich Bullinger's criticisms of the older reformer:

> Remember what a great man Luther is. How marvelous are his gifts, how bravely, how firmly, how ably, how scholarly, how effectively he has constantly labored in the destruction of the Antichrist in the spread of the doctrine of salvation. I hold

to what I have repeatedly said, "Even if he would call me a devil, I would yet honor him and call him an excellent servant of God."[1]

In the Frenchman Calvin the German reformer had a successor of a quality, stature, and strength worthy of himself. It was ironic that their followers did not appreciate the extent of their agreement.

Calvin's development into the second man of the Reformation was in no way predictable, for the initial influences on his young life seemed to head him in quite the opposite direction, and his evangelical conversion seems almost to have caught Calvin himself by surprise. His father, Gerard Cauvin, was a procurator and then an apostolic notary to the cathedral chapter in Noyon, where John was born as the second of five sons in their house off the grain market in the center of town, under the very shadow of the church. Gerard guided his son toward an ecclesiastical career. When he was only eleven John was appointed to a chaplaincy attached to the altar of La Gésine in the cathedral and received the tonsure, although of course he was not ordained. Following a common practice of the time, his father hired a qualified substitute to say mass for him for a small percentage of the benefice. He went to live and study with a noble family, the Hangest de Montmors, where he learned not only grammar but a certain aristocratic bearing that he always retained. Years later, when a French refugee addressed him as "Brother Calvin," Calvin put him off with a chilly "Monsieur Calvin to you!" In August 1523 Calvin went with the young Montmors to Paris, where he lived with an uncle and attended the Collège de la Marche as a day student. One of the best Latin teachers of the time, Mathurin Cordier, there developed in fourteen-year-old Calvin that stylistic clarity and precision which became marks of his writing. When, twenty-seven years later, Calvin dedicated his *Commentary on the First Epistle to the Thessalonians* to Cordier, a "man of excellent piety and learning," he declared that his instruction had been so helpful that it was responsible for all his subsequent progress. "I wish to witness to posterity that if any should profit from my writings, they ought to recognize that it derived in part from you!" Cordier followed his pupil into exile, taught in later years in Neuchâtel, and died in the same year as Calvin in Geneva.

Calvin transferred to the Collège de Montaigu, more scholastic and ecclesiastical in nature, and remained there until 1527. Erasmus and Rabelais had studied in this college and complained of its stultifying atmosphere. There Calvin was enrolled in an elementary arts course. Among his personal friends, besides the Montmors, were the sons of the king's Swiss physician, Michel and Nicholas Cop, and his cousin Pierre Robert, better known by the sobriquet Olivetan, earned by his habit of burning the midnight oil. Calvin left the school about the time that Ignatius Loyola arrived, but Calvin was then only eighteen, while Loyola was thirty-

---

[1] Calvin to Bullinger, November 25, 1544, cited in Emanuel Stickelberger, *Calvin: A Life* (Richmond, Va., 1954), p. 70.

six, and they probably had little or no contact. In September 1527 the canons of Noyon rewarded Calvin's progress with the curacy of St. Martin de Marteville, which he exchanged two years later for the curacy of Pont l'Évêque, a town near Noyons. Though not ordained, he preached a number of sermons and seemed on his way to taking orders in the church. "I was," he commented many years later, "obstinately devoted to the superstitions of popery."

At this very point, however, Calvin began moving in the direction of a secular career. His father had a falling out with the canons and came to favor a more remunerative law career for his gifted son. The fact that his father was under the ban of excommunication at the time of his death in 1531 must have had an unsettling effect upon the son as well. Olivetan had begun serious study of the Scriptures, which led to his pioneering translation of the Bible into French. Olivetan's studies also raised problems in his mind about the nonbiblical foundation of Roman Catholic teachings and practice, problems that he may have discussed with Calvin. In March 1528, at his father's suggestion, Calvin began the study of law at Orléans under Pierre Taisan de l'Étoile, a renowned jurist. He worked furiously and at the same time was captivated by the humanistic study of the classics. In the fall of 1529 he transferred to Bourges to study Roman law under the Italian legist Andrea Alciati. Melchior Wolmar, a German teacher and friend, taught him to read the New Testament in Greek and possibly introduced him to Lutheran theology. Though devoted now to classical scholarship, Calvin remained serious about religion, and he was deeply impressed by an inscription that he read in a church in Bourges: "Fear God, succor the poor, and bear in mind the end." Following the death of his father Calvin left Bourges for the Collège Fortet, where he read Greek and began the study of Hebrew. In April 1532 he published his first work, a commentary in Latin on Seneca's *De clementia*. It was a pedantic piece exhibiting a great deal of erudition. As a good young humanist he sent a copy to Erasmus.

Only eighteen months later Calvin was a convinced evangelical fleeing Paris for his life. In his preface to the *Commentary on the Psalms* Calvin related:

> God by a sudden conversion subdued and brought my mind to a teachable frame, which was more hardened in such matters than might have been expected from one at my early period of life. Having thus received some taste and knowledge of true godliness, I was immediately inflamed with so intense a desire to make progress therein, that although I did not altogether leave off other studies, I yet pursued them with less ardor.

Precisely when this profound change in Calvin occurred remains a mystery. After publishing his book on Seneca he went back to Orléans for a year, visited Noyon in August 1533, and by October returned to Paris. On All Saints' Day his friend Nicholas Cop delivered his inaugural address as the new rector of the university, written under Calvin's influence, in which he praised all the sciences for their usefulness but declared that they mean little next to the time-honored philosophy that "God's grace alone redeems from sins." There was much head-shaking during the oration, and within a matter of hours Cop was summoned before the parlement and had to flee to sanctuary in Basel. Friends warned Calvin and he too escaped, though his room was searched and his books and incriminating letters were taken. Around New Year of 1534 he took refuge under an assumed name with a friend, Louis du Tillet, in Angoulême, and made use of the library of the elder Tillet in preparation for the first version of his *Institutes of the Christian Religion*.

While in the southwest Calvin visited the venerable French humanist Lefèvre d'Étaples, who was spending the evening hours of his life under the protection of Marguerite d'Angoulême, queen of French Navarre and sister of Francis I. Their conversation was symbolic of the confrontation of Christian humanism and the Reformation:

LEFÈVRE: For heaven's sake, be moderate, so that you won't tear down the house of God which you intend to purge!
CALVIN: The building is too rotten to be patched up. It must be torn down and in its stead a new one must be built!
LEFÈVRE: Take heed that you may not be killed by the cracking walls. . . . You are chosen to be a mighty instrument of the Lord. Through you God will erect his kingdom in our land![2]

Calvin had received his great commission from the man who had urged everyone *"Christum ex fontibus praedicare,"* to preach Christ from the very fountains themselves, the Scriptures.

Thereafter, when not in jail, Calvin was on the move. He resigned his prebend in Noyon, was briefly imprisoned twice, went to Paris, and visited Orléans and Poitiers, where in a grotto near the city he celebrated the Lord's Supper according to a reformed rite for the first time, using a slab of rock for a communion table. The situation in France was tense and the Affair of the Placards brought things to a boil. On the morning of October 18, 1534, radical Protestants posted placards headed "True Articles on the Horrible Abuse of the Papal Mass" in Paris and other cities. One was even found tacked to the king's bedroom door in Amboise. Francis I dramatized his horror and outrage by accompanying a solemn procession to Nôtre Dame Cathedral, with tapers burning, to cleanse the city of Paris after this abomination. At a banquet held in the episcopal palace he pledged to purge this poison from the realm. Capitalizing on the subsequent upsurge of popular anger, he imprisoned hundreds of Protestants, burned thirty-five of them, executed

---

2 Theodore Beza, *Vita Calvini*, cited in Stickelberger, *Calvin*, pp. 23–24.

one of Calvin's own brothers, and the following year, to please Pope Paul III, issued a royal decree commanding the thorough suppression of heresy. Calvin fled with Louis du Tillet to Strassburg and then to Basel.

In Basel in March 1536 the printer Thomas Platter published Calvin's *Institutes*. It has recently been argued with some plausibility that although Calvin was under Lutheran influence while still in France, his personal conversion experience did not take place until after his arrival in Basel, and that it was in Basel that he actually wrote the *Institutes*. He wrote it, he said, "first that I might vindicate from unjust affront my brethren whose death was precious in the sight of the Lord, and, next, that some sorrow and anxiety should move foreign peoples, since the same sufferings threatened many." He dedicated the work to King Francis and warned him to desist from persecuting the faithful lest God avenge his own. He made a brief visit in April 1536 to the court of Renée, duchess of Ferrara, a cousin of Marguerite d'Angoulême, whose support he hoped to enlist. The attempt was futile, thanks to the duke's hostility, and Calvin later commented, "I only went to Italy in order that I might have the pleasure of leaving it." He returned to France incognito to arrange his affairs. On the way to sanctuary in Strassburg with his younger brother Antoine and his half sister Marie, he was importuned by Farel into staying in Geneva, his city of destiny.

Like the introduction of Bacon's *Novum organum*, Newton's *Principia*, and Kant's *Critique of Pure Reason*, the publication of the *Institutes* by the twenty-six-year-old John Calvin was an epochal event. Few scholars in Christendom have written so much as Calvin, except perhaps Augustine, Thomas, and Luther. Fewer still have written so much with such tremendous consistency. There is an awesome homogeneity in his writings, though they were produced over three decades. To know Calvin well requires extensive study of his sermons (of which some 2,025 are still extant in the public library in Geneva), his treatises, biblical commentaries, and correspondence, for he could write with anger and gentleness, in sorrow and exultation. And yet in a very special sense Calvin was a man of one book—the *Institutes*. As a systematic presentation of Christian theology it became the handbook of militant Protestantism and exercised an enormous influence upon Western thought, among friends and foes alike. In its French version (1541), done by Calvin himself, it had a formative influence upon the French language. All his life Calvin worked at improving the *Institutes*. The second edition of 1539 was twice the size of the first and the eighth edition of 1559 was twice the size of the seventh. Through these editions and some twenty-five impressions there is amplification but very little change; its theological core remained substantially unaltered. His biographer Theodore Beza relates how Calvin ate frugally, stayed up till midnight, and rose early in the morning to meditate on what he had studied. Calvin, like Dr. Johnson, was a man "born to grapple with libraries."

A "masterpiece of luminous argument," the *Institutes* presented a statement of faith of the persecuted Protestants and served as a manual of instruction for neophytes. The first edition was divided into six books on (1) the law, (2) faith, (3) prayer, (4) sacraments, (5) false sacraments, and (6) Christian liberty, ecclesiastical power, and civil liberty. The centrality of Paul and the influence of Augustine and Luther are evident throughout, although Calvin's comprehensive knowledge of the Scriptures and patristic writers also comes through in force. The law, or the commandment of God to love him above all things and one's neighbor as oneself, reveals to man his complete spiritual inadequacy. In the mirror of God's law man recognizes that he is hopelessly lost when confronted with God's command to be perfect, even as he is perfect. The law strikes fear in the hearts of sinners and is a schoolmaster leading men to Christ. Faith or trust in the promises of God and the benefits of Christ's sacrificial and atoning death is itself a gift of God. Faith is instilled by the Holy Spirit into the hearts of the elect, who approach God in prayers of supplication and thanksgiving and without spiritual pride. With the later Luther he reduced the sacraments to the two dominical institutions of baptism (for infants as well as adults) and the Lord's Supper, both of which are symbolic acts and means of grace because of the promise associated with them. Christ is spiritually present in the Lord's Supper, which is a true communion with him and not a renewed sacrifice of the transubstantiated bread and wine or merely a symbolic memorial. The final two books were highly polemic, attacking the Catholic sacramental-sacerdotal system, assaulting the episcopal hierarchy as unbiblical, and arguing that in the New Testament church the preachers and overseers, who were called shepherds, bishops, and elders or presbyters, served with the consent of the Christian congregations. He followed Luther's views on Christian liberty: that the Christian is the freest of all in being above the law but is the servant of all in acting willingly in love for the good of his fellow man. In the heat of controversy with Catholic foes and more latitudinarian or universalistic Protestant opponents during the decades following the publication of the *Institutes,* Calvin forged more forceful arguments, more rigorously logical and extreme positions, and more refined statements of his basic tenets, but the tenets themselves remained the same.

Melanchthon called Calvin *ille theologus,* the theologian. This tribute from the author of the *Loci communes* must puzzle those who know merely the familiar caricature of Calvin's theology symbolized by the mnemonic TULIP: *t*otal depravity, *u*nconditional election, *l*imited atonement, *i*rresistible grace, and *p*erseverance in faith. To see Calvin's theology in perspective, it is necessary not simply to define its component parts, but to proceed from its fundamental affirmation to its logical extensions. If Luther's central concern was the question of man's justification in the eyes of God, bestowed in mercy through Christ, Calvin's concern was to proclaim the power, grace, and glory of God, who has revealed himself to man in Christ. This order of priority is evident from the table of contents of the final edition of the *Institutes,* in which Book 1 treats of God the Father, Book 2 the Son, Book 3 the Holy Spirit, and Book 4 the Holy Catholic Church. Calvin's entire doctrine was intended to affirm the sovereignty of God and to vindicate his honor. The answers to the opening questions of the Westminster Shorter Catechism, though written a century after Calvin, faithfully reflect his spirit:

> Question 1. *What is the chief end of man?*
> Answer: Man's chief end is to glorify God, and to enjoy Him forever.
> Question 2. *What rule hath God given to direct us how we may glorify and enjoy Him?*
> Answer: The Word of God, which is contained in the Scriptures of the Old and New Testaments, is the only rule to direct us how we may glorify and enjoy Him.

God's providence embraces all reality, is cognizant of the least happening, and directs every occurrence in the natural and spiritual worlds. He who numbers the very hairs of a man's head and knows when a sparrow falls leaves nothing to blind fate or chance, but works in all and through all. Before the great majesty of God natural man stands helpless and uncomprehending. In a passage reflecting the influence of Augustine's phrase *finitum non est capax infiniti,* the finite cannot grasp the infinite, Calvin declared that man the creature cannot fathom the Creator, for to do so "would be to measure with the palm of his hand a hundred thousand heavens and earths and worlds. For God is infinite and when the heaven of heavens cannot contain Him, how can our minds comprehend Him?"[3] Before the great holiness of God sinful man is "brought to nothing by the incomprehensible brightness."[4] If God would "institute no medium of intercourse, and call us to a direct communication with heaven, the great distance at which we stand from Him would strike us with dismay and paralyze invocation."[5] In his favorite allegory of the labyrinth, Calvin described the fatal limitations of man's natural knowledge of God, which perceives "certain symbols of his presence" but can attain to no saving knowledge of him, and underlined the need for special revelation. T. H. L. Parker recapitulates Calvin's labyrinth imagery in this way:

> Man is lost in a maze of which he does not possess the plan, and however much he may attempt to find his way out, he always fails. He can never know God by himself, for his sin has led him into ignorance and a wrong-mindedness that prevents him from thinking his way through to the true idea of God. His mind is a veritable maze, with passages leading off to the worship of this or that idol. He has to worship some god, and he will invent a god, or perhaps many gods, to worship. "Men's conceptions of God are formed, not according to the representations He gives of Himself, but by the inventions of their own presumptuous imaginations. . . .

---

[3] John Calvin, *Commentary on Ezekiel* (1:28), in *Corpus Reformatorum,* ed. J. W. Baum *et al.,* 59 vols. (Halle, 1863–1900), vol. 40, col. 60.

[4] Calvin, *Commentary on Exodus* (33:20), in *ibid.,* vol. 25, col. 111.

[5] Calvin, *Commentary on the Psalms* (132:8), in *ibid.,* vol. 32, col. 346.

They worship, not God, but a figment of their own brains in His stead." For all his capabilities, man is a puzzled, groping creature, surrounded by that which is mysterious to him. He not only does not understand about God, but nor does he understand the world in which he lives; he does not even understand himself—whence he has come, why he lives or whither he goes. If help does not come to him from without he will never know God or find His kingdom.

But God, in His loving concern for man, reaches right to him where he is wandering imprisoned in the labyrinth, and gives him the guidance of the Holy Scriptures, which are like a thread, leading him through this maze of ignorance to the knowledge of God. "The light of the Divine countenance, which the Apostle himself says no man can approach unto, is like an inexplicable labyrinth to us, unless we are directed by the thread of the Word."[6]

Natural reason, even when aided by all the arts and sciences, cannot lead man to faith in the God who reveals himself in Christ. The Holy Spirit must move men's minds to understand that the humanity of Christ was "like a veil by which His divine majesty was concealed," but that in this person God's true nature, both just and loving, is revealed. Jesus Christ is called the image of the Father, Calvin explained, because "He sets forth and exhibits to us all that is necessary to be known of the Father.[7] For the naked majesty of God would, by its immense brightness, ever dazzle our eyes. It is therefore necessary for us to look on Christ, that is to come to the light." In Christ God has taken on mortal flesh, the source of blessing has been made subject to the curse, so that men might be redeemed from spiritual death and become partakers of righteousness and immortality.

Calvin viewed the church in dynamic terms, not merely as an institution or collection of believing individuals, but as God's covenantal people for whom and through whom God's eternal purposes are realized within the development of the total historical process. God's people in ancient times were running a race toward the goal of the full manifestation of God in Christ. God's chosen people, the spiritual Israel of the New Testament, conform to his will as instruments in his grand design for building a holy commonwealth on earth, culminating in the New Jerusalem hereafter.

It is against this background of daring and overpowering religious assertions that Calvin's doctrine of divine predestination must be understood. Only in the final edition of the *Institutes,* as a reaction to the polemical situation, did he spell out with complete clarity his definitive position on this fearful doctrine. The problem of "Why some and not others?" was implicit in the Old Testament concept of the chosen people. In preparing his powerful *Sermons on Deuteronomy* Calvin encountered the Mosaic pronouncement in Deuteronomy 7:7-8:

> It was not because you were more in number than any other people that the Lord set his love upon you and chose you, for you were the fewest of all peoples;

---

[6] T. H. L. Parker, *Portrait of Calvin* (Philadelphia, 1954), pp. 50–51.
[7] Calvin, *Commentary on 1 John* (2:22–23), in *Corpus Reformatorum,* vol. 55, col. 325.

but it is because the Lord loves you, and is keeping the oath which he swore to your fathers, that the Lord has brought you out with a mighty hand, and redeemed you from the house of bondage, from the hand of Pharaoh king of Egypt.

St. Augustine was a high double predestinarian. St. Thomas acknowledged the universality of God's prescience or foreknowledge and his election of a minority among men to salvation. Zwingli had stressed God's absolute right to choose and to reject whomever he willed. Luther found assurance in the belief that the faith of the elect was determined by God's eternal counsel and did not depend upon man's own weak will, but, except for some polemical passages in his treatise *On the Bondage of the Will* in which he overstated his own case, he left the question of why some were lost open, holding with the Scriptures that "the Lord is not willing that any should perish but that all should come to repentance." Men were lost necessarily through some fault of their own under God's permissive or secondary will. Calvin found such a paradoxical position untenable and pressed on to a logical solution that would exalt the sovereignty of God and reduce men to a state of absolute dependence. "It must remain a first principle with us," he wrote, "that there is no event which He has not ordained. Therefore if He has brought us to the saving knowledge of Himself, we must not doubt that His particular providence is watchful for our preservation, never permitting any event which it will not overrule for our eternal benefit." This tenet allowed the later Calvinists to sing with such bold confidence:

> The Lord our God is good,
> His mercy is forever sure;
> His truth at all times firmly stood
> And shall from age to age endure.

Most of Calvin's theological predecessors were perplexed, embarrassed, or anguished over the question of why some men were lost. Some clung to the universalistic hope suggested by Paul's Epistle to the Romans, Chapters 9–11, that just as Adam in the fall plunged all men into sin and death, so Christ will raise all men to righteousness and life. But Calvin was not one to mince words, and he made his meaning so clear that no one could misunderstand him:

> Predestination we call the eternal decree of God by which He has determined in Himself what He would have to become of every individual of mankind. For they are not all created with a similar destiny, but eternal life is fore-ordained for some and eternal damnation for others. Every man, therefore, being created for one or the other of these ends, we say is predestined either to life or to death.[8]

Calvin did not shrink from the consequences of the double predestination theory. He held that since God does not really will all men to be saved, Christ's death on

---

[8] Calvin, *Institutes of the Christian Religion,* trans. John Allen, 7th ed. (Philadelphia, 1936), vol. 2, bk. 3, chap. 21, p. 176.

the cross must have been intended for the salvation only of the elect and a sign of judgment upon the condemned. God created many men whom he had in his eternal counsels appointed for destruction. God could rightly condemn all men, and his decrees could not therefore impudently be called into question by sinful man. In Calvin's teaching even God's love seems to be but an instrument of his justice. This is that "horrible decree," as Calvin himself labeled it, which proved to be so fascinating to his later followers. Starting with Theodore Beza, they gave to it a position of prominence it never held in the total body of Calvin's own homiletical or exegetical writings. Quite tiresome in the English Puritans, it became absolutely terrifying from New England pulpits and in the preaching of the Scottish Presbyterians. The lines of Robert Burns catch the sulfurous odor of the double predestination doctrine:

> O Thou, wha in the heavens does dwell,
> Wha, as it pleases best Thysel',
> Sends one to heaven an' ten to hell
> A' for Thy glory
> And no for any gude or ill
> They've done afore thee.

Calvin cannot be fairly impugned for the games that later Calvinists played with his teachings. In commenting upon even such a ruthless enemy and persecutor of the Reformed Church as the French duke of Guise, Calvin expressly denied that any man could know here and now who belonged among the reprobate. Nor could a man know absolutely whether he himself belonged to the elect, although Calvin proposed three presumptive tests: a man's heartfelt profession of his faith, a decent and godly life, and participation in the sacraments of baptism and communion. Certainly he did not ever suggest that worldly success or material wealth was a sign of election to be coveted or demonstrated. The practical psychological effect of the doctrine was to inspire the children of light with an unshakable fortitude and invincible courage, for a favorite Bible passage of Calvin's read: "Because God is my defence I will not fear what man can do unto me." Calvin spawned a race of stalwart activists.

Calvin's Geneva

THE CITY OF GENEVA to which Calvin came almost by chance was destined to become his model Christian commonwealth and the center of militant Protestantism. Situated at the crossroads of French and Italian trade, the lovely city on Lake Leman was in a borderland position between the Swiss confederacy, still under the nominal overlordship of the empire, and the kingdom of France. During the first decades of the sixteenth century, Geneva, with the help of Catholic Fribourg and Protestant Bern, carried to a successful conclusion its long struggle for independence from its feudal and episcopal masters, the duke of Savoy and the bishop of Geneva, who was related to the house of Savoy. By 1519 the commune had checked the feudal forces repressing its urban development and depressing its commercial enterprise. By 1534 the city had succeeded in permanently exiling the notoriously immoral bishop and repudiating the house of Savoy. On a pattern of city government familiar at that time, the patrician class ruled through the Council of Two Hundred; the Little Council, with twenty-five members, exercised certain executive functions; and four syndics plus the city treasurer were elected by the general assembly. The council announced that it wished to see no changes made in the old religion. Its aristocratic conservative members declared that they wished to possess truth with no admixture of human fables and inventions. While they showed some openness toward new and fresh religious ideas, they wanted no changes in church organization. In his *Life of Calvin* Theodore Beza commented that although the Genevans had staged a political revolt against Savoy, they were still "very imperfectly enlightened in divine knowledge and had as yet scarcely emerged from the filth of the papacy."

Farel, Olivetan, and young Antoine Froment changed all that by undertaking a preaching and propaganda mission in Geneva. When the hapless bishop opened an attack on the city, he also opened up the possibility of allying the evangelical cause with the struggle for freedom and security. In a marathon debate on dogma in June 1535, Farel and Viret routed the incompetent Catholic defenders of the faith, then boldly occupied various churches, including the cathedral. Iconoclasts broke church windows and threw statues of saints down wells. In August the large council suspended celebration of the mass, and in subsequent months the Catholic clergy abandoned the city to the Protestant leaders. In January 1536 Protestant Bern defeated Savoy and occupied Geneva, but after much dickering agreed to independent status for the city. On May 21, 1536, in an exercise of Swiss democracy, with the male heads of families voting, the general assembly congregated in the cathedral and voted unanimously in favor of the evangelical form of worship. The councils undertook the proprietary supervision of the church, and it seemed that a state-church solution reminiscent of Zwingli's Zurich was in the making. At that moment Farel prevailed on John Calvin to remain in Geneva to assist in the reform of the city.

Calvin began his work in Geneva by expounding Paul's epistles in the church of St. Pierre, and a year later the magistrates, with the consent of the people, elected him preacher. He demonstrated his brilliance by defining his position between the Catholics on one side and the radicals on the other in a disputation with Catholic defenders in Lausanne in October 1536 and with the Anabaptists in March 1537. This debate turned into such a rout that the Council of Two Hundred stopped the verbal battle and drove out the hapless Anabaptists. Aiming at good order, the city government legally established the *Articles Concerning the Governance of the Church* on January 16, 1537. When Farel and Calvin drew up twenty-one articles as an *Instruction and Confession of Faith* directed against the radicals, the citizens were required to appear in groups of ten and swear adherence to this statement of belief. The climax to these reformatory efforts came with the adoption of the famous *Ordinances* of 1537. Although Calvin held to the divine sanction of secular authority, he sought to prevent government from encroaching upon the prerogatives of the church and interfering in its purely spiritual concerns. He therefore began moving toward a structure of church government that could be independent of the state. The question of morals, which had traditionally been legislated by the city council through sumptuary laws and moral regulations, he believed to be properly within the domain of the church. He therefore proposed that key people be appointed in every section of the city to oppose immorality and to report vice. Following the steps of admonition outlined by Christ in Matthew 18, the *Ordinances* urged first fraternal remonstrances to the erring brother himself, and then if there was no evident improvement his fault was to be told to the church. If the sinner continued to offend, he might then be publicly denounced by the minister and excluded from the Christian congregation. The visible church of Christ on earth was to preserve the high public morals of her members.

But forces of reaction and opposition were gathering strength. Many Genevans resented the leadership of Frenchmen and the growing number of French refugees within the city. Pierre Caroli, an emotionally unstable convert, as pastor in Lausanne sought to discredit the work of Viret in that city. Caroli held prayers for the dead to be of value, and in the ensuing controversy charged Calvin with anti-Trinitarian tendencies. The Bern city council decided in Calvin's favor and refused to allow Caroli to preach again in its territories, whereupon he returned to France and eventually to Catholicism. But the controversy had weakened Calvin's prestige and helped to undermine his position in Geneva.

In Geneva itself a strong opposition party developed under the leadership of a certain Jean Philippe, who resisted the innovations, the control of morals by the ministers, and the forced confessions of faith. In February 1538 Calvin's foes won election to office and the ministers denounced the victors from the pulpit. The government of Bern, meanwhile, sought to have the Bernese liturgical and sacramental rites introduced throughout its territories, including the use of unleavened bread in communion and the retention of baptismal fonts. Calvin and Farel were reluctant to accede to this demand in Geneva, where they had suspended the Bernese practices. They preached on Easter Day of 1538, although they had been forbidden by the Little Council to do so, but they refused to administer the Sacrament while such an uproar was going on. The next day the Council of Two Hundred met and ordered Calvin and Farel to get out of town within three days.

They left for Bern and from there went to a synodical meeting in Zurich, where they explained their views on ecclesiastical structure and discipline and received general approbation. Farel returned to Neuchâtel, and the leader of the evangelical movement in Strassburg, Martin Bucer, persuaded Calvin to become the pastor of a congregation of some four hundred French refugees there. They were barely able to support him, but Calvin lived modestly and worked conscientiously as both minister and scholar. Bucer's moderation and concern for Protestant unity impressed Calvin very favorably. Calvin prepared a French liturgy, drawing heavily on Bucer's, which became a prototype for Calvinist services. For church music he favored the singing of psalms rather than chants or organ music, and prepared an edition of eighteen psalms set to music. He revised the *Institutes* (1539), did a *Commentary on the Epistle to the Romans,* and published a *Tract on the Lord's Supper,* which showed the influence of Bucer's views on the spiritual presence of Christ in the Sacrament. He lectured on theology at Johannes Sturm's famous secondary school for the liberal arts. He also reflected Bucer's ecumenical concern and accompanied him to the conference on Christian reunion at Frankfort sponsored by Charles V in 1539. The next year he attended the colloquies at Hagenau and Worms, and in 1541 he was sent as an official representative of Strassburg to the colloquy at Regensburg, where he saw the conciliatory Catholic cardinal Contarini and Melanchthon in action.

His tremendous labor so exhausted his strength that Bucer and other friends urged him to marry so that he would be better cared for. He resisted the idea: "I shall not belong to those who are accused of attacking Rome as the Greeks fought Troy, only to be able to take a wife." But soon thereafter Melanchthon commented, "Well, well! It seems to me that our theologue is thinking of taking a future spouse." Calvin came to concede that his friends might have a good idea, and cooperated in the search for a bride. She should be, as he put it quite unromantically, "modest, decent, plain, thrifty, patient, and able to look after my health." History had moved on; whereas Luther had married a former nun, Calvin chose a widow with three children. She was Idelette de Bure, widow of a radical from Liège whom Calvin had converted from Anabaptism. Calvin was an affectionate and considerate husband, though quite prosaic, and the marriage was successful. In a letter largely concerned with other things he referred matter-of-factly to the birth of their only child, Jacques, who was born prematurely on July 28, 1542, but lived only a few days. Idelette never regained her health and died in 1549—of weakness, and not, as some of Calvin's latter-day detractors have asserted, of boredom.

Geneva, meanwhile, had not forgotten Calvin. The city was torn with dissension, for one party, known as the Guillermins after Guillaume Farel, led by a prominent citizen named Ami Perrin, refused to acknowledge the new preachers who had replaced the exiled reformers. The Catholics had renewed hope of regaining the city. At that point, in May 1539, the Erasmian bishop of Carpentras,

Cardinal Jacopo Sadoleto, composed his famous appeal to the people of Geneva to return home to Rome. In the colorful prose of Theodore Beza, Sadoleto, "observing his opportunity in the circumstances which had occurred, and thinking that he would easily ensnare the flock, when deprived of its distinguished pastors, under the pretext of neighborliness ... sent a letter to his so-styled most Beloved Senate, Council, and People of Geneva, omitting nothing which might tend to bring them back into the lap of the Romish Harlot." Sadoleto argued the inerrancy of the Catholic Church, since the "Holy Spirit constantly guides her public and universal decrees and councils." He saw the key question for the Genevans as "whether to accord with the whole Church, and faithfully observe her decrees, and laws, and sacraments, or to assent to men seeking dissension and novelty." The Little Council referred the letter to Bern and the Council of Bern asked Calvin to reply, which he did, composing his answer in six days during mid-August. Calvin's response reflected the impact of his own conversion to evangelical Christianity and argued especially for the conception of the church as the communion of all believers in Christ and in favor of the doctrine of justification by faith alone.

Calvin's remarkable performance made a great impact in Geneva and helped to strengthen the Guillermins. Internal strife increased when the anti-Calvin party in power made too many concessions in legal negotiations with Bern. A riot in June 1540 precipitated the arrest and execution of Jean Philippe on the charge of having killed a citizen in a street brawl. The Guillermins quickly gained control and invited Calvin to return to Geneva. Reluctantly he yielded to pressure and went back to Geneva on September 13, 1541, a fateful step for Christendom. He was welcomed back with public acclaim.

Calvin had matured a great deal during his three years in Strassburg. A man of medium size, he had a pallid complexion and dark hair and beard. Contemporaries commented upon his alert, clear, and lustrous eyes. He dressed simply, ate little, and slept less. He was quick-witted, observant, and gifted with a remarkable memory. He could be lighthearted and even facetious, and he had a special penchant for puns. "We are nowhere forbidden to laugh," he wrote in the section on Christian liberty in the *Institutes*, "or to be satisfied with food, or to annex new possessions to those already enjoyed by ourselves or our ancestors, or to be delighted with music or to drink wine." But his manner was usually grave and he spoke simply and directly, with deliberation and great weight. After his death the Little Council observed that God had given him "a character of great majesty."

The historian Merle d'Aubigné called Calvin "*the* legislator of the renovated church." On his return to Geneva Calvin set about almost immediately to reorder the church. The *Ecclesiastical Ordinances* of 1541 developed a mature Presbyterian polity. The *Ordinances,* which were approved by both councils and by the general assembly on November 20, provided for the rule of the church by four sets of officers. (1) The pastors were the ministers of the gospel; they were coopted by the venerable Company of Pastors, approved by the council, and presented to the people and clergy for approval. (2) The doctors held the very important position of teachers in charge of Christian education. (3) The elders, or presbyters, were twelve outstanding laymen chosen to assist the pastors in looking after the spiritual welfare of the congregations, and with them made up the governing consistory, which came to be known also as the presbytery. (4) The deacons administered civic charities. A city treasurer handled salaries and city councilors supervised the physical plant. Laymen, usually elders, were also chosen to serve as morals police in each of the three parishes; in this capacity they admonished sinners and reported the impenitent or intransigent ones.

Meanwhile Calvin continued his work on a reformed order of worship. He published an edition of fifty psalms in metrical translation by Clément Marot and a revised liturgy and catechism, in which he declared, "For the worship of God we have not found better songs, nor any more suitable for use, than the psalms of David, which the Holy Spirit Himself writ and wrought."

Thanks to his tremendous prestige and imposing personality, Calvin unofficially controlled the consistory, which was primarily a morals court. The consistory exercised the power of excommunication independently of the secular government, and struggled to prevent interference by the government in matters of doctrine and church discipline. It was the central switchboard for the network of morality intelligencers in the city. The minutes of the consistory, preserved from February 16, 1542, on, reveal how it reviewed and judged the most minuscule offenses. Vestigial remains of Catholic folkways and superstitious practices were reviewed and punished. One woman possessed a copy of the *Legenda aurea,* or lives of the saints; a barber had given a tonsure to a priest; a goldsmith had made a chalice for the mass; a man had called the pope a good man; a woman had tried to cure her sick husband by tying a walnut shell with a spider in it around his neck. Lewdness or breaches in strict morality were ferreted out and punished; the investigators even went so far as to question children about their parents. Indecent dancing, a dress with a low neckline, card playing, and drunkenness drew stiff penalties. Calvin was particularly adamant against prostitution, for which Geneva had enjoyed a considerable reputation. Although he urged a stronger punishment, the council decreed in 1558 that second offenders should be marched through the streets wearing a red hat, the strumpet to be heralded by a trumpet. Calvin succeeded in having the taverns closed and replaced by decent and orderly cafés, with a French Bible on the premises for reference during serious discussions, but after a time he had to yield to consumer demand and allow the taverns to be reopened. Serious cases of witchcraft, heresy, adultery, blasphemy, and sedition that threatened the public order were referred to the civil authorities. There is even a story of a citizen jailed for naming his dog Calvin. In one four-year period these cases, which not infrequently involved confessions extorted by torture, resulted in fifty-eight executions and seventy-six sentences to exile. Because of his legal training and civic-mindedness, Calvin was consulted by the syndics and councils on many purely secular matters. But Geneva was far from being the theocracy historical legends have made it. The Company of Pastors was more nearly an administrative body than was the consistory, but it was always subject to the city councils.

Opposition to Calvin and the rule of the consistory naturally arose. One group of foes, whom Calvin labeled the Libertines, reacted against the moralistic regime, and another group, whom he considered heretics, challenged his doctrinal positions. The first real test of strength developed in January 1546, when a playing card manufacturer, Pierre Ameaux, who faced financial losses and possible bankruptcy, denounced Calvin as a foreign meddler, a wicked man, and a purveyor of false doctrine. Calvin was not satisfied when the council sentenced Ameaux to kneel before Calvin in front of the council and ask his forgiveness, for the offense had been made public, he argued, and therefore the punishment should be public; so the council forced the hapless fellow to march through the city streets in a shirt, holding a taper, and imploring divine mercy. When a placard denouncing and threatening the ministers was found on the pulpit of the church of St. Pierre in June 1546, a prime suspect was seized by the councils, tortured, and beheaded. Calvin's erstwhile supporter Ami Perrin, who had helped bring him back to Geneva, turned against Calvin when the consistory disciplined his father-in-law, brother-in-law, and wife, who were members of one of the best families of Geneva. Perrin became a syndic in 1553, a year that saw many Libertines elected to office, and headed a movement to abrogate the consistory's power of excommunication and to restore it to the council. At that point the Servetus case developed and Calvin emerged with his escutcheon unsullied and his prestige and authority thereafter virtually unchallenged.

The Servetus incident was also the last of the major challenges to Calvin's doctrinal definitions. Understandably it was his extreme solution to the predestinarian problem that stirred up the most serious criticisms against him. A Catholic, Albert Pighius, conditioned to the doctrine of prevenient grace and subsequent cooperation in achieving justification before God, questioned Calvin's teaching. But in the subsequent exchange Calvin absolutely overwhelmed Pighius and convinced him of the correctness of his own more Augustinian teaching. It was this same issue that roused the Parisian Jerome Hermes Bolsec, a former Carmelite friar, to oppose Calvin in 1551. Bolsec had renounced his Catholic faith and had fled to Veigny, a village not far from Geneva, in order to practice medicine. It is fascinating to note how many medical people became doctrinal deviationists and heretics in this period, just as many Renaissance humanists and reformers had studied law before turning to classical letters or theology. Bolsec tried to convince the Genevan ministers that Calvin's doctrine made God the author of sin, which was repugnant and false. Calvin denounced Bolsec to the Little Council as a contumelious slanderer and heretic. After consultations with other Swiss city councils, which revealed no consensus on the matter, the council exiled Bolsec from Geneva. He returned to France and to the Catholic Church, taking vengeance on Calvin with a vicious and slanderous biography of him, published in 1577, after Bolsec's death.

Calvin's strength of character never stood out more clearly than during his last illness and death. Though weakened by years of overwork, anxiety, and concern for the church, he continued to labor long hours. "Would you that the Lord should find me idle when he comes?" he asked of friends who urged him to rest. When he was so sick that he could not carry out his duties, he refused to receive his regular clerk's stipend for work he could no longer do. His estate, in fact, amounted to very little, for although his income had been substantial, he had given much of it away to charities. On February 6, 1564, he preached his last sermon. On May 2 he wrote his last letter—to Farel, who hurried from Neuchâtel to be with him during those final days. He was working on a *Commentary on Joshua* at the time of his death and with this he entered into the promised land. At the end, wrote Theodore Beza, "nothing seemed left but his spirit." On May 27, in his fifty-fifth year, he died quietly in Beza's arms. The next day, in accordance with his own wish, he was buried in an unmarked grave in the common cemetery of Plain-palais.

Calvin was indeed a man of great courage and complete dedication. Beza wrote, "I have been a witness of him for sixteen years and I think that I am fully entitled to say that in this man there was exhibited to all an example of the life and death of the Christian, such as it will not be easy to depreciate, such as it will be difficult to emulate." For all his faults, his willful tenacity, his impatience and sudden flares of temper, his lack of spontaneity, generosity, and openness, Calvin stands out as a spiritual giant in a time of great turmoil. "Calvin succeeded," the mild nineteenth-century skeptic Ernst Renan concluded, "because he was the most Christian man of his age." Calvin would have considered this a false or at best an ambivalent judgment.

Calvinism in Europe

CALVINISM IN FRANCE

One of Calvin's devoted followers, François Hotman, wrote to him in 1556 that in Geneva was engendered that spirit which raised up a new race of "martyrs in Gaul, whose blood is the testimony of thy doctrine and thy church." Calvin's heart was with his fellow Frenchmen. His hopes were high that France might someday become a truly Christian commonwealth as he conceived it, and he wished that meanwhile the reformed churches and evangelical Christians would be allowed to worship in peace according to their consciences. From Geneva he sent out an army of missionaries inspired and educated to serve the reformed congregations coming into being throughout France. Calvin carried on a mountainous correspondence with the burghers, nobles, and princes sympathetic to the evangelical cause or already convinced believers. He wrote to such powerful men as King Antoine of Navarre, the prince of Condé, and Admiral Coligny. He wrote as well to young ministers and martyrs, such as the five prisoners of Lyon, who were arrested while they were on their way from Geneva to undertake a ministry in France, and sealed their devotion to the cause with their own blood. No one who asked Calvin's intervention went without aid; he wrote to help the unemployed find jobs, to recommend tutors for the children of gentlemen, to secure admission for pupils to boarding schools, to find aid for the poor, and to encourage evangelists to be mighty in the spirit. His correspondence would easily fill thirty-five volumes. Calvin confided to a friend, "I do not have time to look out of my house at the blessed sun, and if things continue thus I shall forget what it looks like. When I have settled my usual business, I have so many letters to write, so many questions to answer, that many a night is spent without my bringing any offering of sleep to nature."

In the earliest phase of French Protestantism the lines were not very clearly differentiated between Erasmian or mystical reform impulses and Lutheran evangelicalism infiltrating from Germany. By the decade of the 1550s, however, French Protestantism had taken on a Genevan cast as French exiles returned to their homeland to propagate their faith and as Calvinist literature was spread in increasingly wide circles. Small groups of the faithful would meet secretly in private homes or barns, in fields or groves, in caves or any conceivable hideaway. As the nucleus grew into a larger congregation, they often petitioned Calvin to send them a minister, and some prospered to such an extent that they even requested assistant ministers. Calvin sent as many as he could. They traveled by night, hid in attics and false rooms behind chimneys, and used secret routes. They carried with them copies of the Olivetan Bible in French, the Genevan psalter, and Calvin's treatises.

The year 1559 was of tremendous importance for Calvinist expansion, owing to the founding of the Geneva Academy. Once again the influence of Strassburg made itself felt, for the pioneer humanist-reformed gymnasium headed by Johannes Sturm served as a model for the academy. The college offered humanistic training in Latin, Greek, and Hebrew, as well as in philosophy and theology. The consistory, with the approval of the council, appointed the faculty, and it recruited top men from the Lausanne Academy who had been expelled from the canton of Vaud by Bern, such as Pierre Viret and the Greek scholar Theodore Beza, who became the head of the academy. The institution, known today as the University of Geneva, immediately attracted young men from all parts of Europe, who returned home as bearers of Calvin's message. In 1561 the French government lodged a formal protest with the city of Geneva for aiding and abetting Protestant agents in French territory. In that same year the Protestant admiral Coligny estimated that France had some 2,150 Calvinist congregations. The term Huguenots, as the French Calvinists came to be called, perhaps was a corruption of *Eidgenossen,* the Swiss "confederates." The *Aignos* were the Genevan supporters of the rebellion against Savoy, who were friendly to the *Eidgenossen.* The name was later applied to the Genevan Protestants. This etymology appears as early as 1562.

Calvinism made such tremendous advances in France that in the year 1559 a synod met in Paris to organize a nationwide church. As in Geneva, the local congregation was to be governed by a consistory, the district by an assembly or colloquy, and the province by a synod, with the provincial synods organized under a national synod. Calvinism made its greatest progress in Navarre, Dauphiné, eastern Provence, Normandy, Orléans, and Orléanais. But it was unable to consolidate its gains and realize its plans for a national organization, for the French monarchy opposed the movement with ever greater consistency, rigor, and effectiveness. That the monarchy could strike with the fervor and abandon of a medieval crusade was demonstrated in 1545, when it launched a bloody attack on the Waldensians in southern France, taking the lives of hundreds of people who espoused the ideals of poverty and humility taught by Peter Waldo centuries before. The new heretics were to fare no better. King Francis I persecuted the Protestants, fiercely at times but sporadically, for his wars with the Habsburgs kept him preoccupied much of the time. His successor, Henry II (1547–1559), had a sadistic streak, and especially in his last years loved to watch the burning of heretics, though when his own tailor was being burned the man fixed him with a look of such reproach that his majesty was unable to sleep for several nights afterward. In 1548 he set up a special tribunal to try heretics, the *chambre ardent.* In 1551 the Edict of Chateaubriand codified the laws designed to suppress the Protestants. All Protestantism breathed a sigh of relief in 1559 when Henry II breathed his last. He died a few days after a shattered lance pierced his right eye in a tournament. But the death of Henry II coincided with the peace of Cateau-Cambrésis between France and the empire, which was soon followed in the kingdom of France by the wars of religion and in the rest of Europe by the onset of the Counterreformation.

CALVINISM IN THE HABSBURG LANDS

In the year 1543 Calvin admonished Emperor Charles V himself:

> The Reformation of the church is God's work and is as independent from human hope and intention as the resurrection from the dead or any other wonder of this kind. One must therefore, in view of the possibility of doing something for it, not wait for the good will of the people or for a change of circumstances, but one

must break right through the middle of despair. God desires to have his Gospel preached. Let us obey this command and go where he calls us! What the result will be is not for us to ask.[9]

But the one thing Charles V had in common with Francis I was an implacable hostility toward Protestantism. Charles opposed Protestantism because it ran counter to the century-old allegiance of his dynasty to Rome. Francis suppressed it because it threatened the unity of his kingdom, which had moved further than other national monarchies toward consolidation. In the Habsburg Netherlands Charles was able to exert enormous pressure upon the young Calvinist movement, but in the empire it developed under the aegis of favorably disposed princes against the opposition of the established Lutheran churches as well as the Catholics.

The seventeen provinces of the Netherlands belonged immediately to the Habsburg dominions. There Charles V had managed to hold the Lutheran and Anabaptist movements in check by inquisition and execution. But the more militant Calvinism made real headway after it first penetrated into the Walloon or southernmost French-speaking provinces. A Geneva-educated missionary, Guy de Brès, prepared a Calvinist confession that was adopted in 1566 by a synod at Antwerp. The movement gained strength as French refugees came across the border and later as English Protestants arrived, especially in the northern Dutch provinces, where Calvinism became more firmly established than in the south. With the accession of Charles V's son, the narrow and fanatically Catholic Philip II (1556–1598), who was in residence in the Lowlands the first four years of his reign, more systematic repression of the Calvinists began. The cause of religious liberty in the Netherlands coincided with the desire for political freedom. Militant Calvinism paid the Habsburgs back in their own coin by contributing to the fervor of Dutch resistance to Spanish rule.

The empire was an essentially different matter, for there the princes stood as a buffer between the Habsburgs and the people. That Lutheranism became static or dormant after the Peace of Augsburg (1555) is a myth, for it made some striking accessions even after that date, including the Strassburg of Bucer and Calvin, which subscribed to the Lutheran Formula of Concord in 1580. But here and there in the empire Calvinism made gains against established Lutheran churches as well as in Catholic territories. The name Reformed Church was, in fact, first used to distinguish the Calvinist congregations from the more conservative Lutheran establishments. Penetration was evident in Württemberg, lying close to Switzerland in the upper Rhineland; somewhat later in Brandenburg, where the ruler turned Calvinist, although most of the people remained Lutheran; but especially in the Palatinate.

In the Palatinate the elector Frederick III (1559–1576) became convinced that

---

[9] *Corpus Reformatorum*, vol. 6, cols. 510–11.

Calvin's sacramental doctrine was the true interpretation. He appointed Calvinist theologians, educated in Geneva, to professorships at Heidelberg University. In 1563 they prepared the Heidelberg Catechism, Calvinist in essence but moderately formulated, which was widely used both for instruction and as a doctrinal statement by the Reformed churches in the Germanies and in the Netherlands as well. Calvinism in the Palatinate ran into the problem of the proprietary church arrangement, according to which the prince was accustomed to assume the legal governance of the church. A certain Thomas Lüber (*c.* 1524–1583), the elector's physician, better known by his Latinized name, Erastus, argued that the civil government should exercise the power of excommunication. His writings were published posthumously in England (1589), and the term Erastianism was forever after in that country applied to political theories that favored state domination of the church.

CALVINISM IN EASTERN EUROPE

In eastern Europe Calvinism made its most notable gains during the second half of the sixteenth century in Poland and Hungary. Although Lutheranism had made slow but steady progress up to the accession of Sigismund II Augustus in 1548, from then on Calvinism forged ahead until it gained a dominant position in Lithuania and Little Poland. King Sigismund corresponded with Calvin and greatly admired the *Institutes.* In 1554 Calvin sent him a plan for the reform of the Polish church under an evangelical archbishop and Calvinist bishops. For the middle and lower Polish nobility, Calvinism had certain appealing features that Lutheranism lacked. It was not so closely associated with the Germans as Lutheranism was, and in its presbyterian organization it provided for lay participation in the consistories and lay leadership at the provincial and national levels, analogous to the participation these classes were seeking in political government. As a more militant form of Protestantism, Calvinism was opposed both to papal authority and to absolute monarchy, and therefore proved to be congenial to the landed gentry.

In Lithuania the powerful Lithuanian magnate Nicholas Radziwill, Sigismund's chancellor, converted to Calvinism and brought with him all his feudal estates and dependencies. In Little Poland the leading figure was a clergyman of noble descent named John à Lasco. Lasco had been converted to Lutheranism, helped to organize the church in Ducal Prussia, and served refugee congregations in Frankfort and Emden, meanwhile veering over toward Calvinism. For three years he was a pastor of an émigré congregation in England during the reign of Edward VI. Then in 1557 he returned to Poland and there worked without success to establish a united Protestant church with a Calvinist theology and polity. Under his leadership Calvinism as such made considerable headway. But Protestantism eventually failed in Poland, and in the seventeenth century Catholicism won a nearly complete and bloodless victory, because the power of the Catholic clergy was firmly rooted in the state and the kings remained loyal to the old church. Because the kings nevertheless made concessions on freedom of worship, the Protestants were never able to combine their cause with a revolt of the gentry against the kings. After failing to place a Protestant candidate on the throne in any of the three sixteenth-century interregnums, they lost the initiative, and one by one the landed magnates returned to the Catholic Church so that their families would not be excluded from preferred appointments in the kingdom.

The development of Calvinism in Hungary was analogous to that in Poland. Until the middle of the century the Lutherans had a virtual monopoly on evangelizing the kingdom, but then Calvinism developed a powerful appeal for the Magyar landed magnates. Matthias Biró turned the city of Debrecen into a Hungarian Geneva. In Transylvania, where Zapolya had been mighty, the "Transylvania Saxons," or Lutherans, were challenged by a strong Calvinist movement, and a rule of local autonomy was established according to which villages or cities could choose preachers congenial to them, an arrangement celebrated euphemistically as "Transylvanian toleration." Although Calvinism maintained itself better in Hungary than in Poland, the great preponderance of people and of power remained with a resurgent Catholicism.

PROTESTANTISM IN SPAIN AND ITALY

French-speaking Geneva provided a strategic location from which the penetration of Latin or Romance-language Europe could be attempted. Calvin made heroic efforts to launch an evangelical invasion of these Catholic strongholds, but Spain under its most Catholic Habsburg kings remained almost completely impervious, and Italy, though rocked from head to toe with dissent, deviation, and disputes, was saved for the papacy largely by the strong hand of Spain, which dominated the peninsula throughout most of the century.

The church in Spain was extremely well organized and disciplined, primarily because of the work of Cardinal Francisco Ximénez de Cisneros, confessor to Queen Isabella, primate of the Spanish church, humanist founder of the University of Alcalá, and, above all, founder of the Spanish Inquisition in 1480. When he died, in the same year in which Luther posted his ninety-five theses, he left behind a strong church prepared to work hand in iron glove with Charles V and Philip II, who made Spain the main power base of their dynastic empire. Moreover, the successful conclusion of the crusades against the Moors had left the Spaniards with a fanatic zeal in behalf of Catholicism, which in their minds was as inextricably a part of the Spanish identity as Islam was of the Moorish, and with an endemic hostility toward all foreign influences.

Nevertheless, some humanist and Protestant books did penetrate, smuggled in by merchants, hidden in bales of hides, in colporteurs' luggage, in casks or cargo. Even though Erasmus' books were proscribed, his ideas filtered through. The Spanish inquisitors either could not or did not bother to distinguish between Erasmians and Lutherans, and fiercely suppressed them all as heretics. When these "Lutherans" went into exile, they generally ended up as Calvinists. Attempts have been made, however, to trace the influence of Erasmus on Spanish thought all the way down to Cervantes. Even the mystical movement of the *Alumbrados,* who stressed the inwardness of religion and the indwelling of Christ in the hearts of men, centering in a Benedictine monastery nestled high up on a craggy cliff at Montserrat, fell suspect to the prying eye of persecutors. In 1555 Pope Paul IV specifically condemned the *Espiritualistas* of Spain. Small groups of Lutherans gathered clandestinely at Seville and Valladolid, but were ferreted out and tortured, or fled. Some of Spain's best minds chose exile. Juan Luis Vives (1492–1540), a distinguished Erasmian humanist and educational philosopher, lived out his life in France, England, and the Netherlands. The Erasmian Juan de Valdés (1500–1541) and his twin brother, Alfonso, left Spain. After writing *The Dialogue of Mercury and Caron,* Juan moved to Naples in 1530 in fear of the Inquisition; Alfonso turned to politics and served in the entourage of Charles V in the empire, where he died in 1532 in Vienna. Spain has yet to recover from this suppression of the intellectuals and the consequent loss of independent thinkers.

The case of Italy, with Rome and the Papal States in its heartland, was far more complex. Suffering repeated foreign invasions, serving as the battleground of Spanish and French armies, and politically fragmented into small warring states, Italy experienced in the first decades of the sixteenth century a waning of its Renaissance culture and the virtual end of its world of humanism, except in Venice, which enjoyed an Indian summer of civic humanism and an artistic afterglow. In the early years evangelical religion made sporadic headway in various Italian city-states, although it is difficult to distinguish individuals of Protestant and Erasmian Catholic reform leanings, and Lutheranism from native anticlericalism or anti-curialism. Moreover, the extent to which Anabaptism and other sectarian beliefs penetrated the masses needs to be explored further, for there is evidence of Anabaptist congregations in Vicenza and Venice, and of Anabaptist activity elsewhere. Protestant Europe was rapidly dotted with Italian refugee congregations. With the year 1542 Protestantism in Italy entered upon a new phase, for in that year Pope Paul III, under pressure from the zealous Cardinal Caraffa, established the Holy Office of the Roman Inquisition. The Inquisition hounded many free spirits out of the country, most of them gravitating now toward Geneva and western Europe.

In cosmopolitan, antipapal Venice, blessed with at least a modicum of toleration, some of Luther's and Zwingli's works were published. There too appeared Benedetto Luchino's *Most Useful Treatise on the Benefit of Jesus Christ Crucified,* the most widespread Italian Protestant tract, primarily a compilation of translations of Calvin. At the University of Padua in the Venetian domain, as at the University of Bologna, the German students in residence made active Protestant propaganda, and for a long time the local authorities did not intervene for fear of losing revenue. In Padua, too, transpired a poignant human tragedy that epitomized the spiritual agony of many men in that generation. The distinguished lawyer Francesco Spiera was converted to the evangelical faith, and began to preach and distribute literature. After being arrested and tried, he recanted, for he thought that his eleven children would otherwise be disinherited. But then he feared that in denying Christ as the sole author of his salvation he had committed the sin against the Holy Ghost, and sank into a deep melancholy that lasted until he died in despair two years later.

The northeast presented Protestantism with a stalwart advocate in the person of Matthias Flacius Illyricus (1520–1575). Orphaned early, he worked his way through school and studied with the humanist Baptista Egnatius, a friend of Erasmus, in Venice. An uncle who was sympathetic to the Reformation, although he was a provincial of the Franciscans, dissuaded him from becoming a monk and directed him toward university study. He attended the universities of Basel, Tübingen, and Wittenberg, where he was warmly welcomed by Melanchthon and Luther. There in 1544 he was appointed professor of Hebrew. He subsequently feuded with Melanchthon over the compromise Leipzig Interim, and thereafter wandered from Jena to Regensburg, Antwerp, Strassburg, and Frankfort until his death. He was almost Manichaean in his stress on the substantive nature of sin and evil in man. But through his exegetical *Clavis,* or key to the Scriptures, and his historical schema in the *Magdeburg Centuries,* both designed to prove that the papacy rested on false foundations, he had a strong influence upon Protestant thought.

In Naples a second major center of unorthodox belief developed in the literary and religious circle around the Erasmian and mystical Juan de Valdés. Valdés had moved from Naples to Rome in 1531 and served as an attendant to Pope Clement VII. In the fall of 1533 he returned permanently to Naples, where a group of intellectuals gathered around him to study the Scriptures. He translated parts of the Bible from Hebrew and Greek into Spanish and wrote brief commentaries on the epistles of Paul to the Corinthians and the Romans. Pietro Carnesecchi (1508–1567) ascribed to the influence of Valdés his acceptance of the doctrine of justification by faith. Bernardino Ochino and Peter Martyr Vermigli came under his spell, and two remarkable women, Vittoria Colonna and her sister-in-law Giulia Gonzaga, belonged to his coterie. With his death in 1541 the spirit of religious freedom also ebbed away.

The Roman Inquisition lost no time in swinging into action as soon as it was organized. The impatient Caraffa set up instruments of torture in his own house until more spacious quarters could be found. One of the Inquisition's most prominent victims was Valdés' disciple Pietro Carnesecchi. Protonotary to the curia and first secretary to the pope, he was led by Valdés to accept a Pauline view of justification by faith. He fled to Paris but later returned to Venice. When he was summoned to Rome in 1557, he fled to Geneva. Under Pius V pressure was less intense than it had been under Paul IV, and he felt secure in Florence, but in 1565 the Inquisition renewed its activity. Betrayed by Duke Cosimo of Florence, who wished to ingratiate himself with the pope, Carnesecchi was condemned to die. On October 1, 1567, he was beheaded and then burned. He went to his death like a gentleman, Cosimo's agent reported from Rome, "as though to his wedding," wearing a "white shirt, with a new pair of gloves and a white handkerchief in his hand."

A man of great eminence forced into permanent exile was Bernardino Ochino (1487–1564), an earnest religious who rose to become general of the Observantine Franciscan order. In 1534 he joined the new, more austere order of the Capuchins, and four years later was elected vicar general. In 1539 he preached a series of sermons in Venice, at the invitation of Cardinal Bembo, in which a decided emphasis on justification by faith was evident. No sooner had Caraffa established the Inquisition than Ochino was summoned to appear in Rome. Warned by Cardinal Contarini, he fled to Geneva, where Calvin received him with open arms. He published six volumes of tracts defending his conversion to the evangelical faith. In 1545 he became pastor of an Italian refugee congregation in Augsburg and barely escaped when Charles V's troops took the city. He fled through Strassburg to England, where Edward VI gave him a pension. There he published *A Tragedy, or Dialogue of the Unjust Usurped Primacy of the Bishop of Rome* (1549), a prolix piece in which Lucifer, angered at the spread of Christ's kingdom, assembles all the fiends and enthrones the pope as Antichrist. Just when Satan and Antichrist are about to triumph, Ochino exults, God raises up Henry VIII and his "illustrious" son and succeeds in overthrowing them. Queen Mary drove Ochino out of her earthly kingdom. He became pastor of an Italian congregation in Zurich, but in his *Thirty Dialogues* he seemed to make a case for polygamy and to hold unorthodox views of the Trinity, so he was driven out of there too. He fled to Poland, but was banished again, and died toward the close of 1564 in Moravia.

Other men of quality, such as Vergerio, Vermigli, and Acontius, were also driven out of Italy by the Inquisition and were attracted as though by a magnet to Swiss Protestantism. Pietro Paolo Vergerio (*c.* 1498–1564), a man of unusual religious sensitivity, stood high in the ecclesiastical hierarchy. A Venetian trained in canon law, he rose to become a reforming bishop of Capodistria and a papal legate. In 1535 he was sent to Wittenberg to negotiate with Luther about an ecumenical church council and was deeply impressed by the reformer. In Italy he visited Spiera to observe his acute soul struggle. In 1548 Vergerio became convinced of the truth of the evangelical faith, and the next year he left Italy to become pastor of a congregation of Italian Lutherans in Switzerland. As councilor to Duke Christoph of Württemberg, Vergerio, who remained essentially Lutheran in doctrinal outlook, had a powerful influence on the course of religious development.[10]

Peter Martyr Vermigli (1500–1562) and Giacomo Acontius moved from Italy through Switzerland to Protestant England. Vermigli was born in Florence, the son of a devoted follower of Savonarola. He was educated in the Augustinian cloister at Fiesole and in a Paduan monastery, and became a preacher at Brescia, Pisa, Venice, and Rome. In 1530 he became the abbot of an Augustinian monastery at Spoleto and three years later became prior of a convent in Naples. But he meanwhile steeped himself in biblical studies, read Zwingli and Bucer, fell under the suspicion of the Spanish viceroy in Naples, and in 1541 moved to Lucca, where a nucleus of Protestants was in formation. Ordered to appear before his order in Genoa, he consulted with Ochino in Florence and then fled to Zurich, Basel, and Strassburg. In 1547 Thomas Cranmer offered him a pension in England, and the next year he was made regius professor of theology at Oxford. He fled back to Strassburg on the accession of Queen Mary, and ended his days as a professor of Hebrew in Zurich, where his sacramental views blended with Zwinglian teaching.

Giacomo Acontius (1492–1560?) was a real pioneer of religious toleration. Like Vermigli and Ochino, he turned to a more radical form of protest than Lutheranism. His line of flight took him through Switzerland and Strassburg to England, where he arrived soon after the accession of Queen Elizabeth. As an engineer he drained marshes and inspected fortifications; as a religious intellectual he wrote two books, upon which his lasting fame rests. In his *De methodo* he discussed the correct way of investigating the Scriptures. In his *Stratagemata satanae* he argued that dogmatic creeds are the divisive stratagems of Satan and that the least common denominator or fundamentals of the various creeds should be determined and all other disputable matters ruled out as immaterial, a daring thought for that era and one that was generally repudiated.

It seems that the dogmatic line and harsh action of the church and state in Spain and Italy produced an opposite if not equal reaction, for Spain produced Servetus and Italy a company of anti-Trinitarians. Possibly, too, the impact of Neoplatonic philosophy carried over from the Renaissance to condition religious thinkers. The relation of anti-Trinitarians to such radical groups as the Italian Anabaptists is a question still in need of scholarly investigation. Most prominent among the anti-Trinitarians were Lelio Sozzini (1525–1562) and his rambunctious nephew Fausto (1539–1604). Lelio, a jurist, told Melanchthon that his drive toward the *fontes juris* had led him to search also for the pristine fountains of religion and to renounce the "idolatry of Rome." He was a constant wanderer, moving

---

[10] See Anne Jacobson Schutte, "Pier Paolo Vergerio: The Making of an Italian Reformer" (unpublished Ph.D. dissertation, Stanford University, 1969).

through Switzerland, France, England, Holland, Germany, Austria, Bohemia, and Poland. Calvin welcomed him in Geneva and concealed his suspicions of Lelio's speculative flights. He was in Zurich when he died. His family back in Italy was persecuted by the Inquisition, and several of his relatives were imprisoned. His nephew Fausto was perhaps a bit influenced by Lelio's papers, which he claimed in Zurich, but for the most part he was an independent thinker. In his *Explicatio* of the proem of the gospel of John, Fausto ascribed to Christ an official, not an essential, deity. He expressed doubt about the natural immortality of man. For twelve years he was in the service of Isabella de' Medici, but in 1575 he fled to Basel. He then played a role in the anti-Trinitarian movement in Transylvania and in Cracow, Poland, where a mob wrecked his house. He died in retirement on an estate east of Cracow.

John Calvin was intensely interested in the "progress of the gospel" in the papacy's Italian homeland. His extensive correspondence reveals that he hoped, through the conversion of princes by the mysterious power of the word, to win Italy for the evangelical cause. He continued to write to the French duchess Renée of Ferrara, whom he had visited in 1537. But Duke Ercole II opposed him, and in 1559 her own son Alfonso drove her out and back to France, for the Estes family could not afford to alienate the pope or bring Spanish troops down upon them. Calvin, perhaps with Carnesecchi in mind, constantly warned the Italian Protestants not to be like Nicodemus, the young aristocrat who came to Jesus by night for fear of the rulers, but to confess their faith openly. It is easy to fault Calvin on many counts, but there can be no question of his dedication to the cause and his concern for all his brothers in the faith. Goethe once commented that when we elect to find fault with a great man of the past, we should, to be just, do so on our knees.

Bibliography

Calvin:

BENOIT, JEAN D. *Jean Calvin: La vie, l'homme, la pensée,* 2nd ed. Paris, 1948.

BRATT, JOHN H. *The Rise and Development of Calvinism,* rev. ed. Grand Rapids, 1964.

BREEN, QUIRINUS. *John Calvin: A Study in French Humanism,* 2nd ed. Grand Rapids, 1968.

CADIER, JEAN. *The Man God Mastered: A New Biography of John Calvin.* Grand Rapids, 1960.

DOUMERGUE, ÉMILE. *Jean Calvin, les hommes et les choses de son temps,* 7 vols. Lausanne, 1899–1927.

HARKNESS, GEORGIA. *John Calvin: The Man and His Ethics.* New York, 1958.

HUNT, R. N. *Calvin.* London, 1933.

PARKER, T. H. L. *Portrait of Calvin.* Philadelphia, 1955.
STAUFER, RICHARD. *Calvins Menschlichkeit.* Zurich, 1964.
STICKELBERGER, EMANUEL. *Calvin: A Life.* Richmond, Va., 1954.
WALKER, WILLISTON. *John Calvin, the Organizer of Reformed Protestantism, 1509–1564.* New York, 1906.
WARFIELD, BENJAMIN. *Calvin and Calvinism.* New York, 1931.

Calvin's theology:
BIÉLER, ANDRÉ. *The Social Humanism of Calvin.* Richmond, Va., 1964.
BOISSET, JEAN. *Sagesse et sainteté dans la pensée de Jean Calvin.* Paris, 1959.
DOWEY, EDWARD A. *The Knowledge of God in Calvin's Theology.* New York, 1952.
FORSTMAN, H. JACKSON. *Word and Spirit: Calvin's Doctrine of Biblical Authority.* Stanford, 1962.
GANOCZY, ABBÉ ALEXANDRE. *Calvin: Théologien de l'église et du ministère.* Paris, 1964.
HOOGLAND, M. P. *Calvin's Perspective on the Exaltation of Christ.* Kampen, Netherlands, 1966.
JANSEN, JOHN F. *Calvin's Doctrine of the Work of Christ.* London, 1956.
McDONNELL, KILIAN, O.S.B. *John Calvin: The Church and the Eucharist.* Princeton, 1968.
NIESEL, WILHELM. *The Theology of Calvin.* Philadelphia, 1956.
NIXON, LEROY. *John Calvin's Teachings on Human Reason.* New York, 1963.
PARKER, T. H. L. *The Doctrine of the Knowledge of God: A Study in the Theology of John Calvin,* rev. ed. Edinburgh, 1959.
QUISTORP, HEINRICH. *Calvin's Doctrine of the Last Things.* Richmond, Va., 1955.
STROHL, HENRI. *La Pensée de la Réforme.* Paris, 1951.
TORRANCE, THOMAS. *Calvin's Doctrine of Man.* London, 1940.
WALLACE, RONALD S. *Calvin's Doctrine of Word and Sacrament.* Grand Rapids, 1957.
WARFIELD, BENJAMIN. *Calvin and Augustine.* Philadelphia, 1956.
WENDEL, FRANÇOIS. *Calvin: The Origins and Development of His Religious Thought.* New York, 1963.
WILLIS, EDWARD D. *Calvin's Catholic Christology.* Leiden, 1966.

Calvinism and the French Reformation:
DAKIN, ARTHUR. *Calvinism.* London, 1941.
HAUSER, HENRI. *La Naissance du Protestantisme.* Paris, 1940.
IMBART DE LA TOUR, PIERRE. *Les Origines de la Réforme,* 2 vols., 2nd ed. Melun, 1948.
LECERF, A. *Études Calvinistes.* Neuchatel and Paris, 1949.
LOVY, RENÉ. *Les Origines de la Réforme française: Meaux, 1518–1546.* Paris, 1959.
MACKINNON, JAMES. *Calvin and the Reformation.* London, 1936.
McNEILL, JOHN T. *The History and Character of Calvinism.* New York, 1954.
VIENOT, JOHN. *Histoire de la Réforme française des origines à l'Édit de Nantes.* Paris, 1926.

Geneva and the spread of Calvinism:
BERGIER, J. F. *Genève et l'économie européenne de la Renaissance.* Paris, 1963.
BERTHOUD, G., et al. *Aspects de la propagande religieuse.* Geneva, 1957.
CHOISY, E. *La Théocratie de Genève au temps de Calvin.* Geneva, 1897.
GRAHAM, W. F. *Calvin and His City.* Richmond, Va., 1970.

HALKIN, LÉON. *La Réforme en Belgique sous Charles Quint.* Brussels, 1957.
HIGMAN, FRANCIS L. *The Style of John Calvin in His French Polemical Treatises.* Oxford, 1967.
HUGHES, PHILIP E. *The Register of the Company of Pastors of Geneva in the Time of Calvin.* Grand Rapids, 1966.
HUNT, G. L. *Calvinism and the Political Order.* Philadelphia, 1965.
KINGDON, ROBERT M. *Geneva and the Coming of the Wars of Religion in France, 1555–1563.* Geneva, 1956.
———. *Geneva and the Consolidation of the French Protestant Movement, 1564–1572.* Madison, Wis., 1967.
MONTER, E. W. *Calvin's Geneva.* New York, 1967.
NAEF, HENRI. *Les origines de la Réforme à Genève,* 2 vols. Geneva, 1968.

Protestantism in Spain and Italy:
BREZZI, P. *Le origini del Protestantesimo.* Rome, 1961.
CANTIMORI, DELIO. *Bernardino Ochino: Uomo del Rinascimento e Riformatore.* Pisa, 1929.
———. *Eretici italiani del cinquecento.* Florence, 1939.
——— et al. *Ginevra e l'Italia.* Florence, 1959.
CHURCH, FREDERICK. *The Italian Reformers, 1534–1564.* New York, 1932.
LEMMI, FRANCESCO. *La riforma in Italia.* Milan, 1938.
LONGHURST, JOHN. *Luther and the Spanish Inquisition: The Case of Diego de Uceda.* Albuquerque, N.M., 1953.
McNAIR, PHILIP. *Peter Martyr in Italy: An Anatomy of Apostasy.* Oxford, 1967.
RODOCANACCHI, F. *La Réforme en Italie,* 2 vols. Paris, 1920–1921.
ROSSI, PAOLO. *Giacomo Aconcio.* Milan, 1952.
RUFFINI, FRANCESCO. *Studi sui riformatori italiani.* Turin, 1955.
SCHUTTE, ANNE J. "Pier Paolo Vergerio: The Making of an Italian Reformer." Ph.D. dissertation, Stanford, 1969.
TEDESCHI, JOHN A. *Italian Reformation Studies in Honor of Laelius Socinus.* Florence, 1965.

CHAPTER 17

The Reformation
in England
and Scotland

British historians have long been convinced that the Reformation in Great Britain represented one of the great turning points in modern history. Some with Protestant and progressivist Whiggish prejudices have indeed declared it to be the crucial event in Western history. James Froude, for example, wrote: "I believe the Reformation to have been the greatest incident in English history; the root and source of the expansive force which has spread the Anglo-Saxon race over the globe, and imprinted the English genius and character on the constitution of mankind."[1] In spite of its supposed universal significance, the English Reformation is said to have had a special stamp of its own. That peculiar characteristic was the moderation with which an official reformation was carried out. David Hume asserted that the English Reformation represented the *via media* between papalism and radicalism.[2]

The near-ecstatic appreciation of the English Reformation by Britain's patriotic sons has been quite evenly balanced on the other side by an absurd reduction of the Reformation to a matter of the "King's Great Question" and the bright eyes of Anne Boleyn. The mischievous Voltaire quipped that "England separated from

---

[1] James Froude, *The Divorce of Catherine of Aragon* (New York, 1891), p. 18.
[2] David Hume, *The History of England* (Boston, 1854), vol. 4, p. 115.

the Pope because King Henry fell in love." Somewhere between adulation and denigration lies the truth about the English Reformation. Sorting out the essential facts, presenting a narrative as true as brevity allows, distinguishing those features that the English Reformation had in common with the continental Reformation and those that were unique to it, and, finally, assessing its historical significance are no simple matters.

Ironically, the strong desire of the English people for peace and security played a large part in precipitating the disorder of the Reformation. For after the protracted bloody struggle of the Wars of the Roses between the Yorkist and Lancastrian factions, the English longed for quiet and prosperity. But the security of the state depended upon masterful rule by the sovereign and an orderly succession, a fact that explains the widespread acceptance of Henry VIII's moves to assert and to increase the royal power and the general acquiescence in the king's maneuvering to secure a male heir by one queen or another. The English greeted the coronation of vigorous young Henry VIII in 1509 with unrestrained enthusiasm. Expectations ran high.

His father, Henry VII (1457–1509), was the founder of the Tudor dynasty. Henry VII invaded England with French aid and landed at Milford Haven, among his Welsh allies. In the famed battle of Bosworth field, aided at this critical juncture by the noble Stanley's treason to Richard III, he defeated and killed the Yorkist king on August 22, 1485. He was ceremoniously crowned in Westminster on the following October 30. He married Elizabeth, the oldest daughter of King Edward IV, thus uniting in the marriage bed the red and white roses and eliminating all pretexts for further civil war. Nevertheless, conspiracies and insurrections persisted, and Henry VII's reign was far from peaceful. By way of matrimonial diplomacy Henry VII married his oldest son, Arthur, to Catherine, the daughter of King Ferdinand and Queen Isabella of Spain. One of his daughters, Margaret, was married to James IV of Scotland, and another, Mary, was bestowed as wife upon Louis XII of France, gentle private hostages to international security.

The Rule of Cardinal Wolsey

ERASMUS WAS MUCH IMPRESSED with the brilliance of young Prince Henry (1491–1547), whom he saw as a boy at the court in 1499. Educated under the influence of Renaissance tutors, such as the poet John Skelton, Henry was a remarkable young scholar, a gifted linguist, a talented musician, a remarkably learned amateur theologian, and an athlete and horseman who loved to ride to the hunt. He was idolized as a child and became a willful, opportunistic, assertive egotist. After the death of his older brother, Arthur, in 1502, Henry became the hope of the dynasty. On the death of his father on April 22, 1509, Henry succeeded to the throne. He was, as the historian Bishop William Stubbs said, "a man of unbounded selfishness; a man of whom we may say ... that he was the king, the whole king, and nothing but the king; that he wished to be, with regard to the church of England, the pope, the whole pope, and something more than the pope."[3] When he was only twelve he had been betrothed to his brother Arthur's widow, Catherine of Aragon, nearly seven years older than he. Church law forbade marriage between a man and his brother's widow, but Pope Julius II granted a special dispensation so that the marriage could take place. Erasmus lauded the marriage of Henry and Catherine as an ideal example of love and chastity.

During the first two years of Henry's reign, mild Richard Foxe and Archbishop Warham managed affairs of state, while Henry amused himself. But soon one of the most spectacular statesmen Britain has ever had, the clever and ruthless Cardinal Thomas Wolsey (1471–1530), rose to prominence and proceeded to dominate the whole first half of Henry's reign. An ambitious, arrogant, masterful man, Wolsey combined magnificent style with a flair for the dramatic. Local records in Suffolk reveal that Wolsey was the son of a cheating butcher, periodically in trouble with the law for giving short weight, selling spoiled meat, and keeping a disorderly house. Wolsey was saved by those sturdy ladders of upward social mobility, the church and Oxford University. His enemies could say of him without charity, but not without justice:

> Born by butcher, but by bishop bred,
> How high His Highness heaves his haughty head!

A precocious student, Wolsey became bursar of Magdalen College, and early demonstrated unusual administrative skill. Urging a foreign policy actively directed against France in cooperation with Ferdinand of Spain, Wolsey attracted the attention of young King Henry, who named him chancellor in 1515. In 1518 Leo X named Wolsey, who was already archbishop of York and a cardinal, *legatus a latere*, that is, the pope's representative, in the church provinces of both York and Canterbury. As chancellor and legate Wolsey held in his hands the combined powers of state and church, although King Henry VIII always played a very important role in determining policies.

Game for adventure in private life, Wolsey advocated an adventurous foreign policy for the realm. Working in alliance with his father-in-law, Ferdinand, Henry joined Pope Julius II's Holy League (1511), designed to force France out of Italy. He put pressure on France to divert its troops from Navarre, which Ferdinand

---

[3] William Stubbs, *Seventeen Lectures on the Study of Medieval and Modern History,* 3rd ed. (London, 1900), pp. 300–1.

was invading. In 1513 Henry crossed the channel with his army, personally led the successful sieges of Thérouanne and Tournay, and took part in the battle of Guinegate. Wolsey managed the campaign efficiently and manipulated a truce with France in August 1514. Meanwhile James IV of Scotland took advantage of Henry's involvement in France to invade the north, but he died in the battle of Flodden.

The accession to the throne of France of the young Renaissance king Francis I in 1515 led to renewed antagonism between England and France and, naturally, a renewed entente between England and Spain. In 1516 Ferdinand died and in 1519 Emperor Maximilian died, so that their grandson Charles V became heir of all the Habsburg holdings. Now Wolsey maneuvered to make Henry the arbiter who would preside over the balance of power between the Habsburgs and Valois. Charles came to court Henry's favor in Kent before proceeding to his coronation at Aachen. Francis sought his friendship at the meeting on the Field of the Cloth of Gold in 1520, although Francis injured Henry's pride by throwing him in a wrestling match on that occasion. At a conference at Calais in 1521 Henry enjoyed his finest moment playing umpire in Europe. In 1522 and 1523 he sponsored another pointless and unpopular expedition into France, but the support he gave to Charles V upset the fine balance of power, and within a few years Charles came out on top and took Francis captive at Pavia (1525). Spanish fortunes rose to new heights, to the discomfiture of Henry, whose marriage to Charles V's aunt Catherine was beginning to cloy. Henry gradually came to view Wolsey's foreign policy with a more skeptical and finally jaundiced eye.

Wolsey's domestic difficulties were compounded by the economic consequences of his continental adventures. The economy was caught in a squeeze between a decline in the demand for wool (offset somewhat by an increase of textile production and export) and rising prices for commodities. In its incipient stages in the early 1520s, this economic condition became aggravated as the decade wore on. "Money is the sinew of war," said the ancients. Wolsey's cross-channel adventures had to be financed. In 1523 the chancellor found it necessary to summon parliament to ask for subsidies. Sir Thomas More was then the speaker of the House of Commons. Parliament refused to grant the money and Wolsey was reduced to making forced loans, which did not increase his popularity. In 1526 he resorted to recoinage and debasement to relieve the money situation.

As a churchman Cardinal Wolsey had splendid plans for reform. He dissolved some twenty-eight small and understaffed religious houses in order to divert their wealth to the founding of his own college at Oxford, which came later to be known as Christ Church, and to a new school at Ipswich. He could not personally provide much inspiration for reform, however, for he was himself a notorious example of one of the church's greatest abuses, the holding of multiple benefices. He was archbishop of York, bishop of Durham and Winchester, deputy for nonresident alien bishops at Worcester, Salisbury, and Llandaff, and abbot of St. Albans. He made his bastard son dean of Wells and archdeacon of York and Richmond, with two rectories, six prebends, and one appointment as chancellor. But at the same time Wolsey had his good personal qualities: he often protected people of no personal influence against the exploitation of the powerful, attempted to slow the enclosing of common lands, which was forcing the peasants off the land, and exhibited a good deal of tolerance for unorthodox opinions. While he was at the height of his power no one was burned for heresy.

Wolsey was finally undone through no real fault of his own, but because he was not able to obtain a papal annulment of King Henry's marriage. Catherine had had a number of children, but the only one who lived was a girl, Mary. With the exception of Queen Matilda, long before, whose reign had been disputed by Stephen, no queen had yet reigned in England. There was talk of a "divorce" as early as 1514, when relations with Ferdinand were strained. By 1526, when Catherine was forty-one and Mary ten, it was evident that Henry would have no male heir by Catherine. The peace of the realm appeared endangered, since peace depended on an orderly succession. Henry meanwhile had developed a regal passion for dark-eyed Anne Boleyn, one of the queen's ladies-in-waiting. But he was more concerned about the succession than with lust; plenty of outlets for that could be found at the court.

Wolsey undertook to secure from Pope Clement VII an annulment of Henry's marriage to Catherine. The grounds for the annulment were to be the laws of consanguinity, the same laws from which Pope Julius II had exempted them in order to make the marriage possible in the first place. According to Leviticus 18: 6–18, marriages were not to be contracted within five or even six degrees of relationship. Leviticus 20:21 reads: "If a man takes his brother's wife, it is impurity; he has uncovered his brother's nakedness; they shall be childless." Wolsey convinced Henry that Rome would grant the divorce, and at first Pope Clement was inclined to do so. Cardinal Campeggio was dispatched to England with the necessary power. Then suddenly things took a turn for the worse, for Charles V laid Francis low and in 1527 his troops stormed Rome. Under pressure from Charles, who was Catherine's nephew, the pope now refused to annul the marriage. When Campeggio was recalled from England and the case remanded to Rome, Henry had his marriage secretly dissolved by an English tribunal and Cardinal Wolsey fell.

Ironically, Wolsey was arrested under a writ of *praemunire,* accusing him of acting as a papal legate, a foreign agent. He died on the way to his trial, a broken man. The tragedy of his fall is perhaps best expressed by the lines Shakespeare gives him to speak in *Henry VIII:*

> Had I but serv'd my God with half the zeal
> I serv'd my king, he would not in mine age
> Have left me naked to mine enemies.

Popular Protest and Heresy

WOLSEY'S NAME served as a catalyst for an outpouring of anticlerical feeling among the masses. In the popular mind he symbolized the higher clergy's worldly disregard for spiritual values. For throughout England the level of religiosity was higher among the people than among the clergy—a paradoxical and potentially explosive situation. In time the forces of dissidence would have produced a crisis in religion even if King Henry's eyes had never lighted upon the daring décolletage of Anne Boleyn. A look at the church in any part of England reveals many people passionately devoted to religion. The parish church was the center of the people's religious and social life, and was tied in with the details of administration of the local community. To secure the welfare of their souls, people made bequests to provide ornamentation or additions to their beloved churches. But the more they loved the church, the more indignant they became at the obvious faults of the churchmen. This popular protest was predominantly secular or ethical rather than evangelical or theological.

A number of scandalous cases of clerical tyranny stirred up anger against the privileges of the clergy, clerical immunities, and the special ecclesiastical courts. The Convocations of the Clergy had the time-honored right to pass ecclesiastical (canon) laws and fix penalties independently of the will of king and parliament, even though these acts affected laymen. The ecclesiastical courts had jurisdiction over the probating of wills, and often charged excessive fees. The case of Richard Hunne, a London tailor, focused the public eye upon this scandalous situation. In the year 1514 Hunne was imprisoned on a charge of heresy in the Lollards' Tower at St. Paul's. He was found hanged from a beam in his prison cell. The investigating jury at the coroner's inquest leveled a murder charge against Bishop Richard Fitz-James' chancellor. The bishop promptly petitioned Cardinal Wolsey to remand the case to a special board of inquiry, for he was convinced that if the chancellor were to be tried by a jury of "any twelve men in London, they be so maliciously set in favour of heretical depravity that they will cast and condemn my clerk, though he were as innocent as Abel." A special board of inquiry was set up and the chancellor and his men were declared not guilty. It is quite possible that they were in fact innocent. At any rate, Sir Thomas More, who attended the inquiry, firmly believed that Hunne was a heretic who died in despair by his own hand. But the incident does illustrate the distrust of the laity felt by the higher clergy. And of course the special handling of the case added to the popular fury against the clerical class.

The Hunne case was a national scandal; more typical was the case of a butcher, James Hardcastell of Barwick-in-Elmet. The case involved elements of both heretical sentiment and personal hostilities within the parish. On September 24, 1540, a former curate of Barwick, Thomas Mettringham, accused Hardcastell of saying that "there was nothing in the church that could do him good, and he would believe in none of them." There was some talk of burning. Later in the investigation, when Myles Walker, a priest, asked Hardcastell if he did not believe in the Blessed Sacrament of the Altar, the butcher replied, "Yes, marry, that do I believe in." With that he doffed his cap and declared that he had said what he had about the church "to prove what a drunken priest would say thereto."

Rabble-rousing agitators were ready to whip up a furor among the masses with incendiary tracts. Simon Fish, an Oxford student, joined a circle of young men in London who were extremely critical of the hierarchy, and especially of Cardinal Wolsey. A vicious anticlerical pamphleteer, he stirred up the populace against churchmen as early as 1529 by circulating his *Supplication of Beggars*. Dedicated to the king, the *Supplication* spewed out pure venom on the clergy.

Many expressions of anticlerical feeling in these early decades of the sixteenth century were very difficult to distinguish from vestigial remains of Lollardy and other forms of medieval dissent and heresy. By this time the meaning of the term Lollard had become so vague that it was applied quite arbitrarily to any undesirable. The court records, moreover, are not easily analyzed, for the charges and the evidence against the accused were presented in such a way that the defendants' beliefs appeared to conform to the definitions of heresy, so that they would stand little chance of escaping conviction and condemnation under traditional statutes. Evidence does suggest, however, that some Lollardy remained in the back country of Yorkshire, and a good deal in Kent.

The Lollards were followers of John Wycliffe (1320–1384), a sharp critic of the Roman church. While a lecturer at Oxford Wycliffe criticized the wealth and worldly power of the church, soon found fault with sacramental doctrine, and with his disciples undertook the translation of the Scriptures into English. Wycliffe commissioned his Poor Preachers, the Lollards, to bring the gospel into the highways and byways of England. The Council of Constance in 1415 declared Wycliffe's teachings to be heretical and demanded that his books and his body be burned. But Wycliffe died in bed because his English sovereigns were involved in a struggle with the Avignonese papacy and could exploit Wycliffe's ready pen for their own cause, and his ideas were not easily rooted out. Lollardy persisted in the midlands and home counties into the sixteenth century and gradually fused with other strains of anticlericalism and Protestantism. Most of the Lollards belonged to the lower middle and working classes. The key to the movement was the English translation of the Bible, circulated in hundreds of manuscript copies, and with many passages ardently memorized and recited at secret meetings of Lollards. There seem to have been regular contacts between various groups of Lollards. The Lollards questioned the veneration of saints, the sacramental doctrine of transubstantiation, the value of pilgrimages, the necessity for confession to priests, and indeed the need for a priesthood at all.

Some ideas of the continental reformers were so similar to these heretical views of the Lollards that there was a natural fusion between them. The high theological treatises of the reformers seem to have had no direct impact on the lower-class Lollards. The Lollards lacked positions of power and could not have launched a reformation of their own. But they welcomed the new English editions of the Bible by Tyndale and Coverdale which were smuggled in from the continent, and they provided a ready audience for the Protestant message. Periodically Lollards would be brought to trial at episcopal courts. A few were burned at the stake during the reigns of Henry VII and Henry VIII, but the great majority of the accused recanted and were made to do penance by carrying a faggot as a reminder of the punishment that might have befallen them.

Erasmian Humanists and Early Protestants

JUST AS STRANDS of anticlericalism were woven tightly together with threads of medieval heresy among the common people, Erasmian humanism was intimately fused with proto-Protestantism among the learned. The name of Erasmus was associated with English humanism from his first visit to England in 1499. His Christian humanism, with its stress upon the Scriptures, upon the wisdom of the church fathers, upon right living, and above all upon moderation and toleration, had a tremendous impact on English intellectuals of both conservative and liberal leanings. The energetic translation of his works, especially during the critical third and fourth decades of the century, indicates that many intellectuals saw some special relevance of his ideas to English problems. One might argue, in fact, that the Erasmian *via media* was the real basis of the English religious settlement in the early years of Henry's son and successor, Edward VI, and the final resolution in the Elizabethan settlement under Henry's younger daughter, Elizabeth I. On the one hand, Erasmian humanism moderated the orthodoxy of the conservative episcopal party of Warham, Tunstall, Foxe, Longland, Pole, Gardiner, Thomas More, and John Fisher; on the other, it contributed to the repeated failure of dogmatic Protestantism to take deep root and helped to produce a generation of young moderates, such as Thomas Starkey and Richard Morison, to frame Tudor policy. In the widespread infusion of Erasmian humanism into Reformation thought, English developments were much closer to those on the continent than they have traditionally been portrayed.

Through the patronage of Italian humanists by Henry VII and Henry VIII, the crown had itself promoted humanist culture in the realm. Aristocratic patrons such as Lord Mountjoy, the pupil and patron of Erasmus, nurtured the movement further. The Erasmian program for reform and the mild moralism of Erasmus' *philosophia Christi* soon made converts, and an indigenous English movement developed. During the first three decades of the sixteenth century the English universities underwent profound changes. The influence of humanism at Cambridge and Oxford, particularly in extra-official teaching, was stronger than has been commonly supposed. At Cambridge, where Erasmus himself taught, the active humanist enterprise clearly began with the foundations of Lady Margaret Beaufort, mother of Henry VII, and Bishop John Fisher, Christ's College and St. John's. Two years before Luther's attack on indulgences, a student activist at Cambridge denounced Leo X's proclamation of indulgences, posted on the doors of the schools on orders from Bishop Fisher, the chancellor. Fisher excommunicated the boy and he fled to the continent. At Oxford Richard Foxe endowed Corpus Christi College and provided for public lectures in Greek.

The fusion of Christian humanism and Pauline theology in a single mind can be seen in that notable Oxford reformer John Colet. Colet made his break from Oxford in 1504 and became dean of St. Paul's in London. He was an avid student of Paul and an earnest reformer, and he inspired Erasmus to turn more seriously toward theology. In a famous sermon to the Convocation of the Clergy on the appointment of Archbishop Warham in 1512 he laid down a platform for reform. Colet cited St. Bernard's dictum that the wicked life of the clergy damages the church more than heretics. He called for the "reformation of the church's estate, because that nothing hath so disfigured the face of the church as hath the fashion of secular and worldly living in clerks and priests." He chastized the clergy for ambition and greed, criticized the large fees charged by ecclesiastical courts, the worldliness and pomp of the hierarchy, the ignorance of the regular clergy. He spoke so openly, he confessed, because of "very zeal" and as "a man sorrowing the decay of the church."

From reforming humanists such as John Colet to humanist reformers of evangelical conviction was but a short step. England's earliest Protestants were a race of martyrs, some dying at the hands of Henry VIII's ministers and others surviving to fall into the hands of Bloody Mary. In the preface to *The Flower of Godly Prayers* Thomas Becon paid them tribute:

> God, once again having pity on this realm of England, raised up His prophets, namely William Tyndale, Thomas Bilney, John Frith, Doctor [Robert] Barnes, Jerome [Barlowe], [Thomas] Garret, with divers others, which both with their writings and sermons earnestly labored to call us unto repentance that by this means the fierce wrath of God might be turned away from us. But how were they entreated? How were their painful labors regarded? They themselves were condemned and burnt as heretics, and their books condemned and burnt as heretical. O most unworthy act![4]

Although the ideas of Luther, Zwingli, and other continental reformers made little impression on the English masses, their tracts and pamphlets did infect the

---

[4] Cited in Marcus Loane, *Pioneers of the Reformation in England* (London, 1964), p. vi.

merchants who carried on their trade between the east coast and north Germany. Even in Devon and Cornwall the seaports showed signs of Protestant activity. But the critical development was the infiltration of Reformation ideas into the universities, where Lutheran pamphlets were circulated as early as 1519. In March 1521, only a few weeks before Luther made his stand at the Diet of Worms, Archbishop Warham, chancellor of Oxford, wrote to Cardinal Wolsey of subversive influences in the university. "I am informed," he warned, "that divers of the university be infected with the heresies of Luther and others of that sort, having a great number of books of the said perverse doctrine." Wolsey responded by ordering the burning of Lutheran books on Market Hill in Cambridge and at St. Paul's Church in London. There he had a new pulpit and a scaffold built. While John Fisher preached against Luther's "pernicious doctrine," Wolsey graced the platform with an assemblage of bishops and abbots to view the burning of basketsful of Luther's books. He was dressed, Protestants noted, in purple, like a "bloody antichrist."

King Henry VIII now threw the full weight of his theological erudition into the balance. He had written a treatise designed to refute Luther's ninety-five theses, which were known in England even before Erasmus sent a copy to Sir Thomas More on March 5, 1518. Now, enraged by Luther's treatise *On the Babylonian Captivity of the Church,* Henry wrote a defense of the seven sacraments, *Assertio septem sacramentorum,* dedicated to Leo X. Ever since he "knew of Luther's heresy in Germany," the king assured the pope, he "made it his study how to extirpate it." The authorship of the *Assertio* was doubted then and since. Some said John Fisher, Richard Pace, or even Cardinal Wolsey wrote it. In Germany some charged that Erasmus wrote it for the king, and in England some said that Erasmus wrote Luther's reply. "If only they would change sides," Erasmus sighed, "that is, if only the English suspected what the Germans suspect!" Luther was quite convinced that Edward Lee was the true author, but he declared that he would treat it as the king's, for either a fool wrote it or a fool let it go out under his name, so it was all the same. Henry, for his part, doubted that his book would bring the heresiarch to repentance, declaring: "Alas! The most greedy wolf of hell has surprised him, devoured and swallowed him down into the lowest part of his belly, where he lies half alive, and half in death. And whilst the pious Pastor calls him and bewails his loss, he belches out of the filthy mouth of the hellish wolf these foul inveighings which the ears of the whole flock do detest, disdain and abhor." On October 11, 1521, the pope conferred upon Henry the title *fidei defensor,* defender of the faith.

When in the year 1525 Johannes Bugenhagen, pastor of the city church in Wittenberg, addressed a letter to the English people urging them to accept Luther's teachings and not to be misled by slanders against him, he had some reason to hope for a positive response. In those same years a group of fifty or sixty scholars was meeting at the White Horse Inn in Cambridge, known as "Little Germany," to discuss the new evangelical theology of the continental reformers. This company included names prominent in the Protestant movement and martyrology, such as

Robert Barnes, John Frith, perhaps William Tyndale, Hugh Latimer, Thomas Bilney, Nicholas Ridley, John Bale, and John Foxe, the chronicler of their catastrophes. One converted another, as in the early days of Christianity. When in 1524 Latimer presented a denunciation of Melanchthon as his bachelor of divinity thesis, Bilney took him aside and persuaded him that evangelical theology was true. Foxe reported that it was through Tyndale that Frith "received into his heart the seed of the Gospel and sincere godliness." When Cardinal Wolsey recruited Cambridge scholars to man his new college at Oxford in 1526, six of the eight who went were reform-minded. The story of two of England's earliest Protestants, even briefly related, tells us volumes about the movement.

Robert Barnes was a stormy petrel, bold and reckless when he had the ear of a crowd, less daring when alone with antagonists who could exploit his fears and misgivings. His attempt at swift reform failed miserably. Barnes was not in the humanistic avant-garde, even though he and Erasmus were at Cambridge at the same time. While he did not know Greek and Hebrew, he did cite the Latin fathers, schoolmen, and canonists. On Christmas Eve of 1525 he preached a sermon containing heretical statements and twenty-five criticisms of the church. Cardinal Wolsey had his rooms in Cambridge searched for Lutheran books, but he had hidden them elsewhere. Barnes was taken to London, and on the advice of Bishops Gardiner and Foxe he renounced his preaching "against the worldliness of the church." His penance was to kneel during Bishop John Fisher's long sermon at St. Paul's on Sunday, February 11, 1526, and to carry a faggot in procession around the church. In 1528, under house arrest, he decided to flee, but first he wrote a letter to Wolsey, tipping him off as to where he had gone to drown himself, and another to the mayor, reporting that he would find a parchment sealed in wax on his body, advising all men to submit to Wolsey. Then, dressed in layman's clothes, he shipped out to Antwerp, and arrived eventually at Wittenberg.

At Wittenberg, Foxe relates, Barnes was "made strong in Christ and got favor with the learned in Christ," such as Luther, Melanchthon, and Bugenhagen. In 1531 the Wittenberg theologians sent him as their emissary to King Henry, whose chancellor, Thomas More, sought to arrest him as a heretic and apostate monk after his safe-conduct ran out. More charged him with selling the books of the heretics George Joye and William Tyndale as well as his own. Barnes escaped detection by shaving off his beard and disguising himself as a merchant. But finally he fell victim to the conservative reaction during Henry's last years, and was condemned to die for opposing Bishop Gardiner and Henry. He was burned at Smithfield on July 30, 1540. Allowed to speak while he prepared himself for his ordeal, he asked God's forgiveness for his sin and confessed his faith. "I trust in no good works that ever I did," he said, "but only in the death of Christ. I do not doubt but through him to inherit the kingdom of heaven." Thus died "St. Robert," as Luther called him fondly.

The most remarkable of England's earliest Protestants was clearly William

Tyndale, a man whose name will forever be associated with the English Bible. Born about 1495 in Gloucestershire, he took his M.A. at Oxford in 1515 and then studied at Cambridge. While serving as a tutor in Sir John Welsh's household at Little Sodbury, Tyndale encountered opposition to his preaching from local priests whose knowledge of the Bible was sketchy at best, and thus saw clearly the need to make the Scriptures available to the laity in their own language. He decided to do the translating himself, "because," he recounted later, "I had perceived by experience how that it was impossible to establish the lay people in any truth except the Scripture were plainly laid before their eyes in their mother tongue, that they might see the process, order and meaning of the text."[5] Once resolved, he set about laboriously to perfect the linguistic tools needed for the task. Turned down by the bishop of London, Cuthbert Tunstall, he received support from a rich cloth merchant in London named Humphrey Monmouth, a member of the Christian Brethren, a secret society of merchants influenced by Lutheranism and Lollardy. In 1524 he made a pilgrimage to meet Luther in Wittenberg, and his translation of the New Testament, based upon the Greek text of Erasmus, was greatly influenced by Luther's German version. He tried most conscientiously to render a faithful translation. "I call God to record," he wrote, "against the day we shall appear before our Lord Jesus, to give a reckoning of our doings, that I never altered one syllable of God's Word against my conscience: nor would this day, if all that is in the earth, whether it be pleasure or riches, might be given me." In 1525 he started publication of his work in Cologne, but had to flee to Protestant Worms, where he finished the job. Through the years, beginning in March 1526, copies of this and later editions, as well as the Pentateuch and other parts of the Old Testament, streamed into England despite all the frantic efforts of the authorities to dam the flow. At length Tyndale even found an English publisher, John Day, who was willing to publish his work. Day thought it a great joke to arouse his printers and apprentices each morning by calling out, "Arise, 'tis day!" But it was for heresy that he was eventually sought, during Mary's reign, and he too had to flee abroad.

In his later years Tyndale lived for the most part in the English house of the Merchant Adventurers at Antwerp, where he enjoyed immunity from arrest by Habsburg imperial officers. But in May 1535 a traitor named Henry Phillips, posing as a convert, tricked him into leaving the house. He was arrested and imprisoned in the castle of Vilvorde, near Brussels, where he languished for sixteen months before being brought to trial for heresy. On October 6, 1536, he was strangled at the stake and his body burned to ashes. His last words were said to have been: "Lord, open the king of England's eyes." The acerbic preacher known to posterity as "bilious John Bale" wrote of these early Protestant martyrs: "I think within this realm of England . . . the spirit of Elias was not at all asleep in good William

---

[5] A. G. Dickens, *The English Reformation* (London, 1964), p. 70.

Tyndale, Robert Barnes, and such other more whom Antichrist's violence hath sent hence in fire to heaven, as Elias went afore in the fiery chariot."[6]

Cromwell and the Reformation Parliament

WHEN DURING THE SUMMER of 1529 Henry VIII despaired of bringing Pope Clement VII to annul his marriage to Catherine, he turned from persuasion to menace. There was a fourteenth-century precedent for asserting English independence of papal domination. In 1351 the Statute of Provisors had been directed against papal authority within the realm, followed in 1353 by the Statute of Praemunire, which forbade appeals to Rome not sanctioned by the king. Henry saw the possibilities of using parliament to blackmail the pope into permitting him virtual independence from Rome and supremacy in his own land.

Wolsey had always feared Thomas More, but he recognized his abilities and his conservative bent, and recommended him as his successor as lord chancellor. The great seal was transferred to More on October 25, 1529, with nearly universal popular approval. In his initial address to parliament as speaker, More referred to Wolsey most bitterly as "the grete wether which is of late fallen as you all knowe." As a devout layman, More was speaking for all who felt the need for reform, and reform was to be the main concern of this parliament. But events now took a turn that left Thomas More himself in a desperately vulnerable position.

After Wolsey's fall the Cambridge theologian Thomas Cranmer suggested that Henry consult the universities on the question of his divorce, hoping for a consensus that would strengthen the king's case. The result of this inquiry proved disappointing, for even antipapal Wittenberg recognized the legitimacy of his marriage, and Luther later announced how mightily he was praying for Queen Catherine. It was now clear that strong legal measures had to be taken.

At the end of 1530 the king accused the clergy of having violated the Statute of Praemunire, as had Wolsey, and the Convocation of the Clergy agreed to pay over £100,000 rather than risk the loss of all church goods through confiscation. They were forced, moreover, to grant to the king the title of "singular protector, only and supreme lord, and as far as the law of Christ allows even supreme head of the English church and clergy." The House of Commons meanwhile passed a series of bills regulating the fees payable for probate, burials, and other services, and more drastic measures were on the way.

The mastermind behind all this critical legislation was a *parvenu* named Thomas Cromwell, soon to emerge as the strong man of the English Reformation.

---

[6] Cited in Loane, *Pioneers of the Reformation*, p. 48.

Cromwell's design was to exclude the pope from the realm and to deliver a centralized control to the king and parliament. Born around 1485 in Putney, he was the son of a roustabout brewer, fuller, and blacksmith. While still in his teens Cromwell set out to make his fortune, first as a French mercenary and then as a clerk for the Frescobaldi bankers in northern Italy. After two years or so he moved on to become an economic adviser to English merchants in the Netherlands, reporting on developments in the Antwerp market. An urbane man, with a knowledge of Latin and Italian literature, Cromwell approached practical affairs of state with a rationalistic Renaissance flair. He was inspired by Marsiglio of Padua's radical *Defensor pacis* rather than by Machiavelli's *Prince*, as Cardinal Reginald Pole later charged, and was schooled in the practical art of politics in the household of Wolsey himself. Wolsey used him to carry out the liquidation of the monasteries that he had marked for dissolution in the interest of his education fund. When Wolsey fell, Cromwell was visibly shaken. They say he even cried. But soon he dried his eyes and rode off to London to court the king's favor. He held minor offices, and by January 1531 he was sworn into the king's council. He worked on the king's finances and in 1534 became his principal secretary, extending his control to all of his majesty's business.

It is not true, as has often been alleged, that Cromwell attempted to make an absolute monarch of Henry. Schooled in the common law, Cromwell worked through the House of Commons, and thus the legislation of the Reformation Parliament (1529–1536) proved to be decisive. Thomas Cranmer was able to write to the Strassburg reformer Wolfgang Capito in 1537 that Cromwell "had himself done more than all others together in whatever had hitherto been effected respecting the reformation of religion and of the clergy." In five years the juridical reformation effected the complete transformation from papal supremacy over the church in England to royal supremacy over the Church of England.

Cromwell's drive to void the legislative independence of the church began with the Supplication of the Commons Against the Ordinaries, which cleverly combined restrictions on the power of the Convocation of the Clergy to pass ecclesiastical laws without the agreement of the Commons and attacks upon the arbitrary and unjust actions of the ecclesiastical courts, often unfair to the laity. The king spoke to the speaker of the House about his displeasure with the oath of obedience to the pope taken by prelates on their consecration. On May 15, 1532, the convocation adopted the Submission of the Clergy, appealing to the king for his protection against the Commons and giving him control over their legislative functions in return for his protection of their ecclesiastical courts. The next day Thomas More resigned as chancellor. Toward the end of the year an act suspending the payment of annates to Rome was passed, a threat that forced the pope to consecrate the king's candidate, Thomas Cranmer, as archbishop of Canterbury.

In March 1533 Cromwell secured the passage of the most decisive legislation of all, the Act in Restraint of Appeals. Its famous preamble read: "This realm of England is an Empire . . . governed by one Supreme Head and King having the dignity and royal estate of the imperial crown of the same, unto whom a body politic, compact of all sorts and degrees of people divided in terms and by name of spirituality and temporalty, be bounded and owe to bear, next to God, a natural and humble obedience." The act provided that matters involving the king's business were to go to the Upper House of Convocation, which had final jurisdiction without any recourse to appeals outside the realm—to Rome, for example.

One bit of royal business was daily growing more urgent. In January of 1533, nearly six years after Henry's secret divorce from Catherine, he had secretly married Anne Boleyn. Although he and Catherine had separated, the divorce had not been made public, and he was not certain its legality would be upheld. Now Anne was obviously pregnant, and the king needed to ensure the child's legitimacy before it was born if it was ever to be able to succeed him. With the passage of the Act in Restraint of Appeals, Archbishop Cranmer could pronounce the divorce from Catherine and the marriage to Anne valid. In June Anne was crowned queen, and a few days later Henry was excommunicated by the pope. By this time the country was disinterested in papal actions, and Henry boasted that he would not care a straw if the pope promulgated ten thousand excommunications. In September Princess Elizabeth was born. Parliament then obligingly passed the Act of Succession, which established the heirs of Henry and Anne as legitimate successors to the crown. All subjects were required to swear an oath in support of this act. Later in 1534 the Act of Supremacy fully defined the royal headship over the church and authorized royal visitations. The Treason Act of November 1534, designed to protect his majesty and his loving family from subversive opposition, completed the legislative breastworks of the national church and the house of Tudor.

The resistance to Henry's ecclesiastical revolution from the top was surprisingly small, but two prominent martyrs were offered up as token sacrifices: a clergyman, Bishop John Fisher, and a devout layman, Sir Thomas More, who had once considered entering the monastic life and wore a hair shirt to humble his flesh. Fisher and More were unable in good conscience to swear the oath required by the Act of Supremacy, for in effect it repudiated the authority of the pope. Fisher had already been imprisoned for alleged collusion with the so-called Nun of Kent, who had prophesied Henry's perdition for marrying Anne. Now Fisher and More were taken to the Tower and held there for more than a year before being brought to trial. Fisher was marked for the martyr's red when Pope Paul III bestowed on him the cardinal's red. Henry is reported to have sneered, "Well, let the pope send him a hat when he will; but I will provide that whensoever it cometh, he shall wear it on his shoulders, for head he shall have none to set it on." On June 22, 1535, Fisher was beheaded.

Sir Thomas More earned his sainthood by resisting all temptations to yield.

His second wife urged him to think of all the preferments and comforts of life he could enjoy by acknowledging the king's religious supremacy, a temptation he easily rejected. His daughter urged him to consider that he was pitting his single opinion against that of many churchmen who had denied the papal primacy, and that he had turned against his own king, an argument that sorely tried his conscience. "Daughter," responded More firmly, "I never intend to pin my soul to another man's back!" He had a great fear that under the laws of treason he might be disemboweled, not merely beheaded. In prison More, who had been a harsh polemicist against Tyndale and the Protestants, wrote beautiful nonpolitical religious treatises, such as his *Dialogue of Comfort Against Tribulation*. More managed to retain his dry humor to the end. His son-in-law Roper, though he was not present himself, relates that when More mounted the scaffold he said, "I pray you, Master Lieutenant, see me safe up, and for my coming down let me shift for myself." He is said to have asked the executioner to spare his beard, for it had committed no treason. In contrast to More, Reginald Pole chose exile, and was rewarded in due course with a cardinalate.

In February 1536 the Reformation Parliament received reports on the monasteries from Cromwell's inspectors and passed the first Act of Dissolution. Economic necessity combined with religious motives and the anticlerical spirit of the Commons to bring Henry to undertake the suppression of the monasteries. By the act of 1536 parliament suppressed the smaller houses that had incomes of less than £200. The larger monasteries surrendered to the king, most of them under duress; the last to submit was Waltham Abbey in Essex, which capitulated on March 23, 1540. The monasteries were really in much better moral condition than Cromwell's propaganda and later historians supposed. Some orders, such as the Carthusians, had high morale and an exemplary record. They even provided some martyrs to Henry, including the prior of the London Charterhouse. In 1539 the abbots of Glastonbury, Reading, and Colchester were hanged, but they were victims of circumstances rather than heroes or willing martyrs. The monasteries were closed more for expediency than for principle, although even these spoils, which increased the crown's annual income by more than £100,000 by the 1540s, did not provide resources adequate for Henry's needs. With the dissolution of the monasteries the shock troops of the old church were gone, and there could never be a return to things as they had once been.

The monastic lands that passed into the hands of the gentry contributed to the further rise of this class and its participation in national government, while on a lower level the enriched squires increasingly dominated local government. The revenue from the sale of lands and other properties went as pensions to some former monks and nuns, to endow new sees, to support new schools and colleges, and to enrich the king's purse.

The dissolution contributed to a disaffection among the masses which led to the group of uprisings known collectively as the Pilgrimage of Grace. It is difficult to say precisely to what extent the four uprisings were anti-Reformation in character. For in the Lincolnshire rebellion, in the main pilgrimage under Robert Aske in Yorkshire, Lancashire, and the northeastern counties, and in two separate Yorkshire rebellions between October 1536 and January 1537, many bitter local and economic grievances were mixed with religious conservatism, irrational superstitions, and even apocalyptic elements. The pilgrimage can hardly be considered a desperate crusade to confound the heretics, reestablish the monasteries, or restore the papal dominion. The rebellions were easily suppressed.

The Emergence of Anglicanism

THE RENOWNED BRITISH HISTORIAN Thomas Babington Macaulay described the Church of England as "the fruit of the union" between the government and the Protestants, the result of compromise by both parties to its conception. The alliance of the crown and the Protestants was an uneasy one, marked by periods of tension and regression. Henry VIII seems to have believed it possible to dissolve the ties to Rome without changing the doctrine and worship of the church. He remained personally conservative in theology, and from 1532 to 1540 he was caught between the radical group, led by Cromwell and Cranmer, and the conservative group, headed by the duke of Norfolk and Stephen Gardiner, bishop of Winchester. At first the radicals and then, after Cromwell's fall in 1540, the conservatives had their day at court. Henry strove to preside over the rival factions, much as his daughter Elizabeth was to maintain a position above the Anglican and Puritan parties later in the century. As a result, the Reformation followed the comprehensive *via media* in England as it did nowhere else on the continent, except perhaps in Sweden.

The "middle way" of Anglicanism was comprehensive territorially, for it embraced all the inhabitants of the realm except for a few diehard Catholics, who were very much in hiding, and doctrinally, for it sought to include both the conservatives and as many of the radicals as could be accommodated without public scandal and offense. One of the most representative statements pleading for the middle way was the treatise of Thomas Starkey, *An Exhortation to Unity and Obedience.* Starkey, an Erasmian humanist and formerly a member of Reginald Pole's Padua circle, argued that all citizens were bound by God's law and by all good civility to embrace the middle way between "superstition" on the one hand and division, controversy, and sedition on the other. He employed Melanchthon's teaching on *adiaphora,* or things indifferent, to urge that matters of belief or practice that are not specifically defined in the Scriptures and not essential to salvation should not be made binding upon consciences or insisted upon as necessary to orthodoxy. This idea proved to be a seed of toleration that bore fruit in due course. Ironically, however, the *adiaphora* concept was double-edged, for later on, in Elizabeth's reign, instead of leading to a tolerant, comprehensive Anglicanism, the doctrine was used to justify the retention of the episcopal hierarchy, the ceremonial rubrics, and the like, which were then backed up by enforced conformity and submission. In this and other ways Starkey, Richard Morison, and other young humanists contributed to the ideological foundations of Tudor policy.

Even the conservatives had a lofty notion of the divine right of kings, related to the ancient concept of thaumaturgical or sacramental kingship. Stephen Gardiner, for example, in his *On True Obedience* (1535), was close to Marsiglio of Padua in his conception of the obedience owed by true Christians to the king as God's representative on earth, a father to his children and a master to his servants. Since the king and parliament had decreed that the English people should be separated from Rome, all should obey, for theirs was the rightful authority. Poor Gardiner was hard pressed to explain away this book when Catholic Queen Mary ascended the throne. His lame explanation then was that he had written it out of fear that he would suffer the fate of Fisher and More.

The leading role in religious reform was played by Thomas Cranmer (1489–1556), a complex personality of gentle birth, with a kindly disposition and a mind open to change, though he was no great creative thinker or very forceful leader. As a fellow at Jesus College he took priest's orders, earned the degree of doctor of divinity, and seemed headed for the life of a scholar until the king's business intervened. After several missions for the king to the Lutherans, among whom he met and married the niece of Osiander, the reformer in Nuremberg, and to the emperor in Vienna and northern Italy, he was made archbishop of Canterbury in 1533, with the expectation that he would be the king's pliant instrument. With the enthusiastic support of Cromwell, Cranmer promoted the publication of the English Bible and the introduction of an English litany. He received royal permission for the publication of Matthew's Bible in 1537. The text was basically Tyndale's and the polemical notes proved to be so offensive that Miles Coverdale was asked to revise it. This Great Bible appeared upon the lecterns in 1539 and proved to be the surest foundation for the building of Protestantism. Cranmer's theological views moved by gradual stages from a position close to Luther's, on the sacrament, for example, to Swiss interpretations close to those of Oecolampadius. He moved slowly and deliberately in the direction of less conservative Protestant convictions. He was one of the more dependable of Cromwell's partisans.

Cromwell's overthrow by Norfolk and Gardiner was due to his hapless selection of Anne of Cleves, the "Flemish mare," for Henry's fourth sally into matrimony, as well as to his failure to check a dangerous deterioration in the political and religious situation. Anne Boleyn fared no better than Queen Catherine, for she too produced a daughter and no male heir to the throne. She was beheaded for adultery in 1536, the same year that Catherine died. Henry then married colorless Jane Seymour, who gave birth to Edward VI and died in 1537. Henry made some approaches toward the Protestants in authorizing the English Bible and accepting the Ten Articles, which mentioned only three of the seven sacraments, although they did not formally abolish or deny the other four. Fearing a hostile combination of Charles V and Francis I against England, Henry followed Cromwell's diplomatic maneuvering for allies among the German Protestant states, and thus became ensnared in the marriage with Anne, daughter of the Erasmian duke of Cleves. When the Franco-Spanish crusade against England proved to be fictitious and Anne proved to be all too repugnant a reality for Henry, the king reacted by divorcing her and beheading Cromwell on July 28, 1540.

The triumph of the conservative party under Norfolk and Gardiner was celebrated by Henry's marriage to Catherine Howard. The very Catholic Six Articles (May 16, 1539) were intended to restore basic Catholic teachings on transubstantiation, communion in one kind, the celibacy of the clergy, vows of chastity, private masses, and compulsory auricular confessions. The punishments prescribed for violations were so savage that the articles were known as the "whip with the six bloody strings." Spasmodic outbursts of persecution claimed the lives of Protestant martyrs, but the conservatives failed to dislodge Cranmer from his position as archbishop of Canterbury. Luckless Henry sent Catherine Howard to the block for adultery in 1542, and in his final years found solace in the learned company of Catherine Parr, who survived him. He died on January 27, 1547, ministered to by Cranmer, in whom he trusted to the very end. In his will, however, Henry provided that many masses were to be said for his soul.

The Edwardian Reformation

UPON THE ACCESSION of Henry's son, Edward VI (1537–1553), the prophets of doom again intoned one of their favorite texts, "Woe to the land whose king is a boy!" Even though Holbein's portrait of Edward at the age of two shows him as a healthy child, he was really very frail and was never expected to live many years. His childhood was plagued by tutors such as Roger Ascham, who schooled him so thoroughly in Latin and Greek, as well as French, that by the age of thirteen he was able to read Aristotle's *Ethics* in Greek and to translate Cicero's *De philosophia* into Greek. All factions sought to control him in their struggle for power. During his first three years as king real power was in the hands of his uncle, the handsome, affable, sincere Protestant Edward Seymour, earl of Hertford, who took the title duke of Somerset and was known as Protector Somerset. During Edward's remaining years that crafty intriguer John Dudley, earl of Warwick, who became duke of Northumberland, dominated him. The course of the Reformation under Edward VI was determined primarily by social and domestic considerations rather than by issues of foreign policy.

A few hours after nine-year-old Edward was proclaimed king, the council voted Hertford protector. After a few weeks the protector received a patent that enabled him to act with great personal power. He nevertheless proceeded with considerable moderation, and Cranmer, who now enjoyed more freedom of action than he had for years, proceeded to promote Protestantism with surprising restraint. In a session of parliament the new government indulged in what has been called a "self-denying orgy," rescinding Henry's harsh additions to the old treason laws, repealing the Six Articles Act, removing all restrictions on the printing, sale, and expounding of the Bible, and annulling the act that gave royal proclamations the force of law.

In a move that affected the life of the people more directly than the dissolution of the monasteries had done, Edward's first parliament passed a new chantries act, which transferred to the crown all chantries, which were essentially endowments for masses for the souls of the dead, and all free chapels, colleges, fraternities, and guilds. This broad-scale secularization reached into the life of nearly every parish. It coincided with the Protestant rejection of intercession for the souls of the dead in purgatory. It contributed to a reshuffling of wealth in many communities, and brought into question the motives of some Protestants, including the protector, who displayed an inordinate interest in the building of his great house. But even these new resources failed to meet the needs of the royal treasury.

Further religious change came about with official blessing and on the popular level, although it is safe to say that only a minority of the people had real Protestant convictions during Edward's reign. Cranmer's *First Prayer Book* was a brilliant piece of studied ambiguity, sufficiently traditional in form to pacify the Henrician Catholics—although in English, of course—and yet so phrased, even in respect to the Eucharist, as to allow its use in good conscience by the Protestants. An act of uniformity provided sufficiently severe penalties to ensure use of the prayerbook by all the clergy. Calvinism had begun to make inroads during Henry's last years, and Protestant propaganda became even more strident and insistent during the reign of King Edward.

Somerset fell to his enemies in October 1549, helpless before the social, political, and religious unrest, having at the outset given away many instruments of strong government he now desperately needed. By skillful maneuvering the earl of Warwick gathered the dissident forces about him, and the council sent Somerset to the Tower and to eventual execution in 1552. The price of failure in Tudor politics was often death. Warwick, who adopted the title of duke of Northumberland in 1551, was thoroughly unscrupulous. Having deceived the Catholic faction into supporting him, he proceeded to promote the Reformation more radically than Somerset had ever done.

From his initial suggestion early in his career that Henry consult the universities about his "great question," Cranmer had been concerned with England's ties to continental Protestantism. He invited Melanchthon to England, and though the Wittenberg reformer could not accept, other Protestant leaders came in a steady stream from Strassburg, Zurich, and Geneva. The most notable among them was Martin Bucer of Strassburg, the charitable mediating theologian, forced out of his home city by the Interim imposed by Emperor Charles V. Bucer arrived in 1549 and through Cranmer's influence was given the regius chair at Cambridge. He finished writing his *On the Kingdom of Christ* there and contributed to the second Edwardian prayerbook, but his strength was spent and he died in February 1551. In the fall of 1548 the Polish nobleman John à Lasco arrived and consulted with Cranmer. In 1550 he returned from Friesland to become superintendent over four ministers to foreign Protestants. Holding an amalgam of Calvinist and Zwinglian views, Lasco developed a refugee congregation of some five thousand members along Puritan lines, with rule by elected presbyters or elders, rigorously enforced church discipline, and an emphasis upon edification (two-hour sermons) and the Christian life. Two Italian refugees came to England for a time by way of Strassburg, Peter Martyr Vermigli and Bernardino Ochino, as well as a militant Protestant from Scotland, the rambunctious John Knox. The radical Anabaptists, however, were as unwelcome in England as they were elsewhere.

The Edwardian bishops who shouldered the main burden of the Anglican reform covered a somewhat narrower spectrum, from the Puritan-like John Hooper to the more main-line Nicholas Ridley of Rochester and London. Clerical marriage was a subject of considerable controversy. A statute of February 1549 permitted the clergy to marry, and those who did so generally suffered little or no unfavorable reaction from the public, which as usual resolved the problem by condemning the women involved; prejudice against the wives of bishops and priests lasted into and beyond the Elizabethan period. With the introduction of a more distinct Protestant liturgy, the government felt justified in confiscating church plate, vestments, and other valuables. But Northumberland was building up a deep black pool of ill will that was soon to engulf him.

Edward's health began to fail markedly in 1552, and by May 1553 everyone realized that the king was dying, though he did not oblige until July 6. Intent upon securing his personal domination of the government, Northumberland married his son to the sixteen-year-old Lady Jane Grey, grandniece of Henry VIII and a Protestant, and then persuaded Edward to name Jane as his successor in place of his older sister Mary, who was Catholic. But when Edward died, Northumberland committed a fatal blunder in not having Mary in a secure prison. She slipped away to

East Anglia, and the people rallied around her as the heiress designated in law by Henry. Lady Jane, appalled at finding herself queen, reigned just nine days before she and her young husband were imprisoned for treason. Northumberland too was committed to the Tower, and right up to the day of his execution he made frantic last-minute efforts to save his skin by admonishing everyone within earshot to eschew heresy and embrace the Catholic religion. But he could save neither himself, his son, nor Lady Jane. Eventually all three were beheaded.

The Marian Reaction

QUEEN MARY was a high-spirited woman with more than her share of Tudor obstinacy. Her entire life was tragic. When she was still an infant she was used as a pawn in the marriage designs of Francis I and then of Charles V. Her own father had forced her to acknowledge herself a bastard, though later, in the Act of Succession, he had made a place for her as successor to Edward. As the daughter of a Spanish princess, she was brought up an ardent and narrow Catholic. Worse still for her political prospects, she thought of herself not as English, but as Spanish. She further alienated the English by marrying her cousin Philip II, the king of Spain, instead of a sturdy Englishman. In her persecution of heretics, Mary was not inherently cruel, merely fanatical. History has done her an injustice by tagging her with the sobriquet "Bloody Mary."

No sooner was Mary acclaimed queen than she turned Edward's Protestant officials out and returned to office Bishops Gardiner, Tunstall, Heath, Bonner, and Day. Cardinal Reginald Pole came as papal legate to absolve the kingdom of disobedience to the Holy See, and for so renowned a Christian humanist he proved to be a severe and uncompromising leader of reaction. When Mary announced her intention of marrying Philip of Spain, English national resentment ran high. The Commons sent a deputation to beg her not to marry a foreigner, and a series of insurrections broke out. The most serious threat was the rebellion led by young Sir Thomas Wyatt, who stirred up the county of Kent with hatred for the Spaniard and led some four thousand men to the gates of London before he was repulsed. It was this rebellion that determined Mary to have Lady Jane Grey's head. Up till then, though Lady Jane remained in prison, her hopes for a pardon were not unrealistic. Now Mary saw that as long as a Protestant contender for the throne, however unwilling, remained alive, there would be men who would try to put her there. After Wyatt's failure, Mary's second parliament revoked all statutes that had been enacted against papal authority since 1529.

Mary's marriage to Philip was a disappointment all around, and it eventually became clear that she would not succeed in having children by him. Embittered, all but ignored by her husband, she then turned to the suppression of Protestantism. Many prominent Protestant divines were imprisoned: John Rogers, Hugh Latimer, Nicholas Ridley, John Hooper, Miles Coverdale, and others. John Foxe in his *Book of Martyrs* recorded the lurid details of the executions and the courage of those who were ready to die for the faith by which they had lived. Dour Hurrell Froude once remarked that the best that was to be said of the reformers was that they burned well. John Rogers, editor of Matthew's Bible, was the first to go, burned on February 4, 1555. Hugh Latimer, formerly bishop of Worcester and a great Reformation preacher, was led with Ridley to the stake in the great ditch opposite Balliol College, Oxford. Latimer, a man of humility and moderation, died like a saint. He cheered Ridley with the heroic words: "Be of good comfort, Master Ridley, and play the man; we shall this day light such a candle by God's grace in England as (I trust) shall never be put out." He "received the flame," the martyrology recounts, "as it were embracing it. After he had stroked his face with his hands, and (as it were) bathed them a little in the fire, he soon died (as it appeared) with very little pain or none." A recent list numbers the victims of Mary's persecution at 282. Many of those burned for heresy were lowborn artisans; the rich bought their way clear. Some lucky Protestants were merely jailed or flogged. Edmund Bonner, bishop of London, answered a critic who had chided him for having an old man whipped in a "pelting chafe": "If thou hadst been in his case, thou wouldst have thought it a good commutation of penance to have thy bum beaten to save thy body from burning."

Thomas Cranmer was now put to the ultimate test. Philip and Mary requested that his case be reserved for papal disposition. He was ordered to appear in Rome within eighty days, but his trial was finally held in the university church of St. Mary the Virgin at Oxford. Pope Paul IV's representative, Bishop Brooks, sat on a platform ten feet high before the altar, while the royal prosecutors below charged Cranmer with blasphemy, incontinency, and heresy. Found guilty, he was stripped of his insignia of office in a humiliating ceremony and condemned to death. After his degradation, Cranmer, desperately afraid of the fire awaiting him, signed seven submissions and recantations. But the authorities were adamant: he must burn. On March 21, 1556, he was placed on a stage opposite the pulpit in St. Mary's. There he stood, the "very image and shape of perfect sorrow," with tears streaming down his cheeks. When it was his turn to speak he exhorted all men to true obedience toward rulers and to love toward all men. Then he astonished everyone present by reading a recantation of all his recantations:

> And now I come to the great thing, that so much troubleth my conscience, more than anything that ever I did or said in my whole life; and this is the setting abroad of a writing contrary to the Truth; which now here I renounce and refuse, as things written with my hand, contrary to the truth which I thought in my heart, and written for fear of death, and to save my life, if it might be; and that is, all such bills

and papers which I have written or signed with my own hand since my degradation; wherein I have written many things untrue and forasmuch as my hand offended, writing contrary to my heart, my hand shall first be punished therefore; for, may I come to the fire, it shall be first burned.[7]

Then he denounced the pope and acknowledged his own book on the Sacrament as representing his true belief. Cranmer was pulled off the stage, dragged to the ditch where Latimer and Ridley had died, and burned. The martyrologist recounts:

> When the wood was kindled and the fire began to burn near him, stretching out his arm, he put his right hand into the flame, which he held so steadfast and immovable (saving that once with the same hand he wiped his face) that all men might see his hand burned before his body was touched. . . . Using often the words of Stephen, Lord Jesus receive my spirit; in the greatness of the flame he gave up the ghost.

Although the conservative north and west seemed to support Mary quite strongly, the Protestant underground maintained itself in London and elsewhere. Reginald Pole was not a forward-looking leader; he rejected, for example, Ignatius Loyola's offer to train seminarians as ideological shock troops. Mary's Catholic restoration had a backward-looking, medieval, even monastic cast to it, and did not realistically take into consideration the fact that England had undergone fundamental changes in outlook. All the portents pointed toward evil days during the final months of Mary's reign. As the childless queen maneuvered to perpetuate her will in religious matters, nature intervened with disease and pestilence to decimate the number of bishops and lesser ecclesiasts. The Marian exiles were waiting on the continent to fill the vacancies. But Mary died in the early morning hours of November 17, 1558, and her strong man, Archbishop Reginald Pole, died in his sleep just twelve hours later. Young Queen Elizabeth, who succeeded her, was "pure English," and her succession to the throne was greeted with bonfires and revelry in London and throughout the realm.

The Reformation in Scotland

THE SCOTTISH REFORMATION was a Johnny-come-lately in the Reformation movement. By 1560 over four decades had passed since Luther initiated the Reformation and nearly a generation since Henry VIII broke with the pope. An act of parliament in 1525 forbade the importation of Lutheran books into Scotland, but they continued to come in through port towns. The burning of Patrick Hamilton for evangelical preaching in 1528 precipitated a number of executions and iconoclastic

---

[7] F. E. Hutchinson, *Cranmer and the Reformation* (London, 1951), p. 157.

incidents. Cardinal Beaton burned the bold evangelist George Wishart at St. Andrews in 1546 and was himself waylaid and murdered three months later in his own castle at St. Andrews. Much animosity built up before the dam burst in Scotland.

The direction in which Scotland moved was of vital importance to British and European history. A Protestant Scotland would mean a rapprochement with Protestant England. A Catholic Scotland meant a continuation of the alliance with France and intermittent hostilities with England. Scotland was relatively backward economically and was dominated locally by clans of lesser nobility. Certainly there can be no talk of a middle class inclined toward Protestantism or of Protestantism as an expression of class interest, giving impetus to the rise of capitalism. Rather there was a strong current of protest against the ignorance and lewdness of the secular clergy during the decades preceding the critical year 1560. The monks seem to have played little part, either as objects of scorn or as leaders of reform, although the canons regular were a constructive force.

The hero of the Scottish Reformation was the "thundering Scot" John Knox (1513–1572), a strong, stocky, swarthy priest of peasant lineage, who stood guard with a two-edged sword while Wishart preached. After Wishart's death Knox joined the Protestant garrison defending the castle at St. Andrews against French troops determined to preserve the power and the religion of their countrywoman Mary of Guise, widow of James V of Scotland and regent for their young daughter, Mary, queen of Scots. In August 1547 the French captured the defenders of St. Andrews, and for nineteen months Knox was forced to work as a galley slave, chained to a rowing bench, which was his only shelter from the weather. He finally reached England in April 1549, no little embittered against the Catholic French. When King Edward died, Knox fled to Calvin's Geneva. In 1556 he wrote to a Mrs. Locke of his new spiritual haven, "whair I nether feir nor schame to say is the nearest perfyt school of Chryst that ever was in the erth since the dayis of the Apostillis."

In 1559 the Scottish Protestants sent a delegation to Geneva to urge Knox to come home. Calvin declared that Knox must heed the call "unless he would declare himself rebellious unto his God and unmerciful to his country." Knox had attacked Catholic Mary of Guise, calling her an "unruly cow saddled by mistake." In 1558 he had published his *First Blast Against the Monstrous Regiment of Women,* declaring that to "promote a woman to have rule above any realm is repugnant to nature, contumely to God, a thing most contrarious to His revealed will and approved ordinance, and finally it is the subversion of good order, of all equity and justice." Now Knox returned to Scotland, and the English sent an army to help the Protestants drive out the French. Mary of Guise died during the war, and the Treaty of Edinburgh, July 6, 1560, assured the triumph of Protestantism. An act of parliament on August 24 outlawed Catholicism in the land.

John Knox preached in St. Giles' Cathedral with great energy. His student

James Melville related how Knox in the pulpit "behoved to lean at his first entry; but ere he had done with his sermon, he was so active and vigorous that he was like to ding that pulpit in blads [pieces] and fly out of it." When he lectured on the prophet Daniel, Knox made Melville shudder and tremble so much that he "could not hold a pen to write." Knox's Calvinist Presbyterianism is reflected in each of the three basic documents of the Scottish Reformation, the *Confession of Faith,* the *Book of Common Order,* and the *First Book of Discipline.* Knox also impressed his image of what had transpired upon posterity with his *History of the Reformation in Scotland.*

In 1561 Mary, queen of Scots, age eighteen, returned from France on the death of her husband, King Francis II. At first conciliatory, she reverted to a hard line against the Protestants, and was forced to flee to England in 1567. The triumph of Knox and the Reformation was astonishing for both its suddenness and its durability. Watching the outcome of the struggle from Geneva, John Calvin commented, "As we wonder at success incredible in so short a time, so also we give great thanks to God, whose special blessing here shines forth."

Bibliography

The Reformation in England:
CHILD, G. W. *Church and State Under the Tudors.* London, 1950.
DICKENS, A. G. *Lollards and Protestants in the Diocese of York.* Oxford, 1959.
———. *The English Reformation.* London, 1964.
GAIRDNER, JAMES. *Lollardy and the Reformation in England,* 4 vols. London, 1908–1913.
GASQUET, F. A. *The Eve of the Reformation.* London, 1900.
GEORGE, CHARLES, and GEORGE, CATHERINE. *The Protestant Mind of the English Reformation.* Princeton, 1961.
HUGHES, PHILIP. *The Reformation in England,* 3 vols. London, 1950–1954.
KNOWLES, DOM DAVID. *The Religious Orders in England,* 3 vols. Cambridge, 1948–1959.
LOANE, MARCUS. *Masters of the English Reformation.* London, 1954.
McCONICA, JAMES K. *English Humanists and Reformation Politics under Henry VIII and Edward VI.* Oxford, 1965.
MAITLAND, S. R. *The Reformation in England.* London and New York, 1906.
PARKER, T. H. L., ed. *English Reformers,* vol. 26 of *Library of Christian Classics.* Philadelphia, 1966.
PARKER, T. M. *The English Reformation to 1558.* New York, 1950.
POWICKE, MAURICE. *The Reformation in England.* New York, 1941.
THOMPSON, A. H. *The English Clergy and Their Organization in the Later Middle Ages.* Oxford, 1947.
WOODWARD, GEORGE. *Reformation and Resurgence, 1485–1603.* London, 1963.

Henry VIII:
BAUMER, F. L. *Early Tudor Theory of Kingship.* New Haven, 1940.
CONSTANT, G. *The Reformation in England: Henry VIII, 1509–1547.* New York, 1934.

DOERNBERG, ERWIN. *Henry VIII and Luther.* Stanford, 1961.

ELTON, G. R. *England Under the Tudors.* London, 1955.

———. *The Tudor Revolution in Government: Administrative Changes in the Reign of Henry VIII.* Cambridge, 1962.

INNES, A. D. *England Under the Tudors,* 9th ed. London, 1929.

JACOBS, H. E. *The Lutheran Movement in England During the Reigns of Henry VIII and Edward VI.* Philadelphia, 1894.

MACKIE, J. D. *The Earlier Tudors, 1485–1558.* Oxford, 1952.

MATTINGLY, GARRETT. *Catherine of Aragon.* Boston, 1941.

PICKTHORN, K. *Early Tudor Government.* Cambridge, 1934.

POLLARD, A. F. *Henry VIII.* London, 1913.

———. *Wolsey.* London, 1929.

READ, CONYERS. *The Tudors.* New York, 1936.

SCARISBRICK, J. J. *Henry VIII.* Berkeley, 1968.

SMITH, HERBERT M. *Henry VIII and the Reformation.* London, 1948.

SMITH, LACEY BALDWIN. *Tudor Prelates and Politics.* Princeton, 1953.

TJERNAGEL, NEELAK. *Henry VIII and the Lutherans.* St. Louis, 1966.

ZEEVELDT, W. G. *Foundations of Tudor Policy.* Cambridge, Mass., 1948.

Cranmer and other churchmen:

BROMILEY, G. W. *Baptism and the Anglican Reformers.* London, 1953.

———. *Thomas Cranmer, Theologian.* New York and London, 1956.

BROOKS, PETER. *Thomas Cranmer's Doctrine of the Eucharist.* London, 1965.

CHESTER, ALLAN G. *Hugh Latimer, Apostle to the English.* Philadelphia, 1954.

CLARK, FRANCIS, S. J. *Eucharistic Sacrifice and the Reformation.* Westminster, Md., 1960.

CLEBSCH, WILLIAM A. *England's Earliest Protestants, 1520–1535.* New Haven, 1964.

DUFFIELD, G. E., ed. *The Work of William Tyndale.* Philadelphia, 1965.

DUGMORE, C. W. *The Mass and the English Reformers.* New York, 1948.

HUTCHINSON, FRANCIS E. *Cranmer and the English Reformation.* New York, 1951.

MAYNARD, THEODORE. *The Life of Thomas Cranmer.* Chicago, 1956.

MEYER, CARL S., ed. *Cranmer's Selected Writings.* Greenwich, Conn., 1961.

MOZLEY, J. F. *William Tyndale.* London, 1937.

PERRY, E. W. *Under Four Tudors.* London, 1940.

POLLARD, A. F. *Thomas Cranmer and the English Reformation, 1489–1556.* New York, 1904.

RICHARDSON, CYRIL C. *Zwingli and Cranmer on the Eucharist.* Evanston, Ill., 1949.

RIDLEY, JASPER G. *Nicholas Ridley: A Biography.* London, 1957.

———. *Thomas Cranmer.* Oxford, 1962.

RUPP, E. GORDON. *Six Makers of English Religion, 1500–1700.* New York, 1957.

SMYTH, C. H. *Cranmer and the Reformation Under Edward VI.* Cambridge, 1926.

WILLOUGHBY, H. R. *The First Authorized English Bible and the Cranmer Preface.* Chicago, 1942.

Edward VI:

CHAPMAN, HESTER W. *Last Tudor King: A Study of Edward VI.* New York, 1959.

JORDAN, WILBUR K. *Edward VI: The Young King.* Cambridge, Mass., 1968.

POLLARD, A. F. *The History of England from the Accession of Edward VI to the Death of Elizabeth (1547–1603).* London, 1910.

PRIMUS, JOHN HENRY. *The Vestments Controversy.* Kampen, 1960.

Mary Tudor:
GARRET, CHRISTINA H. *The Marian Exiles.* Cambridge, 1938.
HARBISON, E. HARRIS. *Rival Ambassadors at the Court of Queen Mary.* Princeton, 1940.
MULLER, J. A. *Stephen Gardiner and the Tudor Reaction.* New York, 1926.
OXLEY, JAMES. *The Reformation in Essex to the Death of Mary.* Manchester, 1965.
PRESCOTT, HILDA, F.M. *Mary Tudor.* London, 1952.
SCHENK, WILHELM. *Reginald Pole, Cardinal of England.* London, 1950.

The Reformation in Scotland:
BURLEIGH, JOHN H. *A Church History of Scotland.* New York, 1960.
DICKINSON, W. CROFT, ed. *John Knox's History of the Reformation in Scotland.* London, 1949.
DONALDSON, GORDON. *The Scottish Reformation.* Cambridge, 1960.
GORE-BROWNE, R. *Lord Bothwell and Mary Queen of Scots.* New York, 1937.
HENDERSON, T. F. *Mary Queen of Scots,* 2 vols. New York, 1905.
HURLBUT, S. A. *The Liturgy and the Church of Scotland,* 4 vols. Charleston, S.C., 1944–1952.
KNOX, JOHN. *The History of the Reformation in Scotland,* ed. William C. Dickinson. New York, 1950.
MACGREGOR, G. *The Thundering Scot.* Philadelphia, 1952.
MCROBERTS, DAVID, ed. *Essays on the Scottish Reformation, 1513–1625.* Glasgow, 1962.
MAHON, R. H. *Mary Queen of Scots.* Cambridge, 1924.
PERCY, LORD EUSTACE. *John Knox.* London, 1937.
RIDLEY, JASPER G. *John Knox.* New York, 1968.
WATT, HUGH. *John Knox in Controversy.* New York, 1950.
WILLOUGHBY, H. R. *The First Authorized English Bible and the Cranmer Preface.* Chicago, 1942.

CHAPTER 18

The Catholic
Reformation

Pope Clement VII, who faced the shock of the Reformation and suffered the trauma of the sack of Rome, had a medal struck depicting Christ bound to a column and below him the foreboding device *Post multa, plurima restant:* After many things, even more remain. Clement, in a dark apocalyptic mood, believed that the last days of the world were at hand. Just before his own days came to an end he commissioned the great Michelangelo to portray the Last Judgment on the front wall of the Sistine Chapel. And yet only a few decades later baroque artists delighted in portraying the church as triumphant over her enemies. The change in mood was a result of the astonishing success of the Catholic Reformation in spiritually invigorating the old church and in stemming the tide of Protestantism.

It took shock treatment to restore the mental and spiritual health of the church. From the intellectual, religious, and institutional crisis of the Renaissance and Reformation movements the church emerged chastened and scourged, but purer and more vital than she had been for centuries. The increased knowledge, especially derived from new Greek sources, the doctrinal challenges of the evangelicals based upon the Scriptures, and the defection of half of Europe threatened to engulf the ark of the church. For years the church seemed completely impotent, too paralyzed to react to the blows that fell upon her. Good churchmen interpreted the sufferings of Rome as a punishment for her sins. In 1528 Bishop Stafileo declared that the city had been laid low "because all flesh had given way to corruption and because we are no longer the inhabitants of the holy city of Rome, but of the perverted city of Babylon." Many believed that if only the Fifth Lateran Council had responded to Aegidius da Viterbo's admonitions to reform in 1512, the church might have been spared the scourging of the Almighty. But the supreme pontiffs were themselves too confused, stunned, or inept to respond effectively to the thrusts of the reformers.

The Reformation Popes

THE LATERAN COUNCIL in 1512 reaffirmed the full power of the pope, condemned conciliarism, and denounced the tendency toward independence of the national clergies. But the popes of the Reformation era were not the inspired and incisive monarchs needed to act in such a crisis. Some time was lost under Leo X before the full danger of the schism was fully appreciated. But by the time Leo X died, on December 1, 1521, the cardinals recognized the gravity of the situation. On January 9, 1522, they elected a Dutch cardinal with a spotless reputation, Adrian Floriszoon, to lead the church in its own reformation. Adrian VI, as he styled himself, had studied with the Brethren of the Common Life and taught theology at Louvain, and he was a friend of Erasmus and the tutor of young Charles V. In Spain, as archbishop of Tortosa and papal legate in Castile and Aragon, he encountered the severe discipline of the Spanish church. He was no stranger to politics, for he had served as regent of Spain in the absence of Charles. He established a severe discipline upon the prelates under him and had all the makings of an earnest and zealous reformer. But Adrian VI proved to be completely ineffective as pope, for the Italians despised him for his rude Latin, his indifference to art, and his naïveté, by Italian Renaissance standards. He died disappointed and frustrated on September 14, 1523, and his epitaph is an apt commentary on his brief pontificate: "Alas! How the power even of a most righteous man depends upon the times in which he happens to live!"

The cardinals, impressed by the futility of Adrian VI's reform efforts and relieved by the brevity of the reign of the last non-Italian pope, on November 18 proclaimed as the new pope a cousin of Leo X, Giulio de' Medici, who adopted the name Clement VII. Giulio was the son of Lorenzo's brother Giuliano, who had been murdered in the cathedral of Florence at the time of the Pazzi revolt. Clement VII was a witty, easygoing, urbane churchman, a patron of the arts. He had no really ostentatious vices, but he had one basic constitutional flaw: he was indecisive and given to procrastination. He was politically adroit, but not sufficiently forceful for the desperate times in which he ruled. The pope's involvement in Italian intrigues and the conflicts of the major powers—the price that had to be paid for possession of the Papal States—reduced the spiritual prestige and moral influence of the papacy in the eyes of the faithful and foes alike. Clement shared Erasmus' view that sending the supercilious Cajetan and the overbearing Aleander to cope with the Lutheran situation had been a mistake. He sent instead as nuncio to the Diet of Nuremberg in 1524 the moderate, learned, and good-humored Cardinal Campeggio, who went prepared to make such important concessions as allowing the sacramental cup to the laity and marriage to the clergy. But no real progress toward reconciliation was made, for the doctrinal differences ran too deep to be glossed over by offers of wine and women. The Catholic princes of Austria and Bavaria ordered their students to leave heretical universities and return home. It became increasingly clear even to Clement VII that only a church council could possibly cope with the Protestant rebellion. Early in May 1532 he consented to a council, but on September 25, 1534, he died without having actually convoked one.

The new pope, Paul III, was more serious and resolute about reform and a council. In some ways Alexander Farnese was a typical Renaissance prelate. He had a family of illegitimate children, and shortly after his accession to the papal throne he made cardinals of his fourteen- and fifteen-year-old grandsons, Ascanio Sforza and Alexander Farnese, as "props for his old age," as he put it. He encouraged conversations with moderate evangelical theologians such as Martin Bucer and Melanchthon. He bestowed red hats upon a number of Erasmian churchmen between May and December 1536: Gasparo Contarini, Pietro Bembo, Jacopo Sadoleto, Giampietro Caraffa, Jean du Bellay, and Reginald Pole.

During the spring of 1536 the consistory in Rome mastered its fears of conciliarism and consented to the calling of a general church council. Paul III convoked the council to assemble in Mantua on May 23 of the following year. By way of preparation he appointed a commission of nine cardinals, including Contarini, Caraffa, Sadoleto, Pole, Aleander, and Giberti, who were Erasmians. Under the chairmanship of Contarini the commission met almost daily from early in November until mid-February 1537. On March 9 Contarini presented to Paul III their *Counsel ... Concerning the Reform of the Church.* The *Counsel* scored the abuses of nepotism and simony, pluralism and absenteeism, the immorality of secular and regular clergy, easy dispensations, and rampant venality; but it did not come to grips with the basic theological issues raised by the reformers. In the matter of indulgences, for example, the cardinals merely recommended that they should not be given oftener than once a year in each of the larger cities. Through an indiscretion the *Counsel* was revealed prematurely and confirmed the Protestants in their opinion of the corruption of the church. Luther himself published a German edition of the *Counsel* embellished with his own ironic comments.

In spite of Paul III's reluctant but honest intention to assemble a council, he was continually forced to postpone it. In 1537 Mantua proved to be an unsuitable place because of the duke's opposition; in 1538 the delegates did not appear in Vicenza, in Venetian territory; and in 1542 the renewal of the war between Charles V and Francis I prevented all but a few prelates from coming to Trent, and these left shortly thereafter. This tragicomedy of errors at last came to an end in 1545, when the Council of Trent, convoked for March 25, finally convened on December 13 for its first session. Paul III died of old age in 1549. A conclave of cardinals convened to elect his successor was deadlocked for months, but eventually, on February 7, 1550, elected Cardinal del Monte, who took the name Julius III. The new pope was a relaxed Tuscan who lacked strong convictions, but he was persuaded to reconvene the Council of Trent for its second session. He was succeeded upon his death in 1555 by Pope Marcellus II, who died shortly after his election. Then with the election of Cardinal Caraffa as Pope Paul IV (1555–1559) a new spirit of dogmatic rigidity and intransigence asserted itself in the Holy See.

Giampietro Caraffa embodied the spirit of the Counterreformation and in his own person represented the new direction that the church's reaction to Protestantism was taking. He had belonged to a mystical group known as the Oratory of Divine Love, and he was early closely associated with churchmen of an Erasmian Christian humanist type. But his own convictions were narrower than theirs, and he was increasingly offended by their liberal views. As nuncio in Madrid in 1536 he saw the Inquisition move efficiently against the Erasmians and effectively root out their influence in a matter of months. Caraffa was convinced that the hard line alone would be effective, and with his pontificate the repressive Counterreformation moved ahead.

Catholic Spiritual Renewal

THE JESUIT HISTORIAN Pallavicino referred to the era of the Renaissance popes as an age of iniquities "the memory of which cannot be recalled without horror and indignation." And yet even in this dark period of the church, there were signs of new spiritual life not only in the north, where the Brethren of the Common Life were making their tremendous impression upon education, but also in the south and in Rome itself. Italy contributed many first-ranking Renaissance humanists, such as Marsilio Ficino and Pico della Mirandola, whose most earnest desire was to reinvigorate Christian theology with life from new Greek and Near Eastern sources.

Erasmian Christian humanism inspired a number of prelates to write in favor of reform and to improve the administration of their own dioceses. Cardinals such as Pole, Sadoleto, Giberti, and Contarini believed that if learning were improved, if piety were taught and practiced, if the simple teachings of the gospels were made clear, a renewal could be effected in the church. There were many interior correspondences between the teachings and practices of the late medieval church and the tenets of Christian humanism—optimism about the educability of man, respect for ancient or received traditions, the strength of man's will in achieving piety, the meritorious nature of good works. A certain religious superficiality and inability to grapple with the theological issues raised by the reformers was evident in Cardinal Jacopo Sadoleto. He addressed an admonishing letter to the people of Geneva, but when Calvin published a reply, Sadoleto let the matter drop. But Sadoleto nevertheless hoped that the blows of the reformers would have a therapeutic effect upon the body of the church. To Pope Clement he wrote: "If we satisfy God's wrath and justice, if those terrible punishments open the way for purer manners and juster laws, perchance our misfortune will not have been so great."[1]

Cardinal Gian Matteo Giberti (1495–1543), the natural son of a Genoese sea captain, was admitted to the household of Cardinal Giulio de' Medici, where he proved to be a brilliant student of Greek and Latin and was admitted to the Accademia Romana, the famous classical school. He became the cardinal's secretary and an emissary to Charles V. As Pope Clement VII, Giulio appointed Giberti bishop of Verona. Resident in Rome, Giberti advised Clement politically, promoted peace between Francis I and Charles V at Pavia, urged papal support of Francis, and engineered the League of Cognac (1526). After the sack of Rome in 1527 the imperial forces imprisoned him, but he escaped and fled to Verona. There he became a model reform bishop, upgrading the learning and morals of the clergy, sponsoring a printing press that issued splendid editions of the Greek church fathers, and laying down edicts for reform. His dissertation on the restoration of ecclesiastical discipline became the basic platform for the reformatory acts of the Council of Trent. Post-Tridentine churchmen studied his example closely.

Gasparo Contarini (1483–1542), of a noble Venetian family, was a member of the Great Council in Venice, a Venetian ambassador at the court of Charles V, and a celebrant at the coronation of Charles V at Bologna in 1530. In 1535 Pope Paul III made Contarini a cardinal and the next year appointed him to the reform commission. He was of an Erasmian temperament, diplomatically talented, and knew the strength of the Protestants in the empire. When Emperor Charles summoned imperial diets at Worms and at Regensburg in 1540 and 1541, at which theologians of both persuasions were to be present for a discussion of theological points of difference, Contarini and the Erasmians strongly favored participation in spite of Pope Paul III's fears that the emperor might follow the path of Henry VIII to a national church. At Regensburg the discussions were based upon some twenty-one articles largely drawn up by the Lutherans. Melanchthon, Martin Bucer, John Calvin, and other eminent reformers represented the evangelical point of view. Melanchthon and Contarini worked out a verbal formulation of the doc-

---

[1] Cited in Pierre Janelle, *The Catholic Reformation* (Milwaukee, 1963), p. 47.

trine of justification by faith, which pleased the emperor enormously when word of the agreement leaked out. But hopes for unity sank as the discussions proceeded, for questions regarding transubstantiation and the authority of the papacy led to an impasse. When Melanchthon returned to Wittenberg, he found Luther adamant against the compromise formula on faith, and when Contarini returned to Italy, he was accused of heresy. Mercifully he died the next year. The failure of the Erasmians to work out peaceful solutions to the schism in the church opened the way for the militant program of the intransigents.

The religious vitality of the church, especially in Italy, was further evidenced by a renewal within the old monastic orders and the founding of new orders during the first decades of the Reformation. Ascetic renunciation, mystical contemplation, and the religious life of the regular clergy retained strong power to attract the devout. Well before the advent of Luther, Baptista Mantuanus had worked for the reform of his Carmelite order. Among the Franciscans there arose a reformer of Italian peasant stock, Matteo de Bascio (d. 1552), who worked for a restoration of the primitive simplicity of St. Francis. He later became an itinerant evangelist himself. His followers were known as the Capuchins, distinguished by their four-pointed hoods. The Capuchins were recognized by the pope in 1528. In spite of the opposition of the Observant Franciscans, the Capuchins were second in power only to the Jesuits. They survived even the crisis precipitated by the defection to Protestantism of Bernardino Ochino in 1542, though they came close to being suppressed. They gained formal independence in 1619. The Dominicans, too, produced a notable spiritual reformer, Battista da Crema, who through his life and writings exercised a profound influence upon his times.

In 1516 a reformatory movement began close to the heart of Leo X's court in Rome. Certain clerics and laymen met frequently at the Church of Saints Sylvester and Dorothea for prayer, meditation, and mutual encouragement. Under the direction of Gaetano da Thiene, a disciple of Battista da Crema, and Giampietro Caraffa, the group was organized as the Oratory of Divine Love, counting among its members Sadoleto, Giberti, Contarini, and other Erasmian reformers. Later in the century (1575) St. Philip Neri raised the organization to a new prestigious form of religious expression by founding a new community of secular priests who lived a life of obedience for mutual strengthening, but were bound by no vows.

The whole history of monasticism was characterized by gradual decay and a weakening grasp on the original difficult and purist standards, followed by reform within the orders. The evolution of the monastic ideal moved steadily away from hermetic isolation to involvement in the world. The development went from single hermits to cenobitic groups, then to monastic living, such as the Benedictines practiced, apart from the world and behind walls, but for the good of the world through agricultural improvement, the copying of manuscripts, and schools to promote learning and culture. The mendicants emphasized the ideal of poverty, but deliberately entered the world and trod the dusty streets in their sandals. The most important new foundations of the sixteenth century, those of the Theatines and the Jesuits, not only afforded stellar examples of intramundane asceticism, but deliberately entered into contact with the most influential and powerful classes of society, into the courts, patrician houses, and universities. In the world and in the mission field they engaged Protestants and pagans in a contest for the religious allegiance of mankind.

From the Oratory of Divine Love emanated a spirit of devotion that led Gaetano da Thiene, Paolo Consiglieri, Bonifacio da Colle, and Caraffa to found the order of the Theatines, named after the city of Chieti (Theate) in southern Italy, where Caraffa was bishop. On September 14, 1524, the feast of the Exaltation of the Holy Cross, they made their solemn profession before the altar of St. Peter's in Rome. Their main objective was to recall the clergy to an edifying life and all Christians to the practice of virtue. They founded oratories and hospitals, evangelized, and by good example sought to inspire others to virtuous lives. They soon counted many members of the aristocracy among their congregations. They were the first order to undertake foreign missions in the Near East and in the East Indies. Other new foundations, such as the Somatians (1532) and the Barnabites (1533), emulated their example of sincerity and devotion.

Further evidence of sincere lay piety is to be found in such religious brotherhoods as the School of St. George and the School of St. Rochos in Venice. The School of St. Rochos was supported by extremely wealthy and devout merchants and was heavily endowed through testamentary bequests. It supported the painter Tintoretto for life in return for three lavish paintings of biblical scenes each year to ornament the school, a veritable jewel box with its classical Corinthian columns.

Just as Christian humanism and renewed monasticism gave evidence of Catholic vitality, so the appearance throughout the sixteenth century of genuine religious mystics, who combined vision and practicality in the best medieval tradition, provided proof that Catholicism, though suffering, was far from dead. The Spanish milieu seemed most conducive to the mystical life, and in Spain flourished those Carmelite saints who were the finest flower of the mystic garden, St. Teresa of Avila (1515–1582) and St. John of the Cross (1542–1591). St. Teresa grew up in a pious home within the ancient walled city of Avila. As a child she once set out with her younger brother to convert the Moors. At twenty she joined the Carmelite order, devoted herself to its reform, and directed the Discalced (unshod) Carmelites, who established an amazing number of reformed convents all over Spain. It was said that it would be easier to establish four new orders than to reform one old one, but St. Teresa succeeded by skillful administration and tremendous practicality. "The Lord walks among pots and pans" was a favorite expression of hers. Her autobiography was an amazingly sensitive and perceptive account of her early life and inner struggles. Her *Way of Perfection* was intended as a guide to the ascetic life for nuns in the reformed convents. Her masterpiece of mystical writing, however, was *The Interior Castle* (1577), in which she explored the secrets of the contemplative life, the mystical techniques of the soul's communion with God.

St. John of the Cross (1542-1591) was St. Teresa's most celebrated disciple. He led a rigorous life as a Discalced Carmelite, but somehow found the time to write great treatises on the highest reaches of the mystical experience, such as *The Ascent of Mount Carmel* and *The Dark Night of the Soul.*

A mystical poet less fortunate than St. John was Luis de León (1527-1591), who wrote commentaries on the Scriptures, a metrical version of the Song of Solomon, and original odes. But in 1572 he was arrested by the Inquisition on grounds of heresy and disrespect for the Vulgate and was imprisoned at Valladolid. He was eventually exonerated and a few days before his death even appointed provincial of his Augustinian order. The repression of the Inquisition, however, gradually squeezed the life out of Spanish mysticism, which steadily degenerated into a form of quietism.

France also contributed intellectually and spiritually to the Catholic revival. A fascinating French contribution was the slightly mad William Postel (1510-1581), a noninstitutionalized representative of the Catholic Reformation. Postel was in the tradition of Raymond Lull (1232-1315), who over two centuries earlier had undertaken to convert the Moslems by making missionary journeys, writing some three hundred esoteric apologetic works, and establishing a college to teach missionaries the languages and lore of the Near East. Postel studied at the University of Paris and learned Greek, Hebrew, Spanish, Portuguese, and Arabic. He wrote a work on the harmony of the world, *De orbis terrae concordia* (1544), intended to refute Mohammed and win Moslem converts to Christianity. That same year he traveled to Rome and joined the Jesuits, who were happy to have a scholar of such distinction. But very shortly he began to show erratic tendencies, advocating that the papacy be moved from Rome to Jerusalem and that the king of Rome should be the king of France, with his capital in Paris. He was ejected from the Society of Jesus and his works were put on the Index. Still he went to the Council of Trent and undertook to expound his theories to the churchmen there. The Inquisition declared him to be mad, imprisoned him for four years, and then had him held in informal custody in Paris for the final eighteen years of his life. Postel has been all but forgotten by historians, but the Inquisition, the Index, and the Jesuits have gone down in history as characteristic instruments of the Counterreformation.

The Counterreformation

HISTORIANS in these ecumenical days very much prefer the term "Catholic Reformation" to the term "Counterreformation," for the move toward reform within the church had its own spiritual wellsprings within the old church and was not merely a negative response to the Protestant revolt. Nevertheless, in certain important respects the Catholic Reformation was predominantly a reaction, and it did turn to forms of reprisal and repression that the modern church can in retrospect only regret. The major impulses toward the hard line came from Spain, the "hammer of heretics" and "sword of Rome."

Thanks to the centuries of combat with the Moslems and the crusade to drive them out of Iberia, Spain developed a very strong militant orthodoxy and a fanatical spirit. Ferdinand and Isabella had established powerful institutional controls against deviation in any form. Cardinal Ximénez not only had strengthened the hierarchy in Spain by a rigid moral rearmament, but had himself served as a grand inquisitor (1508). Charles V allowed the Inquisition to enlarge its jurisdiction from preventing Moors and Jews from proselytizing to judging questions of faith, not even exempting the regular clergy from its authority. In 1531 Pope Clement VII subjected the episcopacy in Spain to the Inquisition and refused any right of appeal from its sentences. From 1538 on, the Inquisition became very active in combating heretical religious propaganda and suppressing the Erasmians and Lutherans.

Cardinal Caraffa had been very favorably impressed by the effectiveness of the Inquisition in Spain, and suggested introducing its methods into Italy. Popular resistance had held back the Inquisition in the Spanish domains in Italy, so that it did not function in Sicily until 1518, and then primarily in controlling the Jews, and in Naples it even tolerated the followers of Valdés for many years. Caraffa believed that papal support was necessary, and he urged the pope to establish a new congregation in Rome which would reinvigorate the old Dominican tribunal for action against heretics. Paul III was hesitant, for he feared the hostility of the people. But as the number of heretics increased and the mediating efforts of the moderates failed, he reluctantly gave Caraffa a free hand. Caraffa was so impatient to get on with it that he set up interrogation chambers and instruments of intimidation in his own house until the tribunal could be organized. "If our own father were a heretic," he exclaimed, "we would carry the faggots to burn him!" Another time he intoned: "No man is to lower himself by showing toleration toward any sort of heretic, least of all a Calvinist!" The Roman tribunal was given jurisdiction over all Italy, with the same power and organization as the Spanish Inquisition. The judges were by custom Dominicans, and they were subordinated to a congregation of six cardinals who were appointed by the pope to serve as inquisitors general, including Caraffa. On July 21, 1542, Paul III formally sanctioned the Roman Inquisition and extended its authority to all of Christendom. With this step Rome regained the initiative from the reformers.

The cooperation of the reinvigorated monastic orders and especially of the civil authorities made the Inquisition an effective instrument for the suppression of heretics. In March 1547 the Inquisition had the Spanish nonconformist Juan de Enzinas burned at Rome. It summoned Pietro Paolo Vergerio from Venetian territory to Rome. Excommunicated on July 3, 1549, Vergerio fled to safety in Grisons. The narrow-minded grand duke of Florence, Cosimo I, enthusiastically supported the Inquisition in Tuscany, and from 1542 on, it also operated in Milan. In Ferrara it brought pressure on Hercules d'Este to move against the evangelicals whom the duchess Renée was protecting. They fled, and Renée, abused by her fanatical son, retired to France. The Spanish government now felt free to act in its Italian domains. Caraffa became archbishop of Naples on February 22, 1549, and encouraged the final dissolution of the Valdés circle.

The advent of inquisitorial justice in France coincided with the resolution of an embittered King Francis I to suppress the Huguenots. The Inquisition claimed victims in Rouen, Toulouse, Grenoble, and Bordeaux. The royal courts handled heresy in Paris. Even Meaux, where Bishop Briconnet had once sheltered such free spirits as Lefèvre d'Étaples, was no longer a sanctuary, for on October 4, 1546, the authorities arrested sixty-one evangelicals at an assembly and subsequently burned fourteen of them for heresy. The next year a special tribunal of the parlement of Paris was given exclusive authority in the burning issue of heresy. It established such a record of executions by fire that it came to be known as the *chambre ardente*. King Henry II (1547–1559) was very narrow-minded and encouraged restrictive legislation on books, professorships, and communication with Protestant centers. A royal edict in 1549 defined the legal competence of the ecclesiastical and civil authorities in matters of heresy. Throughout Europe there was a direct correlation between the success of the Inquisition and the willingness of the monarchs and lesser rulers to cooperate.

For effective thought control it is essential to burn the books as well as their authors, a point that was not lost upon the zealous Paul IV. From 1521 on, lists of forbidden books were circulated; the theological faculties at Paris and Louvain figured prominently in the compilation. The first complete list, valid for the entire church, was the *Index librorum prohibitorum*, promoted by Paul IV during the last year of his pontificate and published in 1559. This list of prohibited books, however, included titles that less excitable minds than Caraffa's considered harmless, and it was modified by the Index of Trent in 1564. Not only were heretical Protestant writings proscribed, but also humanist classics thought to be injurious to morals, such as Boccaccio's *Decameron*. The works of the prince of the Christian humanists, Erasmus, who had once nearly been given a cardinal's hat, were forbidden and subsequently published in a bowdlerized version. The Renaissance was now clearly a thing of the past.

The Jesuits

THE SHOCK TROOPS of the Counterreformation were the Jesuits. In addition to the traditional monastic vows of poverty, chastity, and obedience, they took a fourth vow of absolute obedience directly to the pope. So efficient and effective was the newly founded Society of Jesus in polemics, politics, education, and mission enterprise that it has been associated too exclusively with the thrust against Protestantism. In reality the Jesuits were an expression of that reservoir of religious sentiment from which a variety of new orders welled up in the first decades of the century. A product of Spanish spirituality, the Society of Jesus considered itself primarily a force for the rejuvenation of the church and the Christianizing of the heathen, rather than a combat force against Protestantism. That it served so well also in the new offensive is a tribute to the genius of its founder, Ignatius Loyola, and to the dedication of its first members.

Ignatius Loyola (1491–1556) was one of the most dramatic figures in the history of Christendom, a man of war who became a soldier for the Prince of Peace. His father was a Basque nobleman and as a boy he served as a page at the court of King Ferdinand. Schooled in courtly manners and military strategy, he served with two brothers in the army of their feudal overlord, the duke of Najera. On May 21, 1521, Loyola was defending a breach in the city wall at Pamplona during an invasion by the troops of King Francis I when a French cannonball smashed his right leg and wounded his left one. A French doctor made a crude attempt to set his leg, but it had to be rebroken and reset twice, and he was lame for life. While recuperating in the family castle he read lives of the saints and Ludolph the Carthusian's *Life of Christ*. Caught up in a vivid religious experience, similar to the conversion struggle and release of Luther and Calvin, Loyola transferred his chivalric ideals to the realm of faith. He envisioned the Christian life as devoted service to Our Lady. The knights in shining spiritual armor formed the army of the righteous King engaged in deadly combat with the forces of Satan. With a flair for the dramatic, Ignatius made a symbolic gesture to mark his change of life. Traveling along the road discussing religion with several companions, he had been unable to convince one of them of Mary's virginity. Furious, he had been momentarily tempted to use his dagger on the insolent fellow. Shocked at his own impulse, a few days later Loyola hung the weapon in the church of Montserrat and dedicated it to the Virgin. He gave away his rich garments to the poor and put on a cloak of sackcloth reaching to his feet. Loyola thus chose a religious solution within the church.

Loyola spent a year in seclusion outside of Manresa, near Barcelona, where he underwent an intense spiritual struggle, wrestling with the question of the ability of man, with the aid of grace, to control his free will in such a way as to make salvation possible. He worked out a sketch of his famous *Spiritual Exercises,* although he did not give them their final form till 1541. He formulated "Rules for Thinking with the Church," even indulging in a bit of hyperbole with the statement: "If we wish to proceed securely in all things, we must hold fast to the following principle: What seems to me white, I will believe black if the hierarchical

Church so defines" (Rule 13). The "first principle and foundation" of the *Spiritual Exercises* expresses the heart of Loyola's religious feeling:

> Man is created to praise, reverence, and serve God our Lord, and by this means to save his soul.
>
> The other things on the face of the earth are created for man to help him in attaining the end for which he is created.
>
> Hence, man is to make use of them in as far as they help him in the attainment of his end, and he must rid himself of them in as far as they prove a hindrance to him.
>
> Therefore, we must make ourselves indifferent to all created things, as far as we are allowed free choice and are not under any prohibition. Consequently, as far as we are concerned, we should not prefer health to sickness, riches to poverty, honor to dishonor, a long life to a short life. The same holds for all other things.
>
> Our one desire and choice should be what is more conducive to the end for which we are created.[2]

Following an honored tradition, in 1523 he made a pilgrimage to Jerusalem. He returned to study at the Alcalá, the university founded by Cardinal Ximénez. There he gathered a group of like-minded followers, but came under the surveillance of the Inquisition and ironically was briefly imprisoned on suspicion of heresy.

In 1528 he moved to Paris, where he studied, as had Erasmus, at the Collège de Montaigu, and later at the Collège de Sainte Barbe. He took his licentiate in theology in 1534 and his M.A. in 1535. He was in Paris at the same time as John Calvin, but there is no evidence that they met. In Paris Loyola was once again denounced by the Inquisition but escaped prosecution. In 1534 Loyola's religious society accepted its first six members, including Diego Lainez, who was to succeed him later as general of his order, Alfonso Salmerón, and Francis Xavier, the great missionary to the Far East. They swore an oath to dedicate themselves to the conversion of the Moors, a further indication that the movement was an efflorescence of the medieval Spanish crusading spirit. It took Loyola several years to persuade the Roman curia of the orthodoxy and the great value of his proposed new order for the propagation of the faith and the support of papal authority, but finally, on September 27, 1540, Pope Paul sanctioned the Society of Jesus with the bull *Regimini militantis ecclesiae.* The Jesuits were an elitist corps. They accepted as members only the most intelligent, physically strong and attractive, energetic, and dedicated men of good character. After two trial years the novices took the usual three monastic vows of poverty, chastity, and obedience. After an additional year of general studies and three years of philosophy, they taught philosophy or grammar to the younger members. Then after studying theology for four years they were admitted to the priesthood, publicly renewing the three vows. They then devoted

---

[2] Louis J. Puhl, S.J., ed., *The Spiritual Exercises of St. Ignatius* (Westminster, Md., 1957), p. 12.

a year to the study of practical theology, preaching, and spiritual exercises. After a second year of proving themselves they were at last admitted to the special obedience to the pope and incorporated into the Society of Jesus. Ignatius spent his last years in semiretirement, handling the order's vast correspondence with its members throughout the world. He passed away peacefully while saying his prayers. At the time of Loyola's death the society numbered around a thousand members. He lived to see the establishment of a hundred colleges and seminaries, and within a century and a half the society had founded over seven hundred schools; today its schools are numbered in the thousands.

The Jesuit order was the last major flowering of monasticism in the Western world. The excellence of its constitution, which reflects Ignatius' organizational talent, explains in part the tremendous efficiency of the society. The exchange of information from the lowest echelons to the general was a model of smooth communication. The discipline emphasized the maintenance of spiritual vitality. The Jesuits advocated frequent communion, individual confessions, and spiritual direction, evidencing special concern for the conscience of each member. Although Jesuitism and Calvinism are usually portrayed as antithetical archetypes of Catholic and Protestant thought, in certain essential ways they were two sides of the same coin. Both were ascetic and inclined toward intramundane asceticism. Both emphasized the importance of education for higher culture and for the promotion of right religious knowledge. Both developed theories to justify resistance to secular authority, pointing toward the contractual political theory. Both had a pessimism and a rigidity in their anthropology that were foreign to the optimism of Christian humanists such as Erasmus. Both believed that the natural will of man must be bent and disciplined, made malleable to receive religious truth. And yet both were fundamentally optimistic regarding the ground of being, seeing the universe created and ruled by a just but merciful God. The differences in their theories of salvation, church doctrines, sacramental teachings, and other theological questions are obvious enough.

The Jesuits were most successful in the areas of education and missions. They set up excellent schools with a curriculum or *ratio studiorum* that incorporated much humanist educational philosophy, although they stressed dialectic at the expense of history for apologetic reasons. They supplied learned tutors for the instruction of princes, a successful strategy, for in this way they exercised powerful influence over future rulers such as Ferdinand of Styria and Sigismund of Poland. An interesting incident in the story of Jesuit influence is the case of the pretender to the Russian throne known to history as the first False Dimitri, who won the support of the Poles and the Jesuits when he converted to Roman Catholicism and married the daughter of a Polish nobleman. After the death of the ruling tsar, Boris Godunov (who is credited with having murdered the real Dimitri, son of Ivan the Terrible), he seemed well on his way to establishing his claim to the throne when he was murdered. He had planned an alliance with the Holy Roman emperor, the pope, Poland, and Venice against the Turks, and if he had lived and succeeded in establishing himself as tsar he might well have replaced the Russian Orthodox Church with a Jesuit-guided Roman Catholic Church.

Jesuits operating in lands where Protestantism was strong utilized all existing resources, libraries, and monastic grounds. Peter Faber and Peter Canisius made tremendous inroads into Protestant areas in the Germanies, training young priests, writing a catechism, and establishing colleges, such as the Jesuit academy in Vienna. The German College in Rome, later directed by Cardinal Bellarmine, was an important center for the reconquest of German lands. William Allen founded a seminary at Douay directed toward the infiltration of England by priests sent in as secret agents. It was there that the Douay English version of the Bible was prepared. This college, as well as the English College in Rome, was of the same type as those of the Jesuits, with whom Allen was on very good terms. The transition from princes' tutors to rulers' confessors was easily made. But Jesuit involvement in politics led to their expulsion from a number of countries, and later even to their suppression for a time by the pope.

During the sixteenth and seventeenth centuries the Jesuits undertook world missions that were perhaps their greatest achievement. In spreading Christianity to all corners of the earth, in serving as a partial counterbalance to the materialistic imperialism of the European merchants and soldiers, in bringing to Europe eye-witness reports of foreign lands and scholarly accounts of their history and geography, the Jesuit missionaries contributed to the European outreach that has been one of the most important features of modern history. This mission endeavor was in line with Christ's commission to "go into all the world and preach the gospel." It was the same generic type as the missionary activities of the fourteenth-century Franciscans and not unrelated to the desire of Vasco da Gama, Columbus, and other explorers to carry the cross to foreign shores.

Although the Franciscans, Dominicans, and Augustinians were the most active in Christianizing Mexico and Peru, the Jesuits played the leading role in Brazil, where Father José de Anchieta directed the early efforts, and in Paraguay. While conditions in Latin America favored the wholesale conversion of the Indian populations, the work was much more difficult in Asia, where more complex ancient cultures with established higher religions were encountered.

Though the older religious orders accompanied the Portuguese explorers to India and the East Indies, the great Jesuit missionary Francis Xavier towers above all the rest as the "apostle of the Indies and of Japan." Xavier was born in his noble family's castle below the Pyrenees in 1506. At eighteen he went to study philosophy at the Collège de Sainte Barbe in Paris, where he met Loyola. Ignatius recognized in this handsome, bright, and cheerful young Spanish nobleman a rare spirit, and won both Xavier and his friend Peter Faber as disciples. Xavier went with Loyola to Venice, where he worked in a hospital for incurables, then to Rome, and then back to Venice, where he was ordained as a priest. When King John III of Portugal asked Pope Paul III to send six Jesuit missionaries to the East Indies, Ignatius named Xavier as one of the two ready to go. Xavier went to Lisbon and then traveled to southern India, where he preached for three years in the Portuguese colonies at Goa, Cochin, San Thomé, and along the coast of Travancore. Then he moved on to the Portuguese colonies in Malacca, Malaya, the Moluccas, and other islands of the East Indies, where he evangelized for two and a half years. His most remarkable undertaking was his mission to Japan, from 1549 to 1551, where he had astonishing success in winning converts at Kagoshima, Yamagutsi, and elsewhere, founding a Christian community that still survives, in spite of severe persecutions in earlier centuries. He died of a fever when only forty-six while attempting to penetrate China with the Christian gospel.

Father Matthew Ricci (1551–1610) undertook to convert the Chinese by starting at the top, winning the mandarins first and then working down. Learned in astronomy and mathematics, he was well received in Peking and favored by the emperor. His adaptations to native customs and traditional beliefs went far, and offended the Dominicans and more conservative parties in the church.

The reports of the Jesuits, known as the Jesuit relations, brought volumes of new knowledge about Asia, Africa, and America to the Europeans. They stressed the great variety of custom and belief, the different standards of aesthetics, and the rule of reason and morality of the noble heathen. Father Ricci so admired the Chinese that he believed that God had endowed them with superior reason and knowledge of natural law. These reports had an unsettling effect upon the European mind, precipitating a real crisis of conscience. They became arsenals for the eighteenth-century European philosophers who developed theories of aesthetic and moral relativity, which have ever since been characteristic of Western thought.

The Council of Trent

THE REFORMATION prompted the convening of the Council of Trent (1545–1563), the most important church council since that of Nicea in 325 A.D. After its adjournment, no other council was held for three hundred years, until the First Vatican Council in the nineteenth century—a span of time between councils without precedent in the history of the church. "It was the answer of the church," writes the contemporary historian of the council, Hubert Jedin, "to the confessional schism and an act of self-definition and self-renewal of this same church." Two simple questions may serve to bring into sharp focus the historical importance of the Council of Trent: If the council had been held in 1525 instead of 1545, would everything have been different? If the council had not been held at all, would anything have been different? It can be argued that a council held before the full force of the Protestant revolt had been deeply felt would have varied little from the bland results of the Fifth Lateran Council (1512–1517). It can also be asserted that the council represented no basic reform, but rather a reaffirmation of accepted positions. Bossuet chided Leibniz, who had urged the suspension of the canons and decrees of the Council of Trent in the interest of Christian unity, with the reminder that this would do his cause no good at all, because every assertion of the Council of Trent was to be found authorized in earlier papal and conciliar documents. That the council was convoked at all, in view of papal suspicion of conciliarism, seems surprising to some observers. Others find it inexplicable that it was delayed so long, in view of the pressure for a council throughout much of Christendom.

Pope Pius II had capped the triumph of the papacy over councils in the year 1460 with his bull *Execrabilis,* in which he declared it "useless, illegal, and wholly detestable" to appeal over the head of the pope to a council, and declared anyone who did so automatically excommunicated. That this decree was not universally accepted is evident from the fact that the Fifth Lateran Council, meeting under Leo X during the greater part of its tenure, found it necessary to reassert the thesis of the *Execrabilis.* Conciliarism was far from dead during the half century following the pronouncement of Pius II. Ulrich von Hutten dared to publish a pamphlet bearing on its title page the refrain "Consilium! Consilium! Consilium!" Girolamo Aleander, the papal legate to Germany and the dedicated foe of Erasmus and Luther, writing from Worms in 1520, complained, "All the world cries out, 'Council, council!'"

Luther was ambivalent about a council. He appealed earnestly for an ecumenical council to effect the reform of the church, but at the same time realism compelled him to expect little of any council called in the prevailing circumstances. On November 28, 1518, he made a stirring appeal for a council, but the next year at Leipzig he argued for the authority of the Scriptures over that of popes and councils, for councils too have often erred and contradicted each other. In his *Address to the Christian Nobility* in 1520 he outlined the worst abuses with which a council would have to deal. When a council had still not been convened by 1539, Luther wrote a treatise summarizing his views *On the Councils and the Church*. "We cry out and appeal for a council and beseech all of Christendom for its advice and help!" he exclaimed. "You say that there is no hope for such a council any longer; I suppose I agree with you." Many people concluded that the popes were merely procrastinating and evading a council in order to save themselves from reform. Luther spoke for a large part of the public when he compared Pope Paul III with the medieval rogue Markolf, who could not find a tree anywhere on which he wanted to be hanged.

The character of the Renaissance papacy, it is true, lent plausibility to the worst construction that could be placed upon the papal opposition to a council. But there were pressing political conditions that dictated such a course, for the kings and emperors of the day exploited the threat of a council to bend the papacy to their will. The French kings Louis XI, Charles VIII, and Louis XII, with their special interest in Italian affairs, made constant use of such threats. Louis XII went so far as to have five cardinals summon a council to convene in Pisa in September 1511, but Julius II outmaneuvered him and in July of that year called the Fifth Lateran Council to meet in Rome in April 1512. Even though Julius died after the first session, this council continued sporadically under Leo X until the fateful year 1517, when it finally adjourned with little accomplished. In 1517 the University of Paris advocated the calling of a general council in protest against the abolition of the Pragmatic Sanction of Bourges. John Major (1470–1550), a professor of philosophy and theology at Paris, who returned to his native Scotland in 1518 to teach first at the University of Glasgow and then at St. Andrews, consistently appealed for a council and even wrote a *Disputation on the Authority of a Council.*

Even the lethargic emperor Frederick III and the quixotic Maximilian resorted to threats of a council and unilateral reform for political ends. But when the Habsburg empire, spanning all of Europe, came into the hands of Charles V, the papacy was placed in a really precarious position, for it was caught between the French and Spanish interests during the course of the Habsburg-Valois wars and was forced to vacillate wildly in order to maintain its own temporal interests.

Charles V, who had to get along with the evangelicals in the empire, insisted upon the calling of a council as one condition for support of the papacy. The Spanish preponderance, following the defeat of Francis I of France at Pavia in 1525 and the sack of Rome by the imperial troops in 1527, dictated the acceptance of Charles's demands. But Pope Clement VII, a Medici, in alliance now with France, still delayed in calling a council, even though the emperor threatened a national council for the empire only, with the Protestants participating. In 1542, after futile attempts to convene a council at Mantua and Vincenza, Paul III convoked a council to meet at Trent, or Trento, in northern Italy but technically on German soil— a concession he made unwillingly. But the Habsburgs had still not reached an accommodation with the French, and it was only after the Peace of Crépy (September 18, 1544) that Charles accepted the pope's proposal. A bull of November 30 announced a meeting for the following March, but the *Bull of Convocation of the Holy Ecumenical Council of Trent* did not arrive until December 11, 1545. The council opened two days later. The *Bull of Convocation* took cognizance of the "evils that have long afflicted and well-nigh overwhelmed the Christian commonwealth," of the princes "filled with hatreds and dissensions," of the "schisms, dissensions, and heresies," of the delays in the assembling of a council due to the plots of "the enemy of mankind," and warned that all who opposed the summons would "incur the indignation of Almighty God and of His blessed Apostles Peter and Paul."

Owing to the halo effect of religious assemblies, there is a natural inclination for the historical imagination to conjure up a scene of sanctity when reflecting on a council like the one that met at Trent. Cardinal Madruzzo, bishop of Trent, who alone represented the empire, had to wrestle with some very earthy problems in providing for the physical needs of the delegates and their entourages. Room rents skyrocketed, the price of wine rose 30 percent, Venice was asked to grant free transit of wheat and oats from the Papal States, oxen and cattle were imported from Germany, and "everything was exceeding dear."

The human element played a predictable part in the proceedings. One skeptical father at the council observed that the Holy Spirit would no doubt come to them from Rome in the courier's bag. After a Spanish prelate had orated interminably, one of the delegates rose and asked, "Is this the Council of Toledo?" When a French delegate had criticized the abuses of the Roman church very harshly, an Italian took the floor and said, *"Ecce!* Behold how the *gallus* [cock] crows!" The Frenchman slashed back with "But in the Scriptures it says that when the cock crowed, Peter roused himself and repented in tears." There were even physical encounters, as when an angered prelate yanked a fistful of hair from the beard of a Greek representative. But for the most part the sessions were conducted with the dignity and ceremony due the occasion.

Attendance was scanty for an enterprise of such significance; when the first session opened it included only four archbishops, twenty bishops, four generals of monastic orders, and a few theologians. The Italians were best represented, with a dozen prelates present, compared with only five Spaniards, two Frenchmen, and one bishop from the empire. The Spaniards turned out to be a difficult quotient, for while they were intransigent in dogma, they were sensitive to the emperor's wishes, and pressed conciliar arguments to put the curia on the defensive. Since the Greek Orthodox and Protestant churches did not take part in the council, it could not really pretend to be ecumenical.

In his opening address the president of the council, Cardinal del Monte, cited as the two main reasons for the convening of the council the growth of heresy and the need for the reform of abuses. He attributed both to the negligence of the bishops, and called on the bishops present (the bishop of Rome not being among them) to confess and to beg God's pardon. All knelt and prayed for forgiveness, although it became clear later that a good number of them resented being singled out in this way while the curia was omitted from censure. The cardinal read the collect and gospel lesson for the day, the choir sang *"Veni, Creator Spiritus"* and the *Te Deum,* and the Council of Trent was declared to be in session.

The council met, as it was summoned, under papal auspices. In deciding to

The Council of Trent. British Museum, London.

debate the issues of reform and dogma simultaneously, the fathers at Trent acknowledged the basically twofold nature of the problem confronting the church, the loss of spiritual idealism reflected in the growing number of abuses and the theological uncertainty and religious degeneration in matters of doctrine. The seventh and fourteenth sessions issued major decrees concerning reform, touching upon such matters as incompetency in cathedral churches, plurality of offices, plurality of benefices, plurality even in positions involving the cure of souls, neglect of visitations, and the like. The twenty-first session struck at illiteracy and the ignorance of the clergy. In matters of dogma, the fourth session pronounced upon the canonical Scriptures and their authority. In the decree *De canonicis scripturis* the council imposed the authority of the Vulgate upon the church. The statement on tradition failed to explain the full sense of its meaning and the extent of its authority. The conclusion was simply that Scripture and tradition were to be considered equally valid, without spelling out clearly whether religious truth is to be found partly in Scripture and partly in tradition or whether the whole truth is to be found in each, with the Scripture as the norm that determines acceptable tradition. The fifth and sixth sessions defined the orthodox position on original sin and justification; many of the remaining sessions were devoted to the number, nature, and celebration of the sacraments. They reaffirmed transubstantiation, the sacrificial nature of the mass, the legitimacy of private masses, and the efficacy of the seven sacraments, which were declared to be efficacious in themselves, independently of faith.

In developing their dogmatic definitions the fathers simply followed the statements in the Lutheran Augsburg Confession of 1530, opposing them with orthodox definitions and adding anathemas. The most acrimonious debates developed around the central problems of original sin and justification. Conciliatory Cardinal Contarini, in his *Epistola de justificatione* (1541), had distinguished an "inherent justification" of a man before God, which results from right action, and an "imputed justification," which the merits of Christ provide when they are appropriated by a man through faith. The righteousness thus acquired constitutes the supreme end of faith. The moderates at Trent wished to subordinate works to faith, without being indifferent to the necessity of good works. Jacopo Seripando, general of the Augustinians, pressed for a solution that would not be entirely offensive to the evangelicals. On instructions from Loyola, the Jesuit theologians Lainez and Salmerón had remained more or less in the background up to that point in the discussions. But now they intervened energetically, insisting on the absolute necessity of good works for justification, and adamantly refused to accept any conditions or to subordinate works to faith. In the end the assembly adopted a statement in harmony with the definition of St. Thomas Aquinas. Chapter 7 of the decree concerning justification promulgated on January 13, 1547, reads in part as follows:

In what the justification of the sinner consists and what are its causes: This disposition or preparation is followed by justification itself, which is not only a remission of sins but also the sanctification and renewal of the inward man through the voluntary reception of the grace and gifts whereby an unjust man becomes just and from being an enemy becomes a friend, that he may be an heir according to hope of life everlasting. The causes of this justification are: the final cause is the glory of God and of Christ and life everlasting; the efficient cause is the merciful God who washes and sanctifies gratuitously, signing and anointing with the holy Spirit of promise, who is the pledge of our inheritance; the meritorious cause is His most beloved only begotten, our Lord Jesus Christ, who, when we were enemies, for the exceeding charity wherewith he loved us, merited for us justification by His most holy passion on the wood of the cross and made satisfaction for us to God the Father; the instrumental cause is the sacrament of baptism, which is the sacrament of faith, without which no man was ever justified; finally, the single formal cause is the justice of God, not that by which He Himself is just, but that by which He makes us just, that, namely, with which we being endowed by Him, are renewed in the spirit of our mind, and not only are we reputed but we are truly called and are just, receiving justice within us, each one according to his own measure, which the Holy Ghost distributes to everyone as He wills, and according to each one's disposition and cooperation....[3]

The scholastic structure of the definition is very striking. But in order to leave nothing ambiguous, the council spelled out thirty-three canons on justification, condemning Protestant positions as the fathers understood them. The definitions of the council hardened and rigidified Catholic dogma where some room for variation and maneuvering had existed before. But in removing theological ambiguity or uncertainty, it presented a dogmatic platform on which the church of the Catholic Reformation could take its stand.

The council was making genuine progress when once again the wheel of fortune upset the political balance and the fathers adjourned in a panic. Charles V had engaged the Schmalkald League of Protestant princes and cities in war and triumphed over them. The Spaniards at Trent began at once to assert themselves with new authority, and Cardinal Cervini feared the emperor might arrive in person with his armies to enforce his will on the council. A serious epidemic provided an occasion for transferring the council to Bologna, where the Italian delegates held the eighth session. Charles V protested violently, demanding that the council return to Trent, and in November the Diet of Augsburg refused to recognize the legality of the council's debates. On February 15, 1548, Pope Paul III ordered the council to recess. Toward the end of 1549 Paul III died without having reconvened it.

The new pope, Julius III (del Monte), was elected on February 7, 1550, and

---

[3] H. J. Schroeder, O.P., ed., *Canons and Decrees of the Council of Trent* (St. Louis and London, 1960), p. 33.

before the year was out he had summoned the council to reassemble at Trent on April 29, 1551. The Italian and Spanish delegates were in the majority, with the Spaniards hostile to the Italian pope, though conservative in dogma. Charles V was apprehensive about his control of the German Protestants, who were secretly negotiating with Henry II for support, and rejected the decisions of the council in advance for not giving their views a fair hearing. Julius III chose the Jesuits Lainez and Salmerón as his spokesmen. Once again reform and dogma were to be discussed simultaneously. Once again the fathers took up the question of the Eucharist, declared for a Thomist definition, and reasserted the legitimacy of the adoration of the host. In the matter of penance they reasserted the necessity of making oral confession before a priest and doing penance or giving satisfaction for sins repented of in the heart and orally confessed. They reaffirmed the time-honored forms in the administration of the last unction.

In October the council met the demands of the emperor and issued safe-conducts to German Protestant delegates. Melanchthon wished to attend but was unable to do so. But other representatives arrived in January 1552 from Saxony, Württemberg, and evangelical cities of south Germany. They were incensed that the council had decided the essential questions before they arrived and would allow them to discuss only communion in both kinds and the marriage of the clergy, which the emperor had already conceded to them in the Interim. At this juncture the wheel of fortune took one more complete turn, when Maurice of Saxony turned against the emperor and nearly captured him. Maurice reorganized the Schmalkald League, gained support from Henry II, and struck fear into the hearts of the fathers at Trent, who expected another invasion of German troops such as that of 1527. On April 28, 1552, Julius III precipitously adjourned the council for two years, but nearly a decade was to pass before it met again. In the meantime the Peace of Augsburg (1555) guaranteed the Protestants their legal right to exist in the empire, and the Treaty of Cateau-Cambrésis (1559) established a new international settlement.

Pope Pius IV (1559–1565) reconvoked the council for April 8, 1561. Called in part to head off a French national settlement, it included for the first time a significant French representation. It became increasingly clear as the debates went on that the papacy had emerged from the struggle with new prestige and authority. The papal representatives initiated proposals for action by the council and the council referred important questions to the pope for decision. The Jesuits were active proponents of papal power. The curia temporized as long as it could in the matter of reform, while pro-imperial churchmen worked desperately for it in order to quiet the criticism of the Protestants. Any question of dogma that was discussed—communion in both kinds, the mass as sacrifice, ordination—was always decided in favor of the traditional interpretation. When the council adjourned at the end of 1563, with fitting ceremony, and the canons and decrees received the formal signatures of the prelates present, 189 of the 255 signatories were Italian churchmen.

Protestant reaction was one of bitter disappointment, though not of surprise, for most of them shared Luther's skepticism about the "irreformability of the church." Even before the first session Luther had written: "Thus the council is settled before it even begins. Nothing is to be reformed, but everything is to be retained in accordance with past usage. What a fine council that is!" The council had a negative effect upon Christian unity, for with its scholastically refined definitions and its canons with anathemas attached, it burned the last bridges to the Protestant side of the stream. But by elevating the papacy anew, by improving the efficiency of the church's organization, and by clarifying dogma, the Council of Trent gave to the Catholic Church a clear-cut confession that it could embrace and for which it could battle in the wars of religion that lay ahead.

Post-Tridentine Reform

ON JANUARY 26, 1564, Pius IV (1559–1565), in the bull *Benedictus Deus,* confirmed the canons and decrees of the council, as it had petitioned him to do, and forbade any commentary on them without papal authority. On August 2, 1564, he created a congregation of cardinals for an authentic interpretation, a renewed assertion of the authority of the teaching office of the church. His bull *Iniunctum nobis,* of November 13, 1564, promulgated the *Professio fidei tridentinae,* which included the Nicene Creed, to which all to whom it was addressed were pledged. In addition the bull demanded, among other things, consent and adherence to apostolic and ecclesiastical traditions and to Holy Scripture, "according to the sense which the Holy Mother Church was held and holds whose right it is to judge regarding the true sense and interpretation of the Holy Scriptures." The pledge demands acknowledgment of the Roman church as the mother and mistress of all and true obedience to the Roman pontiff as the successor of Peter and vicar of Jesus Christ. Finally, it demands acceptance and profession of all sacred canons, particularly of the Tridentine Council, to which the Vatican Council of 1869–70 added a decree concerning the primacy and infallible magisterium of the Roman pontiff.

Charles Borromeo, nephew of Pius IV, may serve as a living model of the Tridentine spirit. As archbishop of Milan, he took for his model St. Ambrose, who more than a thousand years before had won sainthood in the corrupt times of the declining Roman Empire. Borromeo renovated and restored desecrated and deserted churches, reformed the law and the clergy, restored discipline in the religious orders, and established schools and colleges. Without the labors of men like Borromeo the resolutions of the Council of Trent would have been of little value to the church.

Pius V (1566–1572) provided all the bishops with an official edition of the council's decrees for their guidance. Peter Canisius took them to Germany, and they even reached America and the Congo at that early time. In 1566, for the benefit of parish priests, Pius published the Roman Catechism as an introduction to the council's resolutions. This he supplemented with a revised breviary and missal, for which, as well as for the catechism, the council had already made provision.

Gregory XIII (1572–1585) instructed the papal nuncios to ensure the execution of the Tridentine decrees in their respective areas. In response to the council's wish, Sixtus V (1585–1590) and Clement VIII (1592–1605) published a revised text of the Vulgate. The popes were not everywhere successful in their efforts to obtain immediate recognition of the council's acts. They succeeded in Spain, Poland, and the Italian states, but failed in France and Germany. Today the council's decisions are, within the widened borders of later papal definitions, definitive for the Roman Catholic Church everywhere.

The Roman Catechism, composed under Thomist influence, did not meet with favor among the Jesuits, who preferred the triple catechism of their fellow Jesuit, Peter Canisius. Even the catechism of Robert Bellarmine, authorized by Clement VIII and published in 1603 as a true exposition of the Roman Catechism, could not compete with that of Canisius. Canisius' beatification by Pius IX (1846–1878) as one "who stemmed the Reformation" and his canonization by Pius XI (1922–1939) are indications of the continued Jesuit influence in the Roman Catholic Church. (But Pius XI also canonized Bellarmine, thus laying to rest at last a number of controversies that had seemed irreconcilable in their time.)

The issues debated at the Council of Trent were so crucial and its resolutions so decisive for the course of Western history that the events stimulated two great histories that have brought diametrically opposed interpretations into the literature. In 1618 Paolo Sarpi, a Venetian priest, published his *History of the Council of Trent,* the "Iliad of our age." Sarpi was a late Venetian version of the fifteenth-century *uomo universale,* skilled at mathematics and optics, learned in Oriental religions, active in governmental and ecclesiastical affairs. In a crisis between the papacy and Venice, based on old and cherished enmity between them, the pope laid the interdict on Venice. Sarpi emerged as a strong apologist for Venice, and argued that the pope's position in the church was a usurpation. In his history of Trent Sarpi made the papacy a villain and exposed the conniving of the curia to protect the interests of Rome. Sarpi stressed the unpredictable events in history, rather than legality or uniformity, and showed how plans often have results quite different from those intended. Since accidents defeat human designs, chance severely delimits the area in which an individual can maneuver. In answer to Sarpi, the Jesuit historian Pallavicino wrote a history of his own. He had no difficulty in demonstrating that Sarpi had altered documents and manipulated facts to put the Holy See in a bad light. He defended the integrity of the council and warmly approved of its results, which he considered had been achieved through Providential guidance.

In retrospect, it seems quite clear that after the invasions of Italy by the northern powers and the wars on Italian soil, as well as the economic decline of Italy and the loss of vitality and initiative, the Renaissance was dead or dying in Italy even before the Counterreformation gained strength and turned repressive. It lingered on into the sixteenth century in Venice, which produced a version of civic humanism, the Venetian school of art, and intellectuals such as Sarpi. But it was the demise of the Renaissance and the enervation of Christian humanism that allowed the Counterreformation to develop its narrow rigidity and authoritarian character by default. The Spaniards were not alone to blame for the turn things took.

The continuity of the Counterreformation with medieval efforts at reform is very striking. The Council of Trent was reminiscent of the Fourth Lateran Council of 1215, when ecclesiastical reform was tied up with the crusades against the Moslem heretics. The intervention of nascent national interests into the affairs of the church is more fully developed at Trent, but directly related to particularist interests asserted against the universalism of the church during all the last centuries of the Middle Ages. Ideas make for change, institutions make for stability. It may not be too fanciful to see in the systematic response of the world's oldest continuous institution, the Roman Catholic Church, to the prophetic call of the evangelicals to repentance and faith one more grand dramatization of that age-old conflict of prophets and priests which reaches far back into the history of Israel.

To the historian who has some feeling for the great forces of change and continuity in history, the struggle of Reformation and Counterreformation offers a fascinating spectacle. He cannot help viewing with awe and respect the response of the Catholic Church to the most traumatic crisis of her long history, a crisis that, as the Erasmian cardinals observed in 1537, had "well nigh overwhelmed her." Something of this sort of sentiment must have touched the Whiggish English historian Thomas Babington Macaulay when he wrote in his review of Leopold von Ranke's *History of the Popes* (1840):

> There is not and there never was on this earth a work of human policy as deserving of examination as the Roman Catholic Church. . . . She saw the commencement of all the governments and of all the ecclesiastical establishments that now exist in the world; and we feel no assurance that she is not destined to see the end of them all. She was great and respected before the Saxon had set foot on Britain, before the Frank had passed the Rhine, when Grecian eloquence still flourished in

Antioch, when idols were still worshipped in the temple of Mecca. And she may still exist in undiminished vigor when some traveler from New Zealand shall, in the midst of a vast solitude, take his stand on a broken arch of London Bridge to sketch the ruins of St. Paul's.

Bibliography

General:

BRANDI, KARL. *Gegenreformation und Religionskriege,* vol. 2 of *Reformation und Gegenreformation.* Leipzig, 1942.

BURNS, EDWARD M. *The Counter Reformation.* Princeton, 1964.

DANIEL-ROPS, HENRY. *The Catholic Reformation.* London and New York, 1962.

DELUMEAU, J. *La vie économique et sociale de Rome dans la seconde moitié du XVIe siècle.* Paris, 1957.

DICKENS, A. G. *The Counter Reformation.* New York, 1969.

GARSTEIN, OSKAR. *Rome and the Counter-Reformation in Scandinavia (1539–1583).* Bergen, 1963.

HUGHES, PHILIP. *Rome and the Counter-Reformation.* London, 1944.

JANELLE, PIERRE. *The Catholic Reformation.* Milwaukee, 1949.

JEDIN, HUBERT. *Reformation, Katholische Reform, und Gegenreformation,* vol. 3 of *Das Handbuch der Kirchengeschichte.* Freiburg, 1967.

KIDD, B. J. *The Counter-Reformation.* London, 1933.

MOURRET, F. *A History of the Catholic Church,* vol. 5. St. Louis, 1930.

OLIN, JOHN C., ed. *The Catholic Reformation: Savonarola to Ignatius Loyola.* New York, 1969.

TUCHLE, HERMANN; BOUMAN, C. A.; and LEBRUN, JACQUES. *Réforme et Contre-Réforme,* vol. 3 of *La nouvelle histoire de l'Église.* Paris, 1968.

WARD, A. W. *The Counter-Reformation.* London, 1888.

Catholic reform:

BENDISCIOLI, MARIE. *La riforma Cattolica.* Rome, 1958.

BREZZI, PAOLO. *Le riforme Cattoliche dei secoli XV e XVI.* Rome, 1945.

DOUGLAS, RICHARD M. *Jacopo Sadoleto, 1477–1547: Humanist and Reformer.* Cambridge, 1959.

EVENNETT, H. OUTRAM. *The Spirit of the Counter-Reformation,* ed. John Bossy. Cambridge, 1968.

JOURDAN, G. V. *The Movement Towards Catholic Reform in the Early Sixteenth Century.* London, 1914.

McNALLY, ROBERT E., S.J. *Reform of the Church.* New York, 1963.

———. *The Unreformed Church.* New York, 1965.

MAURENBRECHER, WILHELM. *Geschichte der Katholischen Reformation.* Nordlingen, 1880.

PONELLE, L., and BORDET, L. *St. Philip Neri and the Roman Society of His Times.* London, 1932.

PROSPERI, ADRIANO. *Tra evangelismo e controriforma: G. M. Giberti, 1495–1543.* Rome, 1969.

Jesuits:
BÖHMER, HEINRICH. *The Jesuits.* Philadelphia, 1928.
———. *Ignatius von Loyola.* Stuttgart, 1951.
BRODRICK, JAMES. *The Economic Morals of the Jesuits.* London, 1934.
———. *St. Peter Canisius.* London, 1935.
———. *The Origins of the Jesuits.* London, 1940.
———. *The Progress of the Jesuits.* London, 1947.
———. *St. Francis Xavier.* London, 1952.
———. *St. Ignatius Loyola: The Pilgrim Years.* New York, 1956.
CAMPBELL, T. J. *The Jesuits,* 2 vols. New York, 1921.
DUDON, PAUL. *St. Ignatius of Loyola.* Milwaukee, 1949.
RAHNER, HUGO. *Ignatius von Loyola.* Freiburg, 1956.
SCADUTO, MARIO, S.J. *Storia della Compagnia di Gesù in Italia,* 3 vols. to date. Rome, 1964.
SCHURHAMMER, GEORG. *Franz Xaver, sein Leben und seine Zeit.* Freiburg, 1963.
SEDGWICK, H. D. *St. Ignatius Loyola.* New York, 1923.
TACCHI-VENTURI, PIETRO, S.J. *Storia della Compagnia di Gesù in Italia,* 2 vols., rev. ed. Rome, 1950–1953.
VAN DYKE, PAUL. *Ignatius Loyola, the Founder of the Jesuits.* New York, 1926.

Inquisition and Index:
BETTEN, F. S. *The Roman Index of Forbidden Books.* Chicago, 1935.
COULTON, G. G. *Inquisition and Liberty.* New York, 1938.
HAUBEN, PAUL J., ed. *The Spanish Inquisition.* New York, 1969.
LEA, H. C. *History of the Inquisition in Spain,* 4 vols. New York, 1922.
LECLER, JOSEPH. *Toleration and the Reformation,* 2 vols. London, 1960.
ROTH, C. *The Spanish Inquisition.* New York, 1938.
TURBERVILLE, A. S. *The Spanish Inquisition.* New York, 1932.

Council of Trent:
ALBERIGO, GIUSEPPE. *I vescovi italiani al Concilio di Trento (1545–1547).* Florence, 1959.
CRISTIANI, L. *L'Église à l'époque du Conceil de Trente.* Turin, 1948.
EVENNETT, H. O. *The Cardinal of Lorraine and the Council of Trent.* Cambridge, 1940.
HARNEY, M. P. *The Jesuits in History.* New York, 1941.
JEDIN, HUBERT. *A History of the Council of Trent,* 2 vols. to date. St. Louis, 1957–1961.
SARPI, PAOLO. *History of the Council of Trent.* London, 1676.
SCHNÜRER, GUSTAV. *Katholische Kirche und Kultur in der Barockzeit.* Paderborn, 1937.
SCHROEDER, HENRY J., ed. *Canons and Decrees of the Council of Trent.* St. Louis, 1941.
WILLAERT, LÉOPOLD, S.J. *Après le Conseil de Trente: La restauration catholique, 1563–1648,* vol. 18 of *L'histoire de l'Église.* Tournai, 1960.

CHAPTER 19

Civil War in France
and the
Spanish Preponderance

The sixteenth century was the golden age of Spain. Not only did Spain weather the storms of the Reformation as the mightiest Catholic power, not only did it found a new empire throughout the world, but during the second half of the century it overshadowed its old rival France, torn by a confessional crisis and civil war that threatened it with total ruin. During the year 1559, one year after the death of Charles V, a number of crucial events pushed history in the course it would take. In that year the Treaty of Cateau-Cambrésis marked the end of French efforts to conquer Italy and provided relief in foreign affairs which allowed the French to turn their attention to domestic problems. In that year the fanatical King Henry II died and was succeeded by Francis II, a sickly boy of fifteen who in spite of his youth was already married to the queen of Scotland. That was the year in which the Reformed congregations held their first national synod in Paris. Above all, 1559 marked the beginning of the era in which Spain, under its strange and devoted monarch Philip II, assumed the leadership of the Catholic world and undertook to establish its hegemony in Europe. The rise of Spain was a concomitant of the turmoil in France, which was rocked by bloody conflicts between rival political and religious factions.

The Wars of Religion in France

A MOST REMARKABLE WOMAN analyzed with great candor the predicament of France in the second half of the sixteenth century. Queen Catherine de' Medici, the widow of King Henry II and daughter of Lorenzo the duke of Urbino, to whom Machiavelli had dedicated *The Prince,* once wrote to the pope: "It is impossible to reduce either by arms or law those who are separated from the Roman Church, so large is their number." Calvinism was indeed making tremendous inroads in France. Its adherents grew from half a million to a million and a half by 1562, with possibly some decline after that. The conventional statement that Calvinism attracted the bourgeois and lesser nobility whereas the upper nobility and the peasants and urban masses remained Catholic needs to be considerably revised. A good number of the most powerful aristocrats and governmental leaders joined the Reformed cause, and in a number of urban centers the common citizens supplied converts and support for the new movement. In 1559 there were already some two thousand Reformed congregations in France. From 1564 to 1572 French Calvinists considered two competing forms of church government, the congregational and the presbyterian systems. In spite of the pull in two directions, the Calvinists had remarkable cohesion under the guidance of Geneva. But in spite of their reverence for the religious instruction of Calvin and Beza, they ignored their political advice quite freely.

Catherine de' Medici had been condescended to and pushed aside by the haughty French nobility, who considered her the daughter of a "Florentine shopkeeper." But she was a calculating, crafty woman who loved beautiful art and furniture and was indifferent to matters of religion. She was dedicated to maintaining Valois power so long as she or any of her children remained alive to exercise it. She wrote with complete candor: "I am resolved to seek by all possible means to preserve the authority of the king my son in all things, and at the same time to keep the people in peace, unity, and concord, without giving them occasion to stir or to change anything." Opportunistic and skillful, she played the parties within France against each other and fended off her son-in-law, Philip II of Spain, until at last she died in 1588, the year in which his hopes of ruling all of Europe sank with the Armada.

When Henry II died of his jousting wound, the Calvinists hoped for some relief from royal persecution, but their hopes were to be disappointed. Francis II devoted himself with adolescent fervor to his young bride, Mary Stuart, and allowed her fervent Catholic uncles Francis of Guise and Charles, cardinal of Lorraine, to dominate the government. The powerful nobles whom the Guises excluded from influence in the government secured Huguenot support for the opposition. They held that Antoine de Bourbon should serve as regent for the young king, and Constable Montmorency and the Bourbons maneuvered for positions of power. Catherine de' Medici saw an opportunity to put the crown above both parties and had a mediating moderate, Michel de L'Hôpital (1503–1573), appointed chancellor in 1560. But strong Catholics held both the executive and the judicature, and Catherine's attempt to rise above the battle failed. The Conspiracy of Amboise, in March 1560, to capture the king or at least to free him from domination by the Guises, was foiled. The prince of Condé was arrested for complicity in the plot, but at the very moment when prospects for a total victory for the Guises were most promising, King Francis II died (December 5, 1560) and the situation took a new turn.

The new king, Charles IX (1560–1574), was only ten years old, which gave Catherine her opportunity to step in as regent, with Antoine, king of Navarre, as lieutenant general of the realm. Mary Stuart left for Scotland and the Guises were maneuvered to one side, a development they were not about to accept as final. At Easter in 1561 a triumvirate made up of the duke of Guise, Montmorency, and the sieur de St.-André, marshal of France, succeeded in establishing themselves as the real force in the government. Catherine naturally now looked to the Bourbons and the Huguenots for support. Acts of violence multiplied and radical proposals increased. At a meeting of the estates general at Pontoise a Protestant member of the third estate proposed that all the secular possessions of the church should be sold with the exception of a single residence for each benefice holder, and that the proceeds should be used for the support of the church and clergy and to amortize the public debt. The frightened clergy voted a subvention to the regent to relieve the financial difficulties of the state. Catherine pressed for the reconciliation of the parties by sponsoring a colloquy at Poissy in September 1561. The French government invited Beza rather than Calvin to represent the Reformed cause, but there was no real dialogue, for Beza was not permitted to answer the rebuttal of Charles of Guise. Lainez, the general of the Jesuit order, present at the colloquy, urged the Catholics to drive out these "wolves, foxes, and serpents."

Catherine then made an important move toward religious peace. She summoned to St.-Germain-en-Laye the representatives of all the parlements, the principal courts of justice, to discuss the religious question. Then on January 17, 1562, she pronounced through her moderate chancellor, L'Hôpital, the famous edict that for the first time gave the Huguenots official recognition and an important measure of toleration. L'Hôpital had called her the "kindest woman on earth," but her move was dictated by expediency more than by any humanitarian impulse. The edict demanded that the Huguenots return the churches of which they had taken possession, but they were now given permission to hold services outside of towns; inside the cities they would be permitted to worship only in private houses. The preamble of the edict states expressly that the edict was not intended to sanction permanently two religious confessions in one state, but to preserve peace and concord until God restored true unity. Catherine and L'Hôpital were *politiques*, fostering toleration to promote the interest of the state over all religious factions. Still, recognition of the Huguenots' legal right of existence was a development of tremendous importance. The feudal particularist interests of the nobles and the republican sentiment of the burghers were given freer expression. But the Catholic Guises refused to honor the provisions of the edict, and two months after the edict was announced, France was torn by an outbreak of hostilities that were to last over thirty years and leave the land exhausted.

The massacre of Vassy precipitated the first in the series of bloody wars. The Guises maneuvered to win the support of Philip II of Spain for the Catholic side, and at the same time they met in Zabern with the Lutheran duke Christoph of Württemberg in order to forestall Protestant support for the Calvinists. Returning to France, Duke Francis of Guise encountered a congregation of Huguenots worshiping in Vassy in Champagne. His troops attacked them and killed over three hundred. The Catholics celebrated the duke's return to Paris as a great military victory. The triumvirate now forced Catherine to move to Paris from Fontainebleau and to work more closely with the Catholics.

The Huguenots, led by Admiral Gaspard de Coligny and the prince of Condé, now took up arms to enforce the January edict and to free Catherine and Charles IX from the Guises, and captured Orléans, Lyon, and other cities. Calvinist chaplains accompanied the army into battle, conducted services on the field, and led in the singing of psalms. Queen Elizabeth of England sent troops to occupy Le Havre as a hostage for Calais. Catherine hired Swiss and German mercenaries and appealed to the pope and to Philip II of Savoy for help. Duke Francis captured Condé, and an assassin murdered Duke Francis on the Loire bridge in February 1563. This left Admiral de Coligny as leader of the Huguenots, and he greatly rejoiced at God's judgment upon Duke Francis. But after suffering defeat at Rouen and being held to a stalemate at Dreux, the Huguenots were happy to accept the Peace of Amboise (1563), which allowed Calvinist nobles to hold services in their castles and burghers to maintain one church in each bailliage. Calvin and Coligny, however, were critical of the peace, and the pope, the emperor, and Philip II of Spain were equally dissatisfied. Guerrilla bands continued to ransack towns and destroy crops. Catherine made a goodwill tour to sell the peace, but destroyed the effect she was trying to create by meeting (1565) at Bayonne with the hated duke of Alba and her daughter Elizabeth, who had married Philip II after Bloody Mary's death and was now queen of Spain. Fear of a sinister plot to wipe out Protestants goaded the Huguenots into preparing once again for war.

War came again in 1567, the Huguenots crying out that they would "free the king" from Catherine. They nearly captured the court in Meaux and forced Catherine to take precipitous flight, an indignity she never forgave. Both sides were exhausted and agreed to a new peace on March 23, 1568.

Catherine felt desperate, for conciliation and repression alike had failed. Both sides were now organizing politically, and new Catholic leagues, such as the Brotherhood of the Holy Ghost in Burgundy, were forming to serve as vigilantes against the local Huguenots. The Huguenots fortified La Rochelle on the Atlantic coast and other strong points. Condé led some 30,000 men, but in March 1569 he was captured in battle at Jarnac and killed. Admiral de Coligny carried on alone. Happily for him, Catherine now became suspicious of Charles of Guise's proposal that Philip II of Spain inherit the throne if none of her children had heirs, and she moved closer to the Huguenots. The Edict of St.-Germain (August 8, 1570) granted freedom of conscience to the Calvinists and places to worship, as before the war.

Coligny now very unwisely pressed his advantage too far. With four major strongholds in La Rochelle, Cognac, Montauban, and La Charité, the Huguenots felt new unity and strength. Coligny tried to organize the French for a move against Spain, aimed at dividing up the Spanish Netherlands with Ludwig of Nassau and England. Coligny even dared say to Catherine de' Medici that anyone who opposed war with Spain was not a good Frenchman. He had pushed Catherine too far, and she decided that France must be rid of Admiral de Coligny once and for all. She connived in a plot on his life, but the assassin sent to kill him failed to finish him off. The Huguenots demanded an inquiry, and Catherine and the Guises, fearing exposure, agreed that not only Coligny but all the top Calvinist leadership had to go. The result was the massacre of St. Bartholomew's Night, one of the great horrors in Western history, which has seen so many.

Much mystery still surrounds the actual circumstances of the massacre, including the extent of the knowledge and involvement of young King Charles IX. Catherine seems to have been involved in the plot but did not foresee the extent of the slaughter. On the night of August 23–24, 1572, assassins broke into Coligny's chambers in Paris, stabbed him, and hurled his body from the window. That same night other leading Huguenots were murdered. The conspirators had decided in advance that young Condé and Henry of Navarre, who had married another of Catherine's daughters only the week before, would be given an opportunity to save their lives by converting to Catholicism, and they hastily agreed. While the two princes were being taken into custody, fanatical mobs went on a mad hunt for heretics throughout Paris, killing at least three thousand men. The wholesale slaughter spread to the provinces and lasted into October, resulting in death for thousands of Huguenots, in order, as Catherine put it, "to wipe out those subjects who were rebellious to God and to Charles IX." Pope Gregory XIII celebrated the massacre with a *Te Deum* and had a medal struck to commemorate the event.

It is said that when Philip II learned of the massacre, he laughed for the first time in his life.

The massacre was a bad mistake. The Huguenots rallied, won new sympathizers, and determined upon continued armed resistance. Powerful nobles resolved to restore traditional feudal independence and oppose the "despicable despotism" of King Charles. But moderate Catholics, the *politiques,* joined milder Calvinists to form a middle party to work for stability within the state. Through their spokesman, Marshal Damville, son of the constable Montmorency, they declared their loyalty to the king but asked for freedom of worship for the Protestants. At this juncture, in 1574, Charles IX died and his brother Henry III rushed back from Poland to ascend the throne.

Henry III was politically stupid. Catherine's spoiled favorite, he grew up a wastrel, a sensuous roué, given to debauches and lascivious living. He kept a bevy of "darlings," pretty boys in women's dress, for his amusement. The Calvinists responded to the leadership of this new monarch with very little enthusiasm. In 1576, to keep the Huguenots in their place, Duke Henry of Guise, son of the murdered Francis, organized the Catholic League, with local chapters to keep the faith and the king supreme in all the provinces. The league favored the ancient freedoms of the nobility and the medieval prerogatives of the third estate and gained a good deal of support for its cause. Henry III decided that if he could not lick them, he would join them, and made himself head of the league. He thereby alienated the *politiques* and the Huguenots and still failed to placate Henry of Guise and the ultra-Catholics. Alarmed, Henry III declared all leagues dissolved and allied himself with Henry of Navarre, who had renounced his enforced Catholicism at the first opportunity and was now leader of the Huguenots. Civil war and riots went right on. To the surprise of a number of people, Henry III and some of his *mignons* proved to be fine military commanders.

In 1584 Henry III's last brother, Francis, duke of Alençon, died and the Valois line was played out. Duke Henry of Guise tried to exclude Henry of Navarre, a Bourbon, from possible succession to the crown on the grounds of his heretical faith. Henry of Navarre attacked and the "war of the three Henrys" was on. Henry III tried to assert his authority at the meeting of the estates general in Blois, but Duke Henry of Guise and the Catholic Leaguers proved that they were in control. Fearing the duke of Guise, Henry III committed his final blunder. He had the popular Duke Henry murdered in the castle of Blois. He is said to have kicked the dead body and callously remarked, "My, but he is tall." The next day Duke Henry's brother Louis was also killed. Henry III thought that he was at last truly king, but the Catholics were now in open rebellion. Queen Catherine saw at once that Henry III had blundered again. "You have cut out, my son," she exclaimed, "but you must sew together!" Thirteen days later, in January 1589, Queen Catherine de' Medici departed from this vale of tears in despair at having to leave her son in such a spot. Terrified when members of the Catholic League assembled in Paris to avenge the murders of the Guises, Henry III fled to the protection of Henry of Navarre. But on August 1, 1589, a fanatical Dominican murdered Henry III, not realizing that he thereby prepared the way to the throne for the Huguenot. With his last breath Henry III acknowledged Henry of Navarre as his heir and successor to the throne of France.

Handsome, generous, eloquent, soldierly, the thirty-five-year-old Henry IV quickly won the affection of the people, though his religion was unacceptable to the Catholic majority. He issued a statement that he would not harm the Catholics but within six months would assemble a council to deliberate on the religious question. The *politiques* and moderate Protestants such as Philippe du Plessis-Mornay favored him. When the milder Catholic Leaguers declared that their only objection to Henry IV was that he was Protestant, Henry allowed the archbishop of Bourges to declare that he was ready to become Catholic (again). On July 25, 1593, he abjured his Reformed faith, early in 1594 he was anointed in Chartres, and on March 22, 1594, he entered Paris. He is reported to have commented, "Paris is worth a mass."

Henry IV now enjoyed such popular support that he felt confident enough to battle in alliance with England against Philip II of Spain. On May 2, 1598, at the urging of Pope Clement VIII, who was dismayed at a war between Catholic powers, Henry agreed to the Peace of Vervins. A few weeks before the end of the Spanish war, Henry IV moved to aid his former coreligionists with the famous Edict of Nantes (April 13, 1598), the edict of toleration for the Huguenots. The Huguenots could hold church services in two locations in every bailiwick except in Paris and within five miles of the capital, and some other large cities. They were to enjoy all political privileges, including the holding of public offices and membership in the parlements. For eight years some two hundred towns were to be places of security under Huguenot governors, and their garrisons were to be maintained at government expense. Pope Clement VIII, the Paris parlement, and the Catholic clergy opposed these concessions, but Henry pushed them through.

Henry IV now labored with energy and intelligence to heal the wounds of three decades of civil war and to build up France internally once again. Maximilien de Béthune, duke of Sully, the gloomy but honest and efficient Calvinist that he appointed to oversee the economic recovery, fought inflation by cutting expenses and reducing corruption in tax collection. He believed that ultimately land was the true source of wealth, and accordingly worked to improve agriculture, build new farm-to-market roads, drain swamps, dig canals, construct bridges, and protect the peasants from marauding bands of robbers. He set up a commission on commerce to promote industry, such as silk manufacturing in Lyon. Sully even originated Henry IV's grand design to make France the head of a *république chrétienne* for the promotion of peace and order in Christendom. Looking beyond Europe, the crown established new colonies in North America and Asia. In 1608 Champlain established French settlements in Port Royal and Quebec.

When all seemed to be going well, fate once again intervened. Henry IV continued his pressure on Spain, especially in the Netherlands, and he allied himself with several German Protestant princes to keep the small state of Jülich-Cleves from falling into the hands of Spain. While preparing to join his forces on the eastern front, Henry was murdered on a street in Paris on May 14, 1610, by a Catholic fanatic who believed that Henry intended to wage war on the pope. Unhappy France fell victim once again to forces that threatened disintegration.

For seven years Henry's widow, Marie de' Medici, served as regent for her young son Louis XIII (1610–1643). With the great Cardinal Richelieu as his minister from 1624 on, Louis XIII was able to continue successfully the Bourbon policy of making the king supreme in France and France supreme in Europe, which came to full fruition with the reign of his son, Louis XIV. No doubt the fear and fatigue generated by the civil war made the French people readier to accept absolutism than they might otherwise have been. France had come a long way since the rosy days of Francis I, when the humanists hailed the advent of the golden age. The Habsburg-Valois wars had bled her and the wars of religion had ravished her. By the seventeenth century the will to resist absolutism was greatly weakened. The struggle of the Huguenot minority with the Valois, however, stimulated new political theories of sovereignty and the right of resistance that were of great significance at the time and in the subsequent age of democratic revolutions.

The Development of French Political Thought

IT USED TO BE THOUGHT that the French Calvinists went along with the Genevan's teaching on obedience to civil authority until their precarious position was rendered so critical by the St. Bartholomew massacre in 1572 that they then developed full-blown theories of the limitations of the sovereign and the right of resistance to the monarch. The truth is that medieval political theory had in the main reflected the reality of limited monarchy, with sovereignty subject to the good old laws and shared with lesser feudal authorities and with the estates. The canon lawyers who supported papal claims to the *plenitudo potestatis,* or fullness of power, and Renaissance proponents of *The Prince* contributed something to the theoretical basis of absolute monarchy. Such an absolutist theory of monarchy did develop in the France of Francis I, extending the theories of the lawyers from Louis IX onward to enlarge the powers of the crown in every possible direction.

Their conception was that of a monarch ruling as vicegerent for God, independently of popular will and consent. The Roman legists tended to see the very essence of sovereignty as the lawmaking power.

Some theorists, such as the humanist Guillaume Budé, argued that if the king acted contrary to reason and equity or to his own ordinances he was guilty of *lèse majesté,* but the king was ultimately the judge of what constituted right reason. Claude de Seyssel, a bishop who had served as chancellor and as ambassador to England, implied in his *Le grand monarchie de France* (1518) that the whole complex of traditional and actual restraints upon the royal will belonged in a real way to the unwritten constitution of the French monarchy. Monarchy rests on custom and expediency, not on divine right, he argued, and the problem of government is how best to maintain peace, order, and justice. Queen Catherine's chancellor, Michel de L'Hôpital, asserted that the ruler held his authority directly from God. He believed that France's only hope for peace and order lay in the ruler's power to make law and to determine all questions without appeal. The subject was never justified in rebellion, regardless of what the ruler did, and tyrannicide was an abomination. Only the ruler's full sovereignty could maintain unity in the state.

The most powerful political thinker of the sixteenth century was indisputably Jean Bodin (*c.* 1529–1596), author of *The Method for the Easy Comprehension of History* (1566) and of *The Six Books of the Republic* (1576). Bodin taught at the University of Toulouse and then moved to Paris to write on jurisprudence, with all France as his focus. He saw the family, under the natural authority of the father, as the true source and origin of the republic. The state, he argued, is an association of families, over which it has sovereign power, which should be directed toward the realization of all good for mind and body. The government of a well-ordered state will be concerned with justice, defense, and economics. Sovereignty is the recognized and unlimited authority to make law. Bodin considered such sovereignty indispensable to calm the disorders of his times. Nevertheless, he was a proponent of limited monarchy. In a letter to a friend around 1580 he wrote these striking lines:

> What could be more democratic than what I dared to write, that the king was not permitted to exact tribute without the consent of the citizens? Of how great importance is the fact which likewise I stated, that princes are held by divine and natural law, by a sterner bond than are their subjects? That they are held by compacts just like other citizens?[1]

Against the background of such monarchical political theory, the Calvinist theories of resistance to the state stand out as truly revolutionary. In opposition to the ancient French tradition of *un roi, une loi, une foi* (one king, one law, one

---

[1] Bodin to Du Faur, October 3, 1580(?), cited in Beatrice Reynolds, *Proponents of Limited Monarchy in Sixteenth-Century France: Francis Hotman and Jean Bodin* (New York, 1931), pp. 185–86.

faith), dissident nobles challenged the unity of the consolidated state and non-conforming Calvinists pressed the claim for legalized diversity of religion. Calvin had taught a doctrine of nonresistance and had carefully dissociated himself from the Conspiracy of Amboise. But Calvin openly criticized tyrants, and he allowed an important exception to his rule of nonresistance: when the authority of man conflicts with duty to God, one must obey God rather than man. The lesser magistrates, like the Spartan ephors or Roman tribunes, were duty bound to protect the people from tyranny. Later Calvinists went on to develop ideas with truly revolutionary consequences. The shoddy historian Hilaire Belloc was wrong, of course, but not entirely wrong, when he wrote, "No Calvin, no Cromwell."

Some of Calvin's close associates developed theories of resistance even before their situation in France became desperate—new ideas prior to the concrete realities. Theodore Beza (d. 1605) argued as early as 1554 in his treatise *De haereticis* that persons in inferior positions of authority have the right to lead popular uprisings against higher authority in the name of "true religion." This idea he spelled out without any ambiguity in his 1574 treatise *De jure magistratuum*. Beza cited the precedent of the city of Magdeburg, which defended itself—justly, Beza claimed—against the armies of Charles V during the Schmalkald War. Another Swiss reformer, Pierre Viret (1511–1571), followed Calvin in urging obedience to kings, magistrates, and civil laws as a general principle, but criticized tyrants, urged passive resistance, and even declared that he could conceive of instances when the Lord would countenance "righteous disobedience" to tyrannical political edicts that were contrary to God's will.

A prominent Huguenot legist, François Hotman, published in Geneva his *Francogallia,* a passionately rhetorical treatise on French history and constitutional law. Although he published the work in 1573, he actually wrote it during the six months preceding the St. Bartholomew massacre, so it was not merely a *livre de circonstance* prompted by that outrage. His purpose was to prove that from the time of pre-Roman Gaul the sovereignty of the people, expressed through a national representative body, had been traditionally recognized, except for the period of Roman intervention. The right of the representative body, derived from the sovereignty of the people, to make laws, appoint magistrates, and even depose the king, he maintained, had been recognized until the end of the preceding century, and had been usurped by the Valois kings. Hotman's history was bad, but his treatise served as an effective instrument of propaganda.

An even more astonishing tract was the anonymous *Vindiciae contra tyrannos* (1579), which declared that the prince was bound by a contract expressing the immutable will of God, which neither the king nor the people could break with impunity. Although the *Vindiciae* was weak on specifics, the emphasis on contracts suggested the idea of reciprocal obligation, with emphasis on the obligations of the prince. The people in every kingdom were the true lord and sovereign. Rebellion was always justified against a tyrant, since he had broken his contract by his tyrannical behavior and therefore did not have a just title to his throne. When a legitimate prince has become a tyrant, ruling without regard for law, justice, or piety, he is at enmity with God and man. All may judge when the prince has become a tyrant, but a single individual may not act upon his own responsibility. Only the community may act through its representatives, the nobles and magistrates. For all its tentativeness and fuzziness, the *Vindiciae,* in proclaiming the sovereignty of the people, had very revolutionary implications. The evolution of political thought in France, as in John Knox's Scotland and Puritan England, was of great importance for the embryonic development of modern democratic ideas. Though he is often criticized for overstating the case, there is nevertheless much evidence in support of the historian John L. Motley's claim that Calvinist Protestantism inspired and sustained man's most successful effort to break the yoke of unjust authority. "It is certain," he wrote, "that France, England, the Netherlands, and North America owe a large share of such political liberties as they have enjoyed to Calvinism."[2]

The Spanish Preponderance

FOR SPAIN the sixteenth century was a golden age. While its great rival France was torn apart by internecine warfare, Spain rose to a position of preeminence that it had never before enjoyed and which no other power could equal. Spanish armies paraded their triumphs from Sicily to the North Sea. Spanish fleets roamed the waters from the Gulf of Lepanto to Manila Bay. Spanish *conquistadores* crushed great Indian empires. And Spanish authors and artists produced an efflorescence of culture such as the Iberian peninsula had never known before and has not seen again.

Charles V had hoped to see his only legitimate son, Philip II, succeed him on the throne of the Holy Roman Empire, but the plan failed. Instead the Habsburg dominions were divided between Vienna and Madrid, the house of Austria taking the Danubian inheritance and the imperial crown, Philip II inheriting the kingdom of Spain with its possessions in Africa, Italy (Sicily, Naples, Milan), Burgundy, the Netherlands, Asia, and the New World.

KING PHILIP II OF SPAIN

Philip's mother, Isabella of Portugal, was deeply conscious of the great destiny awaiting her child as she lay in labor on May 21, 1527, in Valladolid. She feared

---

[2] John Lothrop Motley, *History of the United Netherlands* (New York, 1900), vol. 4, p. 431.

that any sign of weakness or suffering would diminish the dignity of that auspicious event. When a lady in attendance urged her to cry out to ease the pain and tension, the queen exclaimed, "Silence! Die I may, but wail I will not!" She then commanded that her face be hidden from the light so that no one could see her grimaces. To such a dedicated, devout mother was born the sickly child who became Spain's mightiest ruler. She died when he was only twelve.

Historians have differed wildly in their estimates of Philip II. To Motley he was "the incarnation of evil," to Roger Merriman "the prudent king." To Leopold von Ranke he was a "dilatory hermit of the Escorial," a patient clerk whose heart was in another world and whose mind was lost in myriad administrative details. The "black legend" about Philip as a vicious, monstrous man who betrayed friends, assassinated enemies, burned heretics, murdered his own son Don Carlos, and lurked like a spider in the dark recesses of the Escorial was a product of the calumnies of Antonio Pérez, a secretary who defected to the enemy, and of the Dutchman William the Silent's *Apologia,* a piece of anti-Spanish propaganda. Recent historians see him as a man who was born into a narrowly circumscribed tradition and who never sought to transcend it. He was well intentioned, but was victimized by circumstances. He was a dutiful son, a devoted husband, and a good father.[3]

From the time Philip was sixteen, Charles V left him to rule as regent whenever he himself was out of the country, and he wrote out a number of letters of instruction to guide him. The most characteristic advice he offered his son was to trust no one and to "depend on none but yourself." Philip spent a lifetime fighting to keep his courtiers from dominating him. He was careful to give rival parties equal representation on the governing councils, so that the decisive voice would be his own. Philip had a grave, dignified, and self-possessed bearing, but he tended to be excessively enigmatic, secretive, crafty, and cautious. Though his Germanic inheritance was revealed in his blue eyes, fair hair, and prominent Habsburg jaw, Philip was Spanish to the core. After signing the Peace of Cateau-Cambrésis in 1559, he never left Spain again until the day of his death nearly forty years later, in 1598. The Spaniards loved him as their very own.

Philip's life was personally tragic. Before he was sixty he had already buried seventeen members of his family. His son Don Carlos, by his Portuguese queen Maria, who died soon after giving birth, was physically stunted and mentally retarded, perhaps the hapless victim of too many consanguineous marriages in his lineage. (His own parents were cousins.) To keep him from falling into the hands of his enemies, Philip kept Don Carlos in close custody, and when he died, Philip's enemies accused him of murdering his own son.

After Maria died, Philip married another cousin, Queen Mary of England, hoping desperately to produce an heir who would unite the Spanish and English

---

3 See John C. Rule and John J. Te Paske, *The Character of Philip II* (Boston, 1963).

empires as Catholic dominions. He landed at Southampton on July 20, 1554, bearing gifts for friends and foes alike. Three days later, in the episcopal palace of Winchester, Mary saw Philip for the first time and fell desperately in love with him. He was wearing a suit of white kid covered with gold embroidery and a gray satin French surcoat. Mary was a washed-out little woman eleven years older than he, with virtually no eyebrows. Philip had come to beget an heir and he did not blanch even in the face of this challenge, but he failed in the mission. Mary was perhaps even more anxious than Philip to produce a child, for she loved the man; so anxious, in fact, that when a year had passed and Philip left for Brussels to take over the rule of the Netherlands from his father, she experienced a false pregnancy that lasted many more than the traditional nine months. But there was no child, and still Philip did not come. When at last he did return, after an absence of a year and a half, he stayed only long enough to gain England's assistance in Spain's war against France. That was the last Mary saw of him. After her death he had thoughts of trying again with her half-sister, Elizabeth I, but nothing came of them, and to seal the peace with France he married instead Elizabeth of Valois, daughter of Henry II and Catherine de' Medici, with the duke of Alba standing in as his proxy in Paris.

A Spanish writer of the sixteenth century, Pedro de Medina, observed, "There is and has always been in Spain so much fervor for the Holy Catholic Faith that it is something which is not to be found elsewhere." The fervor of the crusades against the Moors and the strength of the hierarchy in resisting Protestant encroachments paid rich dividends in the high religious spirit of the sixteenth century. Pious Philip was in a sense the very embodiment of this Spanish spirit. Not long after his return to Spain in 1559 he resolved to build a seat of government outside of hot Madrid. That massive granite pile, the Escorial, which he built northwest of the city in the foothills of the Sierra de Guadarrama, was in Prescott's phrase "a palace, a monastery, and a tomb." As a palace it was the center of elaborate courtly ceremonies, a part of the inherited Burgundian tradition. As a monastery it was the home of the Hieronymite monks, and with them the pious Philip practiced his religion with fervor, observing long vigils and fasts, praying for long periods, and doing penance. He attended mass every day, and the Venetian ambassador reported that he regularly consulted his confessor on the effect of proposed actions upon conscience. It is not to be supposed, however, that Philip's religious devotion made him a papal lackey or instrument of the hierarchy. Quite the contrary; as he conceived it, his role as Catholic king required his personal control over the papacy. And finally, when Philip's long reign came to an end, the Escorial became a tomb for him and his descendants.

Philip gave detailed attention to nearly every domestic and foreign problem, poring conscientiously over dossiers and annotating dispatches with loving care. Like Frederick the Great and Napoleon, he looked after details personally, but unlike them, he could not distinguish the significant from the insignificant. The government ground along laboriously. "If God decreed my death through the Escorial," a Spanish official commented, "I would be immortal." At the head of the government was a council of state, which was entirely dependent upon the king. The direction was toward absolutism, and the French ambassador once wrote to Catherine that the king secretly meant "to cut the claws and dock the privileges" of the members of the Aragonese cortes, which made them so "insolent and almost free." Philip reformed the judicial system, promoted public works projects, and tried to be a benevolent ruler.

Economic difficulties mounted during Philip's reign. Spain's highland terrain was hot, desiccated, and largely empty. Nearly six million of its eight million inhabitants lived in Castile. Although production did increase during Philip's reign, Spain's industrial base was still so meager that most of the gold and silver that poured in from the New World merely passed through the hands of foreign bankers on its way to the Netherlands and other commercial and industrial centers of Europe. That which remained in Spain added to inflationary pressures there. The sea battles in the Mediterranean, the attempt to suppress the revolt of the Netherlands, and the adventurous assault on England cost Philip enormous sums. In 1573 the government had already spent its income for the next five years. In 1577 taxes were tripled in Castile. On seven occasions Philip repudiated his debts, and still two-thirds of the state's income was paid out in interest on debt by the end of his reign.

FOREIGN AFFAIRS

Philip was the great-grandson of that Ferdinand whom Machiavelli had so admired, and he inherited all of his cunning but little of his luck. Philip's record in foreign affairs was basically tragic, for his two triumphs, the acquisition of Portugal and victory over the Turks in the Mediterranean, were more than offset by the long and costly revolt of the Netherlands and the disaster of the Armada sent against England.

Portugal Won. As with a majority of the Habsburgs' most impressive gains, Philip owed to family ties his inheritance of Portugal and its overseas possessions in South America, India, and the Far East. In 1578 King Sebastian of Portugal was killed in the battle of Alcazarquivir near Tangiers while on a crusade against the Moslems in Morocco. Since he died without male heirs, his granduncle Cardinal Prince Henry assumed the rule until his death early in 1580. Philip, who was the grandson of Manuel I of Portugal (his mother was Manuel's daughter), now saw the need to reinforce his claim to the inheritance by armed intervention. By autumn his army under the duke of Alba had crushed the feeble opposition and

Portugal was united with Spain under the personal sovereignty of the king, though it retained a great deal of autonomy.

The Turks Defeated.   Philip continued the crusading tradition of Ferdinand and Isabella and the warfare at sea of Charles V against the Ottomans. He completed the integration or elimination of the Moslems still living in southern Spain, but gaining control of the sea was another matter. In 1559 the Ottoman Turks and their North African vassals still dominated the Mediterranean. Philip commissioned the viceroy of Sicily to attack Tripoli in alliance with the Knights of St. John on Malta. They scored some successes as long as Suleiman I was preoccupied with his war against Persia, but in 1565 the Turks struck back and took Malta itself, except for a single fortification. The Spaniards drove off the Turkish fleet and Suleiman died on a campaign against Hungary. Philip II, urged on by Pope Pius V, dreamed of dealing the Turks a fatal blow, but the Netherlands were giving him trouble and he could not give full attention to the Turks.

Philip was rocked by the revolt of the *Moriscos* in Granada at the end of 1568, aided by North African Moslems. Don Juan of Austria, an illegitimate son of Charles V, assumed command of the royal army, crushed the *Moriscos,* and went on to plan a counterattack against the Turks. With support from the Venetian, papal, and Genoese fleets, Don Juan maneuvered a weaker Turkish fleet into the bay of Lepanto near Corinth in Greece. On October 7, 1571, he directed the allies in an attack on the Turks that has gone down in history as one of the great sea battles of the century. Of some 208 Turkish galleys and 66 smaller ships, the Spanish forces sank 15 and captured 177, and freed from 12,000 to 15,000 Christian galley slaves. The battle was not so decisive as the West jubilantly believed, for the very next year the Turks sent a fleet of some 250 ships to rove through the Mediterranean. But it was nevertheless the first massive defeat of the Ottomans at sea, and it relieved the pressure on western sea lanes.

The Netherlands Revolt.   The revolt of the Netherlands against Spain has long captured the imagination of Western man. It has all the pathos and heroism of David's battle with Goliath or the Greeks' struggle with mighty Persia. It has appealed to all the deepest emotions of liberal, republican, progressivist Protestant historians. John Lathrop Motley, for example, in his three-volume *Rise of the Dutch Republic,* saw Spanish Catholicism and absolutism as the powers of darkness, while Dutch Protestantism was a force for liberty, democracy, and light. The revolt was indeed one of the most moving spectacles in European history, but the issues at stake were far too complex to be depicted in simple black and white.

During Philip's rule most of the seventeen provinces of the Netherlands rebelled, but only the seven northernmost provinces, located above the great rivers that flow into the North Sea, managed to gain independence, and it took them eighty years to secure Spain's official acknowledgment of the freedom they had won. The seven United Netherlands, together with certain territories to the south and east, comprise the present-day kingdom of the Netherlands. The core of the remaining provinces, which continued under Spanish rule, comprises the present-day kingdom of Belgium. The larger part of the Netherlands was inhabited by people who spoke a Low German dialect, whereas in the Walloon area to the south and to the west French was the predominant language; the division can be traced back to the Frankish invasions of the sixth century. Economically some of the medieval centers of trade, such as Ghent and Bruges, were in decline, while Antwerp and other cities were on the rise. The textile industries were suffering from increased competition from England and other areas. In spite of the inflation produced by the influx of bullion from the New World through Spain, which worked a hardship on certain classes, economic life was not so vigorous as it had been, and as it would be again with Dutch imperial expansion.

Unlike his father, who was at home in the Netherlands, Philip II was a Spaniard and a foreigner. Although his policies were the same as his father's, coming from him the measures were *a priori* less acceptable to the people. Philip attempted to win over the nobility, but disaffection actually developed first among the privileged upper classes and gradually spread to the commoners.

Protestantism had made early inroads into the area. In spite of Charles V's harsh repressive measures, first Lutheranism, then Anabaptism, but then most successfully Calvinism won many adherents. Guido de Bray composed the Calvinist creed *Confession de foi des églises des Pays-Bas*. But Calvinism was professed by only a tiny fraction of the population at the time of the revolt. The burnings of heretics and executions of Reformed pastors added fuel to a growing anticlerical feeling. Economic and ideological elements coalesced into a stubborn determination to rid the land of foreigners.

Although the earlier governor of the Netherlands, Charles V's sister Mary, had got by with few incidents, Philip II had hardly taken command before serious opposition began, in the fall of 1555. There was general resentment over the taxes levied to support the war against the French, which they considered to be a Spanish affair. Margaret of Parma, Philip's half-sister, appointed as governor, seemed very much a foreigner to the people. When one of her officials, Cardinal Granvelle, reorganized the church dioceses and established himself at their head, the estates and upper nobility feared that their traditional privileges were in jeopardy. Resistance to the extranational tendencies of Philip's rule, to excessive centralization, to the loss of ancient rights, to religious persecution, to the presence of Spanish troops arose first among the politically privileged classes and centered around William of Nassau and Orange, lord of Breda and governor of Holland, Zeeland, and Utrecht.

William of Orange has most inappropriately come to be called William the

Silent, a sobriquet earned by his great discretion during early years under Catholic surveillance, though he was by nature articulate and loudly assertive. Born in Dillenburg in 1533, William was brought to his family's lowland possessions as a boy. He was not a man of strong religious feeling, but since he was pacific and tolerant, he strove to unite the Calvinists and Lutherans in opposition to Granvelle's measures in 1564. In response to Philip's harsh religious edicts the next year, William of Orange, the count of Egmont, and the count of Hoorne-Montmorency withdrew from the council of state. In April 1565 the nobles who were inclined toward resistance petitioned Margaret in Brussels to mollify the harsh religious edicts and end the Inquisition. The president of the council on finance referred to the petitioners as "beggars" (*gueux*), a name taken up with pride by the resistance movement. Although Margaret promised amelioration, she reserved the final decision for Philip, a half measure that enfuriated everyone. Religious opposition to "papal idolatry" grew, and Calvinism gained new adherents. A few radicals attacked Vlissingen and Antwerp in February 1567. Alarmed, Philip ordered the duke of Alba from Italy to the Netherlands with an army of Germans, Walloons, and Spaniards to suppress the dissidents.

The duke of Alba rode into Brussels on August 22, 1567, and began his reign of terror by having Egmont, Hoorne, and other nobles arrested. Then he set up a "blood council" to punish everyone who had contributed to the disturbances of the preceding year. Believing that the interest of the state demanded the intimidation of all its subjects, he was inhibited by neither law nor equity. Even while the people were spreading rumors of a general pardon in January 1568, Alba was writing to the king:

> A great deal remains to be done first. The towns must be punished for their rebelliousness with the loss of their privileges; a goodly sum must be squeezed out of private persons; a permanent tax obtained from the States of the country. It would therefore be unsuitable to proclaim a pardon at this juncture. Everyone must be made to live in constant fear of the roof breaking down over his head. Thus will the towns comply with what will be ordained for them, private persons will offer high ransoms, and the States will not dare to refuse what is proposed to them in the King's name.[4]

On one day in March 1568 over five hundred new arrests were made. City officials of high position were "pinioned, manacled, and handcuffed like the meanest criminal." On June 1 Alba had eighteen noblemen beheaded in Zavel Square in Brussels and four days later he executed Egmont and Hoorne at the Great Market Square in that city. The "Iron Duke" paralyzed the people with fear.

If the duke of Alba was the villain of the piece, William of Orange was its hero. He made a feeble effort to invade Flanders, but had to take refuge in France. The

---

4 Pieter Geyl, *The Revolt of the Netherlands (1555–1609)*, 2nd ed. (New York, 1958), pp. 102–3.

Dutch took to their ships, and the Sea Beggars, reinforced from England and La Rochelle, whittled away at the Spanish fleet and liberated towns along the coast. William of Orange now became a Calvinist and led the opposition, with Holland and Zeeland as the main base of the resistance.

When Alba was recalled, Luis de Requeséns continued his nonsensical policies without concessions. Following his death in 1576, Don Juan of Austria, the victor of Lepanto, arrived as governor. Don Juan tried to move toward a peaceful settlement and made concessions on the quartering of Spanish troops, but he insisted upon the restoration of Catholicism in all the provinces. In January 1578 the Spanish troops won a telling victory over the soldiers of the estates general. England's Queen Elizabeth supplied subsidies and the Protestant John Casimer, elector of the Palatinate, sent auxiliary troops to the Beggars. William's brother, John of Nassau, organized the Union of Utrecht to resist Alexander Farnese, duke of Parma, who replaced Don Juan upon his death.

Treachery now robbed the resistance forces of their leader. Philip II put a high price on the head of William of Orange, for there was a movement to make William sovereign over the Netherlands. On July 10, 1584, a Catholic fanatic who had posed as a Calvinist shot William in Delft. The man whom Philip II had called the "plague of Christendom" was gone. Although William's son Maurice took over the leadership of the revolt, the Dutch were badly demoralized by their great loss, and Alexander Farnese took many cities. Elizabeth's expeditionary force under the earl of Leicester was ineffective. Shortly before his death, Philip loosened

the tie to Spain by making Archduke Albert of Austria, husband of his daughter Isabella, governor of the Netherlands, a rule that extended from 1598 to 1621.

The syndics of the urban centers were men of wealth and independence. A leader representative of this Dutch bourgeois class, Johan van Oldenbarneveldt (1547–1619), promoted the organization of the Dutch East India Company in 1602, a step that led to further commercial and naval rivalry with the Spanish fleets around the world. At last, after four decades of warfare, combat fatigue took its toll. In March 1609 the Spaniards agreed to a twelve-year truce with the northern Netherlands, which became virtually an independent republic. Even though fighting was resumed at the end of the long truce, the statehood of the northern Netherlands was secure, and at the Peace of Westphalia in 1648, which brought an end to the wars of religion in Europe, its independence was finally internationally acknowledged.

The Armada Fails. Philip's most disastrous and desperate venture was dispatching the Spanish Armada against England in 1588. Few episodes have gone down in history as such arrogant acts of aggression, and few events have been so commonly misrepresented. For the truth is that Philip, far from being carried away by "o'erweening pride," was exceedingly apprehensive about the plan, and regarded it as a last resort in a seemingly lost cause. He had been maneuvered into a duel to the death with Elizabeth, the "English Jezebel," through a long series of diplomatic misfortunes. Melanchthon, the fifteenth-century astronomer Regiomontanus, and other seers had found ominous indications in the books of prophecy that the year 1588 would be a year of disaster. It seemed almost as though Philip were being drawn to his rendezvous with destiny by irresistible forces.

In the early years of Elizabeth's reign, Philip had been a source of strength to her, for he shared her fear of Mary Stuart, queen of Scots. As the daughter of James V of Scotland, Elizabeth's first cousin, Mary was next in the line of succession to the English throne and was considered the only legitimate heir by the Catholics, who refused to recognize the marriage of Elizabeth's mother, Anne Boleyn; as the niece of the powerful French duke of Guise, Mary also posed a threat to Philip, for if her English supporters ever succeeded in placing her on the throne, England would then be allied with France, which coveted Flanders and other Habsburg holdings in the Low Countries. As long as Spain feared France, Philip had to allow Elizabeth many liberties. Her privateers engaged in piracy and smuggling, ran cargoes of Negro slaves to Spanish colonies in the New World, seized Spanish treasure ships, and supported the Sea Beggars in their raids on Spanish strongholds. She repeatedly interfered in the revolt of the Netherlands. This situation persisted for some two decades, until at last the political situation within France deteriorated to such an extent that Philip, relieved of his fears in that quarter, felt free to act against his Protestant foe and imperial rival, Elizabeth of England. Elizabeth in turn, fearing Catholic plots to put Mary Stuart on her throne, had her executed on February 18, 1587. The situation had become deadly serious.

Philip spun a web of intrigue from the Escorial, and when none of his plots against Elizabeth succeeded, he resolved on a direct frontal attack, an invasion of the island, which he anticipated would be greeted by an uprising of the Catholics in England and put an end once and for all to the machinations of the illegitimate queen of heretics. Philip, who habitually counseled others "to enjoy the benefits of time," now was impatient to get on with his grand design. "In so great an enterprise as that of England," he had once written, "it is fitting to move with feet of lead." Now he wrote to his captains, "Success depends mostly upon speed. Be quick!"

The assurance of a papal subsidy strengthened Philip in his resolve to undertake the expedition promptly. Pope Sixtus V sent a special observer to Lisbon to note the progress of the enterprise. This observer reported a conversation with one of the highest and most experienced officers of the Spanish fleet which was most revealing in a number of ways:

PAPAL EMISSARY: And if you meet the English Armada in the Channel, do you expect to win the battle?
SPANISH OFFICER: Of course.
PAPAL EMISSARY: How can you be sure?
SPANISH OFFICER: It's very simple. It is well known that we fight in God's cause. So, when we meet the English, God will surely arrange matters so that we can grapple and board them, either by sending some strange freak of weather or, more likely, just by depriving the English of their wits. If we can come to close quarters, Spanish valour and Spanish steel (and the great masses of soldiers we shall have on board) will make our victory certain. But unless God helps us by a miracle, the English, who have faster and handier ships than ours, and many more long-range guns, and who know their advantage just as well as we do, will never close with us at all, but stand aloof and knock us to pieces with their culverins, without our being able to do them any serious hurt. So we are sailing against England in the confident hope of a miracle.[5]

The miracle was denied the Spaniards and the Spanish commander's analysis proved to be remarkably accurate.

One of Philip's most experienced admirals, Santa Cruz, urged that the English sea power should be totally destroyed before a landing operation was undertaken. Although Philip ignored this perfectly sound advice, Santa Cruz literally worked himself to death in preparing the fleet for the risky venture. Instead Philip planned to have the Armada transport the army of Alexander Farnese in the Netherlands to England for a direct assault on the island. In the spring of 1587 Sir Francis Drake made a preventive attack upon Lisbon and Cádiz, wreaking such havoc upon the Spanish ships and supplies that the expedition was delayed a whole year.

---

[5] Garrett Mattingly, *The Defeat of the Spanish Armada* (London, 1959), pp. 191–92.

At last on May 29, 1588, the Armada set sail from Lisbon with 130 ships and more than 30,000 men under the command of the duke of Medina Sidonia. The ships were galleon types with high, vulnerable wooden hulls and banks of oars, useful in the Mediterranean but of far less value than sails on the open sea. Severe storms hit the fleet between Lisbon and La Coruña, and the ships had to put into La Coruña for refitting and could not go to sea again until July 22. When the Armada reached the channel, on July 29, Lord Howard of Effingham set sail from Plymouth with the English fleet—a larger number of low-slung, fast, and maneuverable ships, with longer range guns. Medina Sidonia might have bottled the English up in the harbor and repeated the victorious Spanish tactic of Lepanto, but his orders were to proceed to the Straits of Dover to take aboard the army of Farnese, and he tried to do as he had been told. He realized too late that the English were behind him. On August 6 the Armada lowered anchor off the coast at Calais, but the Dutch blockaded Farnese's fleet of small transport ships at Nieuport and Dunkirk, so that the Spanish army never reached the Armada. The next night the English sent fire ships against the Armada, and in a panic the Spanish captains cut the anchor ropes and put out to sea.

The English and Dutch now had the Armada between them, and attacked from both sides. With water and munitions running low, the Spaniards did not dare risk running the channel again, and fled instead into the North Sea. As the fleet took the long way home, northward around Scotland and Ireland, severe storms drove many ships onto the rocky coasts. Only fifty-three of the larger vessels ever again reached the safety of a Spanish harbor. King Philip received the news of the disaster with calm resignation, as though the defeat of the Armada were what he had expected all along, despite the wild reports of victory that he received from Don Bernardino de Mendoza, his ambassador in Paris. He was gracious and generous toward his defeated commander, for he realized that he had been defeated as much by the forces of nature as by the enemy.

Philip had trained himself to control his emotions with a near iron will. Moreover, his piety and devotion were so deeply rooted that even the disaster that befell the Armada could not shake his faith in Providence. On October 13 of that fateful year he wrote the news of the Armada's fate to the Spanish bishops, reminded them of the uncertainties of warfare on the high seas, and concluded:

> We are bound to give praise to God for all things which He is pleased to do. Now I give thanks to Him for the mercy He has shown. In the storms through which the armada sailed, it might have suffered a worse fate, and that its ill fortune was no greater must be credited to the prayers for its good success, so devoutly and continuously offered.[6]

The next year Elizabeth added insult to injury by sending a punitive expedition of twenty thousand men to raid La Coruña and attack Lisbon. In 1595 the

---

[6] *Ibid.*, p. 327.

Spaniards hit the Cornish coast to aid Irish rebels against the English. In 1596 Howard of Effingham retaliated with an attack by ten thousand troops under the earl of Essex and five thousand Dutch troops under Louis of Nassau. They captured Cádiz and held it for ransom. Philip planned to send another fleet against England, but it was scattered by storms before it was able to set sail. "An admiral, like a doctor, must have fortune on his side," a Spaniard commented at the time.

THE SPANISH EMPIRE

If Philip fared badly in the Old World, the fortunes of Spain still prospered in the New World. The personal union of Iberia under Philip brought together the widespread Portuguese domain with the mighty Spanish empire. While the French, Dutch, and English challenged Spain's power abroad, they were not able to destroy it for many decades.

Tiny Portugal, with its small population of about two million, was able, thanks to the ability and energy of its commanders, to control an empire several hundred times its own size. The explorations of Henry the Navigator, the explorations along the coast of Africa and around the Cape of Good Hope to India, and the discovery of Brazil by Cabral in 1500 established Portugal as a power around the world. By 1503 the Portuguese had already discovered that a few thousand soldiers in garrisons at strategic coastal spots could dominate a large populous hinterland. The great admiral Francisco Almeida worked out a comprehensive plan resting upon sea power and without emphasis upon political domination. The viceroy Albuquerque contemplated a territorial empire fanning out from power centers such as Goa, Calcutta, and Malacca. Lisbon became a great new center of commercial activity, the capital of the profitable spice trade. The king of Portugal received 25 percent of the commercial profits, but the Portuguese largely confined their operations to transporting cargoes and failed to take advantage of the opportunities of selling them in the European markets. The Portuguese were overextended, and during the second half of the century the attrition began to make itself evident.

The rise of Spain's colonial empire is one of the grand sagas of Western history. The iron will, the supreme self-confidence and national pride of the *conquistadores* as they sailed with small ships out into the "ocean sea," explored vast lands never before seen by Europeans, fought native bands, conquered empires, and won vast treasures will forever command the awe and respect of small boys and grown men. The Catholic kings of Spain and many of their captains in all sincerity viewed their enterprise as a mission to extend the blessings of the church and save the souls of the heathen even more than a search for earthly treasure. The stories of Hernán Cortés (1485–1547), who conquered the Aztec civilization with a band of unreliable soldiers, and Francisco Pizarro (*c.* 1471–1541), who took the mountain redoubts of the Incas and seized their vast treasures, will always remain stirring chapters in the history of Spain.

The Spanish colonial policy differed from the Portuguese in attempting to control an entire area, not just the key ports. Spanish colonial government, administered by viceroys in Mexico and Peru, was superior to that of the Portuguese. Men of established fortunes took posts for honorific reasons (though it is doubtful that they lost any money by their devotion to duty). An advisory council, or *audiencia,* was established in the main city of each of the larger provinces to supervise the operations of the viceroyalty. From time to time the viceroy sent inspectors to gather firsthand information on the local administrations. Finally, there were *residencias* to review the viceroy's record after his term was completed. In Spain the Council of the Indies, drawing on the experience of retired viceroys and administrators, directed the overseas possessions. But the areas controlled by the viceroys were so vast and so diverse that the viceroys could seldom keep abreast of local conditions, and the overdirection and control of the viceroys from the homeland stifled initiative and had an inhibiting effect upon colonial development.

Even though the Spaniards exercised such close political control over their colonies, they did allow private initiative in the development of landed estates (*encomiendas*) and trade. Under the *encomienda* system, the crown made a Spaniard responsible for the education, protection, and religious training of a particular group of Indians, in return for which the Spaniard was entitled to their labor. The system permitted penniless Spaniards who had taken part in the conquest to build up vast landed estates and other economic enterprises, and there was no supervision of the education, protection, or religious training the Indians received. The evils of the system became so notorious that attempts were made to replace it with the *repartimiento,* under which the Indians were still forced to work for the Spaniards, but under contract, on a temporary basis, and for wages. Actually the *encomienda* system lingered on into the eighteenth century, and for a long period the two systems were employed simultaneously.

Twenty percent of all treasure taken from the Indians and of the income of private entrepreneurs went to the king; the "king's fifth," it was called, and it came off the top, before any other allocation was made. Spanish economic policy was aimed at obtaining bullion and raw materials for the homeland; there was to be no colonial competition with such home industries as wine and olive oil production. The influx of silver and to a lesser extent of gold created an inflationary spiral in Andalusia, then in all Spain, and finally in the Spanish Netherlands and other parts of Europe. Spanish prices were 3.4 times higher at the start of the seventeenth century than they had been a hundred years before. In economics even gold does not always glitter.

The Spaniards were not bad maritime organizers at all. In order to protect the ships bearing the silver, gold, and other cargo from pirates, English sea dogs (from 1562 on), and Dutch raiders, they developed the convoy system, which they used down to 1800. Contrary to English legend, there were very few successful raids on Spanish convoys.

Immigration to the Spanish colonies was carefully controlled, and no foreigner, religious irregular, or anyone who was even related to anyone who had been charged by the Inquisition was allowed entry. An exception was made in the case of an English Catholic priest named Thomas Gage, since, like most Englishmen who wished to become priests in those days of militant Protestantism, he had been trained in a Spanish seminary. But Gage only proved the soundness of the rule. After twelve years in Guatemala he became discouraged about his prospects for preferment, returned to England, became a vicar of the Church of England, and wrote a splendidly biased account of conditions in the Spanish colonies, which nevertheless gives revealing insights into the workings of the colonial system. This, for example:

> The miserable conditions of the Indians . . . is such, that though the kings of Spain, have never yielded to what some would have, that they should be slaves, yet their lives are as full of bitterness as is the life of a slave. . . . Thus are the poor Indians sold for threepence a peece for a whole week's slavery, not permitted to goe home at nights unto their wives, though their worke lie not above a mile from the Town where they live; nay some are carried ten or twelve miles from their home who must not returne till Saturday night late, and must that week do whatsoever their Master pleaseth to command them. The wages appointed them will scarce find them meat and drinke. . . . This same order is observed in the city of Guatemala and Townes of Spaniards, where to every family that wants the service of an Indian or Indians, though it be but to fetch water and wood on their backs, or to goe of arrants, is allowed the like service from the neerest Indian townes.[7]

Bishop Bartolomé de Las Casas was a remarkable advocate of the humane treatment of Indians, although he was more influential in Spain than in the colonies. He had a medieval conception of the duty of the ruler toward his subjects, and as a Thomist he employed all the arguments derived from reason and natural law to oppose the colonial *encomiendas* as unjust and tyrannical. Ironically, his concern for the welfare of the Indians led him to recommend the importation of Africans, who could do heavy labor in the heat without the ill effects suffered by the Indians, who, as a Mongoloid people genetically adapted to cool climates, could survive in the tropical lowlands only by adopting a slow rhythm of life—or, as the Europeans liked to say, by being "lazy." It is noteworthy that today the populations of most of the hot coastal regions of Latin America are heavily black, while in the cool mountain regions a black man is a distinct rarity.

The Latin peoples were less loath to cross color lines than were the English and Dutch, and a colorful spectrum of peoples emerged in the Latin colonial areas. The *castillanos* were the Spaniards born in Spain; the *criollos,* or creoles, were people born in America of Spanish parents; the *mestizos* were part Spanish or creole, part Indian; the *mulatos* were part white, part Negro; and the *zambos* were part Indian and part Negro.

---

[7] Thomas Gage, *The English-American His Travail by Sea and Land: Or a New Survey of the West Indies* (London, 1648), pp. 139–40.

PHILIP THE PRUDENT

Philip II was called "the Prudent," which was perhaps the most charitable epithet that could be applied to this dedicated but essentially uninspiring king. He was more fit for the pen and desk than for the sword and saddle. Unlike his father, who traveled incessantly and looked after his empire in person, Philip was bound to the Escorial. Had his capital been Antwerp or Brussels, he would have been able to control his dynastic holdings more effectively, and the revolt in the Netherlands might not have become an albatross around his neck, bringing him endless grief and disaster.

Many circumstances worked against him. The enormous debt of some fifty million ducats bequeathed to him by Charles V gave him an initial financial handicap that he never overcame. New taxes, monopolies, the sale of offices, the "king's fifth" from the New World, all together never came close to meeting the enormous expenditures for government and warfare. At its height the income from America met no more than one-fourth of the government's requirements, which were sent skyrocketing by the wars against the Netherlands and England.

If all these circumstances lay beyond Philip's control, he must nevertheless bear the responsibility for his laborious, meticulous paternalism, for his lack of insight into the financial and economic predicament of Spain, and for his failure to create policy that would slow the forces of debility and disintegration, if it could not halt them.

Bibliography

French political history and the wars of religion:
ARMSTRONG, EDWARD. *The French Wars of Religion,* 2nd ed. Oxford, 1904.
BAIRD, H. M. *History of the Rise of the Huguenots,* 2 vols. New York, 1900.
———. *The Huguenots and Henry of Navarre,* 2 vols. New York, 1909.
BATTIFOL, LOUIS. *The Century of the Renaissance.* London, 1927.
CHARTROU-CHARBONNEL, J. *La réforme et les guerres de religion.* Paris, 1936.
ELLIOTT, J. H. *Europe Divided, 1559–1598.* New York, 1968.
ENGLAND, SYLVIA. *The Massacre of Saint Bartholomew.* London, 1938.
JACKSON, C. *Last of the Valois, and Accession of Henry of Navarre,* 2 vols. London, 1898.
JENSEN, DE LAMAR. *Diplomacy and Dogmatism: Bernardino de Mendoza and the French Catholic League.* Cambridge, Mass., 1964.
LIVET, GEORGES. *Les guerres de religion.* Paris, 1962.
NEALE, J. E. *The Age of Catherine de' Medici.* London, 1943.
PALM, F. C. *Politics and Religion in Sixteenth-Century France.* Boston, 1927.
———. *Calvinism and the Religious Wars.* New York, 1932.
RANKE, LEOPOLD VON. *Französische Geschichte vornehmlich im 16. und 17. Jahrhundert,* 6 vols. Leipzig, 1868–1876.

ROELKER, NANCY L. *The Paris of Henry of Navarre.* Cambridge, Mass., 1958.
————. *Queen of Navarre Jeanne d'Albret, 1528–1572.* Cambridge, Mass., 1968.
SALMON, J. H. M. *The French Religious Wars in English Political Thought.* Oxford, 1959.
————, ed. *The French Wars of Religion: How Important Were Religious Factors?* Boston, 1967.
SEDGWICK, H. D. *Henry of Navarre.* Indianapolis, 1930.
————. *The House of Guise.* Indianapolis, 1938.
STÉPHAN, RAOUL. *L'épopée huguenote.* Paris, 1945.
————. *Histoire du protestantisme française.* Paris, 1961.
SUTHERLAND, N. M. *The French Secretaries of State in the 16th Century.* London, 1962.
————. *Catherine de' Medici and the Ancien Régime.* London, 1966.
THOMPSON, J. W. *The Wars of Religion in France.* Chicago, 1909.
VAN DYKE, PAUL. *Catherine de' Medici,* 2 vols. New York, 1922–1927.
VIENOT, JEAN. *Histoire de la réforme française des origines à l'Édit de Nantes.* Paris, 1926.

French political thought:
ALLEN, J. W. *A History of Political Thought in the Sixteenth Century.* London, 1928.
CHURCH, W. F. *Constitutional Thought in Sixteenth-Century France.* Cambridge, Mass., 1941.
DODGE, G. H. *The Political Theory of the Huguenot Dispersion.* New York, 1947.
FRANKLIN, JULIAN. *Jean Bodin and the Sixteenth-Century Revolution in the Methodology of Law and History.* New York and London, 1963.
————. *Constitutionalism and Resistance in the Sixteenth Century: Three Treatises by Hotman, Beza, and Mornay.* New York, 1969.
GIESEY, RALPH. *The Royal Funeral Ceremony in Renaissance France.* Geneva, 1960.
GÖRING, MARTIN. *Weg und Sieg der modernen Staatsidee in Frankreich.* Tübingen, 1946.
KINGDON, ROBERT M., and LINDER, ROBERT D., eds. *Calvin and Calvinism—Sources of Democracy?* Lexington, Mass., 1970.
LINDER, ROBERT. *The Political Ideas of Pierre Viret.* Geneva, 1964.
REYNOLDS, BEATRICE. *Proponents of Limited Monarchy in Sixteenth-Century France.* New York, 1931.

The Spanish preponderance and Philip II:
ALTIMIRA Y CREVEA, RAFAEL. *A History of Spain from the Beginnings to the Present Day.* New York, 1949.
BERTRAND, LOUIS. *Philippe II à l'Escorial.* Paris, 1928.
———— and PETRIE, CHARLES. *The History of Spain.* London, 1952.
BRATLI, CARL G. *Philippe II, roi d'Espagne: Étude sur sa vie et son caractère.* Paris, 1912.
DAVIES, R. TREVOR. *The Golden Century of Spain, 1501–1621.* London, 1937.
ELLIOTT, J. H. *The Revolt of the Catalans: A Study in the Decline of Spain (1598–1640).* Cambridge, 1964.
FORNESON, H. *L'histoire de Philippe II,* 4 vols. Paris, 1887.
HAUSER, HENRI. *La prépondérance espagnole,* vol. 9 of *Peuples et civilisations.* Paris, 1948.
HUME, MARTIN A. S. *Spain: Its Greatness and Decay, 1479–1788.* Cambridge, 1925.
LIVERMORE, HAROLD. *A History of Spain.* London, 1958.

LYNCH, JOHN. *Spain Under the Hapsburgs*, vol. 1 of *Empire and Absolutism, 1516–1598*. New York, 1964.

MAASS, E. *The Dream of Philip II*. Indianapolis, 1944.

PETRIE, CHARLES. *Philip II of Spain*. New York, 1963.

PRESCOTT, W. H. *History of the Reign of Philip II*, 3 vols. Philadelphia, 1874.

Spain's foreign affairs and the Spanish empire:

BLOK, P. J. *A History of the People of the Netherlands*, 5 vols. New York and London, 1898–1912.

BRAUDEL, FERNAND. *La Méditerranée et le monde méditerranéen à l'époque de Philippe II*. Paris, 1949.

CADOUX, C. J. *Philip of Spain and the Netherlands*. London, 1911.

CHUBODA, BOHDAN. *Spain and the Empire, 1519–1643*. Chicago, 1952.

GEYL, PIETER. *The Revolt of the Netherlands (1555–1609)*, 2nd ed. New York, 1958.

HAMILTON, EARL J. *American Treasure and the Price Revolution in Spain, 1501–1650*. Cambridge, Mass., 1934.

HARING, C. H. *Trade and Navigation Between Spain and the Indies in the Time of the Habsburgs*. Cambridge, Mass., 1918.

KOENIGSBERGER, H. G. *The Government of Sicily Under Philip II of Spain*. London, 1959.

LEWIS, MICHAEL. *The Spanish Armada*. London, 1960.

MATTINGLY, GARRETT. *The Defeat of the Spanish Armada*. London, 1959.

MERRIMAN, ROGER B. *The Rise of the Spanish Empire*, 4 vols. New York, 1918–1934.

MOTLEY, J. L. *The Rise of the Dutch Republic*, 3 vols. New York, 1864.

CHAPTER 20

England
Under
Elizabeth

The reign of Queen Elizabeth (1558–1603) may well be described as a forty-five-year love affair between her majesty and the English people. Seldom in history has there been such a happy correspondence of purpose and program between sovereign and subjects as prevailed during that greatest age in English history. Elizabeth's long reign saw England turn thoroughly Protestant and become the leader among Protestant nations. As a national state on the Atlantic, England won a world empire during those decades and experienced a cultural flowering that was its true renaissance. Historians are now inclined to revise downward their estimates of what Elizabeth contributed personally to the government of England. They feel that she improvised and temporized, "muddled through," rather than providing statesmanlike guidance and vision. But when the effusions of her admirers have been recognized as the patriotic pieties they are, and Elizabeth herself has been reduced to human scale, she remains a remarkable woman who presided over England in an exciting era.

By the time Elizabeth ascended the throne at the age of twenty-five, she was an experienced and worldly-wise young woman, moderately tall, with pale red hair, an olive complexion, striking, expressive eyes, graceful hands, and a dignified bearing. Shrewd, calculating, dissembling, capable of playing coquette or the cold administrator, with the self-confidence to make quick decisions and the strength of nerve for Fabian tactics, Elizabeth was far better suited to occupy the throne of her royal father than either Edward or Mary had ever been.

The transfer of power from Mary to Elizabeth took place smoothly, for while Mary lay dying at St. James's the people were already rallying to Elizabeth at Hatfield. Feria, the Spanish ambassador, reported, "She is much attached to the people and is very confident that they are all on her side, which is indeed true." Her coronation took place on January 15, 1559.

A certain antifeminist bias was widespread and people generally expected the queen to marry. There were suitors enough for her royal hand. Her brother-in-law, Philip II, offered to do the honors, but Elizabeth was far too astute to marry the Catholic monarch, especially after Mary's unhappy experience. Her passionate lover Robert Dudley, earl of Leicester, was spoiled, impulsive, and undependable. The uncertainty about the cause of his wife's death, either from an accidental fall or by suicide, created a public scandal. Although Elizabeth was strongly attracted to him, she characteristically allowed her head to rule her heart and put the "weal of the kingdom" above her personal feelings. A "modern woman" who could speak French, Latin, and Italian, Elizabeth was also skilled at double-talk, and kept many ambitious men living in hope and at her service. The Scottish ambassador remarked to her, "Madam, I know your stately stomach: ye think if ye were married, ye would be but queen of England, and now ye are king and queen both; ye may not suffer a commander." To Protestants the "virgin queen" was a heroic Judith; to Catholics she was a Jezebel, a servant of infamy, the refuge of evil men.

The Elizabethan Settlement

ELIZABETH CHOSE as her closest adviser William Cecil, later Lord Burghley, a moderate Protestant who had served under Somerset and Northumberland, and even for a short time under Queen Mary. He served Elizabeth during nearly all of her reign, first as secretary of state and then as lord treasurer, counseling to action with moderation, to decisiveness with discretion. Elizabeth appointed only Protestants to her council—men more devoutly Protestant and more favorable to Puritans than she herself was. Her secretary of state from 1573 to 1590, Sir Francis Walsingham, followed a policy of active support for the beleaguered Protestants on the continent, especially the Dutch Reformed and French Huguenots. He was energetic in exposing Catholic intrigues against Elizabeth, employing an elaborate counterespionage system against the Spaniards and Jesuits.

Elizabeth recognized England's great need for peace and tranquillity and pursued a religious policy of moderation, seeking the *via media* for the church and the realm. She had a certain religious depth (when she was only eleven she had translated Marguerite d'Angoulême's *Mirror of the Sinful Soul*) and an aesthetic and sentimental appreciation for religious rites and ceremonies; but the rapid religious changes of the preceding reigns had taught her to be tentative and tolerant, and secular in her interests. She once observed that she would sooner hear a thousand masses than be guilty of the millions of crimes done by some who suppressed masses. As a matter of personal choice as well as a policy of state, Elizabeth fostered an Anglican settlement in doctrine and discipline, and held both the Catholics and the radical Protestants in check. John Knox once observed that Elizabeth was "neither good Protestant nor yet resolute Papist." As archbishop of Canterbury she appointed Matthew Parker, a moderate who had once served as her mother's chaplain and as her own tutor. Parker had been a disciple of Martin Bucer, was married, and had long friendships with many of the Marian exiles. Elizabeth had to choose most of her bishops from among the returning exiles, most of whom were considerably more radical in their Protestantism than she was.

The success of her policy was assured by action of parliament, where the religious issue was neatly settled, or nearly settled itself. At the beginning of the sixteenth century parliament was basically a legislative and taxing body, meeting only intermittently. During the course of the century it became an increasingly powerful political force as the House of Commons grew in prestige, position, and initiative. Henry VIII had been party to a marriage of convenience with the Commons, increasing its power because it largely shared his aims. Under Elizabeth the will of the crown and the will of parliament, which is another way of saying the will of the gentry of England, were often at odds. But there was still romance in the marriage, and with a bit of cajoling and manipulating the queen could usually have her way.

Parliament assembled on January 25, 1559, to act on the religious question, for Elizabeth realized that parliament would have to initiate the reformation of the clergy; the Convocation of the Clergy, with most of the bishops appointees of Queen Mary, held to the Catholic doctrines of transubstantiation and the sacrifice of the mass. A combination of the Protestants on the council and in the House of Commons forced a more rapid settlement than Elizabeth actually wanted. She and Cecil hoped for an act of supremacy, with an act of uniformity later. But neither she nor Cecil was able to control the first parliament.

In April parliament passed an act of supremacy that recognized the queen as head of the English church. All royal officials, judges, and the clergy were to take a loyalty oath acknowledging the supremacy of the crown over the church, on pain of deprivation of office. To uphold the authority of any foreign prince or prelate was high treason, punishable by death. Mary's Catholic legislation having been rescinded, the Act of Uniformity restored the ecclesiastical statutes of Henry VIII and reintroduced the *Second Prayer Book* of Edward VI, modified somewhat by the addition of a few more traditional passages from the 1549 edition. Members of the clergy who refused to conform were replaced, so that the sees were eventually filled by appointees favored by Elizabeth.

When the second parliament met in 1563, it reaffirmed the Act of Uniformity and passed measures ensuring its strict enforcement. That same year the Convocation of the Clergy at Canterbury worked out the doctrinal platform of the new dispensation. Edward VI's Forty-two Articles were slightly revised to become the Thirty-nine Articles, the basic Anglican confession. The articles were designed to accommodate moderate beliefs, avoiding overly subtle distinctions and extremes. The definition of the real presence of Christ in the Eucharist was carefully phrased to accommodate private main-line evangelical interpretations, expressly denying the Catholic doctrine of transubstantiation on the one hand and the Zwinglian symbolic interpretation on the other. The Scriptures were declared to be the source and norm of faith. Predestination was accepted, but not in an extreme Calvinist form. The bishop of Salisbury, John Jewel, an able defender of the national church, presented the first systematic statement of the Anglican position in his *Apology for the Anglican Church* (1562). The next year a work of even greater importance was published, the first English edition of John Foxe's *Acts and Monuments,* which for many generations was read nearly as faithfully as the Bible and the prayerbook by the clergy and the literate laity of both England and the American colonies. This crimson martyrology helped to create a specifically Protestant, anti-Roman consciousness that blended with the nationalistic sentiment of the Protestant English-speaking world.

CATHOLICS

At the outset of Elizabeth's reign the great mass of the English people were Catholic in their religious views, as were also a great many of the conservative upper nobility. But the most prominent men of the time, the younger men rising to positions of influence and power in business and government, were Protestants. The House of Commons reflected these energetic and progressive elements. Only about two hundred of nine thousand clergymen would not take the oath acknowledging royal supremacy during the first six years after the act was passed. In the course of Elizabeth's rule the Roman Catholics in England dwindled to a tiny minority, until they constituted only a small percentage of the population of some four million. Nevertheless, between the years 1569 and 1588, Catholicism, aided and encouraged by Spain, seemed to the English to be a real menace. The Catholic-feudal northern rising in 1569–1570, instigated by the duke of Norfolk to advance Mary Stuart's cause, failed to involve more than a limited area. The rebels did not even come close to taking York. The papacy was at a loss as to how to proceed against Elizabeth. The queen had refused to send representatives to the third session of the Council of Trent, citing as one of the main reasons the Catholic efforts to stir up sedition against her.

At last Pope Pius V completed the alienation of England by using the bull *Regnans in excelsis,* excommunicating Elizabeth, on February 25, 1570. The bull asserted that since the Roman pontiff had power over all nations and kingdoms, and since Elizabeth, the slave of vice, had usurped the place of the supreme head of the church, had sent her kingdom to perdition, and had celebrated the impious mysteries of Calvin, she was cut off from the body of Christ and deprived of her rule, and all her subjects were absolved of their oaths of allegiance. During the last three decades of Elizabeth's reign the Seminarists and Jesuits redoubled their efforts to win converts for Rome, and in certain areas they had some success. A decade after the bull of excommunication, the Jesuit mission in England claimed 120,000 converts, although it offered no substantiation for the figure. Whatever the number of "converts," most of them were undoubtedly Catholics from the start, rather than newly won followers. There had always been a fringe of people who remained loyal to Rome, but it is impossible to determine their numbers. The priests in this Catholic underground came often from aristocratic families and were trained abroad by the Jesuits or in Cardinal Allen's colleges in Douay and Rome. They lived precarious lives, moving in disguise from one country house to another, ministering to the households of Catholic squires. Recurrent rumors of assassination plots by recusants or foreign agents kept Lord Cecil on the alert and filled the popular imagination with dread and hate. Pope Gregory XII stated that the bull of Pius V justified taking up arms against "that guilty woman of England" in any way whatsoever, and even sanctioned a plot to murder her.

Elizabeth responded to the papal bull with a statesmanlike proclamation that she

> would have all her loving subjects to understand that, as long as they shall openly continue in the observation of her laws, and shall not wilfully and manifestly break them by open actions, her majesty's means is not to have any of them molested by any inquisition or examination of their consciences in causes of religion, but to accept and entreat them as her good and obedient subjects.

In 1571 parliament passed several antipapal laws forbidding bringing the papal bull into England and declaring it treason to say that Elizabeth should not be queen, or that she was a heretic, usurper, or schismatic. In 1585 an act banishing the Jesuits was passed in order to temper public outrage and fanatical attacks upon ordinary Catholics. Throughout Elizabeth's forty-five-year reign, only 221 Catholics suffered death for their faith, compared with 290 Protestants who died during the five years of her sister Mary's rule. Most of these were executed for treason rather than for heresy, a significant shift in emphasis, though the victims were quite as dead.

Elizabeth's firmness in dealing with Catholic dissidents was due in large part to the fact that their disloyalty played into the hands of her enemies at home and abroad. Fear of a general Catholic resurgence was largely responsible for her handling of Mary Stuart. The switch on the part of the most Catholic king of Spain to an aggressive policy culminating in the assault of the Spanish Armada brought the question of treason at home into sharp focus. But if the Anglican solution was plagued with a persistent Catholic minority, it was itself intimately involved in a broad general religious movement known as Puritanism and harassed by a few extremists of a Protestant variety.

PURITANS

That Puritanism was potentially more explosive and dangerous to the Anglican establishment than Catholicism became evident in the civil war of the seventeenth century. Particularly after 1640, separatism and Presbyterianism emerged as rival forms of doctrine ready to struggle for mastery over church policy. When we think of Puritanism during the reign of Elizabeth, we must take care not to read back into the sixteenth century the developments of later decades. Puritanism was a movement, to borrow Milton's phrase, "for the reform of reformation." The term first appeared around 1564, and was applied to those Protestants, all at that time safely within the fold of the national church, who wished to eliminate any trace of "popery" and "Roman superstition" from the Anglican establishment. A broad stream of younger clergy, including many Marian exiles, had been inspired by the theology emanating from Geneva and continued to look to the Reformed churches and theologians on the continent for learning and inspiration. Very few at this time thought of separatism. Calvin, Bucer, and Knox had not specifically denounced the episcopal office, so that one quite "reformed" in outlook could still live within the established church.

Elizabeth's religious posture was really quite conservative. She had no time for Protestant evangelicalism or for its demands for a preaching ministry. Although many of her bishops were willing to tolerate diversity in matters indifferent and were even ready to drop practices offensive to the reformers, Elizabeth forced Archbishop Parker to issue his "advertisements" in support of conformity. She dismissed Grindal, her own archbishop, for his defense of preaching and prophesying, which offered the best chance of incorporating Puritan evangelicalism within the establishment. It was not until she discovered John Whitgift that she found an archbishop anywhere near as conservative as she was, and she even rapped him on the knuckles for promulgating the Lambeth Articles in 1595. Given Elizabeth's stance and at the same time the growing pressure in the direction of evangelical Protestantism, the religious situation during her reign was bound to be one of tension and occasional confrontation.

A series of controversies during Elizabeth's reign led to more serious troubles later. The vestiarian controversy of 1563 hardly compared with the Arian controversy of the ancient church, and there was more noise than damage. The Puritans felt that the vestments prescribed for the clergy should not be a matter of compulsion. They scrupled about the clerics' practice of wearing cap and gown during the week and the surplice on Sunday. Very shortly they added to the list of Roman practices offensive to conscience such things as making the sign of the cross at baptism, kneeling at communion, observation of what they felt to be an excessive number of church holidays, the ring in marriage ceremonies, and (shades of Zurich!) the use of organs in churches. When a petition was presented to the Convocation of the Clergy to abolish various Roman practices and all vestments except the surplice, it lost out by a single vote.

Agitation about a weightier issue developed in 1572, when Thomas Cartwright and a Puritan group in London pressed for a Presbyterian form of church government to replace the Episcopal system. The "First Admonition," published in that year, urged that the congregations elect their ministers, who would supplant the bishops. The "Second Admonition" developed a Presbyterian model for church government, drawing heavily on Calvin's *Institutes,* urging the organization of presbyteries to administer church discipline, the congregational calling of ministers, and a directory of public worship. This threat to order and stability roused Elizabeth and her counselors, who seemed to recognize that bishops and the crown needed each other. Cartwright fled into exile in 1574, but the Presbyterian movement lingered on. John Field, the devoted organizer of the Presbyterian underground, died in 1589. By 1592 the system had been destroyed, and one might say that the Presbyterian episode was over. It enjoyed no serious renewal until the time of the civil wars.

A more radical departure was advocated by Robert Browne of Cambridge, the first separatist. Browne was a cantankerous character who was hauled up on one occasion for wife-beating. The account of the episode reveals the intellectual subtleties of which he was capable: "Old father Browne, being reproved for beating his old wife, distinguished that he did not beat her as his wife but as a curst old woman." He developed a congregational theory of the church as the body of those who were "called out" or "gathered" from the great mass of men and voluntarily associated with each other in a local church. In his *Book Which Showeth the Life and Manners of All True Christians* he argued that each congregation should be free of state control and independent also of bishops and presbyteries. The congregation should elect the pastors, teachers, and elders, not necessarily the well educated, and its worship should follow a very plain order of service. Around 1580 Browne actually gathered such a congregation at Norwich. Alarmed, the government set the wheels of repression in motion.

Elizabeth's new archbishop of Canterbury, John Whitgift, undertook the task of bringing the deviationist Puritans back into line. Although he severely disciplined Puritans who opposed the use of surplices, Whitgift was theologically a strong Calvinist who at one point even criticized Cartwright for conceding that the doctrine of free will was not "repugnant to salvation." Archbishop Whitgift, whom Elizabeth referred to as "my little black husband," in his first sermon at St. Paul's Cross, on November 17, 1583, let it be known that the Puritans would have to conform to the established order. The Six Articles that same year made mandatory the assent to royal supremacy in church as well as state and the acceptance of the *Book of Common Prayer* and the Thirty-nine Articles as authority and norm. The Court of High Commission brought offenders to justice and a total of some two hundred parish priests were suspended. In 1586 he established censorship for theological works, hoping to check Puritan extremists, but the shocking "Martin Marprelate" tracts appeared in spite of his efforts, attacking the bishops as "petty antichrists, proud prelates, intolerable withstanders of reformation, enemies of the gospel and covetous wretched priests." In 1593 the Conventicle Act demanded exile or death for all who refused to attend the established church and worshiped in separate groups. Whitgift's Lambeth Articles in 1595, however, still held to a consistent and severe predestinarian doctrine.

Not until Elizabeth's last years was there a shift in the theological views of the top leadership, when Richard Bancroft, bishop of London, began virtually to exercise the power of primate in the interest of more latitudinarian churchmen in 1599. At the Hampton Court Conference in 1604 Bancroft prevented the Puritans from making Whitgift's Lambeth Articles a part of the official credal statement. The most influential and characteristic work to emerge from the Anglican Reformation was the work of a modest cleric who was never prominent as a churchman or academician, Richard Hooker's *Laws of Ecclesiastical Polity,* the first four books of which appeared in 1593. Hooker's *Laws* were directed against a Puritan divine, Walter Travers, who attacked the established church on biblical grounds. Hooker rejected the Puritan arguments and in a masterful literary style worthy of the theme laid down the platform for Anglican polity as a proper structure for the church. He stressed the necessity for humility before God, the need for unity, peace, reason, and good order for attaining to tranquillity on earth and happiness in eternity. He appealed to the laws of God, nature, and the Scriptures to support the soundness of the Anglican establishment.

Mary Stuart, Queen of Scots

WHEN MARY STUART fled to England in 1568, she brought with her an implicit threat to Elizabeth's security that kept the English queen uneasy for nineteen years. One of her bishops remarked that Elizabeth had a "bear by the tail." It was the circumstance of Mary's birth as the only legitimate child of James V of Scotland, her Catholicism, her potential as a pawn in the international political game rather than anything formidable about her person that made her a threat. Mary was in many ways the antithesis of her cousin Elizabeth. She grew up in the gay and brilliant French court, was educated with the dauphin and his sisters, and developed into a woman of the world who preferred chivalric romances and Rabelaisian satires to the classics. She had a passionate temperament given to violent loves and virulent hates. Not strong physically, she nevertheless had remarkable endurance. If not the equal of Elizabeth in regal qualities, she was a worthy rival. The first fateful decision Mary made was to return from France, where the enmity of her mother-in-law, Catherine de' Medici, made her life at court difficult, to Scotland, a poor and backward country, but her own. James V, Mary's father, died on December 14, 1542, just one week after she was born. Six years later she was sent to France. In 1558 she was married to the dauphin, Francis. When Queen Mary of England died that same year, Mary and her husband adopted the royal arms of England. The next year, on the death of King Henry II, she became queen consort of France. Meanwhile the Scottish lords revolted, and the Reformed forces and their English allies forced Mary's French garrison to surrender. Mary's representatives signed the Treaty of Edinburgh, ending the civil war, in 1560; but since one of its provisions acknowledged Elizabeth as queen of England, Mary herself procrastinated and managed never to sign it. On December 5 her husband died and Mary resolved to return to Scotland as queen, to which the reformers reluctantly agreed. Mary arrived in Scotland on August 19, 1561.

For some time Mary ruled but did not really govern, for the clans were powerful and the reformers were persuasive. In 1565 Elizabeth allowed Henry Stuart, Lord Darnley, a great-grandson of Henry VII, to return to Scotland. He was a Catholic and in other ways eligible to be Mary's consort, and from Elizabeth's point of view he was less dangerous than a French or Spanish alliance. Mary, now twenty-three, fell violently in love with him. Protestant nobles rebelled, but Mary defeated them and married young Darnley. As a husband he proved to be mean and murderous. Jealous of Mary's Italian secretary, David Rizzio, a cheerful fellow who entertained Mary with music and handled her foreign correspondence, Darnley plotted his death. On March 9, 1566, a band of assassins burst into the queen's apartment while she was present, dragged Rizzio just outside the door, and stabbed him to death. Mary was imprisoned, but escaped and lived to despise her contemptible husband. She turned now to James Hepburn, earl of Bothwell, who was willing to go to extraordinary lengths for her.

Darnley lay sick in Mary's lodgings at Kirk o'Field when between two and three o'clock on the morning of February 10, 1567, the place blew up. Darnley and his page were found strangled in the garden. It appeared as though Darnley had discovered he was about to be blown up and managed to get out at the last moment, so that the conspirators were forced to leave telltale evidence of murder at the scene of what was supposed to look like a mysterious accident. Placards with Bothwell's picture appeared on the streets with the legend "Here is the murderer of the king." Bothwell was charged with murder but naturally was acquitted by his peers, who had been glad enough to see Darnley disposed of. He carried Mary off to Dunbar, seemingly by force but probably with her consent, since only a public scandal would force his wife to seek a divorce and the courts to grant it, and without the appearance of innocence betrayed Mary could not hope to win acceptance of their marriage so soon after Darnley's death. As it happened, any such hopes were misplaced. Mary and Bothwell were married on May 15 and a month later the Protestant lords rose against them. They allowed Bothwell to escape but imprisoned the queen in Lochleven Castle.

How guilty was Mary of complicity in Darnley's murder? The "casket letters," said to have been written by Mary to Bothwell during the fatal crisis, are very damaging, but their authenticity is still questioned by some apologists, who also accept Mary's protests that it was only a lucky coincidence that on the night of Darnley's death she had suddenly remembered she had promised to attend a wedding reception, which providentially kept her away from Kirk o'Field until after the explosion had demolished it.

Mary managed to escape and raise an army, but it was defeated at Langside on May 13, 1568, and Mary fled to England, where she threw herself on Elizabeth's mercy. Cecil had her tried and an open verdict was found: "Nothing has been sufficiently proved whereby the Queen of England should conceive an evil opinion of her good sister." Elizabeth was not a fool, but it seemed to her quite possible and infinitely preferable to clip Mary's wings without destroying her. Mary was kept confined in a series of castles and country estates, with a household of thirty of her own servants, full use of her French dowry, and the deference customarily accorded a queen. She had the freedom to receive guests in private and had little difficulty in corresponding with her supporters.

The rising of Catholics in the north in 1569 and the pope's excommunication of Elizabeth in 1570 compromised Mary, but no further measures were taken against her. An Italian banker, Roberto Ridolfi, was caught in a plot to murder Elizabeth and, with papal sanction, to arrange the marriage of Mary with the duke of Norfolk. Cecil's agents broke up the plot and the duke was beheaded on June 2, 1572.

Mary's imprisonment, insupportable to a woman of her temperament and ambition in spite of its luxuries, continued for fourteen more years. Her eventual undoing came when once again she placed too much confidence in a man. This time the man was Thomas Morgan, an agent who passed letters for her but betrayed her secrets to Sir Francis Walsingham, who headed Elizabeth's secret service. Learning of Mary's complicity in another plot against Elizabeth, Walsingham arranged to have some of his own agents infiltrate the circle of conspirators, and they compiled damaging evidence against Mary. In October 1586 she was tried for plotting against the queen. Mary confessed to seeking escape, but denied that she had "procured or encouraged any hurt against her majesty." The evidence against her was more persuasive than her denials, however, and she was condemned to death as "Mary Stuart, commonly called Queen of Scotland."

She was more magnificent in death than she had been in life. "Mr. Dean," she told the dean of Peterborough, who admonished her to repentance, "I shall die as I have lived, in the true and holy Catholic faith. All you can say to me on that score is but vain, and all your prayers, I think, can avail me but little." Although Mary had married Bothwell in a Protestant ceremony, she was determined now that the world should know that she was dying not only in the Catholic faith, but for it. When the ax fell, her blood would wash away all the plots and accusations and would cry out for vengeance. Mary acted out her last scene to perfection. Holding a crucifix high, she prayed her Catholic prayers, asked God's grace for England and mercy for Elizabeth, and forgave her enemies. Her black velvet gown fell to her feet and she stepped forward in silk of brilliant red, the color of martyrs. She knelt over the chopping block and commended her soul to God, and then the executioner's ax struck twice. The axman, his face covered by the customary black mask of the executioner, stooped, picked up the head to show it to the crowd, and shouted, "Long live the queen!" But all he held in his hands was an auburn wig. At the edge of the platform lay the gray-stubbled head of Mary, queen of Scots.

England's Relations with France and Spain

ENGLAND'S RELATIONS with Scotland and Ireland and Elizabeth's with Mary fitted into the larger pattern of England's struggle for survival against two larger, wealthier, more powerful Catholic rivals, France and Spain. Elizabeth dubbed her policy "underhanded war," as she sent aid to the Huguenots in France and to the Protestant Netherlands. During the first five years Cecil played the game cautiously while Elizabeth consolidated her position at home; after that England became increasingly independent and aggressive in order to escape from the slough in which Mary had left the land.

Philip II had induced Mary to declare war on France, with the result that England lost Calais in 1558. But Elizabeth was glad to have Philip's support in the peace negotiations at Cateau-Cambrésis in 1559. For the time being Philip was more interested in using England as a counterbalance to France than he was in wiping out Protestantism in the island. The French king was also virtually the ruler of Scotland, through his regent, Mary of Guise. Mary Stuart was then the wife of the French dauphin. England thus lay within the jaws of a French vise, and for a decade Elizabeth had to play Spain's game. But even though Philip was now married to the daughter of the French king, France still posed a threat to Spain, so for a time Philip permitted England to develop unmolested. Elizabeth took advantage of the opportunity and by decisive intervention saw the French thrown out of Scotland bag and baggage. England's back door was barred at last.

Elizabeth's policy toward Ireland was not so wise or so successful. "Ireland for the English" was the aim. English Protestantism was forced upon the Irish at the point of the soldiery's pikes. Irish feeling for the ancient faith grew even more fervent under oppression, and hostility to England was driven deep into the Irish soul. England's policy was shortsighted, impractical, and inconsistent. English statesmen who crossed the channel as viceroys or lord deputies returned beaten down and dispirited, determined never to go there again. In his last years Henry VIII had promoted a plan to convert the Irish land system into English tenures, with the collaboration of the Irish chiefs. Edward's "statesmen" turned to conquest and extermination. Mary followed with a policy of expropriation and the establishment of English military colonies.

The Ireland that Elizabeth inherited in 1558 was a land lacking political cohesion and racial homogeneity, and with religion at low ebb. Elizabeth was less concerned about introducing her Protestant state church to Ireland than she was about civilizing a barbarous people and making them safe for English imperial control. A plan for colonization of the island evolved, sponsored for a time by Sir Walter Raleigh. The Spaniards sought to exploit Irish hostility to England and even planned to use Ireland as a base of attack. But clan feuds kept the Irish disunited and weak, so that while they could damage the English, they could not offer a serious threat to English security. From 1594 on, a crafty leader, Tyrone, proved a wily and stubborn foe who cost the English enormously in money, men, and arms. The final four and a half years of the war with Ireland cost the English treasury £1.25 million. England at last completely subjugated Ireland by cruel measures. Mountjoy crushed Ulster by the deliberate and systematic destruction of all livestock, crops, and dwellings. By the time Tyrone surrendered, the English found many of the Irish who survived this genocidal policy living in caves and eating grass and roots. Elizabeth succeeded in establishing a policy of "pacification," but the emerald isle remained a sullen, unreliable part of the realm, ready to break into rebellion again when it could.

During the early years of Elizabeth's reign Spain was considered a protector against France, the traditional enemy across the channel; but a shift in power soon pitted England against Spain in a desperate struggle for survival and eventual leadership. England was much relieved when Francis II, Mary Stuart's husband, died in 1560, and the effective power passed into the hands of Catherine de' Medici, who had little love for Mary or the Guise family. The wars of religion soon paralyzed France, and Elizabeth felt she had less to fear from France than from Spain. By the Treaty of Blois in 1572 France became an ally of sorts with England. The new-found friendship was severely tested but not destroyed when the massacre of St. Bartholemew enraged English Protestant feelings. A series of artificial marriage negotiations between Elizabeth and the duke of Anjou, who later became Henry III, and then with his brother the duke of Alençon, served the diplomatic purpose of making Anglo-French relations appear to be more cordial than they were in actual fact. The alliance at least served to prevent a Franco-Spanish coalition against Protestant England. While it inhibited the role Elizabeth could play in behalf of the Huguenots, it gave her a freer hand to support the Protestant Netherlands.

England's aid to the Dutch and the raids of English seamen on the Spanish main enraged Philip II and convinced him that he would never end the rebellion in the Netherlands or secure his Spanish-Portuguese empire overseas until England had been conquered. A series of events ignited the final conflagration: the murder of William of Orange in 1584, the expulsion from England of the Spanish ambassador Mendoza for plotting with Elizabeth's foes in 1586, and the death of Mary Stuart in 1587. Mary's execution eliminated Philip's hope for a Catholic rebellion if he were to assault England. But he also came to believe that he could take over England as he had taken over Portugal, for Mary had left to Philip her claims to the English throne. There followed then the attack of the "invincible" Spanish Armada in 1588, the Spanish seizure of Calais in 1596, the "invisible armada" of 1599, England's counterattacks on Portugal, and its establishment of "vantage at sea." Now France under Henry IV rebuilt its internal unity and strength to serve as a barrier to Spain's ambitions. England had stood up to the mightiest power in the world and won; a new surge of confidence and pride lifted the British on a wave of patriotism and ambition.

England Expands

TUDOR ENGLISHMEN were not by nature or tradition world explorers or empire builders. It took the attractions of the Spanish main, the gospel, and gold to draw the seafaring folk of southwest England into the game of global expansion. Giovanni Caboto, a Venetian navigator, had voyaged to the northeast coast of North America under the English flag, first in 1497 and again in 1498. The English called him John Cabot and hailed him as a hero, but their enthusiasm for his explorations was largely focused on his reports of an abundance of fish in the waters off Newfoundland. A new cod fishing station might make them independent of·the Icelandic fishermen. But it was a great distance to go for fish, and eventually the excitement died down. Another sixty years passed before England became actively involved again in overseas expansion. During these years England was preoccupied with domestic and religious issues. Moreover, there was little risk capital available for large-scale piracy or colonial development until after the collapse of the cloth trade in 1551. The final closing of Antwerp in the 1570s added to the economic impetus toward geographical exploration and the search for new markets and sources of raw materials abroad. Now Protestant England had a special incentive to contest the papal allocation of the New World to Spain and Portugal. The privateers sailed the seas with Elizabeth's blessing, but without official authorization, plundering Spain's ships and raiding its colonies. Hawkins, Drake, Frobisher, Raleigh, and dozens of others were really buccaneers, raiding outside the law, and knowing full well that if they were caught they could expect to be hanged for piracy.

Although during these decades the actual results in permanent colonies were slight, the idea took root and the vision of empire caught the English eye. "Planting of countries," wrote Francis Bacon in his essay "Of Plantations," "is like planting of woods; for you must make account to lose almost twenty years' profit, and expect recompense in the end." The Elizabethans had little patience for this tedious cultivation of colonies. They wanted quick profits, and nothing compared with raids on Spanish ships for procuring sudden wealth easily.

In 1561 Cecil shocked the bishop of Aquila, Álvarez de Quadra, by declaring that the pope had no right to partition the earth and bestow kingdoms on whom he pleased. The very next year John Hawkins of Plymouth tested the validity of the Spanish monopoly by cutting himself into the Negro slave trade. He procured a cargo of Negroes by raiding the coast of Africa south of Cape Verde and by purchase from Portuguese slavers, then crossed the Atlantic to Hispaniola and sold the Negroes as slaves on the Spanish plantations. His profits were enormous in gold, silver, jewels, sugar, hides, and other wealth of the Indies. The queen, Cecil, and other nobles bought shares in Hawkins' second expedition, two years later. The Spanish government had issued orders that its colonies were not to trade with the English, so Hawkins armed his flotilla, expecting the worst. But again the Spanish planters bought his Negroes and again he returned home with a great profit. Now the Spanish colonial administrators were aroused, however, so on his third expedition, in 1567, Hawkins sailed with a convoy of seven battleships, with Captain Francis Drake in command of the *Judith*. On this trip Hawkins blockaded the port of Río de la Hacha and fought a pitched battle on land with the Spaniards. He burned the town, seized its treasure, and forced the settlement to trade. Trapped in the harbor at San Juan de Ulloa in 1568, Hawkins had to shoot his way out, and lost 120 men and several ships, including the *Jesus,* a round-bottomed boat acquired from the Hanse.

The most persistent and implacable foe to sail the Spanish seas was Francis

Drake. Drake's ire was aroused by the disastrous humiliation at San Juan de Ulloa. He had returned from that battle a ruined man. From then until he died, in 1595, he lived with two goals in mind: to recoup his personal losses and to strengthen England by weakening Spain. With each act of plunder he tightened the garrote around the throat of the Spanish monarchy. A superb seaman, Drake operated most effectively beyond the line and outside the law. The Spanish treasure ships crossed the Atlantic in well-regulated, heavily protected convoys. Not until 1580 did anyone dare to attack them in European waters. Drake's keen eye spotted the weakest link in the silver chain that stretched from the mines of Peru to Lima, across the spine of the Isthmus of Panama to Nombre de Dios, and from there across the Atlantic to Spain. In 1572 Drake raided Nombre de Dios, ambushed the treasure convoy on the way to the port, and escaped with the loot before the Spanish troops at Panama could act. Not all English seamen had Drake's good fortune. When John Oxenham tried to repeat this exploit a few years later he ran into an armed transport column, was caught, and was hanged in Lima as a pirate. Andrew Barker was killed in a skirmish with the Spaniards while raiding the coast of Central America and his ship sank on the way home.

Francis Drake next moved the theater of operations to the Pacific. He sailed around the tip of South America through the Strait of Magellan into the Pacific (1577–1580). A storm blew him far into the Antarctic Ocean and made it evident that no land bridge ran from South America all the way to the pole. Drake scourged the Spanish, but beyond this mischief he had a tremendous vision of founding a New England in California, an empire for Elizabeth reaching from the beautiful Pacific coast to Florida. He explored the California coast, looking for harbors and bays suitable for ports and colonies. The western end of the legendary Northwest Passage was not to be found, and Drake gave up the search around Vancouver. From there he proceeded westward across the Pacific and Indian oceans, rounded the Cape of Good Hope, and headed home. When his ship nosed into Plymouth in September 1580, it carried aboard a treasure of £1.5 million, or nearly half of the Spanish treasure yielded in a year's exploitation of the mines of the New World. Drake was compensated for the losses he had sustained at San Juan de Ulloa over a decade before and the rest of the enormous treasure was kept in the Tower of London, despite the protests of Ambassador Mendoza, until the accounts between Elizabeth and Philip, including compensation for the Spanish role in the Irish rebellion, could be settled.

Sir Francis Drake—for Elizabeth now knighted him—was to play a further role in settling accounts with Philip. Elizabeth unleashed him again in 1585, when he set sail in his great corsair accompanied by a fleet of thirty ships to raid the Spanish ships and harbors. He sailed first to the Canaries and the Cape Verde Islands, burning Santiago and Praia. Then he struck at Santo Domingo, the jewel city of the Caribbean colonies, extracting a ransom of twenty-five thousand ducats for sparing most of the town, and hit Cartagena on the South American mainland the same way. He took the Spanish fort at St. Augustine, Florida, then rescued the survivors of the faltering colony that Sir Walter Raleigh had founded at Roanoke Island and took them home to England. Not only had Drake cost the Spaniards an enormous toll in booty; he had demonstrated the vulnerability of King Philip and helped to drive him to that measure of desperation, the launching of the Armada, which proved to be his undoing. The English were well informed about Spanish preparations for the invasion. When the fleet in the harbor of Cádiz was nearly ready in the spring of 1587, Drake sailed from Plymouth, took the Spaniards by surprise, destroyed thousands of tons of shipping and supplies, including vital barrel staves, and even gutted the admiral's own galleon. Drake had indeed singed Philip's beard. In the final confrontation with the Armada in 1588, Drake, in charge of a smaller squadron out of Plymouth under the fleet command of Lord Howard, acquitted himself well, although the wind and waves made truly heroic deeds dispensable. A ballad of 1591 about a triumphant duel of an English corsair with a Spanish galleon celebrated Elizabeth as the "Lady of the Sea." The scepter of the seas had passed from Spain to England.

Other adventurers followed Drake's pattern of exploration and plunder. Thomas Cavendish roamed the seas from 1586 to 1588, and sailed back to London with his ships adorned with sails of blue damask and each man sporting a golden chain. But of more lasting value were the geographic and navigational expeditions, which, though less thrilling than the buccaneering, were in the long run more significant. The greatest impetus was the search for trade, especially the search for a northwest passage to Cathay, and eventually also the search for lands suitable for colonizing.

The English initiated the search for a northeast passage, although in later years it was taken over by Dutchmen and Danes. "The company of merchant adventurers for discovery of regions, dominions, islands and places unknown," whose first master was John Cabot's son Sebastian, in 1553 sent out a fleet of three ships under Sir Hugh Willoughby, headed for China. Two of them were frozen in near the North Cape and all aboard perished, but the third, under the senior navigator, Richard Chancellor, reached Archangel. The Russians there treated the Englishmen well but warily until they were able to get word to Moscow of the foreigners' arrival and receive instructions on what to do with them. Tsar Ivan IV, who was a young man then and not yet so Terrible as he was later to become, invited them to Moscow and offered them favorable terms for trade. As a direct result of this exploration, a group of merchants organized the Muscovy Company in 1555 to initiate trade with Russia.[1] The year after its founding the company commissioned Stephen Burrough to discover a passage to China around

---

[1] J. H. Parry, *The Age of Reconnaissance* (New York, 1964), pp. 222–23.

the North Cape, an effort doomed to founder in the ice and fog. Another agent penetrated Asia overland as far as Bokhara in search of markets. The Merchant Adventurers exploited the continental markets in Antwerp and up the Rhine and Elbe. In 1579 the Eastland Company began to compete with the remnants of the Hanse in the Baltic.

Humphrey Gilbert, a scholarly gentleman, was caught up in the idea of finding a northwest passage to Cathay. He gathered every scrap of information he could from ancient chronicles and accounts of voyages, and wrote his famous *Discourse to Prove a Northwest Passage*. Martin Frobisher, an experienced seaman, was so obsessed with the idea that he made three voyages (1576–1578) to look for the passage north of Labrador. Although his efforts were foredoomed to failure, he did discover the strait that still bears his name. The efforts of the Muscovy Company to find a northeast passage (1580) were no more successful. The following year the Levant Company was organized to develop trade in the Near East, with some success. The final and most dramatic efforts to find the Northwest Passage were undertaken by John Davis in three voyages (1585–1587). He reached the Northumberland Inlet, north of Frobisher Strait, at latitude 66° 40′, but once again the ice pack blocked the way. These adventures, for all the excitement they aroused, were not so rewarding commercially as the English had hoped. Gradually the idea took shape that colonies on the American seaboard peopled by Englishmen would provide sources for raw materials and markets for English products. The day of colonization was dawning.

Richard Hakluyt, famous as the author of *Voyages and Discoveries* (1589), was one of the fathers of the colonial idea and one of its principal publicists. Raw materials, new markets, a way station to Cathay, a dumping ground for England's vagabonds and unemployed, the opportunity to Christianize the Indians—none of these motives were overlooked in Hakluyt's argument. In 1578 Sir Humphrey Gilbert procured a royal patent to found a "plantation" in the New World and a few years later he undertook to establish a colony in Newfoundland. He lacked the stability to see the project through, however, and he was himself lost at sea.

In 1584 Queen Elizabeth transferred Gilbert's patent to his half-brother Walter Raleigh, who had become her favorite at court, and the following year she knighted him. As the site of his proposed colony Raleigh chose Roanoke Island in the territory he called Virginia, after the Virgin Queen, where the climate was mild and the natives were reportedly friendly. The island lies off the coast of what is now the state of North Carolina. Under Raleigh's auspices, a hundred colonists were settled on Roanoke by Sir Richard Grenville in the spring of 1585, but when Grenville returned in June of the next year he found the colony thoroughly demoralized, half-starved, and at odds with the Indians. Drake repatriated the remnants on his way back from his famous raids of 1585–1586. In 1587 Raleigh tried again at the same location, but when the governor of the second colony, John White, returned to Roanoke with new supplies in 1590, he could find no one, alive or dead. These pioneers had probably been massacred by the Indians, although they may have attempted to resettle in a new location and been lost to the sea or forest. Raleigh claimed to have spent £40,000 on the undertaking, and in 1589, before the final disaster at Roanoke, he signed over his rights in the colony to a company of merchants, keeping only a small rent and a fifth of any gold that might be discovered in the territory. There was of course no gold, but neither was there any need for Raleigh to provide for his old age, since enemies he had acquired as Elizabeth's favorite contrived his downfall after her death.

When Elizabeth died in 1603 Raleigh had long since ceased to be her favorite. She had even had him thrown into the Tower for a time when she discovered he had secretly married one of her ladies-in-waiting. But her vindictiveness passed, and in 1595 he sailed for the Orinoco River with dreams of finding a way to penetrate the Spanish empire in South America. His *Discoverie of Guiana,* published the following year, described in overenthusiastic terms the empire awaiting England in Guiana.

At Elizabeth's death she was succeeded by James VI of Scotland, Mary Stuart's son, who had his own favorites and his own reasons for washing his hands of Elizabeth's. When Raleigh's enemies brought charges of treason against him, he was stripped of his possessions and once again lodged in the Tower. This time it was thirteen years before he was able to contrive his release in order to lead an expedition up the Orinoco and establish his empire. Raleigh seems to have had a touch of piracy in mind even before he crossed the Atlantic. He was in a desperate situation and desperate measures seemed all that remained to him. But he found no treasure, and his own son was killed in an attack on a Spanish outpost guarding the approach to Guiana—an action specifically forbidden the expedition, since England wanted no trouble with Spain. Raleigh was doubtless correct in believing that if the attack had succeeded, it would have been considered no trouble at all. But it did not succeed, and Raleigh was returned to England and executed in 1618.

Englishmen followed him to the coastal regions around the Orinoco, developing plantations, logging camps, and small trading operations, but the dream of an English empire to rival Spain's in Latin America died with Raleigh.

The Economy

IN INDUSTRY AND COMMERCE the reign of Elizabeth was anything but a golden age. Problems mounted in the crucial textile trade and a severe general inflation created difficulties for nearly everyone. The boom years in textiles, which were England's major export—approximately 75 to 90 percent by value—came in the late 1530s and

1540s. The remainder of England's exports was made up of raw wool, tin and lead from marginal mines, grain, beer, and fish. A severe economic crisis in 1551 cut trade drastically, and although there was a partial recovery, England's exports still remained well below the levels of 1548–1550. Elizabeth's reign was marked by periodic depressions, which became most serious in the 1590s. England gradually lost its old established markets for cheap unfinished cloth, and the new "draperies" did not begin to compensate for this loss until the seventeenth century. Cecil's major motive in pushing the Statute of Apprentices or Artificers in 1563, as his own memoranda reveal, was to freeze labor in the land. He hoped to prevent industrial expansion, since this seemed to be the only solution to the periodic depressions in the textile industry, which tended to expand its output beyond the market's ability to absorb it.

The population was increasing, and so were the prices. The cost of food was a particularly acute problem, for in bad years England did not produce enough food to feed the population. Industrial prices lagged and by the end of the century inflation had seriously reduced real wages. The propertied classes on the whole managed to raise rents enough to keep up with the rising prices, but the peasants and town proletariat suffered severe privations. The depressed state of the economy made it impossible to provide jobs or land for continually greater numbers of people, which led to a great deal of concern about overpopulation. The desirability of shipping excess population abroad provided a negative motive for overseas expansion. The depressed state of the economy persisted through the early Stuart period. There were major depressions in the early 1620s and between 1629 and 1633; a great expansion of commerce was achieved only after 1660.

At the beginning of Elizabeth's reign agriculture was in the final phase of its evolution from a manorial structure to a system of individual enterprise. The gentry continued to fence in lands that had previously been allotted to the common use of the peasantry. The story of the "deserted village" was often repeated as people forced off the land moved into town or drifted about in increasingly hopeless search of work. The lands thus enclosed were given over to the raising of sheep, which brought great profits because of the demand for English wool, acknowledged to be the best in the world. Furthermore, during the last half of the century a gradual growth in acreage given over to grain production became noticeable, another use of land more efficient than subsistence farming by peasant families. Because of the ease of storage and transportation, grain production was important in sustaining the growing urban population.

Social change reflected these gradual alterations in the agrarian economy. Servile labor and villeinage were now virtually nonexistent. The tenancy at will, the copyhold, and the leasehold, all old by Elizabeth's reign, continued to be important forms of landholding. The freeholders were the most enterprising element in the lower agrarian echelons, although many yeomen made a very good living out of leaseholds. They enjoyed the benefit of fixed rents in a period of rising prices. This happy development gave them a profit margin that enabled them to educate their sons, who in turn could climb a few rungs higher on the social ladder.

There is a tempest in the scholarly teapot over the gentry, the landed families who ranked above the yeomen but below the old aristocratic families. Historians have traditionally held that the gentry (like the middle class) was always rising and that the old aristocracy was in decline. More recent opinion holds that the aristocrats, far from playing out their useless days riding to hounds, were actually remarkably adaptable. A good name and a good seat on a horse, after all, never had been enough in themselves to keep power from slipping into the hands of able, ambitious newcomers. Now that economic conditions were facilitating upward social mobility on a larger scale than before, it was the aristocratic families more than the gentry that began to educate their sons at the universities and the "legal university," the Inns of Court, so that they could enter commerce and branches of government service that required practical knowledge for success. The gentry, less secure in their social authority and thus more reluctant to risk their prestige by going into trade, formed a conservative corps that eventually trapped many of them in a social backwater. Meanwhile, middle-class families of means were buying their way into the countryside as gentry. Historical facts always tend toward the more complex rather than the simple solution. When the dust of controversy settles, in all likelihood some truth will still be found in the old hypothesis, but the revisionist view will probably be more generally accepted.

With a population of 120,000, London was already in Elizabeth's day the economic hub of England. Although the London merchants were far less wealthy than the Medicis, Albizzis, Welsers, and Fuggers had been in their day, English merchants exerted themselves to find new markets and sources of wealth. English industry was simply not so well developed technically as that of the Rhineland, northwest France, and Italy. In introducing new industries such as silk, lace, glassware, needles, thread, felt, and so on, the English were often obliged to import skilled craftsmen to do the work and train apprentices. A naïve display by the *nouveaux riches* was almost inevitable. The new town houses, sumptuous dress, exaggerated costuming, and elaborate posturing of Elizabethan gentlemen made a colorful display. They made a grand audience at the Globe for Shakespeare's plays.

Elizabeth's End

THE ACHIEVEMENTS of the English people in the sixteenth century have not without justice been credited to the fortunate circumstance of Elizabeth's long reign. She was a symbol of victory, the idol of the people, the emblem of national unity and purpose. And yet when one examines her acts of state with care, one is amazed to see how little initiative she showed and how few programs of a progressive nature she contributed. Basically conservative, she performed a holding action, presided over developments that she could not prevent or control, reigned rather than ruled. She even failed to develop a creative solution to the problem of her own succession. But perhaps what the nation believed to be true of its chief of state was more important for its history than anything she actually did or left undone. Myth is a powerful force upon history as well as upon historians.

As Elizabeth aged, her face grew thin and seemed longer than ever, her teeth were yellow and uneven, and to top it all off she wore a massive reddish wig. Still she played her love games, making an asset of her greatest liability as sovereign, her femininity. Her affection for one of the young bloods at court, the earl of Essex, led to a final heartbreak for her. Essex was a spendthrift and incompetent as a military commander, but he was her weakness. Exploiting her love for him, believing that if he were persistent enough there was no limit to the heights he might reach, the handsome Essex played a dangerous game. During a luckless siege of Rouen he wrote:

> Most fair, most dear, and most excellent Sovereign. . . . The two windows of your Privy Chamber shall be the poles of my sphere, where, as long as your Majesty will please to have me, I am fixed and unmovable. When your Majesty thinks that Heaven too good for me, I will not fall like a star, but be consumed like a vapor by the sun that drew me up to such a height. While your Majesty gives me leave to say I love you, my fortune is as my affection, unmatchable. If ever you deny me that liberty, you may end my life, but never shake my constancy, for were the sweetness of your nature turned into the greatest bitterness that could be, it is not in your power, as great a Queen as you are, to make me love you less.[2]

Elizabeth gave him the chance to prove his mettle on the battlefield. The Irish revolt was still raging, and Essex, a young hawk, cried for the armed conquest of the island. Elizabeth appointed him lord deputy of Ireland against his will, for he was loath to leave the court. At a meeting of the queen's counselors he once disagreed with the queen, and when she rejected his views he turned his back on her. Furious, she boxed his ear, and Essex put his hand on his sword declaring that he would not have taken such an insult from Henry VIII himself. Essex was indulging in that pride which goes before a fall. With 22,000 men at his command he put down little rebellions in Munster but failed to destroy Tyrone, the Irish rebel. He allowed his men to plunder, made a quick peace with Tyrone, and hurried back to Elizabeth.

Essex had made powerful enemies who undermined his position at court, and he was soon put under house arrest. The privy council received word that he was gathering a military force at his estate and summoned him to appear. Instead he

---

[2] Cited in J. E. Neale, *Queen Elizabeth* (New York, 1934), pp. 322–23.

marched into London, expecting the city to rise in his behalf, a vain hope. He was accused of treason, tried, and found guilty. Then Elizabeth had to sign the death warrant of the foolish young man she had loved. On Ash Wednesday, February 25, 1601, Essex emerged from his room in the Tower dressed in a suit of black velvet and satin and walked to a scaffold in the courtyard. He bowed to all present, made a gracious courtly speech, confessed his sins, removed his hat, and placed his head upon the wooden block. It was severed with three blows of the executioner's ax.

Elizabeth never recovered from the shock of all this, and during her last years she frequently fell into periods of deep depression. In 1601 she summoned her last parliament to provide funds for a final effort in Ireland. Lord Mountjoy succeeded in suppressing the revolt, forced the Spanish forces there to surrender, and negotiated terms with Tyrone. The victory in Ireland was a last gleam of success for her.

Elizabeth's health had been reasonably good most of her life, but now time was taking its toll. On September 7, 1602, she reached her sixty-ninth birthday. Many of her old counselors and friends had already died. Christmas of that year saw a final flickering of that bright gaiety for which her court had been renowned. Then soon after the first of March in 1603 Elizabeth fell ill. "I am not sick," she said, "I feel no pain, and yet I pine away." Weak of body but strong in will, she refused to take the doctors' medicines, which might have prolonged her life. On Wednesday, March 23, the privy counselors made bold to ask her to perform her final duty as sovereign, to name her successor. She named her "nearest kinsman, the king of Scots," James VI, son of Mary Stuart, who was to rule after her as James I of Great Britain.

Shortly after six o'clock that evening she summoned Archbishop Whitgift to her bedside. He spoke to her of her Christian faith and of the final glory she was soon to know when she would appear before the King of Kings. She moved her hand and eyes in agreement, and prayed with him until she fell asleep. Between two and three in the morning she passed away.

Bibliography

Elizabeth I:
BLACK, J. B. *The Reign of Elizabeth.* New York, 1936.
BROWNING, A. *The Age of Elizabeth.* New York, 1935.
CHAMBERLAIN, F. *Elizabeth and Leicester.* New York, 1939.
HURSTFIELD, JOEL. *Elizabeth I and the Unity of England.* London, 1960.
JENKINS, ELIZABETH. *Elizabeth the Great: A Biography.* New York, 1959.
McNALTY, ARTHUR S. *Elizabeth Tudor: The Lonely Queen.* London, 1954.
MAYNARD, THEODORE. *Queen Elizabeth.* Milwaukee, 1940.
NEALE, JOHN E. *Queen Elizabeth.* New York, 1934.

————. *Elizabeth I and Her Parliaments*, 2 vols. London, 1953–1957.

OAKESHOTT, WALTER F. *The Queen and the Poet*. London, 1960.

READ, CONYERS. *Mr. Secretary Walsingham and the Policy of Queen Elizabeth*. Cambridge, Mass., 1925.

————. *Mr. Secretary Cecil and Queen Elizabeth*, 2 vols. New York, 1955–1960.

————. *Lord Burghley and Queen Elizabeth*. New York, 1960.

STRACHEY, LYTTON. *Elizabeth and Essex*. New York, 1928.

WALDMAN, MILTON. *England's Elizabeth*. Boston, 1933.

————. *Elizabeth and Leicester*. London, 1945.

————. *Queen Elizabeth*. London, 1952.

WILLIAMS, NEVILLE. *Elizabeth the First, Queen of England*. New York, 1968.

WILSON, ELKIN. *England's Eliza*. Cambridge, Mass., 1939.

Kingdom and empire:

ANDREWS, K. R. *Elizabethan Privateering During the Spanish War, 1585–1603*. Cambridge, 1967.

BINDOFF, S. T. *Tudor England*. Harmondsworth, 1950.

BOWDEN, PETER J. *The Wool Trade in Tudor and Stuart England*. London, 1962.

BYRNE, M. *Elizabethan Life in Town and Country*. London, 1947.

CAM, HELEN MAUD. *England Before Elizabeth*, 3rd ed. London, 1967.

CAMPBELL, M. *The English Yeoman Under Elizabeth and the Early Stuarts*. New Haven, 1942.

CECIL, ALGERNON. *The Life of Robert Cecil*. London, 1915.

ELTON, GEOFFREY R. *England Under the Tudors*. London, 1955.

HARRISON, DAVID. *Tudor England*, 2 vols. London, 1953.

HEXTER, JACK. *Reappraisals in History*. London, 1961.

LOCKYER, ROGER. *Tudor and Stuart Britain, 1471–1714*. New York, 1964.

MORRIS, CHRISTOPHER. *Political Thought in England: Tyndale to Hooker*. London, 1953.

NEALE, JOHN E. *The Elizabethan House of Commons*. London, 1949.

NEF, JOHN U. *Industry and Government in France and England, 1540–1640*. Philadelphia, 1940.

QUINN, D. B. *Raleigh and the British Empire*. London, 1947.

ROWSE, A. L. *Tudor Cornwall*. London, 1941.

————. *The England of Elizabeth*. London, 1950.

————. *The Elizabethan Age*, 2 vols. London, 1950–1955.

————. *The Expansion of Elizabethan England*. London, 1955.

RUDDICK, A. A. *Italian Merchants and Shipping in Southampton, 1270–1600*. Southampton, 1951.

SHIRLEY, F. J. *Richard Hooker and Contemporary Political Ideas*. London, 1949.

STONE, LAWRENCE. *The Crisis of the Aristocracy, 1558–1641*. Oxford, 1965.

TAWNEY, R. H. *The Agrarian Problem in the Sixteenth Century*. London, 1912.

TAYLOR, EVA. *Tudor Geography, 1485–1583*. London, 1930.

————. *Late Tudor and Early Stuart Geography, 1583–1650*. London, 1934.

TREVOR-ROPER, H. R. *The Gentry, 1540–1640*. Cambridge, 1953.

WILLIAMSON, JAMES A. *Maritime Enterprise, 1485–1558*. Oxford, 1913.

————. *The Life and Growth of the British Empire*. Oxford, 1940.

————. *The Ocean in English History*. Oxford, 1941.

————. *The Age of Drake.* London, 1946.
————. *Hawkins of Plymouth.* London, 1949.

Religion:
BABBAGE, STUART B. *Puritanism and Richard Bancroft.* London, 1962.
BIRT, H. N. *The Elizabethan Religious Settlement.* London, 1907.
BOOTY, JOHN E. *John Jewel as Apologist of the Church of England.* London, 1963.
BROOK, V. J. K. *Whitgift and the English Church.* London, 1957.
————. *A Life of Archbishop Parker.* Oxford, 1962.
CLAYTON, J. *The Historical Basis of Anglicanism.* London, 1925.
COLLINSON, PATRICK. *The Elizabethan Puritan Movement.* Berkeley, 1967.
CREMEANS, CHARLES. *The Reception of Calvinist Thought in England.* Urbana, Ill.,
 1949.
DAVIES, E. T. *The Political Ideas of Richard Hooker.* London, 1946.
————. *Episcopacy and Royal Supremacy in the Church of England in the Sixteenth
 Century.* Oxford, 1950.
DAWLEY, POWEL M. *John Whitgift and the English Reformation.* New York, 1954.
HALLER, WILLIAM. *The Rise of Puritanism.* New York, 1938.
————. *Elizabeth I and the Puritans.* Ithaca, N.Y., 1964.
HAUGAARD, WILLIAM P. *Elizabeth and the English Reformation.* Cambridge, 1968.
JORDAN, WILBUR K. *The Development of Religious Toleration in England,* 4 vols. Cam-
 bridge, Mass., 1932–1940.
KNAPPEN, M. M. *Tudor Puritanism.* Chicago, 1939.
KNOX, S. J. *Walter Travers, Paragon of Elizabethan Puritanism.* London, 1962.
McGINN, DONALD J. *John Penry and the Marprelate Controversy.* New Brunswick, N.J.,
 1966.
McGRATH, PATRICK. *Papists and Puritans Under Elizabeth I.* New York, 1967.
MEYER, CARL S. *Elizabeth I and the Religious Settlement of 1559.* St. Louis, 1960.
NEW, JOHN. *Anglican and Puritan.* Stanford, 1964.
PEARSON, A. F. SCOTT. *Thomas Cartwright and Elizabethan Puritans.* Cambridge, 1925.
POLLARD, ARTHUR. *Richard Hooker.* London, 1966.
POLLEN, J. H. *The English Catholics in the Reign of Queen Elizabeth.* London, 1920.
RUPP, E. GORDON. *The English Protestant Tradition.* Cambridge, 1947.
SEAVER, PAUL S. *The Puritan Lectureships: The Politics of Religious Dissent, 1560–1662.*
 Stanford, 1970.
SOUTHGATE, W. M. *John Jewel and the Problem of Doctrinal Authority.* Cambridge,
 Mass., 1962.
THORNTON, LIONEL S. *Richard Hooker: A Study of His Theology.* London, 1924.
TRIMBLE, WILLIAM. *The Catholic Laity in Elizabethan England, 1558–1603.* Cam-
 bridge, Mass., 1964.
USHER, ROLAND G. *The Reconstruction of the English Church,* 2 vols. New York, 1910.
WALZER, MICHAEL. *The Revolution of the Saints: A Study in the Origins of Radical
 Politics.* Cambridge, 1965.
WOODHOUSE, H. F. *The Doctrine of the Church in Anglican Theology, 1547–1603.* Lon-
 don, 1954.
WOODWARD, G. W. O. *Reformation and Resurgence, 1485–1603.* London, 1963.
WRIGHT, LOUIS B. *Religion and Empire: The Alliance Between Piety and Commerce in
 English Expansion, 1558–1625.* Chapel Hill, N.C., 1943.

CHAPTER 21

The Impact
of the Renaissance
and the Reformation
on Society and Culture

The student of history nearing the end of a subject such as ours, one of the great ages of the past, can appreciate Thomas Carlyle's modest disclaimer: "Listening from the distance of centuries across the death chasms and howling kingdoms of decay, it is not easy to catch everything." Around 40 B.C. the ancient Roman historian Sallust pronounced the writing of history the most difficult of tasks. The collation of facts and description of events, however, seem easier (though the ease is deceptive) than the analysis of their influence on society and culture. The pages that follow must therefore be thought of as suggestive and tentative, open, as history must always remain, to discussion.

The Protestant Whig interpretation of history very naturally saw the Renaissance and Reformation movements as great progressive forces toward modernity. Lord Thomas Babington Macaulay asserted flatly that since the sixteenth century the Protestant nations have made decidedly greater progress than their neighbors. In his *History of England* he pronounced his judgment that under the church of Rome

> the loveliest and most fertile provinces of Europe have . . . been sunk in poverty, in political servitude, and in intellectual torpor, while Protestant countries, once proverbial for sterility and barbarism, have been turned by skill and industry into gardens and can boast a long list of heroes and statesmen, philosophers and poets.

> ... Whoever passes in Germany from a Roman Catholic to a Protestant principality,
> ... in Ireland from a Roman Catholic to a Protestant county, finds that he has
> passed from a lower to a higher grade of civilization.[1]

Such grossly prejudiced and unqualified value judgments are today considered neither acceptable nor respectable. By whose standard is a competitive industrialized country superior to a traditionalist agrarian society? What of Catholic France as a "modernized" land? What role did the difference in religion actually play compared with other factors? Was the Reformation a more powerful solvent of the medieval cultural system than the Renaissance? Questions come crowding in like harpies upon anyone who ventures a dogmatic judgment.

That the era of the Renaissance and Reformation saw revolutionary changes in European culture comparable to those that occurred at the end of the eighteenth century seems obvious to many historians, but is contested by others. The humanists and reformers, looking to the standards of the past for guidance, propelled Western man at an accelerated rate of speed toward the future. The clever comment of Francis Bacon clearly applies to them: "By show of antiquity they introduce novelty."

State, Church, and Political Theory

THE REFORMATION forced men to reconsider the concepts and relationships of church and state in radically new terms. This development meant more than merely another chapter in the old story of the struggle between the spiritual and temporal powers. The political circumstances had altered, for the Renaissance state had burst the bonds of the feudal system. The secular state, freed from any de facto control by the church, provided a sanctuary for the development of Renaissance culture and the possibility of independent churches. The medieval church could not maintain itself against the twofold attack of the secular state from without and increased religious concern from within. With the coming of Calvinism, Protestant piety took on a more polemical cast and provided a religious ideology for the nationalistic struggles during the half century that followed. The so-called confessional wars stemmed from the close ties of political and ecclesiastical-religious commitments. The *raison d'état* of the princely dynasties and, after 1789, of the nations was a natural concomitant of the more sharply delineated particularism of the various secular states as they developed during the fifteenth and sixteenth centuries.

The ecclesiastical-political pattern was nearly stabilized by the end of the sixteenth century and was altered only in border states by the wars of the seven-

---

[1] Thomas Babington Macaulay, *The History of England from the Accession of James the Second*, 7th ed. (London, 1850), vol. 1, pp. 47–48.

teenth century. In Spain the Habsburg monarchy faithfully served the Roman Catholic Church. In France, which was moving toward princely absolutism (though less absolute than historians formerly thought), Catholicism became a national faith, much as in the various states of Italy. England and the Scandinavian countries adopted an episcopal form of Protestantism well suited to the alliance of altar and throne. The Netherlands offers the most interesting spectacle, for its linguistic and confessional base was mixed, Walloon and Flemish, Catholic and Calvinist. The tensions between its high predestinarian Calvinism, enshrined in the confessional statement of the Synod of Dort (1618–1619), and the latitudinarian position further complicated its religious history. The homeland of Erasmus, the Netherlands transmitted a tradition of tolerance to modern liberalism. Hugo Grotius, the founder of an enlightened doctrine of natural law and of a new concept of international law, owed much to this tradition.

Recent research has disclosed that the Reformation did not contribute immediately to an increase in the power of the Protestant princes in their own territories. Many of them were placed in personal jeopardy by declaring for the new faith, and lesser landholders and commoners profited more than they from the expropriation of ecclesiastical property, since 60 to 80 percent of the income from secularized monastic and church lands was subsequently devoted to education, hospitals, and charity. Some territorial estates actually increased their own prerogatives at the expense of princely authority during the sixteenth century. Petty absolutism developed later, under altered circumstances.

In establishing reforms based on the conception of the church as a community of believers rather than an institution under rigid hierarchical control, the reformers gave renewed emphasis to the importance of each individual member of the fellowship and challenged the hierarchy's claims to temporal power. They taught with Paul that Christ alone is the true head of the church and that all believers are members of its body. This invisible church, known only to God, is the true communion of saints. The visible church of Christ on earth is marked by the gospel and the sacraments. Martin Bucer declared at Strassburg in 1523 that the kingdom of Christ and the true church are surely where the word of Christ is heard with pleasure and observed with diligence. Zwingli added discipline and Calvin ceremonies as aids for distinguishing the true evangelical church.

In urging men to avoid "papal assemblies," Bucer declared in his *Instruction in Love* that the true apostolicity of the church is established when the church's ministers, as well as all its members, have the mind of Christ (Philippians 2:5) and of his apostles; that is, when they enjoy no special status or power, but live in service to the brethren and in deeds of love for their neighbors. The reformers thus effectively removed the church from the juridical area, challenging the religious propriety and legal validity of canon law as well as the political use of the great ban. The history of the preceding period had already made the effectiveness of papal

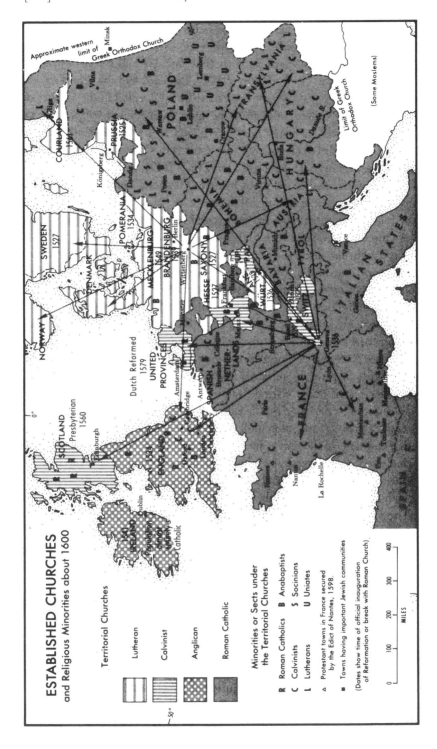

ESTABLISHED CHURCHES
and Religious Minorities about 1600

Territorial Churches

Lutheran

Calvinist

Anglican

Roman Catholic

Minorities or Sects under
the Territorial Churches

R Roman Catholics   B Anabaptists
C Calvinists   S Socinians
L Lutherans   U Uniates

△ Protestant towns in France secured
    by the Edict of Nantes, 1598.

■ Towns having important Jewish communities

(Dates show time of official inauguration
of Reformation or break with Roman Church).

MILES
0   100   200   300   400

political actions questionable, and now the reformers further weakened the papacy as a counterpoise to temporal rulers. The Vatican's political maneuvering had the debilitating effect of bringing the church's spiritual mission into question and of producing the kind of hostility toward the church that was all too evident in the sixteenth century.

Luther left the matter of church polity open, suspended midway between a congregational ideal and an organization directed by council or consistory. From the Christian congregation the minister received his call to serve by preaching and administering the sacraments. Goethe once joked that by limiting the office of the ministry to a service, Luther had scraped the butter off his colleagues' bread. In holding that the priest or minister is of the same estate as all other Christians and is distinguished only by his office, Luther did introduce a leveling process into the structure of the church. Holding up Paul himself as his model, Luther insisted that "the man to whom has been committed the office of preaching has committed to him the highest office in the Christian church." In 1520 he wrote, "If they [the clergy] were forced to admit that as many of us as have been baptized are all equally priests, as we truly are, and that only the ministry was committed to them but with our consent, they would soon know that they have no right to rule over us except in so far as we freely agree to it." Calvin, too, held up the ministry as the first office of usefulness in the church, since God employs ministers as instruments in the performance of his work. The *Second Book of Discipline of the Kirk of Scotland* reflects Calvin's position, in which Knox concurred, referring to all office-holders in the church as ministers, since all are ordained for serving. A reverse current in the direction of high clericalism and bureaucracy developed quite early. Melanchthon and Osiander tried to upgrade ordination by suggesting that the minister was called to an especially holy life. The younger "Christians in authority" had fewer compunctions than Luther did about assuming roles of command.

Betrayed by his own patriotism and personal involvement, Zwingli made more concessions to state-churchism than did the other major reformers. A recent study, however, shows that the traditional charge against Zwingli, that he fostered a theocracy or fusion of church and state, is not justified. Calvin tried to achieve a form of church government based on the New Testament pattern and developed an organization that, although closely commingling the church and the Genevan government, in the context of the larger states achieved real independence for the church. The Anabaptists turned in a minority report on questions of ecclesiology. They held—if one may speak of these splinter groups collectively—that the visible church must be a sanctified body and remain separate from civil society, abjuring oaths. The Church of England meant to many of its clergymen the universal church in England, so that in spite of the obvious factor of nationalism involved, the idea of Christendom persisted in England through the sixteenth century.

With their new ethos of Christian vocation the reformers transcended the medieval dualism of sacred and secular callings. The natural order was for them no longer on a lower plane than the spiritual order. God's majesty was revealed in the created world, to which government belonged as a divine ordinance. With their strong sense of God's immanence the reformers saw the state as subject to God's will and judgment, the "kingdom of God's left hand." They knew nothing of a strictly secular state divorced from "natural law" or freed from ethical ties. The reformers, preeminently Calvin, sought to quicken the conscience of rulers. They enlarged the state's area of competence in social welfare and education, extending a trend already under way in the centuries preceding. Rulers should act like Christians, although the basis of their authority was in natural law under God and not in their church membership.

In accordance with Christ's injunction to "render unto Caesar the things that are Caesar's and unto God the things that are God's," the reformers asserted an absolute distinction between the secular and spiritual authorities. Protestant states were caught up in the general tendency toward tight political cohesion on a territorial or national level. Especially after the revolts and wars of religion, men felt the need for centralized control and strong rulers. The step from the distinction of secular and spiritual authorities to the principle of the separation of church and state, advocated most vigorously by the smaller sects and nonconformists, came only in later centuries.

Religious pluralism had a loosening effect on society. Protestant and Catholic minorities responded to the biblical injunction that one must obey God rather than man. When the need to act according to conscience is affirmed, an explosive potential is introduced. Faith in the King of Kings put earthly rulers in a proper perspective. Luther's sharp criticism of the princes found appreciative readers in subsequent centuries. The Calvinist stress upon predestination and the covenantal theology (the idea that at creation God made a compact with man, each agreeing to do his work) served as a leveling device, for believing oneself to be of the elect was not conducive to a submissive mentality. The famous confrontation between Mary Stuart and John Knox is illustrative. Queen Mary, exasperated at having to discuss her marriage with a commoner, exclaimed to Knox, "What have ye to do . . . with my marriage? Or what are ye within this commonwealth?" Knox retorted, "A subject born within the same, madam. And albeit I neither be earl, lord, nor baron within it, yet has God made me (how abject that ever I be in your eyes) a profitable member within the same."

Reformation thought contributed several basic elements essential to the growth of representative government and democratic institutions. The conception of the universal priesthood of all believers was essentially antihierarchical and corrosive of a pyramidal political structure. There is a link between congregationalism and a democratic ethos. As Knox once declared, "Take from us the freedom of assemblies, and take from us the evangel." The covenant idea in Calvinism, along with the stress on natural law as a basis for positive law, contributed to the idea of the social contract. The doctrine of vocation contributed to the development of an industrious and self-reliant citizenry, the kind of men useful to any government but absolutely essential to a democracy. Calvin concluded the final edition of his *Institutes* with these telling words: "And that our hearts may not fail us, Paul stimulates us with another consideration—that Christ has redeemed us at the immense price which our redemption cost him that we may not be submissive to the corrupt desires of men, much less be slaves to their impiety."[2]

Constructing a model of the good Protestant layman who possesses the qualities of which a perfect republic can be created, as we have just done, is easy enough. "Puritanism," burbled James Russell Lowell, "believing itself quick with the seed of religious liberty, laid without knowing it the egg of democracy." But at least three other important considerations need to be developed in order to put the Protestantism-democracy thesis into perspective.

First, socioeconomic factors had to come into play in conjunction with ideas to produce change in the political patterns. "Thoughts dwell closely together," Goethe observed, "but things jostle one another in space." Only as concrete circumstances produced disaffection toward monarchs did popular forces successfully assert themselves. When the truly revolutionary breakthrough came at the end of the eighteenth century, effecting a thorough destruction of the old religious and political authorities in Europe, it came under the auspices of "enlightened" leadership and in France, a nominally Catholic country.

Second, Catholic thinkers, too, contributed in an important way to natural law and social contract theory. St. Robert Francis Bellarmine (d. 1621), known for his unhappy involvement in the Galileo case—he was obliged to inform Galileo that the pope forbade the teaching of his heliocentric theory, although he himself was in sympathy with both Galileo and his teachings—developed a social contract theory that was antiroyalist in nature, reflecting the views of the Italian church. Bellarmine joined the Jesuit order in 1560 and rose to high positions: rector of the Roman College, provincial of Naples, theologian to Clement VIII, cardinal, examiner of bishops, and consultor of the Holy Office. Involved in an acrimonious controversy with antipapal Venice and concerned about the disabilities of the Catholics in England, Bellarmine argued on Thomist premises that as the supreme bearer of the spiritual sword the pope had indirect authority over secular rulers. Moreover, he contended, the authority of secular rulers is derived from the community by a social contract. The king was thus subject to deposition by the pope, who could absolve the allegiance of the people if the ruler defaulted in his duties. Although Bellarmine was considered a controversial figure in his lifetime, he was canonized and proclaimed a doctor of the church in the 1930s.

---

[2] John Calvin, *Institutes of the Christian Religion*, trans. John Allen (Philadelphia, 1936), vol. 2, bk. 4, chap. 20, p. 806.

The vehement Spanish Jesuit Juan de Mariana (d. 1624), author of a lengthy history of Spain, defended the deposition and killing of tyrants in *The King and Institution of the King* (1599), which he wrote as a "mirror of princes" for the education of future kings. This book stirred up such a storm in France that the Jesuit general had to forbid members of the order to preach that it is lawful to kill despots.

Francisco Suárez (d. 1617), who joined the Jesuits in 1564, distinguished himself not only as a scholastic philosopher but as a political theorist. In his *Treatise Concerning the Laws and God the Legislator* (1612) Suárez argued that the pope, as the spiritual head of the family of Christian nations, was the proper spokesman of all its members. Thus the pope had indirect power to regulate secular rulers for spiritual ends. The state originates in the voluntary agreement of the heads of families, for the power of society to govern itself rests with the social group. Since political power is inherent in the group, no form of political structure is absolute and unchangeable. Government therefore rests upon natural law and is subject to change if it fails to meet its obligations.

Third, certain natural law doctrines, the conception of an international law, and ideas of toleration developed out of a secularized thought not derived by necessity from a theological basis. The doctrine of natural law as Suárez developed it really set politics apart from theology. In spite of his intention to elevate the papal position, his doctrine was not far removed from the thought of the Dutch Calvinists Johannes Althusius (d. 1638) and Hugo Grotius (d. 1645). Althusius continued the line of the antiroyalist French Calvinists. He identified natural law with the law of Moses, but his political theory depended logically upon the central idea of social contract. Men naturally associate in groups and sovereignty necessarily resides in the people as a corporate body. This corporate body bestows its power upon the administrators for effective management of collective affairs. But should the administrators default in their duties, they forfeit this power, which thereupon reverts to the people.

Grotius, in some ways very traditional, filled his concept of natural law with the heady wine of the ancients: substantial justice, good faith, the sanctity of covenants. The definition of natural law which he offered in his great book *On the Law of War and Peace* (Book 1, Chapter 1) was not really revolutionary:

> The law of nature is a dictate of right reason, which points out that an act, according as it is or is not in conformity with rational nature, has in it a quality of moral baseness or moral necessity; and that, in consequence, such an act is either forbidden or enjoined by the author of nature, God.

It was his methodology that was of greatest importance, for his appeal to reason provided the kind of rational thinking that men of his century could regard as a scientific method for arriving at a body of propositions underlying political arrangements within a state, its positive laws, and the laws that should govern relations between nations. To say that Grotius' system was not dependent upon theological premises is not to say that he was not moved by religious considerations. He was himself a product of the meliorating, tolerant Christian humanist tradition of his homeland. Commenting upon the gains of totalitarianism in the twentieth century, the distinguished Cambridge historian Herbert Butterfield has ventured to say in his *Liberty in the Modern World:*

> Because Christianity cannot forgo the basic principle of freedom—the right to worship the true God even against the requirements of the majority of a given society—it is possible, in view of the way in which the world is developing, that all the props of freedom and individualism will fail except the religious one.[3]

Protestantism and Capitalism

THE GREAT DEBATE continues as to whether the Protestant Reformation, especially Calvinism, had a decisive influence upon the rise and development of modern capitalism. But it is less acrimonious than in previous decades and the outlines of a scholarly resolution have begun to emerge. The controversy began over half a century ago, when the great German sociologist Max Weber published his essay on *The Protestant Ethic and the Spirit of Capitalism* (1904–1905). Weber defined the rational organization of free labor as the essence of capitalism. He argued that the spirit of capitalism was reinforced by the religious ethic of Calvinism. Sobriety, thrift, stewardship, rational and systematic behavior, high ethics, a sense of vocation, earthly rewards as signs of grace, social constraints as well as self-discipline— all of these elements were related to Calvinistic "worldly" asceticism. These values contributed to the development of a well-ordered capitalistic way of economic life. The thrust of Weber's argument was directed against materialistic determinism and stressed the importance of a religious movement to an economic development. R. H. Tawney, in his *Religion and the Rise of Capitalism* (1926), supported Weber's general position, but broadened the argument to include all of Protestantism and the socioeconomic and political circumstances at that critical juncture. While Weber never claimed a unicausal link between Calvinism and capitalism, many of his less sophisticated supporters and critics fought over just this issue. As a result, there has been extensive research and much revisionism, so that a far more complicated picture has emerged.

Capitalism clearly antedated the Reformation by many centuries. Certain instruments of capitalism were preserved in the eastern half of the Roman Empire and were transmitted to the West during the Middle Ages. East-West trade was never totally suspended, and commercial capitalism developed with the towns, very

---

[3] Herbert Butterfield, *Liberty in the Modern World* (Toronto, 1952), p. 8.

noticeably from the twelfth century on. The great Italian banking houses of the Renaissance made a highly refined and astonishingly successful use of the financial methods of mercantile and industrial capitalism. Double-entry bookkeeping was of medieval origin. During the Reformation period most of the major banking families were and remained Catholic. The great financial centers, such as Genoa, Venice, Lyon, and Antwerp, were in Catholic countries. In the seventeenth century the Jesuits encouraged the same "economic virtues," thrift and an orderly life, as the Calvinists and Puritans.

The reformers were personally opposed to the practices of unfettered capitalism. Luther drew upon "nature" and the Scriptures for his economic norms. He considered agrarian life more natural and wholesome for man than industry or commerce. As the son of a relatively small but highly successful mining entrepreneur, he was hostile to such big-time operators as the Fuggers, who built up monopolies, squeezed out the little men, and used their money to manipulate politics. Luther espoused a labor theory of value and endorsed just-price theories and a self-sufficient economy for each country. He saw worldly goods as useful and had little sympathy with the radical sects that abolished private property. But he held with the traditional theological opposition to usury or high interest on loans, applying to capitalists the Old Testament injunction against "taking usury or increase" from a brother in need. In his "Little Sermon Against Usury" (1519), his "Large Sermon Against Usury" (1520), and his "Admonition to Pastors to Preach Against Usury" (1540) he reaffirmed his stand, but with little hope that the rising tide of interest-charging finance capitalism could be stemmed. On the basis of Matthew 5 Luther declared that Christ had distinguished three levels in the giving of temporal goods to one's fellow man. The highest was to give more to a man who had already taken from you. The next was to give to a neighbor in need. The lowest was to lend to someone. He would leave it to the law to decide under what circumstances 4, 5, or 6 percent interest could be justified, but he was certain that any higher rate was a sign of greed.

Geneva, at the crossroads of Europe, had long been a lively trading center. Calvin's bourgeois background and legal training made him less medieval and conservative than Luther, and he was in tune with the city's commercial life. In his reply to Claude de Sachins's questions on usury in 1545 he cut through some of the traditional church restrictions on usury, but he still hedged his position so carefully with restrictions of all sorts that it can hardly be said that he "unleashed" finance capitalism. On the contrary, he fought greed and avarice, self-aggrandizement, and exploitation, and he opposed speculative operations such as buying interest without security.

Calvin certainly never pointed to material success as a sign of God's election to salvation. Such a distortion does appear in seventeenth-century Calvinism, but obsessive concern with worldly possessions developed only when genuine religious feeling began to wane. One can, of course, point to extremely wealthy Protestant financiers in the seventeenth century, capitalists such as de Geer, d'Herworth, Rambouillet, and de Witte, who made political loans not only to the Protestant monarchs Christian IV of Denmark and Gustavus Adolphus of Sweden, but to Cardinal Richelieu of France and the Habsburgs of Spain and Austria. But these men were "cool" Calvinists who showed no trace of religious asceticism, wheelers and dealers in the big-time money markets of Antwerp and Liège. Catholicism of the Counterreformation often drove the anticlerical bourgeois of the city-states into exile with their republican notions. Except for a few court favorites who were granted special privileges and monopolies, the Catholic rulers in the southern Netherlands, Spain, and Italy (with the exception of republican Venice) harassed and even drove out their progressive merchants and bankers, forcing able men into difficult situations that by a kind of challenge-and-response mechanism further stimulated their drives toward economic compensation and security.

It would be a mistake to identify seventeenth-century Calvinism mainly with those very wealthy financiers who all too easily attract the eye, for Calvinism's major appeal was to the "little men," the tradesmen and craftsmen. The sense of sobriety, good order, and spiritual strength it conveyed was much more congenial to them than the radical ideas of the sects or the seemly lax and liberal teachings of the Dutch theologian Jacobus Arminius, who opposed the strict predestinarian doctrine and held that salvation was possible for all. H. T. Buckle was more correct than he often was when he wrote, "Calvinism is a doctrine for the poor, Arminianism for the rich. . . . In the republics of Switzerland, North America, and of Holland, Calvinism was always the popular creed. . . ."[4] At least in the Netherlands the regent class opted for the liberal theology of the seventeenth century. In view of all the evidence, the Weber-Tawney hypothesis on the relationship of Protestantism and capitalism scarcely seems to retain any validity as an overall explanation. And yet by instilling into the laboring classes a view of life that raises work from drudgery to a source of self-respect, Protestantism and especially Calvinism helped to build up a group of productive and reliable people, a solid base for a capitalist society.

The Heritage of Humanism

THE POET T. S. ELIOT spoke of culture as "the incarnation of religion" or "lived religion."[5] The theologian Paul Tillich wrote in *The Protestant Era*, "Religion is the substance of culture and culture the form of religion."[6] No cultural creation, he believed, can hide its religious ground. If there is truth in such assertions, one might

[4] H. T. Buckle, *History of Civilization in England,* 4th ed. (London, 1864), vol. 1, pp. 775–76.

[5] T. S. Eliot, *Notes Towards the Definition of Culture* (London, 1948), pp. 15, 33, 67–82.

[6] Paul Tillich, *The Protestant Era* (Chicago, 1938), p. 57.

well expect that an age that saw the juxtaposition of the Renaissance and the Reformation would reveal intimate cultural ties connecting the two movements. And although the Reformation was a far more radical movement than the Renaissance, strong cultural ties did bind the two together.

EDUCATION

One such tie was the deep concern of humanists and reformers for education. "Civilization," as H. G. Wells once remarked, "is a race between education and catastrophe." The humanists made important contributions to education through their renewed emphasis on the classics, the introduction of new studies into the curriculum, and new methods of instruction. They were, of course, elitist in their philosophy of education and served the interests of aristocratic and upper bourgeois circles. The reformers owed them a double debt, for their enthusiasm for learning and their appreciation of the classical languages and literature; but they went beyond the humanists in their stress upon popular education and universal literacy as well as in their special emphasis upon teaching as a divine vocation.

Luther urged compulsory universal education for both boys and girls, with special opportunities for children of exceptional ability. No labor or expense should be spared in educating the youth, he wrote. All who had the wit should be taught to read, so that the Scriptures might be widely studied and known. Education was to prepare men for service in the state as well as in the church, for, as Melanchthon put it, "the ultimate end which confronts us is not private virtue alone but the interest of the public weal." In the same vein Calvin wrote in the *Ordinances* of 1541: "Since it is necessary to prepare for the coming generations in order not to leave the church a desert for our children, it is imperative that we establish a college to instruct the children and to prepare them for both the ministry and civil government." In 1536 the citizens of Geneva had taken an oath that they would "maintain a school to which all would be obliged to send their children." In this tradition the great seventeenth-century educator Comenius admonished, "Let none therefore be excluded unless God denied him sense and intelligence." In 1560 John Knox and his co-workers drew up *The First Book of Discipline,* which envisioned a national system of education. It was no accident that universal literacy was first achieved in Scotland and in several German Protestant states.

The reformers were at one in their praise of the teaching vocation as a service of love to man. "If I had to give up preaching and my other duties," Luther wrote in 1530, "there is no office I would rather have than that of schoolteacher. For I know that next to the ministry it is the most useful, greatest, and best; and I am not sure which of the two is to be preferred." Melanchthon admonished teachers "to take up a school vocation in the same spirit that you would take up the service of God in the church." Theodore Beza believed that in working as a professor of Greek he was performing as great a service in promoting religion as he would have done in the pulpit.

Luther, who considered the Renaissance revival of learning the direct forerunner of the Reformation, urged the cultivation of Latin, Greek, and Hebrew. "Let this be kept in mind," he wrote,

> that we will not preserve the Gospel without the languages. The languages are the scabbard in which the Word of God is sheathed. . . . Therefore it is evident that where the languages are not preserved, there the Gospel will become corrupted. . . . It is our evident duty to cultivate the languages, now that God has restored them to the world through the revival of learning.

He took the initiative in reforming the curriculum of the University of Wittenberg, replacing Aristotle and scholastic philosophy with Augustine, the Scriptures, and the classics. "I am persuaded," he wrote, "that without knowledge of literature pure theology cannot at all endure." The study of poetry and rhetoric fitted people as nothing else could "for grasping sacred truth and for handling it skillfully and happily." Melanchthon was a prime mover in the founding of the new gymnasia or secondary schools with humanist curricula in Nuremberg and elsewhere. He held sound instruction in letters to be a necessary condition for the teaching of religion.

Calvin, who had been a French humanist in his youth, always retained his love of literature. He admired Cicero especially, and his pages sparkle with citations from the classics. He also believed that much could be learned from the classical treatises on science and the practical arts. And he practiced what he preached, for in founding the Geneva Academy he established a curriculum that included the ancient languages and humanist disciplines. The Calvinists founded new universities in Edinburgh, Leiden, Amsterdam, Groningen, Utrecht, Franeker, Nimes, Montauban, Saumur, and Sedan. They reformed others in Calvinist areas, such as Heidelberg, and founded Emmanuel College at Cambridge. For the reformers higher education was a *negotium cum deo,* an activity carried on together with God. Higher culture, too, was a "sphere of faith's work."

Johannes Sturm, the founder of the evangelical gymnasium in Strassburg, which became a model for all the secondary schools of Europe, adopted as his motto "Wise and eloquent piety," revealing his conviction that faith and literary culture fitted well together. Here and in the other schools of the reformers, Protestant seriousness combined with humanist ideals to produce an educational enterprise of which Europe has every right to be proud.

In the new Jesuit schools the students read Cicero's epistles and *Tusculan Disputations,* Terence or Virgil's *Eclogues,* Ovid's *Tristia,* Sallust, and Horace's *Arts poetica.* By 1551 there were Jesuit colleges in Rome, Bologna, Florence, Ferrara, and Venice, and in many parts of northern Europe. But in Catholic and Protestant schools alike, classical studies dwindled in time to a school discipline. What they gained in technical precision they lost in spontaneity. The "safe classics," useful for moral instruction, were taught, but this pedagogical humanism lacked the zest and abandon that had characterized Poggio, Filelfo, and Aretino.

No one would argue that the Reformation ushered in a new Periclean age. The education of a creature so limited and self-centered as man is always a struggle. In the first stormy years of the Reformation, while the reformers attacked scholastic studies and society was in turmoil, enrollments at the universities plummeted downward; Erlangen, for example, which had 311 students in 1520–1521, had only 14 in 1527. Wittenberg, too, dropped briefly, but soon began attracting great numbers. The reformers constantly complained about the lack of talent and wrong motivation of the students. Martin Bucer growled:

> Nobody will learn anything nowadays except what brings in money. All the world is running after those trades and occupations which give least work to do and bring the most gain, without any concern for their neighbor or for honest and good report. The study of the arts and sciences is set aside for the basest kinds of manual work. . . . All the clever heads which have been endowed by God with capacity for the nobler studies are engrossed by commerce.

Nearer the end of the century the minor French humanist Louis Le Roy found the young virtually uneducable: "Students, if they are poor, apply themselves to gainful arts in order to have something to live on, after profiting only moderately from letters. If they are rich, they want pleasure, seeking the easy surface of learning and not its painful depths." By the late seventeenth century the universities had lost their position of leadership and did not rise again in preeminence until the nineteenth century.

THOUGHT AND LETTERS

"Learning, wisdom, and writers should rule the world," Luther pontificated in one of his *Table Talks*, "and should God ever in his wrath take away all learned men from the world, what else would the people who are left be except beasts!" The magisterial reformers took a positive attitude toward letters, a happy circumstance, for if the attitude of certain anti-intellectual sects or the cultural atavism of the practical types had prevailed, the golden ideals of the Renaissance might have sunk forever out of sight.

Italy. Apollo moved his habitation to the north during the sixteenth century as the homeland of the Renaissance groaned under the weight of Spanish occupation, petty tyrannies, and Counterreformation repression, and Italian letters went into decline. Spain controlled Milan and Naples. In Rome Julius III was the last Renaissance pope, and then the Inquisition moved in to suppress free thought and creativity. Cosimo I, duke of Florence, set up a repressive regime. Eleanor of Toledo introduced Spanish etiquette to the Palazzo Vecchio. The many academies that sprang up in Florence, Ferrara, Bologna, and Rome cultivated an elegant Ciceronian style in speech and fine manners suited to the court life of a decadent period.

By mid-century many of Italy's best intellectuals were dead. Cardinal Sadoleto, the Erasmian humanist, died in 1547. Lazzaro Buonamici and Romolo Amaseo, the leading Ciceronians in Padua and Bologna, died in 1552. Petrarchism was barely perpetuated by very mediocre writers. Erotic poetry withered away under the hot breath of the inquisitors. Rhetoric as a discipline declined to the level of banal posturing. Pietro Bembo (d. 1547) continued in the Platonic tradition of the Florentine Academy, but he and his generation contributed virtually nothing original or noteworthy. After the death of the logician Marco Antonio Zimara in 1532, the University of Padua failed to produce any new Aristotelian philosopher of note. The sixteenth century in Italy has, in fact, been nicknamed the *saeculum victorianum*, after the Florentine Vettori or Victorius, an eminent but dull scholar who edited numerous Greek and Latin texts, wrote commentaries on Aristotle, and published thirty-eight books of *Variae lectiones*. Classical studies had moved from the piazza into the study.

Italian historiography accompanied classical studies into decline. Dominated by foreigners and even more disunited than before, Italians had little confidence that historical analysis could be of any profit to political leaders who seemingly had neither the ability nor the opportunity to apply its lessons. Not a single general history of Italy appeared after Guicciardini's until far into the following century. At the end of the sixteenth century the Florentine historian Scipione Ammirato wrote his official *Florentine Histories,* replete with erudite and antiquarian detail, providing many data but little understanding.

Near the close of the century there was a brief flowering of historiography in Venice, reminiscent of the days when civic humanism and patriotism had flourished in Bruni's Florence. Niccolò Contarini, who later became doge, wrote a substantial history of Venice, which was candid about the deficiencies of the age and offered a broad view of developments. Paolo Paruta, who became the official historian of Venice and ambassador to the Holy See, wrote a series of dialogues in praise of the civic life. Paolo Sarpi, author of a history of the Council of Trent, belonged to this Venetian group of historians. The fact that Venice was able to retain its independence, cultivate civic pride, and enjoy the triumph of Lepanto gave the republic an élan that had withered and died elsewhere in Italy. Its civic humanism, like its renaissance in art, came late and glowed in autumn colors.

The Empire. While Italy suffered the effects of its political ordeal and the repression of the Counterreformation, the states of western Europe moved on toward greater national cohesion and more independent cultural traditions. During the half century following the Peace of Augsburg (1555), much energy went into theological controversy and confessional writings. During the two decades following the peace, Protestantism continued in the ascendancy in the empire. The evangelical faith came very close to becoming the universal creed of Germany. If it had succeeded, the religious ideological ground for conflict would have been removed. But three developments prevented such an easy solution: the expansion of militant Calvinism, internal dissension within Lutheranism, and the success of the Counterreformation within the empire.

The Peace of Augsburg provided for a mutual toleration of Catholics and Lutherans, but deliberately excluded concessions to Calvinism. Calvinism, refusing to be thus ignored, penetrated in depth among the learned doctors of theology at Heidelberg. It won the heart of Elector Frederick III of the Palatinate, although he continued to protest his loyalty to the Augsburg Confession. In 1540 Melanchthon published a revised version of the Augsburg Confession (*Confessio augustana variata*) in which he rephrased certain passages to make them more acceptable to other Protestants. In Article 10, for example, he worded the sentences on the Lord's Supper in such a way as to allow for a Calvinist spiritual interpretation. After Melanchthon's death Frederick III published the Heidelberg Catechism, which became a basic text in all Calvinist or "Reformed" churches in Europe and America.

During the decades after Luther's death, Lutheranism was torn by internal dissension and dogmatic quarrels that threatened to fragment the movement and render it impotent. Political rivalries played a part in the development. The Schmalkald War, through which Ernestine Saxony lost to Albertine Saxony the privilege of taking part in the election of the emperor, sowed seeds of discord in both Saxonies, and there was constant tension between the Saxonies and Hesse over the leadership of evangelicals. But beyond politics, the emphasis upon right belief in the sense of correct dogmatic formulation, the readiness to condemn the views of others, and a professional tendency to join schools and factions produced intolerance and an intolerable situation.

The leadership of Lutheranism fell very naturally to Philipp Melanchthon, the brilliant scholar for whom Luther had always felt the deepest affection. Because of his broad humanist background, his peaceful persuasion, and his desire to see good in the ideas of others, Melanchthon came to deviate from a strict Lutheran doctrinal position on a number of central points. He was, for example, willing to grant the cooperation of the human will in the reception of divine grace (synergism). He and his followers, called the Philippists, were attacked by the Gnesio-Lutherans (literally, true or genuine Lutherans), led by the very conservative and polemical Matthias Flacius Illyricus (1520–1575), the watchdog of orthodoxy.

The doctrinal controversies that followed fill shelvesful of pamphlets, dogmatic tomes, reports on conferences and synods, attacks and apologies. The need for doctrinal unity and peace within Lutheranism became increasingly urgent. Jakob Andreae, chancellor of Tübingen, supported by moderate Lutheran theologians and princes, worked toward a doctrinal formula to which all Lutherans might agree. The result was the Formula of Concord (1577), which became the definitive confession of a large majority of the Lutheran principalities and kingdoms. On June 25, 1580, precisely fifty years after the presentation of the Augsburg Confession to the diet of the empire, the *Book of Concord* was published, bringing together the three ecumenical creeds and the specifically Lutheran confessions.

It has been estimated that by 1570 seven-tenths of all the people in the empire were evangelical. The two immediate successors to Emperor Charles V, Ferdinand I (1558–1564) and Maximilian II (1564–1576), were in no position to suppress Protestantism. But as the century moved on, internal strife weakened the evangelical cause and the Catholic Counterreformation picked up momentum.

Even in the 1540s individual Jesuits were at work in the empire. Peter Canisius (1511–1597) wrote a popular catechism as an answer to Luther's and established excellent Jesuit schools. From 1549 on the Jesuits worked in the Habsburg domains, in Bavaria, and in the archepiscopal territories along the Rhine. Their appeal to the common people rested upon their genuine piety, religious ceremonies of great emotional appeal, processions, pilgrimages, and impressive architecture. The Collegium Germanicum in Rome trained German priests in the Jesuit spirit. Pope Gregory XIII (1572–1585) was especially zealous about bringing the Germanies back to the faith. He appointed able nuncios to the empire and in 1573 he established the Congregatio Germanica, a permanent committee of cardinals to handle the "German question."

The results of these efforts were remarkable and to the evangelicals most alarming. By 1600 Bavaria, Baden-Baden, Styria, Carinthia, and Carniola were once again safely Catholic. In the south, Bamberg, Würzburg, and Salzburg, which had large evangelical populations, became overwhelmingly Catholic again. Even in the north several key ecclesiastical territories were recatholicized: Eichsfeld, Fulda, Münster, Paderborn, and Cologne. The battle for Cologne was particularly critical, for it was the key to Westphalia and the lower German Rhineland. As Catholicism gained in power, the possibility of a religious war between fairly evenly matched opponents became a real threat.

The interest and energies absorbed during this period by theological controversy and the ecclesiastical struggle for supremacy limited intellectual creativity and aesthetic accomplishments in the Germanies. A few men of unusual ability appeared in other areas of endeavor—the Silesian poet Martin Opitz, the Augsburg architect Elias Holl, the Tübingen Aristotelian Jakob Schegk, the Saxon musician Heinrich Schütz. In religion itself there was a dearth of creative thought, and a theologian such as Johann Valentin Andreae stands out largely for lack of competitors. Popular religious writing—devotional literature, books of sermons, hymnals—made up an important part of the literature of Protestant Europe.

One literary genre that achieved notable successes was history. During the course of the Leipzig debates Luther had cited historical precedents against Eck and called history "the mother of truth." During his last years he read histories of all kinds and even wrote an introduction to a history by Galeatius Capella, a Sforza historian. Melanchthon wrote an introduction to a chronicle by Carion and rewrote a large part of the chronicle itself. The spiritualistic Sebastian Franck wrote a world history that in originality, independence of viewpoint, and cultural scope may be judged superior to Melanchthon's. But the most impressive work was that of Johannes Philippson, or Sleidanus, as he was called, after the town of Schleiden in the Rhineland. In 1555 Sleidanus published his *Commentaries on the State of Religion and on the Reign of Charles V,* in which he sought to write objectively and impartially, as he explained with care:

> All these things I recite plainly, simply and truly as everything was done: neither use I also any color of rhetoric, nor write anything in the hatred or favor of any man.... I frame my style only and use mine own words, that the speech may be always like and equal, and I bestow each thing in its place, as they follow in order.

The *Bavarian Chronicle* of Johannes Aventinus (d. 1534) was a notable history, going back to the sources in the humanist tradition. Reformation historiography followed the humanist assumption that history, like philosophy, has pragmatic utility, teaching by example. Protestant historians, sharing the humanists' view of the medieval period as a dark age, frequently saw the hand of God in history, rewarding and punishing. The ways of looking at history that had developed during the Renaissance and the Reformation, including its periodization, lived on into modern times, and some still persist today.

France.   French letters continued to prosper during the second half of the sixteenth century, despite the fact that King Henry II and his successors were never as enthusiastic patrons of literature as Francis I had been. The religious wars took their toll, but some remarkable literary figures emerged during those decades. Calvin was himself an accomplished French stylist, and his *Institutes* especially exercised a most constructive influence upon the French language and literature.

The imitation of classical models and the influence of Italian Renaissance thought continued to be very much in evidence in French literature. A group of writers known as the Pleiades cultivated the French language, but at the same time believed that literary perfection was to be achieved by a close study and imitation of classic authors such as Cicero and Virgil. Joachim du Bellay's *Defense and Illustration of the French Language* (1549) developed these theories of the Pleiades. Du Bellay (1522–1560), inspired by both Plato and Christ, adhered to theories of tender and delicate love. Pontus de Tyard, an exquisite poet, was a student of Marsilio Ficino's writings and reflected his Neoplatonic theories of love. Pierre de Ronsard (1524–1585), the best known of the group, met du Bellay in a hostel in Touraine and became his fast friend. Ronsard was voluptuous, sensual, even lewd, not at all in the spirit of Ficino, but his theories of poetic madness were derived from Plato. He spoke of France as the "mother of the arts."

It is fascinating to note the development of rationalism and skepticism side by side with Catholic orthodoxy and Calvinist fideism in sixteenth-century France, in part in reaction to the religious controversies. A real intellectual fluke was the Averroist doctrine of Francesco Vimercati, a Lombard student of the Paduan neo-Aristotelians, who became the physician of Francis I and received a chair of philosophy, protected by the church. Between 1550 and 1556 he published commentaries on Aristotle in which he presented the Averroist doctrine of the one eternal intellect and argued for the eternity of the universe, determinism, and the constancy of natural laws. He was opposed by Gentien Hervet and others, but his most publicized critic was Peter Ramus (Pierre La Ramée), who launched an all-out attack upon Aristotle himself.

Peter Ramus (1515–1572) was a writer of extraordinary brilliance and force. The thesis he defended when he took his M.A. at Paris in 1536 suggests the direction of his thought: "All Aristotle's doctrines are false." He remained throughout his life the fierce opponent of Aristotelianism. Fighting Aristotelianism was a tough assignment indeed, for throughout Europe it remained the predominant philosophy of the universities, including even Wittenberg, where it made a comeback under Melanchthon's aegis. In 1543 Ramus published his two major works, *Aristotelicae animadversiones* and *Dialecticae institutiones,* written in a fine humanist style. The University of Paris condemned his work, and eventually Francis I appointed a committee to judge a disputation between Ramus and his major critic, Anthony of Gorea. The committee condemned Ramus as "rash, arrogant, and impudent," a judgment the king confirmed. Ramus objected to the sterility of Aristotelian logic as it was then being officially taught. He favored enlarging the area of rhetoric in combination with logic and a closer union of the arts of exposition and argumentation. Ramism was opposed in most continental universities, but it had a considerable influence in England and in the American colonies. Thanks to the protection of the cardinal of Lorraine, Ramus secured a "royal lectureship" at the College of Navarre after the accession of Henry II. In 1562 he left the Catholic Church and became a Calvinist. Ten years later he paid the price of his nonconformity and defection by being murdered in the massacre of St. Bartholomew.

The greatest man of French letters in that era, some would say in all times, was that urbane, exquisite intellectual Michel de Montaigne (1533–1592). Montaigne was the scion of a wealthy Bordeaux family and grew up with all the advantages of skilled tutors and schooling. He studied at the College of Guyenne for seven years, then spent two years in logic and dialectics at Bordeaux and studied law before entering public life as a counselor and member of the parliament. At the age of thirty-eight he retired to the Château de Montaigne, where from 1571 to 1580 he wrote his *Essays*. He spent a year and a half traveling through Alsace, Switzerland, Bavaria, Venice, and Rome, recording his experiences in his *Journal*. His life in his rural retreat was reminiscent of the *vita solitaria,* the contemplative life away from the marketplace cultivated by Petrarch, Sadoleto, and other humanists. Embellished by a library of classics and the company of intellectual friends, his urbane style of life anticipated the eighteenth-century salon. Through the wit and charm of his writing shines the evanescent quality that Matthew Arnold must have had in mind when he spoke of a "sad lucidity of soul."

The *Essays* are a long, polished relation of Montaigne's reflections and recollections, his experiences garnered in life and gained vicariously by reading. Although he himself is the subject of the book, it reflects the foibles and strengths of all humanity. Highly rational, Montaigne had a strong sense of the limitations of reason when confronted by the big questions of life. When he considered the variety of customs and ethical and aesthetic standards revealed in the cultures of Asia, Africa, and the New World, he concluded that such matters are relative to the cultural experience of the people concerned. His skepticism has brought down upon him charges of Pyrrhonism. "I generally observe," he commented wryly, "that when a matter is set before them, men are more ready to waste their time in seeking the reason of it than in seeking the truth of it . . . so much uncertainty is there in all things." An unbending elitist as a young man, he learned that the unlettered peasant and fisherman may possess a practical wisdom not to be found in books. Montaigne's humane, witty, pithy, and often wise observations on the human condition place him in the best humanist tradition. Many of his theories on education were very influential in later years. But his acute sense of the limitations of human reason and the frailty of mankind set him apart from the ebullience and naïveté of some Renaissance men. In that sense his work marks the end of an era.

Spain.   During the reign of Philip II Spain experienced its golden age of culture. Thomist theology revived and an Erasmian tradition persisted in letters. Lope de Vega and Pedro Calderón de la Barca flourished. But above all the incomparable Miguel de Cervantes (1547–1616), author of the classic *Don Quixote,* raised Spanish literature to new triumphs. In painting, the names of Velázquez and El Greco became immortal.

The Spanish cultural efflorescence is an intriguing phenomenon, coming as it did in a period of absolutistic tendencies and inquisitorial repression. Perhaps the imperial glory proved inspiring, so that for the first time in their history Spaniards felt themselves culturally superior to other Europeans. In art and literature Spain developed strong traditions of its own and Spanish intellectuals exuded a new confidence, revealing a predilection for ethical, legal, and religious problems rather than for science and philosophy. The decline from greatness was gradual but seemingly inevitable in the century that followed.

England. It can be argued with some plausibility that the real English Renaissance began during the age of Elizabeth. The earlier efflorescence of culture during the reigns of Henry VII and Henry VIII, the days of Latimer, Grocyn, Linacre, Colet, More, and Erasmus, were pale compared with the flowering of native genius during Elizabeth's reign. The first phase was indispensable to the second and the Italian influence was of critical importance to both. Essential carriers were the English who went to Italy, such as the earl of Surrey and Sir Thomas Wyatt. "They," wrote the Elizabethan poet and critic Richard Puttenham, "having traveled into Italy, and there tasted the sweet and stately measures of the Italian poesie, greatly polished our rude and homely manner." Italians who came to England, such as Polydore Vergil, brought with them the finest literary products of the Renaissance, and courtly manners in addition.

The new and improved schools spread learning among increased numbers of Englishmen. In 1531 Sir Thomas Elyot, in *The Boke Named the Gouvenour,* fused the literary aims of Vives and Erasmus with the idea of the "gentleman" promoted by Castiglione. He urged a Renaissance approach to education, Latin as a living language, tutors for the children of "governors" or public servants, and the teaching of music, art, and physical education. The aim of education was to be the cultivation of wisdom learned from the ancients and applied for the good of society. In this humane tradition the greatest English educator of all, Roger Ascham (1515–1568), wrote *The Schoolmaster,* published two years after his death. It was the best treatise in English on classical education, and stressed the need for gentleness in teaching the very young and for cultivating "hard wits" rather than "quick wits." Ascham argued that by education a man learns vicariously and safely in one year what would take twenty to learn by experience. The educational theories and curricula recommended by such distinguished Renaissance humanists as Juan Luis Vives were put into practice in schools even in remote northern provinces. As humanist learning spread out from court circles to a larger segment of the population, the way was prepared for the secular cultural rejuvenation in the age of Elizabeth. There is a unity in the cultural developments that came to a climax in the triumphs at the end of the century and ripened to maturity in the decades after Elizabeth's death.

Although it is difficult to document the correlation between the adventures of the Elizabethans on the sea, the naval triumph over the greatest Catholic power, the growth of a national spirit, and the upward surge of literary and artistic culture, the sense of exhilaration and exuberant energy is evident throughout all aspects of English life, including literature. The writings of greatest genius and most enduring quality were universal in concept rather than merely national. But it was Elizabeth as Gloriana, a symbol of Britain's greatness, and the heroic deeds of Englishmen advancing England's interests that quickened men's minds and set their pens in motion. An age of action leads men to think in epic terms. Just as the Italian

Renaissance produced great chronicles and accounts of Italian affairs by Bruni, Machiavelli, and Guicciardini, so now pride and patriotism led the Tudor historians to relate Britain's greatness to events of the past, now seen as glorious.

A certain sense of destiny that ran deeper than mere chauvinism and self-glorification informed this new historical consciousness. John Lyly's pedagogical moralistic novel *Euphues and His England* (1580), for all the stilted language and affectation that made it the object of much ridicule, provided a key to this new English mystique and helped to develop a Protestant mythology. England, Lyly piously intoned, was the new Israel, the chosen people of God, destined to carry the gospel and to do his will. William Camden, headmaster of Westminster School, published his *Britannia,* an antiquarian geography of every county in England, in order to "restore Britain to antiquity and antiquity to Britain." This Renaissance genre, made famous by Biondo's *Italy Illustrated* and Celtis' *Germany Illustrated,* served the purposes of a people in the process of rediscovering its own heritage. Camden's annals of Elizabeth's reign, written after her death, proved him to be more than a mere antiquarian. Another student of antiquity, John Stow, was so eager a scholar that he "wasted his substance, neglected his business, and spent all his money" in pursuit of his studies, until in old age he had to receive from King James I permission to beg from the churches. His creditors are long forgotten, but Stow is still remembered for his *Survey of London,* on the early history of England's queen city. William Harrison's *Description of Britain* was the most outstanding account of Elizabeth's England. Raphael Holinshed enjoyed the good fortune of having his *Chronicles* exploited by Shakespeare, so that their names are intertwined in luxuriant tangles of Elizabethan scholarship.

History attracted some of the strongest minds of the age. Francis Bacon's *History of Henry VII* had real literary quality and gained considerable renown. But perhaps the most remarkable achievement was Sir Walter Raleigh's outstanding *History of the World,* written to keep his mind occupied during his long years of imprisonment. His preface reveals some of the presuppositions of the age about history. Hearing boys outside his prison window arguing over things that had happened only a short time before, he reflected upon how much more difficult it is to be certain about events of ages gone by. The general notions of a cyclical pattern in history, the pragmatic use of history as philosophy, the assumption that the lessons of history can be applied to daily life and present times—these were typical Renaissance conceptions and were derived immediately from classical theories of history. The fact that Shakespeare's historical plays (*King John, Richard II, Richard III, Henry IV, Henry V*) belong to the years between 1592 and 1600 may suggest that the historical subject matter is related not only to Shakespeare's personal development, but also to the exuberant patriotism and interest in England's national dynastic history in that period.

Classical and Italian models were important to the development of *belles lettres*. Translations became increasingly numerous and some gained lasting fame, such as Chapman's version of Homer's *Iliad*, Harrington's translation of Ariosto's *Orlando furioso*, and Fairfax's rendition of Tasso's *Jerusalem Delivered*. But the classical forms were now filled by native genius. Secular literature came to replace religious poetry as sonnets, lyrics, odes, and popular ballads and madrigals rose to prominence. In a beautiful treatise *In Defence of Poesie* Sir Philip Sidney vindicated the power of the poetic imagination against the dull and prosaic limitations that mere nature imposes upon man. Nature, he wrote, "never set forth the earth in so rich tapestry as divers poets have done, neither with so pleasant rivers, fruitful trees, sweet-smelling flowers, nor whatsoever else may make the too much loved earth more lovely. Her world is brazen; the poets only deliver a golden." Sidney offered a noble argument for the glories of Elizabethan letters. His own masterpiece was his *Arcadia*, which in a somewhat confused mixture of medieval and classical surroundings offered a pastoral story of love and chivalry, setting a high standard for the age. His sonnets reflected his own love experiences and helped to popularize that relatively easy Italianate poetic form. Sidney was important in his own times as the exemplar of the new ideal of Protestant knighthood. In later centuries Raleigh and Essex came to represent the epitome of Elizabethan courtier culture, but their Protestant gentlemen contemporaries saw Sidney as the cultural hero of the age.

Elizabethan men of letters, like the men of affairs, were concerned for the most part with the real world about them. There is very little romantic longing for an imagined golden age of the past. With some justification literary historians have traditionally dated the birth of Elizabethan letters from the *Shepheards Calendar* of 1579, a satire by Edmund Spenser. Spenser was educated at Cambridge, was patronized by the earl of Leicester, and in 1580 went to Ireland as secretary to the viceroy. He lived there, near Cork, for nearly two decades, until the Irish rebels under Tyrone burned his house and forced him to flee to England in 1598. He died in London a year later. A friend of Sir Walter Raleigh, active in Munster, Spenser was close to the Elizabethan scene in spite of his seclusion in Ireland. His *Faerie Queen* was the great epic of the age, revealing the influence of Tasso and Ariosto. Spenser imagined a day when chivalry was more than idle form, peopled his world with such knights and ladies as never were, and carried his readers with him on rhythmic waves of poetry to a land of aesthetic delight. And yet it would be a mistake to interpret his poetry as merely romantic in its use of old forms, for his legends and chivalric symbols carry the spirit of a new age in politics and religion. The *Faerie Queen* is quite simply a masterpiece, and in his devotion to the Protestant ethic as well as his literary concerns, Spenser was a spokesman for his age.

Few men of the time so incorporated in their own persons the Renaissance gentleman, the Elizabethan politician and man of affairs, the genial man of letters, and the serious philosopher as did Francis Bacon. This courtier was only forty-two when Elizabeth died. His career as rival of the formidable legist Sir Edward Coke, his disgrace, and his trial for bribery came during the reign of James I, but he was formed as an Elizabethan, published his famed *Essays* during her reign (1597), and was in many ways typical of the brash, aggressive, profane circle of Elizabethan statesmen. His thoughts on society and science have had enduring influence. His moral essays reflect practical political wisdom derived from an unsentimental observation of Elizabethan politics. His thoughts were weighty but of a practical kind, expressed in short, pithy sayings easily transformed into clichés. Like Erasmus' *Adages*, Bacon's essays grew in number from ten in the first edition to fifty-eight in the edition of 1625. In later life he displayed his pride in the English past by writing a *History of Henry VII*, a lively narrative with a skillful characterization of the monarch.

The fame of Francis Bacon will always rest on his philosophical treatises, which contributed so much, though deviously, to the rise of the modern scientific method. While still a student at Cambridge he came to the conclusion that the methods employed in various sciences were erroneous and sterile. Although he retained a certain respect for Aristotle as a thinker, he reacted strongly against the prevailing Aristotelian philosophy. "The knowledge whereof the world is now possessed," he wrote, "especially that of nature, extendeth not to magnitude and certainty of works." All his life Bacon poured out a stream of treatises, some, such as *On the Advancement of Learning*, of enduring value. His major work on natural philosophy, *Novum organum* (1620), was written in Latin, the language of scholars.

Bacon's basic criticism of philosophy was that men had been too much concerned with "the satisfaction which men call Truth" and too little concerned with operation. In a famous section he analyzed the "idols," the kinds of fallacies or general classes of error into which the mind is apt to fall. There are four false ways of looking at nature, he wrote. The first kind of error he called the idols of the tribe, common to all mankind, such as the tendency to suppose greater order in nature than actually exists, the inclination to support a preconceived opinion, the readiness to generalize on a few instances, and the proneness to give concreteness to the abstract constructs of the mind. The second class, idols of the cave, is a product of the individual's mental and physical peculiarities, the inclination, for example, to prefer the ancient to the modern or vice versa, the tendency to exaggerate similarities or differences, and the like. The third class, idols of the marketplace, arises from the tyranny exercised over the mind by mere words. The fourth class, idols of the theater, is the mistaken modes of thought resulting from traditional philosophical systems and from fallacious methods of demonstration. Against these systems Bacon opposed his new method.

Science was for Bacon really natural philosophy, which is concerned with God, nature, and man, of which the most significant to the scientist is nature. He had a firm grasp of the physical character of natural principles; the "forms" that the natural philosopher studies are not abstract ideas but highly general physical properties. The *prima philosophia,* or first philosophy, undertakes to demonstrate the unity of nature by organizing into one system the general principles of the various individual sciences. The three levels in this philosophy are experience or natural history, physics, and metaphysics. The new method is *induction,* the thread that leads the mind through the great labyrinth of nature. Through natural history— that is, experience—the scientist collects the facts by observation. Man as interpreter of nature must follow a natural and experimental history, moving by induction from particular observations, properly excluding, rejecting, and eliminating data, to the general principle. Bacon made no application of the method to achieve scientific discoveries of his own, nor did he really lay down the basic experimental method of modern science. But as an index to the growing concern with nature and as an inspiration for scientific thought his intellectual contribution has had lasting value.

The true genius of that dramatic age was given its most perfect expression in Elizabethan drama. Christopher Marlowe began to write in the turbulent years just before the Armada. Marlowe lived a wild, dissolute life, and was stabbed to death in a tavern brawl in 1592, when he was only twenty-eight. His dramas, too, displayed the lack of restraint and the *terribilità* of the Italian Renaissance, giving vent to the most extravagant passions and fearful deeds. In his *Tamburlaine the Great* (1586) he portrays the Tatar emperor caught up in *hybris,* false pride that tempts fate, as he rages against God and man. In *The Rich Jew of Malta* (1589) he has Machiavelli recite a prologue, mocking religion as "a childish toy" and holding that "there is no sin but ignorance." His most famous play was *Dr. Faustus* (1588), based on the medieval legend of the Rhenish doctor who sold his soul to the devil in exchange for knowledge and the power it gives. Marlowe's characters, like the Elizabethan adventurers, all seemed larger than life-size.

There were others in Marlowe's day much like him, though less skillful. Notable among them was Robert Greene (1560?–1592), a pamphleteer, novelist, and dramatist who managed to live a little longer than Marlowe but no less extravagantly. After leaving Cambridge he wandered through Italy and Spain, and was impressed by Italian literary models. A restless soul, he did as he pleased, abandoned his wife, and followed the precept that "what is profitable ceases to be bad." His own dramas were hurriedly written and did not approach the excellence of Marlowe's. Yet he ventured to call young William Shakespeare an "upstart crow beautified with our feathers," a mere actor who dared to invade the profession of the playwright.

Shakespeare came to London when Marlowe's earliest play was first appearing. The son of a Stratford tradesman down on his luck, Shakespeare was only nineteen when he married Anne Hathaway, who was eight years older. Poverty and a charge of poaching on a noble's land led him to abandon Stratford to try his fortunes in London, where he became an actor at twenty-two. His invasion of the dramatists' guild was a most happy event. He began with comedies. His earliest play, *Love's Labor Lost,* was a spoof on pedantry and contrived style and verbiage. His *Comedy of Errors* was an adaptation of a Latin play, amusing but lacking in depth of ideas and characterization. In his *Midsummer Night's Dream* he conjured up a fairyland of elves and clumsy clowns. As his fame grew, Queen Elizabeth herself listened with delight, and it is said that he wrote *The Merry Wives of Windsor* to amuse the queen, who had expressed a wish to see Falstaff in love.

After the premature death of so many leading playwrights, Shakespeare virtually had the stage to himself from 1592 to the end of the century, years in which his historical plays responded to the patriotic fervor of the English. From 1601 to 1608 a pessimistic strain crept into his "gloomy comedies," such as *Measure for Measure* and *All's Well That Ends Well,* and into his tragedies, *Hamlet, Othello, King Lear, Macbeth,* and *Timon of Athens.* During the last eight years he softened some, toning down the harsh, tragic element and adding a note of tolerance and romance to leaven the disillusionment and futility in his last plays, as in *The Winter's Tale* and *The Tempest.*

Shakespeare was the universal genius, surpassing all others in depth of insight, in inventiveness, in power of characterization, in versatility and charm. He was a culmination and summation not only of the Elizabethan awakening, but of the entire Renaissance. The major themes of Renaissance humanism found unexcelled expression in the lines of Shakespeare. Consider, for example, how the whole Renaissance discussion of the dignity and misery of man is given its ultimate poetic expression in Hamlet's soliloquy (Act II, Scene 2):

> What a piece of work is a man! How noble in reason! how infinite in faculty! in form, in moving, how express and admirable! in action how like an angel! in apprehension how like a god! the beauty of the world! the paragon of animals! And, yet, to me, what is this quintessence of dust? man delights not me; no, nor woman neither, though, by your smiling, you seem to say so.

Shakespeare was a genius, but his genius was always controlled. He could drink with the cleverest wits of London at the Mermaid Tavern, but he bought land near Stratford and lived out his last years in ease and comfort. He died there in 1616 at the age of fifty-two. Not even Ben Jonson, whose plays *Volpone, or the Fool* (1605), *Epicene, or the Silent Woman* (1609), *The Alchemist* (1610), and

Bartholemew Fair (1614) were of high order, equaled Shakespeare's sympathetic bond with all mankind.

THE FINE ARTS

The Reformation and Counterreformation made a visible impression upon the fine arts, which were more easily correlated than literature with the religious thrust. The Protestant areas in the north suffered a decline of quality and creativity in the visual arts, although music continued to flourish. The Catholic areas suffered at first from the puritanism of the Counterreformation, but in due course developed from mannerism to high baroque, a style expressive of the new religious ardor of the Catholic resurgence.

Architecture and Art in Protestant Europe. Luther was capable of returning from a visit to Cologne and commenting later on nothing more than the poor acoustics in that grand cathedral. His trip to Italy was hurried and of far shorter duration than Erasmus'. But like Erasmus he could return to the north without reacting in the least to Italy's artistic wonders. Luther did admire the skill of artists and craftsmen, and he had no objection to ecclesiastical art in churches so long as it was recognized as adornment and not put to idolatrous use. In fact, when Luther learned of the radicals' destruction of religious statuary and stained-glass windows in Wittenberg while he was in hiding at the Wartburg Castle, he rushed back to stop them. But that very incident shows the danger to religious art inherent in the Puritan component of Protestantism. That tendency was full-blown in Zwingli, who was convinced that artistic representation of Christ and the saints was inherently idolatrous and prepared the people of Zurich for the iconoclastic "cleansing of the temple," when the Great Minster was stripped of its artwork and whitewashed. Calvin had a more positive attitude toward ecclesiastical art, though he favored simplicity. The Anabaptists had little positive to say and nothing constructive to offer in the arts.

The Reformation as a whole affected architecture and art in three major ways. First, the attitude of the reformers toward art, especially ecclesiastical art, affected its fortunes. Second, their religious teachings were reflected in art. Third, the social, political, and military events in which religious issues were involved affected the prosperity of the artists and art itself. The Protestants had no real need to develop a distinctive architecture, for they inherited many more churches and chapels in the overchurched cities and towns than they had need for. Because of the rejection of the veneration of saints and, especially in Calvinist areas, the warning against graven images, sculpture fell into a precipitous decline. It persisted only in Catholic Bavaria and in Austria, thanks to the Italian influence imported by the Jesuits.

Artists still flourished in the early years of the Reformation, but no second generation equal to those masters emerged. Albrecht Dürer (1471–1528), the Nuremberg genius, became Luther's faithful follower. Luther's teachings had helped him "out of great anxieties," and he lived thereafter and died a "good Lutheran." His art reflected his conversion both in subject matter and in style. While he was still a Catholic, Dürer had done more than any other artist to show the north the Renaissance spirit of pagan antiquity. After his conversion to Lutheranism he practically abandoned the depiction of secular subjects except in scientific illustrations, travelers' records, and portraits (of Melanchthon and others), gave up the "decorative style" almost entirely, and concentrated increasingly on religious subjects. The lyrical and visionary element gave way to a scriptural virility that ultimately tolerated only the apostles, the evangelists, and the passion of Christ. His style changed from scintillating splendor and freedom to a forbidding yet strangely impassioned austerity.[7]

Hans Baldung Grien died in 1545. Hans Holbein the Younger, famous for his portraits of Erasmus, reformers, and English royalty, died in London in 1543. Lucas Cranach, the Wittenberg apothecary who produced a host of portraits, group pictures, and altarpieces for evangelical churches, died in 1553, leaving no successors equal to him.

Architecture and Art in Catholic Europe. Dilettantes of universal history have offered grandiose explanations for the cultural differences between north and south. Thus northern Europe, cold and rugged, is said to represent the male principle. There philosophy and scientific theology, the products of hardheaded thinking, flourished. Southern Europe, warm and soft, represents the female principle. There the fine arts and music, the offspring of sensuous, sensitive living, flourished. Such theories, so simple yet apparently so profound, have always had their followers, but unfortunately they fail to take into account the flourishing of philosophy in Athens, Florence, and Rome and the glories of Flemish painting from van Eyck to Rembrandt. The causal factors involved—church patronage, theology, the social cohesion of the city-state, foreign domination, inquisitional repression, personal decision and dedication, traditions, economic base—all offer a better chance of understanding the reasons for the differences between Catholic and Protestant Europe. In the case of the arts such differences are very real and very striking.

Italy's political and military catastrophes had a depressing effect upon Renaissance art. Artists were now subjects of despots, domestic or foreign, rather than citizens of free states. The contrast is not absolute, for in better days Leonardo had served the Sforzas, and Titian, Veronese, and Tintoretto now prospered in republican Venice. But Italy's political humiliation and the Counterreformation produced a most important change in art and architecture. The immediate effect

---

7 Erwin Panofsky, *The Life and Art of Albrecht Dürer* (Princeton, 1955), p. 199.

ALBRECHT DÜRER. *Perspective.*

of the puritanical rigor and prudery of the Counterreformation was a reaction against some of the finest work of the Renaissance. The nudes in the Borgian apartments of the Vatican were dressed. The papal court hired a "breeches painter" to clothe some of the nudes in Michelangelo's *Last Judgment* on the wall of the Sistine Chapel. Ammanati, the sculptor who had done the exquisite nudes on the fountain of Neptune in Florence, repented publicly for his indiscretion.

The high Renaissance in art, which one may date from about 1500 to the death of Raphael in 1520, was followed by a disturbed and unsettled period in which art took on new characteristics that reveal the frustration and uncertainty of the times. The transition from classical measure and balance, characteristic of Renaissance painting, to the new phase is to be seen in the later work of three great masters of the sixteenth century, Michelangelo, Titian, and Tintoretto. All three lost the decorum of their more confident period and gave way in some of their work to less controlled emotion. The younger generation followed their lead in giving violent and unmasked expression to deep and sometimes unpleasant emotions. Their style has in recent years been called mannerism.

The term "mannerism" is awkward, but so was the situation, for the sixteenth-century artists were in a transitional period between two major styles, Renaissance and baroque. In some ways they retained elements of the old and in others pointed toward the new. Mannerism as a term may suggest the eclecticism of the new art, for the younger artists are said to have painted *in the manner* of the late Michelangelo or of Titian. The message of that greatest of all art historians, Giorgio Vasari, seemed to be a commendation of eclecticism. In his indispensable *Lives of the Most Eminent Painters, Sculptors, and Architects* (1550) he lauded extravagantly such a variety of artists as to suggest that the *belle manière* meant many different things. But mannerism has another, less flattering connotation, the quality of excessive singularity; these artistic creations were artificial, affected. The giants of the era—Michelangelo (1475-1564), the architect Andrea Palladio (1518–1580), Titian (*c.* 1477-1576), and Tintoretto (1518-1594)—carried on the best traditions of the Renaissance, modified by their own individual styles. But the artists of lesser stature were more extravagant in their eclecticism and lack of emotional restraint.

Abandoning the effort to achieve verisimilitude in the portrayal of nature, Parmigianino (1503-1540) attempted to express an inner aesthetic vision of the beauty that he seemed to remember from an earlier age when men were still united with the deity. The result was a self-conscious and highly affected style. In his *Madonna del Collo Longo,* done around 1535, for example, the Madonna has a swanlike neck and a curving, serpentine body. The child Jesus is long-limbed, lying lightly and precariously on Mary's lap. The abstract figures are posed against a sensuously draped background. This is a total departure from the natural, classical, decorous idealism of Raphael and Leonardo. The *Deposition* and *Joseph in Egypt* of Pontormo (1494-1557), the *Moses Defending the Daughters of Jethro* of

Il Rosso Fiorentino (1494–1540), the *Portrait of a Young Man* of Bronzino (1503–1572), all exhibit the extravagance, uncertainty, affectation, and strange personal vision that collectively are called mannerism.

The artistic style that gave the most characteristic expression to the religious revival of the Catholic Church was the baroque. Rome itself gave birth to baroque. After the first repressive years of the Counterreformation, it became increasingly clear that Catholicism would not be able to regain the half of Europe lost to Protestantism, and the papacy then undertook to celebrate the glories of Catholicism in those areas where the people had remained steadfast. Pope Sixtus V (1585–1590) was singularly successful in bringing the Papal States under effective control, implementing the decrees of the Council of Trent, and beautifying Rome as a proud capital of a resurgent Catholicism. He enlarged the Vatican, built the Vatican Library, and saw the dome of St. Peter's finished at last. Designed by Bramante, the great church had been begun in 1506. Michelangelo took charge in 1547, redesigned it, and by the time of his death had completed the drum beneath the dome. Now under Sixtus V Giacomo della Porta completed the dome. Significantly, the great colonnades around the magnificent piazza, the baldacchino, and much of the church's interior were the creations of Giovanni Bernini (1590–1680), the greatest artist of the baroque.

A plausible argument can be made that the universal genius Michelangelo created the baroque style, for nearly all its elements are to be found somewhere in his works, including the tendency toward heroic proportions. Baroque artists and architects executed grand designs, and baroque buildings and piazzas are as large as the funds available allowed. If classical forms produced a sensation of solidity, stability, symmetry, and completion, the baroque set things in motion. A Greek column is complete in itself; the baroque architect held that no part of a structure should be self-sufficient, but that each must depend on another. Columns became serpentine and curved into vaulting arches. The forces pulling away from each other were constrained by a rigorous overall balance. Order was superimposed upon turbulence. All surfaces were ornamented with bright colors, curving lines, and a wide variety of shapes. The baroque painter had a predilection for biblical scenes and classical allegories filled with large crowds of people. Apotheosis scenes, showing the bodily elevation of Christ or the Virgin into heaven, were ideal for the high ceilings and domes of baroque buildings. The themes were often derived from the special emphases of Counterreformation theology: the assumption of Mary, Mary as queen of heaven, Corpus Christi processions, regnant pontiffs holding the keys of Peter.

The prototype of baroque churches was the Gesù, the central church of the Jesuits of Rome. Michelangelo offered to design the church and it is possible that the architects who actually constructed it after his death followed his advice or even his plans. Giacomo Vignola (1507–1573) supervised its construction, which features a wide tunnel-vaulted nave, a modest-sized dome over the crossing, and a series of small side chapels instead of the aisles that normally run along each side. Light streams down from the dome, and the use of light through oval apertures became a marked characteristic of the baroque style. Giacomo della Porta (1541–1604) designed the façade, which became a model for churches throughout Catholic Europe in the centuries that followed. The great monastery-palace of Philip II of Spain, the Escorial, and the Louvre in Paris are only two of the architectural monuments erected during the baroque age.

Two of the many artistic creations of the most prominent baroque artist in Europe, Giovanni Bernini, illustrate the impact of the Catholic Reformation upon art. The first is Bernini's sculpture *The Ecstasy of St. Teresa.* The Spanish mystic is portrayed as a young woman swooning at the moment when the arrow of divine love pierces her breast. Only El Greco (*c.* 1548–1614), with his elongated figures and high color, had a comparable feeling for the religious fervor of Spanish piety. The second is Bernini's shrine for the chair of St. Peter in the cathedral. The mighty throne encloses a wooden stool, which allegedly had once been St. Peter's own. It is held aloft by the four great doctors of the church who supposedly had supported papal supremacy in their times. Christ's presentation of the keys of the kingdom to St. Peter ornaments the back of the chair. Above, *putti* carry aloft the papal triple tiara and the keys to the kingdom. At the very top the Holy Spirit hovers in the form of a dove. This whole creation gives powerful expression to that sense of triumph which characterized the resurgent Catholicism of the Counterreformation.[8]

Music.   The sixteenth century has been called the golden age of music. Masters of the Flemish school, such as Jean d'Okeghem (d. 1495) and Jacob Obrecht (d. 1505), had developed polyphony by introducing the technique of imitation, by which the individual voices begin not simultaneously, but one after the other. This repetitive device made for elasticity and intricate polyphonic patterns. A pupil of Okeghem, Josquin Des Prez (d. 1521), was a master composer, combining pleasing symmetries and contrasts so that his music heightened the expressiveness of the text it accompanied.

The two greatest centers of music in Italy during the sixteenth century were Rome and Venice. Giovanni da Palestrina (*c.* 1525–1594) was perhaps the most famous composer of the century. He employed all the advances made by Flemish composers and his style was the exemplar of Flemish contrapuntal technique. His music embodied the loftiest impulses of the Catholic Reformation. For over forty years he served various churches in Rome and became the composer for the papal choir. The Council of Trent sanctioned his work as the official model for all composers in the service of the church. In Venice a Flemish musician, Adrian Willaert (*c.* 1480–1562), became the choir director in St. Mark's Cathedral. The greatest

---

[8] See John Ives Sewall, *A History of Western Art,* rev. ed. (New York, 1961), pp. 665–77, on sixteenth-century mannerism; pp. 678–87 on the origins of baroque art.

Venetian composer, Giovanni Gabrieli (1557–1612), developed a unique concert style, using two choirs, and in compositions for vocalists and instruments he assigned independent parts to the instruments. He influenced several prominent German composers, such as Jacob Handl (1550–1591) and Heinrich Schütz (1585–1612).

The grandest musical invention of the sixteenth century was opera. All the techniques of polyphonic music needed to interpret musically the visual scenes of a drama on stage—the fusing of solo voices, choral groups, and instruments, the expression of personal emotions vocally and instrumentally, and orchestration—had been developed during the course of the century. The Italians' feel for the visual fused with their love of music in the development of opera. A group of Florentines met between the years 1580 and 1589 at the house of Count Giovanni dei Bardi, a wealthy gentleman scholar. This group included Vincenzo Galilei, a lutist and the father of the famous astronomer Galileo; Ottavio Rinuccini, a poet; and Jacopo Peri and Giulio Caccini, musicians. They recognized from their study of Greek drama that the ancient texts had been delivered in a declamatory manner, and they believed the effects of dramatic poetry would be intensified by the addition of music. In that group opera was born. Peri's *Dafne* (1597) was the earliest opera. His setting of Rinuccini's dramatic poem *Euridice* was actually performed in 1600 for the wedding festival of Marie de' Medici and Henry IV of France. The great operatic composer Claudio Monteverdi (1567–1643) composed *Orfeo,* produced at Mantua in 1607, just a decade after *Dafne.* It is still presented in opera houses today.

The Catholic parts of the empire, the courts of Bavaria and Austria, tended to follow the musical lead of Rome. At the Bavarian court Orlandus de Lassus (*c.* 1532–1594), from Flanders, was perhaps the most versatile composer of the time. His two thousand compositions covered secular and sacred music in nearly every form, madrigals, *chansons,* motets, masses, and magnificats. Very cosmopolitan, he used for his texts everything from Petrarchan sonnets to the verses of Hans Sachs. Music is an interfaith as well as an international language. Luther greatly admired the compositions of the Catholic Swiss musician Ludwig Senfl (*c.* 1492–1555) at the Wittelsbach court in Munich, and even wrote him a fan letter. Luther considered music the noblest of the arts. He once wrote:

> I am not satisfied with him who despises music, as all fanatics do; for music is an endowment and a gift of God, not a gift of men. It also drives away the devil and makes people cheerful; one forgets all anger, unchasteness, pride, and other vices. I place music next to theology and give it the highest praise. And we see how David and all saints put their pious thoughts into verse, rhyme, and songs, because music reigns in times of peace.[9]

Luther was himself a talented musician and composed at least eight original hymns, the most famous of which is, of course, "A Mighty Fortress Is Our God."

---

[9] Ewald Plass, *What Luther Says* (St. Louis, 1959), vol. 2, p. 980. See also Helmut Huchzermeyer, "Luther und die Musik," *Zeitschrift der Luthergesellschaft,* 39 (1968):14–25.

He also composed the first part of the German mass. In addition, he provided sacred texts for familiar German folk tunes. Congregational singing became an important part of the evangelical church service. The Lutheran chorale, or congregational hymn, gave expression to the faith and prayers of all the members of the church. Music in worship was no longer the exclusive province of the chanting priest or choir, while the congregation stood mutely by. The first Lutheran hymnbook was published in 1524. It is impossible to conceive of the great hymns of Paul Gerhard (1607–1676) or the glorious creations of Johann Sebastian Bach (1685–1750)—the *St. John Passion,* the *St. Matthew Passion,* the *Mass in B Minor*—outside the tradition of evangelical music initiated by Luther.

Zwingli too, as we have seen, had a personal love for music and was quite accomplished in it. In regard to music he owed a somewhat ambivalent debt to humanism. He presumably learned from humanists such as Conrad Celtis a new appreciation for Renaissance music, but at the same time he also learned from the humanists a profound dissatisfaction with musical practices in the churches. Zwingli's radical formal principle that only those liturgical practices that were derived from the Scriptures were acceptable gave to his Reformed Church its peculiar stamp. The whitewashing of the church walls in Zurich was accompanied by the removal of organs as well. But years after Zwingli's death there was a resurgence of music even in the Great Minster; congregational singing was introduced and an organ was even installed. Music continued to prosper in Zurich, as did the visual arts, at least in secular settings.

Calvin favored the singing of the Psalms, and in 1562 the first completed edition of the French Psalter was published with Calvin's approval. The French poet Marot composed the majority of the 150 or so versified renditions of the Psalms and Theodore Beza completed the edition. This popular songbook adapted popular French *chansons* to the versified Psalm texts and was such a success that it was translated into twenty languages. Claude Goudimel (1505–1572), one of the best Calvinist composers, published several editions of musical settings for the Psalms.

The Reformation and Science

THE AMERICAN INTELLECTUAL HISTORIAN Carl Becker once commented that we moderns necessarily think of everything in terms of history or of science. The scientific revolution, which made its first giant strides in the seventeenth century, has won such a total victory through its apparent domination of nature that the Western mind has virtually capitulated to its criteria of truth. The relation of the Reformation and science, therefore, presents a fascinating historical problem. Why did modern science and technology develop as a socially significant force in the

West rather than in other cultures? Why in Christian countries rather than, say, Moslem? And why did it follow so closely upon the heels of the Reformation?

The role of Protestantism in the rise of modern science is still one of the most controversial issues among contemporary historians. A nineteenth-century French Protestant historian, Alphonse de Candolle, pointed out that of the ninety-two foreign members elected to the Academy of Sciences in Paris from its founding in 1666 to 1866, some seventy-one were Protestant, sixteen Catholic, and the remaining five either Jews or of indeterminate religious position. Correlating these statistics with the number of European Catholics (107 million) and Protestants (68 million) outside of France, Candolle concluded that there were six times as many Protestants as Catholics sufficiently eminent to rate election to the academy. Checking the statistics of the Royal Society of London (founded 1662) at two points in the nineteenth century confirmed his conclusion that Protestants tended to predominate over Catholics among the great scientists of Europe. Other studies brought to light the connections between Puritanism and science in seventeenth-century England. No one can deny the preponderance of Protestants among scientists after the 1640s. Lutherans, Anglicans, and preeminently Calvinists made more scientific discoveries than Catholics and appeared to be more flexible in putting them to use. Moreover, the most rigorous Calvinists contributed proportionately more scientists than did Anglicans, and after the astronomer Johannes Kepler, who died in 1630, the Lutherans produced no scientist of major stature until the nineteenth century.

These circumstances, about which there is a considerable amount of agreement among historians, have released a great flow of speculation as to the relation of religion to the rise of modern science. Were the fragmented Protestants merely less able than the Catholics to prevent the rise of science? Was the sociologist Max Weber right when in 1905 he suggested that ascetic Calvinism had a propensity toward empiricism, which was an essential element in scientific method? Were forces operative that had nothing whatsoever to do with religion, or which had at most only a tenuous connection to it? Is the situation after 1640 actually relevant to the problem of the *origins* of modern science, since by 1640 the work of Galileo, Harvey, and Descartes was virtually complete and science had thus already risen? It is, of course, impossible to rehearse all the arguments or marshal even a respectable fraction of the facts here. But these big questions may profitably be kept in mind while we scan scientific developments after the Reformation.

Among the causes alleged by some historians for the disproportionate number of Protestant scientists, at least after 1640, are (1) a certain concordance between the early Protestant ethos and the scientific attitude in the questioning of authority and spiritual individualism; (2) a certain congruity between the more abstract elements of the Protestant theologies and the theories of modern science, such as the anti-hierarchical implications of the concept of the priesthood of all believers and the idea that man is a microcosm of the great macrocosm; and (3) the use of science by the later Calvinists, especially the English Puritans, for the attainment of their religious aims, for they considered the study of nature a duty, included scientific research among the good works beneficial to humanity, and even considered scientific success, like material prosperity, to be a reassuring indication that a man had been elected for salvation.

Luther has frequently been referred to as the Copernicus of theology and Copernicus as the Luther of astronomy. The identification of the reformation in religion with the revolution in science is very old. Thomas Sprat, an Anglican clergyman and an early fellow of the Royal Society, commented on the

> agreement that is between the present design of the Royal Society, and that of our church in its beginning. They both may lay equal claim to the word Reformation; the one having compassed it in Religion, the other purposing it in Philosophy. . . . They both have taken a like course to bring this about; each of them passing by the corrupt copies, and referring themselves to the perfect originals for their instruction, the one to the Scripture, the other to the huge volume of creatures. They are both accused unjustly by their enemies of the same crimes, of having forsaken the Ancient Traditions, and ventured on Novelties. They both suppose alike that their ancestors might err; and yet retain sufficient reverence for them. They both follow the great Precept of the Apostle of trying all things. Such is the harmony between their interests and tempers.[10]

Luther himself believed that the world was seeing a new sunrise that would bring not only a reform of religion but a new appreciation of nature. He objected to scholastic philosophy, to Neoplatonic cosmology (although in his commentary on Genesis he used the concept of man as a microcosm), and to the humanists' bookishness. They all failed to take nature seriously and to appreciate it as fully as the doctrines of creation and the incarnation warranted. In one of his *Table Talks* he expressed this feeling and took a sideswipe at Erasmus in passing:

> We are at the dawn of a new era, for we are beginning to recover the knowledge of the external world that we had lost through the fall of Adam. We now observe creatures properly, and not as formerly under the papacy. Erasmus is indifferent, and does not care to know how fruit is developed from the germ. But by the grace of God we already recognize in the most delicate flower the wonders of divine goodness and omnipotence. We see in His creatures the power of His word. He commanded and things stood fast. See that force display itself in the stone of a peach. It is very hard, and the germ it encloses is very tender; but when the moment has come, the stone must open to let out the young plant that God calls into life. Erasmus passes by all that and takes no account of it, and looks upon external objects as cows look at a new gate.

This biblical naturalism of Luther's is of the same genre as the "Gothic" naturalism of St. Francis, which is said to have been an important ideological factor in the rise of Franciscan physics during the thirteenth and fourteenth centuries.

---

[10] Thomas Sprat, *The History of the Royal Society of London, for the Improving of Natural Knowledge* (London, 1667), p. 371 (misprinted as 363). Pt. 3, secs. 14–23 are particularly significant for the science-religion problem.

As an intensification of certain main-line attitudes toward nature unique to the Judeo-Christian (and "heretical" Moslem) West, Reformation theology contributed to certain essential presuppositions important to natural science in its incipient stages. The dogma that God created the universe by fiat out of nothing (*creatio ex nihilo*, an interpretation dating from the rabbinical commentators at the time of the Maccabees) underlined the qualitative gap between Creator and creation. Creatures are not extensions or emanations of God's being, and therefore do not share in his divinity. They are thus subject to examination without taboos. God's commission to Adam to "subdue" all creatures established man's sovereignty over nature. The idea that a "reasonable God" is the author of natural laws as well as of human reason was reassuring to the inquirer. The Western mind, trained in legal concepts by Roman and canon law and by exegetic and hermeneutic rules, was easily directed into concepts of law in natural philosophy. When the use of experiment was combined with rational interpretation, preferably expressed in the language of mathematics—and here the Hellenic inheritance was of crucial importance—the ingredients for the rise of science were brought together. The scientific mentality, described by the philosopher Alfred North Whitehead as the passionate interest "in the application of reason to stubborn facts," owed much to this cultural inheritance, which was revitalized by the Reformation in the religious sphere.

Luther and Calvin meant by "philosophy" the sum total of human sciences. They believed that the world of nature was subject to reason and open to its probing power. The Scriptures were the carriers of the word of God to man, not a textbook of natural science. The major reformers were not biblical literalists, and where there was an apparent conflict between the word of God and natural philosophy, they usually resolved the difficulty not on the basis of a "double theory of truth," but by a concept of multiple discourse, two separate levels of knowledge, divine and natural. They did, nevertheless, consider it legitimate to refute scientific theories by citing Scriptures.

Luther was quite open to the authentic scientific advances of the age and expressed wonder at the mechanical inventions of the day. The Germanies were hospitable to the sciences. Georg Agricola studied mining techniques and metallurgy up to 1555. The mathematician and geographer Sebastian Münster offered his *Cosmographie* (1544) in German. Gerard Kremer (Mercator), from Ruppelmonde in Flanders, famous for his great map of the world published in 1539, entered the service of Jülich-Cleves and made Duisburg an active center of geographic studies. Luther referred at least once to the new overseas discoveries when in 1522 he commented that "recently many islands and lands have been discovered, to which this grace [of God] has not appeared for fifteen hundred years." Luther attacked the superstition of the astrologers, but he was quite ready to accept the conclusion of astronomers that the moon was the smallest and lowest of the stars. He suggested that when the Scriptures called the sun and moon "great lights," they were merely accommodating themselves to man's everyday way of looking at things. If the same principle of accommodation had been developed further by Calvin, the conflict about Copernicus' heliocentric theory would have been unnecessary. But a conflict did develop during the second half of the sixteenth century and became a *cause célèbre* in the case of Galileo.

The year 1543 saw the publication of two of the most important books of modern times, *The Structure of the Human Body* by the Flemish anatomist Vesalius and *On the Revolutions of the Heavenly Bodies* by the Polish astronomer Nicolaus Copernicus. On the basis of his own dissections of cadavers Vesalius demonstrated the errors of Galen, who had been accepted since the second century A.D. as the greatest authority on anatomy. This brave beginning was followed up in the seventeenth century by important advances in physiology based upon further observation and laboratory experiment. In 1628 William Harvey's *On the Movement of the Heart and Blood,* based upon laboratory work that included the vivisection of animals, established the continuous circulation of blood through the arteries and veins. An Italian scientist, Marcello Malpighi, who had the advantage of using the newly discovered microscope, confirmed Harvey's theory in 1661 by finding the networks of capillaries that connected arteries and veins. The Dutchman Anton van Leeuwenhoek used the microscope to discover bacteria, blood corpuscles, and spermatozoa. Science was truly an international enterprise. While some scientists were exploring the infinitely small through the microscope, others pondered the great universe above, eventually with the telescope.

Copernicus' heliocentric theory was the most sensational hypothesis to be advanced, for it clearly upset the time-honored order of the cosmos. Ever since Copernicus, Nietzsche once observed, man has been falling away from the center of the universe. The implications of the Copernican theory were contrary to the cherished assumptions of reformers and humanists alike. Beyond that, the Copernican theory defied the authority of the second-century Alexandrian astronomer Ptolemy, who had described the cosmos as geocentric. At the center of the universe, Ptolemy held, was the earth, which was surrounded by a series of transparent crystalline spheres, each carrying a luminous heavenly body that revolved around the earth. Nearest to the earth was the moon; then came Mercury, Venus, the sun, outer planets, and finally the outer sphere containing the fixed stars, which circled the earth majestically like a jeweled curtain. Aristotle's cosmos was even simpler than Ptolemy's, for he made no real effort to explain mathematically the difference in the planets' brightness and size at their nearest and farthest points from the earth as they revolved about it, as he assumed they did. Aristotle's prestige and authority were so enormous, especially in the universities, that any theory that challenged his cosmology inevitably produced fierce opposition.

Copernicus, born in Poland of Polish and German background, came from

a family of merchants, but he had an uncle who was a high churchman and a learned man. Copernicus studied in Italian universities, where he encountered Novara, a Platonist, and others who questioned the Greeks' measurements of the earth's latitude and the mathematical precision of Ptolemy's observations. When he returned to the north, Copernicus made further observations of the skies and realized that if the planets were assumed to revolve around the sun rather than around the earth, the mathematical calculations necessary to accommodate their observed movements would be greatly simplified. His interest was theoretical, and he even credits certain ancient Pythagoreans with inspiring him to develop his hypothesis that the sun was the center around which revolved the fixed stars and the planets, of which the earth was one. This heliocentric theory enabled him to eliminate some of the cycles and epicycles that had been introduced to make the Ptolemaic system seem workable.

Among the "most eminent and learned men" who were interested in his work, Copernicus wrote in his dedicatory preface to Pope Paul III, were certain Lutherans. Copernicus may have had the manuscript of his major work completed as early as 1530. The *Commentariolus,* a brief account of his ideas, which Copernicus had written during the first decade of the century, had been circulated in manuscript among his friends. In the spring of 1539 one of Melanchthon's protégés, Georg Rheticus, a mathematics professor at Wittenberg, journeyed to Frauenburg in Ermland, where Copernicus was a canon in the cathedral chapter, to consult the great astronomer himself. He became convinced that Copernicus was right, and published a report on the theory of the astronomer who, as Melanchthon said, "has caused the sun to stand still and the earth to move." Rheticus was commissioned to publish the great work. The Lutheran theologian Osiander wrote a favorable, if tentative, preface, and the theologian Caspar Cruciger and the mathematician Erasmus Reinhold, colleagues of Luther's, openly advocated his theory. Reinhold even published astronomical tables based upon it.

Luther himself made one disparaging remark in one of his rambling *Table Talks.* Someone had mentioned some new "astrologer," he reported, who was trying to prove that the earth moves and not the sun and moon; that to believe otherwise was to be like a man in a moving boat who thought that he himself was standing still while the earth and trees were moving. That's the way it is nowadays, Luther commented; anyone who wants to be clever can't be satisfied with the opinions of others, but has to produce something of his own, "as this man does, who wants to turn the whole of astrology upside down. But even though astrology has been thrown into confusion, I, for my part, believe the sacred Scripture; for Joshua commanded the sun to stand still, not the earth." Luther made no further mention of the matter and certainly no attempt at repression. Melanchthon, of course, defended Aristotle's position and used scriptural arguments against Copernicus. Calvin actually seemed to be unaware of the Copernican theory, for the one negative comment often ascribed to him turns out to be spurious.

During the first fifty years after 1543 opposition to the theory was quite defensible. But after Kepler and Galileo, no informed man could continue to support the "common-sense" observation of the rising sun, and it took a dedicated obscurantist to carry on opposition to the new theory. Yet acceptance of the theory required such a radical readjustment of ideas that the gradualness of its reception is understandable. Tycho Brahe (1546–1601), the leading expert on the positions and movements of the heavenly bodies in the decades after Copernicus, did not accept the Copernican system in its entirety. Johannes Kepler (1571–1630), his assistant and successor, did accept it, and refined it by demonstrating that the orbits of the planets were ellipses. He was ecstatic about the mysterious harmonies of mathematical forms, and the correspondence he found between mathematics and observed astronomical phenomena was not only personally exciting to him, but very useful in his careful preparation of horoscopes for the emperor.

Galileo Galilei (1564–1642) constructed a telescope in 1609 and observed that the moon, far from being a perfect orb, had pocks, valleys, and mountains, that the sun had spots, that the planets had breadth, and that Jupiter had satellites. He believed the fixed stars to be an incalculable distance from the earth. In developing the concept of inertia, according to which matter remains at rest or in uniform motion unless acted upon by some external force, he continued the line of inquiry developed by the fourteenth-century Franciscans. Galileo's difficulties with the Inquisition and his subsequent retraction and house arrest were due as much to academic conservatism and personal hostilities as to the opposition of Catholic theologians to his views.

The indispensable language for science, especially for astronomy and physics, which long overshadowed the other disciplines, was mathematics. The sixteenth and early seventeenth centuries witnessed important advances in this field. Niccolò Tartaglia (1500–1537) first solved the cubic equation and developed the use of coefficients, thus going far beyond the achievements of the Hindus and Moslems. Another Italian mathematician, Girolamo Cardano (1501–1576), developed a theory of numbers and an algebraic synthesis. Simon Stevin (1548–1620) of Bruges helped develop the decimal system. The Scotsman John Napier (1550–1617) unveiled logarithms in 1614. The noted French philosopher René Descartes (1596–1650) helped to prepare the way for coordinate geometry. These steps forward were followed by Pascal with his theory of probabilities and by the simultaneous development of calculus by Newton in England and Leibniz in Germany. The precision and the complexity of quantitative measurements made possible by these advances were indispensable to modern scientific developments.

Other major discoveries in physics and chemistry were made during this period. William Gilbert (1540–1603), Queen Elizabeth's physician, in his book *On the Magnet, on Magnetic Bodies, and on the Earth as a Great Magnet,* developed theories on magnetism and electricity based on his own laboratory experiments. He attributed the rotation of the earth to its magnetic character. The erratic Swiss doctor Paracelsus (1493–1541) was proud of his originality. "For even as Avicenna was the best physician of the Arabs," he boasted, "Galen of the men of Pergamon, and Marsilius of the Italians, so also most fortunate Germany has chosen me as her indispensable physician!" He experimented with victims of mining disasters and tried cures with new drugs, the "science" of iatrochemistry. His greatest contribution may have been his bombastic attacks upon old authorities, as when he dared to burn the books of Galen in the courtyard of Basel University. The Flemish doctor Jean Baptiste van Helmont (1577–1644), although a superstitious pedant, was a better medical chemist than Paracelsus. He invented the term "gas," discovered carbon dioxide, and made basic observations on the qualities and behavior of gases. The Swiss biologist Conrad Gesner (1515–1565) contributed to the systematic observation and cataloging of plants and animals. The German botanist Leonard Fuchs (1501–1566) wrote a glossary of botanical terms and produced a fascinating collection of woodcuts of plants. As the seventeenth century wore on and the body of knowledge structured about the new scientific theories grew in substance, geniuses such as Evangelista Torricelli, Christian Huygens, Otto von Guericke, and the incomparable Sir Isaac Newton (1642–1727) entered the scene. Confidence in man's ability to conquer nature mounted. One can well appreciate Alexander Pope's ecstatic outburst in the eighteenth century, as he reflected on the beauties of the Newtonian system:

> Nature and nature's laws lay hid in night;
> God said, "Let Newton be," and all was light.

Was the Reformation important for the rise of modern science? It is quite clear that a conflict of theology and science leading to the repression of science is scarcely in evidence, and that the opposition to science was hardly effective. Possibly academic conservatism was as great a hindrance as religious fanaticism. The introduction of religious pluralism and theological novelty eventually made for greater toleration of new and nonconforming scientific views as well. Much of the driving force behind these early scientists' explorations of nature was the zeal of religious men to discover and admire God's handiwork. They were "thinking God's thoughts after him," as Kepler put it. Even considerably later the Prussian Academy of Sciences announced as its purpose "the propagation of the gospel through the sciences." The English pneumatician Robert Boyle (1627–1691), who experimented with the weight of air and devised the law that the pressure exerted by a given quantity of gas is directly proportional to its density, stated in his will that he wished the fellows of the Royal Society a most happy success in their laudable attempts to discover the true nature of the works of God, and [prayed] that they and all other searchers into physical truths may cordially refer their attainments to the glory of the Author of Nature and the benefit of mankind.[11]

It is quite obvious that before 1640 many of the greatest scientists were Catholic, others Lutheran and Anglican, and only some Calvinist. No particular confession had anything essential to contribute to the origins of science. There was no distinctively "Protestant ethic" yet at work. That the Puritan ascetic ethic may have reinforced the empirical approach to science later in the seventeenth century can still be asserted, but there were certainly other factors operative by then. For the interest in invention and practical discoveries was in large part a response to economic need, the exigencies of a lively maritime enterprise in the Netherlands and England, of mining in the empire, of war and disease everywhere. As southern Europe regressed economically and politically in comparison with northern and western Europe and Great Britain, its contributions to science fell behind as well.

The Reformation had one effect upon the rise of science which has been little noticed: By stimulating controversy in religious matters, it made the study of nature seem safe and uncontroversial in comparison, a neutral ground where men could forget their theological differences. Science provided an escape from dogmatism on the one hand and skepticism on the other, for it provided knowledge that was intellectually and emotionally satisfying, and apparently certain, safe, and incontrovertible. Men of the seventeenth century can hardly be blamed for their failure to foresee the controversies that Darwin's evolutionary theory would precipitate two centuries later; and what eighteenth- or nineteenth-century scientist, transfixed by the glory of Newtonian physics, could have anticipated Einstein? Descartes tells in his *Discourse on Method* that he preferred mathematics to the humanities because the humanities never came to any conclusions. Pascal had a similar experience, and as a result built up a great enthusiasm for Archimedes. Thomas Sprat wrote in his fascinating *History of the Royal Society of London* of the satisfaction to be found in scientific studies, in which "philosophical heads unite with mechanical hands." Natural philosophy, he wrote, was the best subject for study if one wished to breathe free air. Politics and theology were excluded from debate for nature alone could entertain pleasantly, without controversy. "If only more Englishmen would turn to science," wrote Sprat, "they would be less violent and dogmatical and more certain." So perhaps the Puritans did, after all, make a distinctive, though negative, contribution to the progress of science. Science seems to have been the child of the new religious thinking rather than its sire. That sci-

---

[11] He even published a volume entitled *The Excellency of Theology, Compared with Natural Philosophy* (London, 1674).

ence has shown itself to be less incontrovertible than was once supposed and in the long run has proved to be only a very inadequate substitute for religious faith constitutes one of the problems of contemporary humanity.

Bibliography

Religion and culture:

BOYER, MERLE. *Luther in Protestantism Today.* New York, 1958.

BREEN, QUIRINUS. *Christianity and Humanism.* Grand Rapids, 1967.

BROWN, ROBERT McAFEE. *The Spirit of Protestantism.* New York, 1961.

———. *The Ecumenical Revolution: An Interpretation of the Catholic-Protestant Dialogue.* Garden City, N.Y., 1967.

BRUNNER, PETER, and HOLM, BERNARD. *Luther in the Twentieth Century.* Decorah, Ia., 1961.

CUSHMAN, ROBERT E., and GRISLIS, EGIL, eds. *The Heritage of Christian Thought.* New York, 1965.

FORELL, GEORGE W., et al. *Luther and Culture.* Decorah, Ia., 1960.

FRAME, DONALD M. *Montaigne's Discovery of Man.* New York, 1955.

FRIEDLAENDER, WALTER F. *Mannerism and Anti-Mannerism in Italian Painting.* New York, 1957.

GARRISON, WINFRED E. *A Protestant Manifesto.* New York, 1952.

GELDER, ENNO VAN. *The Two Reformations in the Sixteenth Century.* The Hague, 1961.

HARBISON, E. HARRIS. *The Christian Scholar in the Age of the Reformation.* New York, 1956.

———. *Christianity and History.* Princeton, 1964.

HOLL, KARL. *The Cultural Significance of the Reformation.* New York, 1959.

HOOGSTRA, JACOB T. *John Calvin, Contemporary Prophet.* Grand Rapids, 1959.

LECLER, J. *Toleration and the Reformation,* 2 vols. New York, 1960.

PAUCK, WILHELM. *The Heritage of the Reformation.* Boston and Glencoe, Ill., 1950.

PELIKAN, JAROSLAV. *From Luther to Kierkegaard.* St. Louis, 1950.

———. *Obedient Rebels: Catholic Substance and Protestant Principle in Luther's Reformation.* New York, 1964.

———, ed. *Interpreters of Luther.* Philadelphia, 1968.

PREUS, ROBERT D. *The Theology of Post-Reformation Lutheranism.* St. Louis, 1970.

RABB, THEODORE, and SEIGEL, JERROLD E., eds. *Action and Conviction in Early Modern Europe.* Princeton, 1969.

RUPP, E. GORDON. *The Old Reformation and the New.* Philadelphia, 1967.

SCHWOEBEL, ROBERT, ed. *Renaissance Men and Ideas.* New York, 1970.

TROELTSCH, ERNST. *Protestantism and Progress.* New York, 1912.

Church and state:

BAINTON, ROLAND H. *Christian Attitudes Toward War and Peace.* New York, 1960.

BATES, MINER SEARLE. *Religious Liberty: An Inquiry.* New York, 1945.

MUELLER, WILLIAM A. *Church and State in Luther and Calvin,* 2nd ed. Garden City, N.Y., 1965.

SPITZ, LEWIS W. "The Impact of the Reformation on Church-State Issues," in *Church and State Under God,* ed. Albert Huegli. St. Louis, 1964.

TROELTSCH, ERNST. *The Social Teaching of the Christian Churches,* 3 vols. New York, 1931.

Protestantism and capitalism:

BARGE, HERMANN. *Luther und der Frühkapitalismus.* Gütersloh, 1951.

BENDIX, REINHARD. *Max Weber.* New York, 1959.

GREEN, ROBERT W., ed. *Protestantism and Capitalism: The Weber Thesis and Its Critics.* Boston, 1959.

HILL, JOHN E. CHRISTOPHER. *Reformation to Industrial Revolution: The Making of Modern English Society, 1530–1780.* New York, 1968.

KITCH, M. J. *Capitalism and the Reformation.* London, 1967.

NELSON, JOHN O., ed. *Work and Vocation.* New York, 1954.

SAMUELSON, KURT. *Religion and Economic Action. A Critique of Max Weber.* New York, 1961.

WEBER, MAX. *The Protestant Ethic and the Spirit of Capitalism.* London, 1930.

Elizabethan Renaissance:

BRADNER, LEISTER, ed. *The Poems of Queen Elizabeth I.* Providence, 1964.

CHAMBERS, SIR E. *A Short Life of William Shakespeare.* Oxford, 1935.

CRAIG, HARDIN. *The Enchanted Glass: The Elizabethan Mind in Literature.* New York, 1936.

———. *An Interpretation of Shakespeare.* New York, 1948.

———. *A New Look at Shakespeare's Quartos.* Stanford, 1961.

———. *A History of English Literature,* rev. ed. New York, 1962.

GOTCH, JOHN A. *Early Renaissance Architecture in England.* London, 1901.

HOOPES, ROBERT. *Right Reason in the English Renaissance.* Cambridge, Mass., 1962.

LEVY, FRED J. *Tudor Historical Thought.* San Marino, Cal., 1967.

NUGENT, ELIZABETH M., ed. *Thought and Culture of the English Renaissance.* Cambridge, 1954.

RYAN, LAWRENCE. *Roger Ascham.* Stanford, 1963.

SPENCER, THEODORE. *Shakespeare and the Nature of Man.* New York, 1942.

SPINGARN, JOEL. *Literary Criticism in the Renaissance.* New York, 1963.

TALBERT, ERNEST W. *The Problem of Order: Elizabethan Political Commonplaces and an Example of Shakespeare's Art.* Chapel Hill, N.C., 1962.

TILLYARD, E. M. W. *The Elizabethan World Picture.* London, 1943.

——— *The English Renaissance: Fact or Fiction?* London, 1952.

WATSON, C. B. *Shakespeare and the Renaissance Concept of Honor.* Princeton, 1961.

Protestantism and science:

BOAS, MARIE. *The Scientific Renaissance, 1450–1630.* New York, 1962.

CALLOT, E. *La renaissance des sciences de la vie au XVIe siècle.* Paris, 1949.

CROMBIE, ALISTAIR C. *Medieval and Early Modern Science.* Garden City, N.Y., 1959.

DILLENBERGER, JOHN. *Protestant Thought and Natural Science.* New York, 1960.

HILL, CHRISTOPHER; KEARNEY, H. F.; and RABB, T. K. "Science, Religion, and Society in the Sixteenth and Seventeenth Centuries." *Past and Present,* July 1965, pp. 97–126.

HOOYKAAS, R. *Humanisme, science, et réforme.* Leyden, 1958.

KEARNEY, HUGH F. *Origins of the Scientific Revolution.* London, 1964.

KOCHER, PAUL. *Science and Religion in Elizabethan England.* San Marino, Calif., 1953.

KUHN, THOMAS S. *The Copernican Revolution.* Cambridge, 1957.

———. *The Structure of Scientific Revolutions.* Chicago, 1962.

MERTON, ROBERT K. *Social Theory and Social Structure,* rev. ed. New York, 1967.

O'MALLEY, DONALD. *Andreas Vesalius.* Berkeley, 1964.

PAGEL, KARL. *Paracelsus.* New York, 1958.

PAULI, WILHELM. *The Interpretation of Nature and Psyche.* New York, 1955.

PRICE, DEREK J. DE SOLA. *Science Since Babylon.* New Haven, 1961.

SANTILLANA, GIORGIO DE. *The Crime of Galileo.* Chicago, 1959.

WIGHTMAN, WILLIAM. *Science and the Renaissance,* 2 vols. New York, 1963.

WOLF, ABRAHAM. *A History of Science, Technology, and Philosophy in the Sixteenth and Seventeenth Centuries,* 2nd ed. London, 1950.

Index

Abano, Pietro d', 186
Abelard, Peter, 146
Acciaiuoli, Agnolo, 108
Acciaiuoli, Donato, 180
Acontius, Giacomo, 436, 437
Acton, Lord, 92, 329, 332
Adelmann, Bernhard, 304
Adelmannsfelden, Adelmann von, 134
Adolf of Nassau, Holy Roman emperor, 65
Adrian VI, pope, 59, 295, 317–18, 358, 367, 470
Adriani, Marcello Virgilio, 242
Aegidius of Viterbo. *See* Egidio da Viterbo
Affair of the Placards, 415
Africans, enslavement of, 259, 519, 536
Agincourt, Battle of, 73–74
Agricola, Georg, 135, 583
Agricola, Michael, 373
Agricola, Rudolf, 277–78, 315
Agriculture:
  in Elizabethan England, 541–42
  in Middle Ages, 7–9
Ailly, Pierre d', 29, 32, 35, 255
Alba, duke of, 499, 508, 509, 512–13
Albert, archduke of Austria, 514
Albert, duke of Prussia, 371, 372
Albert of Brandenburg, archbishop of Magdeburg
      and Mainz, 315, 335, 360, 375
Albert of Saxony, 185–86
Alberti, Leon Battista, 149, 197–99, 229
  as architect, 158, 198–99, 210
  as art theoretician, 199
  as social thinker, 119, 163, 199
Albizzi, Maso degli, 105–6
Albizzi, Piero degli, 105
Albizzi, Rinaldo degli, 106
Albornoz, Gil de, 95

Albrecht, Holy Roman emperors:
  Albrecht I, 65
  Albrecht II, 68
Albret, Charlotte d', 241
Albret, Henry d'. *See* Henry, kings of Navarre:
      Henry II
Albuquerque, Affonso de, 517
Alciati, Andrea, 414
Alcuin, 3
Aldine Press, 176, 189. *See also* Manutius, Aldus
Aleander (Italian humanist), 275
Aleander, Girolamo, 329–30, 338, 350, 471, 484
Alençon, Duke Charles of, 286
Alençon, Duke Francis of, 501, 535
Alexander, popes:
  Alexander V, 31
  Alexander VI, 50–52, 54, 57, 235–36, 240
    division of Spanish and Portuguese possessions
        by, 54, 270
    and Pico della Mirandola, 54, 178
    and Savonarola, 239
Alexander II, tsar of Russia, 15
Alexander of Aphrodisias, 180–81
Alfonso I, king of Sicily and Naples (Alfonso V of
      Aragon), 96, 100, 163, 166, 235–36
Alfonso V, king of Portugal, 258
Allen, William, 482, 527
Almeida, Francisco, 263, 517
Althusius, Johannes, 554
Álvarez Cabral, Pedro, 263
Amadeo, counts of Savoy:
  Amadeo VI, 99
  Amadeo VII, 99
  Amadeo VIII, duke of Savoy, 99. *See also* Felix V,
      pope
Amaseo, Romolo, 561